# OUTSTANDING ACCLAIM FOR THE CUCKOO'S EGG

"A mammoth manhunt. . . . A sobering message about today's Information Age."

—*Washington Post*

"A computer-age detective story, instantly fascinating to the computer generation and astonishingly gripping to the rest of us."

—*Smithsonian*

"An intriguing introduction to the futuristic world of international computer networking."

—*The New York Times Book Review*

"Fascinating! . . . *THE CUCKOO'S EGG* could be science fiction, except that it is true; it could be a spy novel—except that it actually happened. . . . Clifford Stoll is a blend of Indiana Jones and Tron, with a big dash of Berkeley counterculture thrown in."

—William Press, Professor of Astronomy and Physics, Harvard University

**A Literary Guild Editor's Choice Selection**
**A Doubleday Book Club Alternate Selection**

# The Cuckoo's Egg

## Tracking a Spy Through the Maze of Computer Espionage

Cliff Stoll

POCKET BOOKS
New York London Toronto Sydney Singapore

POCKET BOOKS, a division of Simon & Schuster, Inc.
1230 Avenue of the Americas, New York, NY 10020



Published by arrangement with Doubleday, a division of Bantam Doubleday Dell Publishing Group, Inc.



Library of Congress Cataloging-in-Publication Data

Stoll, Clifford.
The cuckoo's egg : tracking a spy through the maze of computer espionage / Cliff Stoll.
p. cm.
Originally published: New York : Pocket Books, 1990.
Includes bibliographical references.
ISBN 0-7434-1146-3
1. Hess, Markus. 2. Stoll, Clifford. 3. Espionage, Soviet—United States. 4. Espionage, Soviet—Germany—Hannover. 5. Defense information, Classified—United States—Databases. 6. Computer crimes—United States. 7. Computer crimes—Germany—Hannover. I. Title.

UB271.R92 H477 2000
364.16'8'0973—dc21 00-033654

First Pocket Books trade paperback printing October 2000

10 9 8 7 6 5 4 3 2 1

POCKET and colophon are registered trademarks of Simon & Schuster, Inc.

Cover design by Carolyn Lechter; front cover photo by Ed Holub/Photonica

Printed in the U.S.A.

# Acknowledgments

How do you spread the word when a computer has a security hole? Some say nothing, fearing that telling people how to mix explosives will encourage them to make bombs. In this book I've explicitly described some of these security problems, realizing that people in black hats are already aware of them.

I've tried to reconstruct this incident as I experienced it. My main sources are my logbooks and diaries, cross-checked by contacting others involved in this affair and comparing reports from others. A few people appear under aliases, several phone numbers are changed, and some conversations have been recounted from memory, but there's no fictionalizing.

For supporting me throughout the investigation and writing, thanks to my friends, colleagues, and family. Regina Wiggen has been my editorial mainstay; thanks also to Jochen Sperber, Jon Rochlis, Dean Chacon, Winona Smith, Stephan Stoll, Dan Sack, Donald Alvarez, Laurie McPherson, Rich Muller, Gene Spafford, Andy Goldstein, and Guy Consolmagno. Thanks also to Bill Stott, for *Write to the Point*, a book that changed my way of writing.

I posted a notice to several computer networks, asking for title suggestions. Several hundred people from around the world replied with zany ideas. My thanks to Karen Anderson in San Francisco and Nigel Roberts in Munich for the title and subtitle.

Doubleday's editors, David Gernert and Scott Ferguson, have

helped me throughout. It's been fun to work with the kind people at Pocket Books, including Bill Grose, Dudley Frasier, and Gertie the Kangaroo, who's pictured on the cover of this book. To them, as well as my agent, John Brockman, thanks for your continued encouragement and wise advice.

To each of these people, I'm indebted; I owe most of them boxes of cookies as well.

Lawrence Berkeley Laboratory supported me throughout this quest; the people of Smithsonian Astrophysical Observatory—especially Joe Schwarz and Steve Murray—have been most gracious and supportive while I've been writing this book. My deep thanks go to my friends at both institutes, and my hopes that I'll now be able to return to astronomy.

I was ten years old when Ernst Both of the Buffalo Museum of Science invited me to look through a telescope, opening up a universe of astronomy. I wonder if I'll ever be able to thank him properly.

—Cliff Stoll
Electronic mail addresses:
Internet: cliff@cfa.harvard.edu
Compuserve: 71660,3013
AOL: cliffstoll

# THE CUCKOO'S EGG

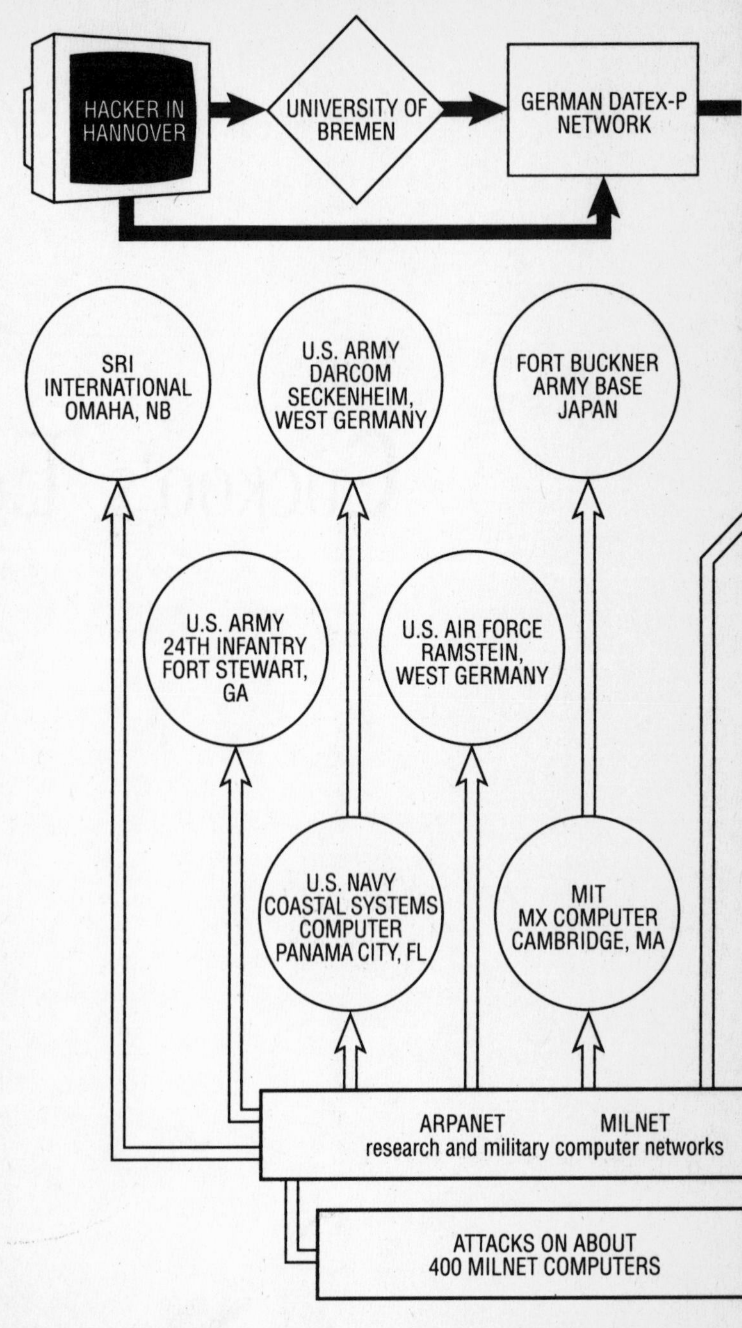
HACKER IN HANNOVER
UNIVERSITY OF BREMEN
GERMAN DATEX-P NETWORK
SRI INTERNATIONAL OMAHA, NB
U.S. ARMY DARCOM SECKENHEIM, WEST GERMANY
FORT BUCKNER ARMY BASE JAPAN
U.S. ARMY 24TH INFANTRY FORT STEWART, GA
U.S. AIR FORCE RAMSTEIN, WEST GERMANY
U.S. NAVY COASTAL SYSTEMS COMPUTER PANAMA CITY, FL
MIT MX COMPUTER CAMBRIDGE, MA
ARPANET
MILNET
research and military computer networks
ATTACKS ON ABOUT 400 MILNET COMPUTERS

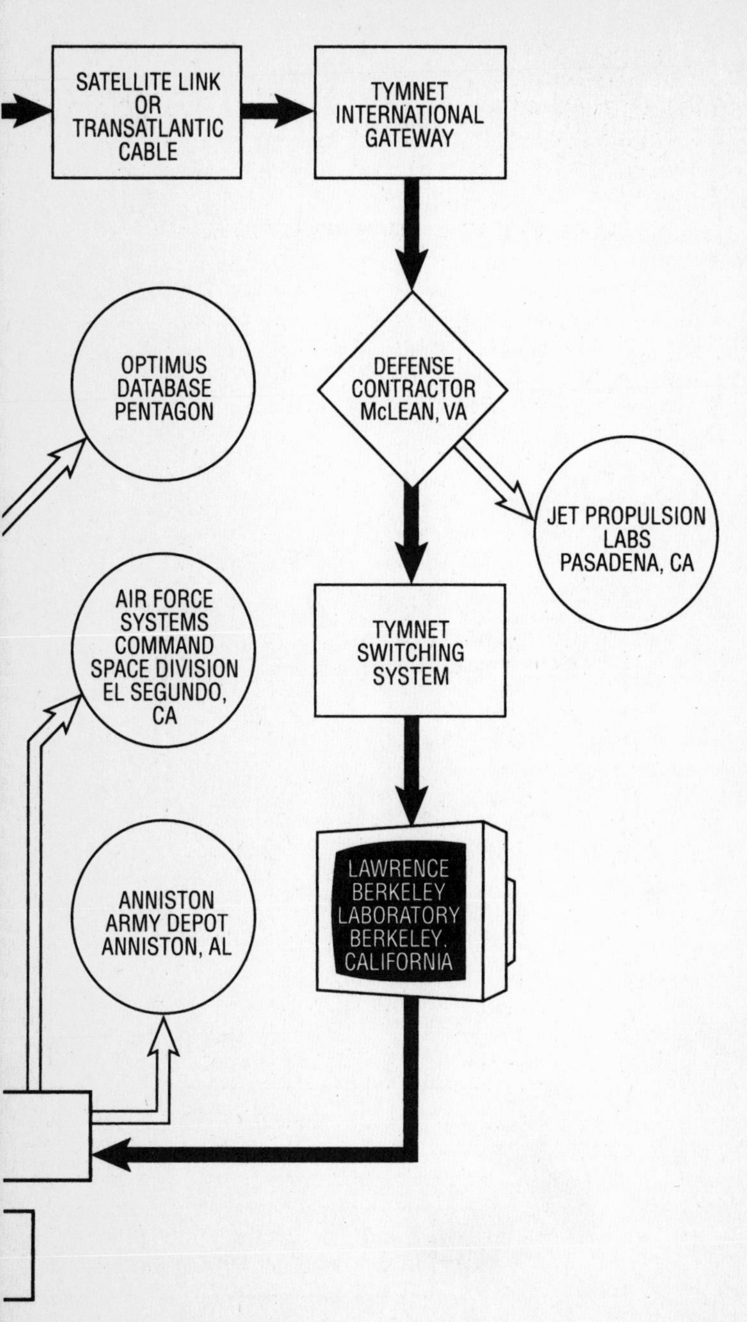
SATELLITE LINK OR TRANSATLANTIC CABLE
TYMNET INTERNATIONAL GATEWAY
OPTIMUS DATABASE PENTAGON
DEFENSE CONTRACTOR McLEAN, VA
JET PROPULSION LABS PASADENA, CA
AIR FORCE SYSTEMS COMMAND SPACE DIVISION EL SEGUNDO, CA
TYMNET SWITCHING SYSTEM
ANNISTON ARMY DEPOT ANNISTON, AL
LAWRENCE BERKELEY LABORATORY BERKELEY, CALIFORNIA

# 1

ME, A WIZARD? UNTIL A WEEK AGO, I WAS AN ASTRONomer, contentedly designing telescope optics. Looking back on it, I'd lived in an academic dreamland. All these years, never planning for the future, right up to the day my grant money ran out.

Lucky for me that my laboratory recycled used astronomers. Instead of standing in the unemployment line, I found myself transferred from the Keck Observatory at the Lawrence Berkeley Lab, down to the computer center in the basement of the same building.

Well, hell, I could fake enough computing to impress astronomers, and maybe pick it up fast enough that my coworkers wouldn't catch on. Still, a computer wizard? Not me—I'm an astronomer.

Now what? As I apathetically stared at my computer terminal, I still thought of planetary orbits and astrophysics. As new kid on the block, I had my choice of a cubicle with a window facing the Golden Gate Bridge, or an unventilated office with a wall of bookshelves. Swallowing my claustrophobia, I picked the office, hoping that nobody would notice when I slept under the desk. On either side were offices of two systems people, Wayne Graves and Dave Cleveland, the old hands of the system. I soon got to know my neighbors through their bickering.

Viewing everyone as incompetent or lazy, Wayne was crossthreaded with the rest of the staff. Yet he knew the system thoroughly, from the disk driver software up to the microwave antennas. Wayne was weaned on Digital Equipment Corporation's Vax computers and would tolerate nothing less: not IBM, not Unix, not Macintoshes.

Dave Cleveland, our serene Unix buddha, patiently listened to Wayne's running stream of computer comparisons. A rare meeting didn't have Wayne's pitch, "Vaxes are the choice of scientists everywhere and help build strong programs twelve ways." Dave retorted, "Look, you keep your Vax addicts happy and I'll handle the rest of the world." Dave never gave him the satisfaction of getting riled, and Wayne's complaints eventually trailed off to a mutter.

Great. First day on the job, sandwiched between two characters who were already ruining my daydreams with their periodic disputes.

At least nobody could complain about my appearance. I wore the standard Berkeley corporate uniform: grubby shirt, faded jeans, long hair, and cheap sneakers. Managers occasionally wore ties, but productivity went down on the days they did.

Together, Wayne, Dave, and I were to run the computers as a lab-wide utility. We managed a dozen mainframe computers—giant workhorses for solving physics problems, together worth around six million dollars. The scientists using the computers were supposed to see a simple, powerful computing system, as reliable as the electric company. This meant keeping the machines running full time, around the clock. And just like the electric company, we charged for every cycle of computing that was used.

Of four thousand laboratory employees, perhaps a quarter used the main computers. Each of these one thousand accounts was tallied daily, and ledgers kept inside the computer. With an hour of computing costing three hundred dollars, our bookkeeping had to be accurate, so we kept track of every page printed, every block of disk space, and every minute of processor time. A separate computer gathered these statistics and sent monthly bills to laboratory departments.

And so it happened that on my second day at work, Dave

wandered into my office, mumbling about a hiccup in the Unix accounting system. Someone must have used a few seconds of computing time without paying for it. The computer's books didn't quite balance; last month's bills of $2,387 showed a 75-cent shortfall.

Now, an error of a few thousand dollars is obvious and isn't hard to find. But errors in the pennies column arise from deeply buried problems, so finding these bugs is a natural test for a budding software wizard. Dave said that I ought to think about it.

"First-degree robbery, huh?" I responded.

"Figure it out, Cliff, and you'll amaze everyone," Dave said.

Well, this seemed like a fun toy, so I dug into the accounting program. I discovered our accounting software to be a patchwork of programs written by long-departed summer students. Somehow, the hodgepodge worked well enough to be ignored. Looking at the mixture of programs, I found the software in Assembler, Fortran, and Cobol, the most ancient of computer languages. Might as well have been classical Greek, Latin, and Sanskrit.

As with most home-brew software, nobody had bothered to document our accounting system. Only a fool would poke around such a labyrinth without a map.

Still, here was a plaything for the afternoon and a chance to explore the system. Dave showed me how the system recorded each time someone connected to the computer, logging the user's name, and terminal. It timestamped each connection, recording which tasks the user executed, how many seconds of processor time he used, and when he disconnected.

Dave explained that we had two independent accounting systems. The ordinary Unix accounting software just stored the timestamped records into a file. But to satisfy some bureaucrat, Dave had built a second accounting system which kept more detailed records of who was using the computer.

Over the years, a succession of bored summer students had written programs to analyze all this accounting information. One program collected the data and stashed it into a file. A second program read that file and figured how much to charge for that session. Yet a third program collected all these charges and printed out bills to be mailed to each department. The last program added up all user charges and compared that total to the result from the computer's internal accounting program. Two accounting files, kept in parallel by different programs, ought to give the same answer.

For a year, these programs had run without a glitch, but weren't quite perfect this week. The obvious suspect was round-off error. Probably each accounting entry was correct, but when added together, tenths of a penny differences built up until an error of 75 cents accumulated. I ought to be able to prove this either by analyzing how the programs worked, or by testing them with different data.

Rather than trying to understand the code for each program, I wrote a short program to verify the data files. In a few minutes, I had checked the first program: indeed, it properly collected the accounting data. No problem with the first.

The second program took me longer to figure out. In an hour I had slapped together enough makeshift code to prove that it actually worked. It just added up time intervals, then multiplied by how much we charge for computer time. So the 75-cent error didn't come from this program.

And the third program worked perfectly. It looked at a list of authorized users, found their laboratory accounts, and then printed out a bill. Round-off error? No, all of the programs kept track of money down to the hundredths of a penny. Strange. Where's this 75-cent error coming from?

Well, I'd invested a couple hours in trying to understand a trivial problem. I got stubborn: dammit, I'd stay there till midnight, if I had to.

Several test programs later, I began actually to have confidence in the mishmash of locally built accounting programs. No question that the accounts didn't balance, but the programs, though not bulletproof, weren't dropping pennies. By now, I'd found the lists of authorized users, and figured out how the programs used the data structures to bill different departments. Around 7 P.M. my eye caught one user, Hunter. This guy didn't have a valid billing address.

Ha! Hunter used 75 cents of time in the past month, but nobody had paid for him.

Here's the source of our imbalance. Someone had screwed up when adding a user to our system. A trivial problem caused by a trivial error.

Time to celebrate. While writing this first small triumph into the beginning pages of my notebook, Martha, my sweetheart, stopped by and we celebrated with late-night cappuccinos at Berkeley's Cafe Roma.

A real wizard would have solved the problem in a few minutes. For me, it was unknown territory, and finding my way around hadn't been easy. As a consolation, I'd learned the accounting system and practiced a couple obsolete languages. Next day, I sent an electronic mail message to Dave, preening my feathers by pointing out the problem to him.

Around noon, Dave stopped by to drop off a pile of manuals, and casually mentioned that he had never added a user named Hunter—it must have been one of the other system managers. Wayne's curt response: "It wasn't me. RTFM." Most of his sentences ended with acronyms, this one meaning, "Read the fucking manual."

But I'd read the manuals. Operators weren't supposed to add a new user without an account. At other computer centers, you just log into a privileged account and tell the system to add a new user. Since we also had to make several bookkeeping entries, we couldn't run such a vanilla system. Ours was complex enough that we had special programs which automatically did the paperwork and the systems juggling.

Checking around, I found that everyone agreed the automatic system was so superior that nobody would have manually added a new user. And the automatic system wouldn't make this mistake.

Well, I couldn't figure out who had made this goof. Nobody knew Hunter, and there wasn't an account set for him. So I erased the name from the system—when he complained, we could set him up properly.

A day later, an obscure computer named Dockmaster sent us

an electronic mail message. Its system manager claimed that someone from our laboratory had tried to break into his computer over the weekend.

Dockmaster's return address might have been anywhere, but signs pointed to Maryland. The e-mail had passed through a dozen other computers, and each had left a postmark.

Dave answered the message with a noncommittal "We'll look into it." Uh, sure. We'd look when all our other problems disappeared.

Our laboratory's computers connect to thousands of other systems over a dozen networks. Any of our scientists can log into our computer, and then connect to a distant computer. Once connected, they can log into the distant computer by entering an account name and password. In principle, the only thing protecting the networked computer is the password, since account names are easy to figure out. (How do you find account names? Just use a phone book—most people use their names on computers.)

Dockmaster's electronic mail message was a curiosity, and Dave passed it to Wayne, attaching a question, "Who's Dockmaster?" Wayne forwarded it to me with his guess—"Probably some bank."

Eventually, Wayne bounced the message to me. I guessed Dockmaster was some Navy shipyard. It wasn't important, but it seemed worth spending a few minutes looking into.

The message gave the date and time when someone on our Unix computer tried to log into Dockmaster's computer. So I scrabbled around the accounting files, looking at Saturday morning's records. Again, the two accounting systems disagreed. The stock Unix accounting file showed a user, Sventek, logging in at 8:25, doing nothing for half an hour, and then disconnecting. No timestamped activity in between. Our home-brew software also recorded Sventek's activity, but it showed him using the networks from 8:31 until 9:01 A.M.

Jeez. Another accounting problem. The time stamps didn't agree. One showed activity when the other account said everything was dormant.

Other things seemed more pressing, so I dropped the problem. After wasting an afternoon chasing after some operator's mistake, I wasn't about to touch the accounting system again.

Over lunch with Dave, I mentioned that Sventek was the only one connected when Dockmaster reported the break-in. He stared and said, "Joe Sventek? He's in Cambridge. Cambridge, England. What's he doing back?" Turned out that Joe Sventek had been the laboratory's Unix guru, a software wizard who built a dozen major programs over the past decade. Joe had left for England a year ago, leaving behind a glowing reputation throughout the California computer community.

Dave couldn't believe Joe was back in town, since none of Joe's other friends had heard from him. "He must have entered our computer from some network," Dave said.

"So you think Joe's responsible for this problem?" I asked Dave.

"No way," Dave replied. "Joe's a hacker of the old school. A smart, quick, capable programmer. Not one of those punks that have tarnished the word 'hacker.' In any case, Sventek wouldn't try to break into some Maryland computer. And if he did try, he'd succeed, without leaving any trace."

Curious: Joe Sventek's been in England a year, yet he shows up early Saturday morning, tries to break into a Maryland computer, disconnects, and leaves behind an unbalanced accounting system. In the hallway I mention this to Wayne, who's heard that Joe's on vacation in England; he's hiding out in the backwoods, far away from any computers. "Forget that message from Dockmaster. Sventek's due to visit Berkeley RSN and he'll clear it up."

RSN? Real Soon Now. Wayne's way of saying, "I'm not sure when."

My worry wasn't Sventek. It was the unbalanced accounts. Why were the two accounting systems keeping different times? And why was some activity logged in one file without showing up in the other?

Back to the accounting system for an afternoon. I found that the five-minute time difference between the time stamps came from our various computers' clocks drifting over the months. One of our computer's clocks lost a few seconds every day.

But all of Sventek's activities should have appeared in both tallies. Was this related to last week's accounting problem? Had I screwed things up when I poked around last week? Or was there some other explanation?

# 2

THAT AFTERNOON, I SAT THROUGH AN IMPRESSIVELY boring lecture on the structure of galaxies. The learned professor not only spoke in a monotone, but filled the chalkboard with a snake's nest of mathematical equations.

Trying to stay awake, I tossed around the problems I'd bumped into. Someone screwed up when adding a new account. A week later, Sventek logs in and tries to break into some computer in Maryland. The accounting record for that event seems garbled. Sventek's unavailable. Something's amiss. It's almost as if someone's avoiding the accounting program.

What would it take, I wondered, to use our computers for free? Could someone have found a way around our accounting system?

Big computers have two types of software: user programs and systems software. Programs that you write or install yourself are user programs—for example, my astronomy routines which analyze a planet's atmosphere.

Alone, user programs can't do much. They don't talk directly to the computer; rather, they call upon the operating system to manipulate the computer. When my astronomy program wants to write something, it doesn't just slap a word on my screen. Instead, it passes the word to the operating system, which, in turn, tells the hardware to write a word.

The operating system, along with the editors, software

libraries, and language interpreters, make up the systems software. You don't write these programs—they come with the computer. Once they're set up, nobody should tamper with them.

The accounting program is systems software. To modify or bypass it, you have to either be system manager, or somehow have acquired a privileged position within the operating system.

OK, how do you become privileged? The obvious way is to log onto our computer with the system manager's password. We hadn't changed our password in months, but nobody would have leaked it. And an outsider would never guess our secret password, "wyvern"—how many people would think of a mythological winged dragon when guessing our password?

But even if you became system manager, you wouldn't fool with the accounting software. It's too obscure, too poorly documented. Anyway, I'd seen that it worked.

Wait—our home-brew software worked properly. Someone had added a new account without using it. Perhaps they didn't know about it. If someone had come in from the cold, they'd be unaware of our local wrinkles. Our system managers and operators knew this. Joe Sventek, even in England, surely would know.

But what about someone from the outside—a hacker?

The word "hacker" has two very different meanings. The people I knew who called themselves hackers were software wizards who managed to creatively program their way out of tight corners. They knew all the nooks and crannies of the operating system. Not dull software engineers who put in forty hours a week, but creative programmers who can't leave the computer until the machine's satisfied. A hacker identifies with the computer, knowing it like a friend.

Astronomers saw me that way. "Cliff, he's not much of an astronomer, but what a computer hacker!" (The computer folks, of course, had a different view: "Cliff's not much of a programmer, but what an astronomer!" At best, graduate school had taught me to keep both sides fooled.)

But in common usage, a hacker is someone who breaks into

computers.* In 1982, after a group of students used terminals, modems, and long-distance telephone lines to break into computers in Los Alamos and the Columbia Medical Center, the computing people suddenly became aware of the vulnerability of our networked systems.

Every few months, I'd hear a rumor about someone else's system being invaded; usually this was at universities, and it was often blamed on students or teenagers. "Brilliant high school student cracks into top security computer center." Usually it was harmless and written off as some hacker's prank.

Could the movie *War Games* actually happen—might some teenage hacker break into a Pentagon computer and start a war?

I doubted it. Sure, it's easy to muck around computers at universities where no security was needed. After all, colleges seldom even lock the doors to their buildings. I imagined that military computers were a whole different story—they'd be as tightly secured as a military base. And even if you did get into a military computer, it's absurd to think you could start a war. Those things just aren't controlled by computers, I thought.

Our computers at Lawrence Berkeley Laboratory weren't especially secure, but we were required to keep outsiders away from them and make an effort to prevent their misuse. We weren't worried about someone hurting our computers, we just wanted to keep our funding agency, the Department of Energy, off our backs. If they wanted our computers painted green, then we'd order paintbrushes.

But to make visiting scientists happy, we had several computer accounts for guests. With an account name of "guest" and a password of "guest," anyone could use the system to solve their problems, as long as they didn't use more than a few dollars of computing time. A hacker would have an easy time breaking into

---

*What word describes someone who breaks into computers? Old style software wizards are proud to be called hackers, and resent the scofflaws who have appropriated the word. On the networks, wizards refer to these hoodlums of our electronic age as "crackers" or "cyberpunks." In the Netherlands, there's the term "computervredebreuk"—literally, computer peace disturbance. Me? The idea of a vandal breaking into my computer makes me think of words like "varmint," "reprobate," and "swine."

that account—it was wide open. This would hardly be much of a break-in, with time limited to one minute. But from that account, you could look around the system, read any public files, and see who was logged in. We felt the minor security risk was well worth the convenience.

Mulling over the situation, I kept doubting that a hacker was fooling around in my system. Nobody's interested in particle physics. Hell, most of our scientists would be delighted if anyone would read their papers. There's nothing special here to tempt a hacker—no snazzy supercomputer, no sexy trade secrets, no classified data. Indeed, the best part of working at Lawrence Berkeley Labs was the open, academic atmosphere.

Fifty miles away, Lawrence Livermore Labs did classified work, developing nuclear bombs and Star Wars projects. Now, that might be a target for some hacker to break into. But with no connections to the outside, Livermore's computers can't be dialed into. Their classified data's protected by brute force: isolation.

If someone did break into our system, what could they accomplish? They could read any public files. Most of our scientists set their data this way, so their collaborators can read it. Some of the systems software was public as well.

Though we call this data public, an outsider shouldn't wander through it. Some of it's proprietary or copyrighted, like our software libraries and word processing programs. Other databases aren't for everyone's consumption—lists of our employees' addresses and incomplete reports on work in progress. Still, these hardly qualify as sensitive material, and it's a long way from classified.

No, I wasn't worried about someone entering our computer as a guest and walking off with somebody's telephone number. My real concern centered on a much bigger problem: could a stranger become a super-user?

To satisfy a hundred users at once, the computer's operating system splits the hardware resources much as an apartment house splits a building into many apartments. Each apartment works independently of the others. While one resident may be watching TV, another talks on the phone, and a third washes dishes. Utilities—electricity, phone service, and water—are supplied by the apartment complex. Every resident complains about slow service and the exorbitant rents.

Within the computer, one user might be solving a math problem, another sending electronic mail to Toronto, yet a third writing a letter. The computer utilities are supplied by the systems software and operating system; each user grumbles about the unreliable software, obscure documentation, and the exorbitant costs.

Privacy within the apartment house is regulated by locks and keys. One resident can't enter another's apartment without a key, and (if the walls are sturdy), one resident's activity won't bother another. Within the computer, it's the operating system that ensures user privacy. You can't get into someone's area without the right password, and (if the operating system is fair about handing out resources), one user's programs won't interfere with another's.

But apartment walls are never sturdy enough, and my neighbor's parties thunder into my bedroom. And my computer still slows down when there's more than one hundred people using it at one time. So our apartment houses need superintendents, and our computers need system managers, or super-users.

With a passkey, the apartment house superintendent can enter any room. From a privileged account, the system manager can read or modify any program or data on the computer. Privileged users bypass the operating system protections and have the full run of the computer. They need this power to maintain the systems software ("Fix the editor!"), to tune the operating system's performance ("Things are too slow today!"), and to let people use the computer ("Hey, give Barbara an account.").

Privileged users learn to tread lightly. They can't do much damage if they're only privileged to read files. But the super-user's license lets you change any part of the system—there's no protections against the super-user's mistakes.

Truly, the super-user is all-powerful: she controls the horizontal, she controls the vertical. When daylight savings time comes around, she resets the system clock. A new disk drive? She's the only one who can graft the necessary software into the system.

Different operating systems have various names for privileged accounts—super-user, root, system manager—but these accounts must always be jealously guarded against outsiders.

What if an outside hacker became privileged on our system? For one thing, he could add new user accounts.

A hacker with super-user privileges would hold the computer hostage. With the master key to our system, he could shut it down whenever he wishes, and could make the system as unreliable as he wishes. He could read, write, or modify any information in the computer. No user's file would be protected from him when he operates from this privileged high ground. The system files, too, would be at his disposal—he could read electronic mail before it's delivered.

He could even modify the accounting files to erase his own tracks.

The lecturer on galactic structure droned on about gravitational waves. I was suddenly awake, aware of what was happening in our computer. I waited around for the question period, asked one token question, then grabbed my bike and started up the hill to Lawrence Berkeley Labs.

A super-user hacker. Someone breaks into our system, finds the master keys, grants himself privileges, and becomes a super-user hacker. Who? How? From where? And, mostly, why?

# 3

IT'S ONLY A QUARTER MILE FROM THE UNIVERSITY OF California to Lawrence Berkeley Labs, but Cyclotron Road is steep enough to make it a fifteen-minute bike ride. The old ten-speed didn't quite have a low enough gear, so my knees felt the last few hundred feet. Our computer center's nestled between three particle accelerators: the 184-inch cyclotron, where Ernest Lawrence first purified a milligram of fissionable uranium; the Bevatron, where the anti-proton was discovered; and the Hilac, the birthplace of a half-dozen new elements.

Today, these accelerators are obsolete—their mega-electron volt energies long surpassed by giga-electron volt particle colliders. They're no longer winning Nobel prizes, but physicists and graduate students still wait six months for time on an accelerator beamline. After all, our accelerators are fine for studying exotic nuclear particles and searching out new forms of matter, with esoteric names like quark-gluon plasmas or pion condensates. And when the physicists aren't using them, the beams are used for biomedical research, including cancer therapy.

Back in the heyday of World War II's Manhattan project, Lawrence's cyclotron was the only way to measure the cross sections of nuclear reactions and uranium atoms. Naturally, the lab was shrouded in secrecy; it served as the model for building atomic bomb plants.

During the 1950s, Lawrence Berkeley Laboratory's research

remained classified, until Edward Teller formed the Lawrence Livermore Laboratory an hour's drive away. All the classified work went to Livermore, while the unclassified science remained in Berkeley.

Perhaps to spread confusion, both laboratories are named after California's first Nobel Laureate, both are centers for atomic physics, and both are funded by the Atomic Energy Commission's offspring, the Department of Energy. That's about the end of the similarity.

I needed no security clearance to work in the Berkeley Lab—there's no classified research, not a military contract in sight. Livermore, on the other hand, is a center for designing nuclear bombs and Star Wars laser beams. Hardly the place for a long-haired ex-hippie. While my Berkeley Lab survived on meager scientific grants and unreliable university funding, Livermore constantly expanded. Every since Teller designed the H-bomb, Livermore's classified research has never been short of funds.

Berkeley no longer has huge military contracts, yet openness has its rewards. As pure scientists, we're encouraged to research any curious phenomena, and can always publish our results. Our accelerators might be peashooters compared to the behemoths at CERN in Switzerland, or Fermilab in Illinois; still, they generate huge amounts of data, and we run some respectable computers to analyze it. In fact, it's a source of local pride to find physicists recording their data at other accelerators, then visiting LBL to analyze their results on our computers.

In raw number-crunching power, Livermore's computers dwarfed ours. They regularly bought the biggest, fastest, and most expensive Crays. They need 'em to figure out what happens in the first few nanoseconds of a thermonuclear explosion.

Because of their classified research, most of Livermore's computers are isolated. Of course, they have some unclassified systems too, doing ordinary science. But for their secret work—well, it's not for ordinary mortal eyes. These classified computers have no connections to the outside world.

It's just as impossible to import data into Livermore from the outside. Someone designing nuclear bomb triggers using Livermore's classified computers has to visit the lab in person, bringing his data in on magnetic tape. He can't use the dozens of networks crossing the country, and can't log in from home, to see how his program is running. Since their computers are often the first ones off the production line, Livermore usually has to write their own operating systems, forming a bizarre software ecology, unseen outside of their laboratory. Such are the costs of living in a classified world.

While we didn't have the number-crunching power of Livermore, our computers were no slouches. Our Vax computers were speedy, easy to use, and popular among physicists. We didn't have to invent our own operating systems, since we bought Digital's VMS operating system, and grabbed Unix from campus. As an open lab, our computers could be networked anywhere, and we supported scientists from around the world. When problems developed in the middle of the night, I just dialed the LBL computer from my home—no need to bicycle into work when a phone call might solve it.

But there I was, bicycling up to work, wondering if some hacker was in our system. This just might explain some of my accounting problems. If some outsider had picked the locks on our Unix operating system and acquired super-user privileges, he'd have the power to selectively erase the accounting records. And, worse, he could use our network connections to attack other computers.

I ducked my bike into a corner and jogged over to the cubicle maze. By now it was well past five, and the ordinary folks were at home. How could I tell if someone was hacking inside our system? Well, we could just send an electronic mail message to the suspicious account, saying something like, "Hey, are you the real Joe Sventek?" Or we could disable Joe's account, and see if our troubles ended.

My thoughts about the hacker were sidetracked when I found a note in my office: the astronomy group needed to know how the quality of the telescope's images degraded if they loosened the specifications for the mirrors. This meant an evening of model building, all inside the computer. I wasn't officially working for them anymore, but blood's thicker than water . . . by midnight, I'd plotted the graphs for them.

The next morning, I eagerly explained my suspicions about a hacker to Dave Cleveland. "I'll bet you cookies to doughnuts it's a hacker."

Dave sat back, closed his eyes, and whispered, "Yep, cookies for sure."

His mental acrobatics were almost palpable. Dave managed his Unix system with a laid-back style. Since he competed for scientists with the VMS systems, he had never screwed down the security bolts on his system, figuring that the physicists would object and take their business elsewhere. By trusting his users, he ran an open system and devoted his time to improving their software, instead of building locks.

Was someone betraying his trust?

Marv Atchley was my new boss. Quiet and sensitive, Marv ran a loose group that somehow managed to keep the computers running. Marv stood in contrast to our division head, Roy Kerth. At fifty-five, Roy looked like Rodney Dangerfield as a college professor. He did physics in the grand style of Lawrence Laboratory, bouncing protons and anti-protons together, looking at the jetsam from these collisions.

Roy treated his students and staff much as his subatomic particles: keep them in line, energize them, then shoot them into immovable objects. His research demanded heavy number crunching, since his lab generated millions of events each time the accelerator was turned on. Years of delays and excuses had soured him on computer professionals, so when I knocked on his door, I made sure we talked about relativistic physics and ignored computing.

Now, Dave and I could guess Roy's reaction to our problem: "Why the hell did you leave our doors wide open?"

Our boss's reaction might be predictable, but how should we react? Dave's first thought was to disable the suspect account and forget about it. I felt we ought to send a nasty-gram to whoever was breaking in, telling him to stay away or we'd call his parents. After all, if someone was breaking in, it was bound to be some student from down on campus.

But we weren't certain that someone was breaking into our system. It might explain some of our accounting problems—someone learns the system manager's password, connects to our machine, creates a new account, and tampers with the accounting system. But why would someone use a new account if they already had access to the system manager account?

Our boss never wanted to hear bad news, but we swallowed hard and called a lunchtime meeting. We had no clear proof of a hacker, just circumstantial pointers, extrapolated from trivial accounting errors. If there was a break-in, we didn't know how far it extended, nor who was doing it. Roy Kerth blasted us. "Why are you wasting my time? You don't know anything and you haven't proven a whit. Go back and find out. Show me proof."

So how do you find a hacker? I figured it was simple: just watch for anyone using Sventek's accounts, and try to trace their connection.

I spent Thursday watching people log into the computer. I wrote a program to beep my terminal whenever someone connected to the Unix computer. I couldn't see what each user was doing, but I could see their names. Every couple minutes my terminal beeped, and I'd see who had logged in. A few were friends, astronomers working on research papers or graduate students plugging away on dissertations. Most accounts belonged to strangers, and I wondered how I could tell which connection might be a hacker.

At 12:33 on Thursday afternoon, Sventek logged in. I felt a rush of adrenaline and then a complete letdown when he disappeared within a minute. Where was he? The only pointer left for me was the identifier of his terminal: he had used terminal port tt23.

Sitting behind a computer terminal, fingers resting on his keyboard, someone was connecting into our lab. My Unix computer gave him the address of port tt23.

Well, that's a start. My problem was to figure out which physical wires corresponded to the logical name tt23.

Terminals from our laboratory and modems from dial-in telephones are all assigned "tt" labels, while network connections show up as "nt." I figured that the guy must be either from our laboratory or dialing in on a phone line over a modem.

For a few seconds, I'd sensed a hesitant feeler into our computer. Theoretically, it must be possible to trace the path from computer to human. Someone must be at the far end of that connection.

It would take six months to track that path, but my first step was to trace the connection out of the building. I suspected a dial-in modem, connected from some telephone line, but it conceivably might be someone at the laboratory. Over the years, well over five hundred terminals had been wired in, and only Paul Murray kept track. With luck, our homegrown hardware connections were documented better than the home-brew accounting software.

Paul's a reclusive hardware technician who hides in thickets of telephone wire. I found him behind a panel of electronics, connecting some particle detector to the lab-wide ethernet system. Ethernets are electronic pipelines connecting hundreds of small computers. A few miles of orange ethernet cable snaked through our lab, and Paul knew every inch of it.

Cursing me for surprising him in the middle of soldering a wire, he refused to give me any help until I proved that I had a legitimate need to know. Aw, hell. Hardware technicians don't understand software problems, and software jockeys know nothing about hardware.

Years of ham radio had taught me to solder, so Paul and I had at least one common denominator. I picked up his spare soldering iron and earned his grudging respect after a few minutes of burning my fingers and squinting. Finally, he disentangled himself from the ethernet cables and showed me around the LBL communications switchyard.

In this roomful of wires, the telephones, intercoms, radios, and computers were all interconnected by a tangle of cables, wires, optical fibers, and patch panels. The suspicious port tt23 entered this room and a secondary computer switched it to one of a thousand possible terminals. Anyone dialing into the lab would be randomly assigned to a Unix port. The next time I saw a suspicious character, I'd have to run over to the switchyard and unwind the connection by probing the switching computer. If he disappeared before I disentangled the connection, well, tough. And even if I did succeed, I'd only be able to point to a pair of wires entering the laboratory. I'd still be a long way from the hacker.

By lucky accident, though, the noontime connection had left some footprints behind. Paul had been collecting statistics on how many people used the switchyard. By chance he had recorded the port numbers of each connection for the past month. Since I knew the time when Sventek was active on port tt23, we could figure out where he came from. The printout of the statistics showed a one-minute 1200-baud connection had taken place at 12:33.

1200 baud, huh? That says something. The baud rate measures the speed that data flows through a line. And 1200 baud means 120 characters per second—a few pages of text every minute.

Dial-up modems over telephone lines run at 1200 baud. Any lab employee here on the hill would run at high speed: 9600 or 19,200 baud. Only someone calling through a modem would let their data dribble out a 1200-baud soda straw. And the anonymity and convenience of these dial-in lines are most inviting to strangers. So pieces were beginning to fit together. I couldn't prove that we had a hacker in the system, but someone dialed into our lab and used Sventek's account.

Still, the 1200-baud connection was hardly proof that a hacker entered our system. An incomplete trace, especially one that went no farther than my building, would never convince my boss that something was up, something weird. I needed to find incontrovertible evidence of a hacker. But how?

Roy Kerth had shown me the high-energy particle detectors attached to the Bevatron: they find jillions of subatomic interactions, and 99.99 percent are explainable by the laws of physics. Spending your time exploring each particle trail will lead you to conclude that all the particles obey known physics, and there's nothing left to discover. Alternatively, you could throw away all the explainable interactions, and only worry about those that don't quite satisfy the canonical rules.

Astronomers, distant cousins of high-energy physicists, work along similar lines. Most stars are boring. Advances come from studying the weirdies—the quasars, the pulsars, the gravitational lenses—that don't seem to fit into the models that you've grown up with. Knowing cratering statistics on the planet Mercury tells you how often the planet was bombarded in the early solar system. But study the few craters intersected by scarps and ridges and you'll learn how the planet shrank as it cooled during its first billion years. Collect raw data and throw away the expected. What remains challenges your theories.

Well, let's apply this way of thinking to watching someone visiting my computer. I've got a terminal on my desk, and can borrow a couple others. Suppose I just watched the traffic coming into the computer center. There's about five hundred lines entering the system. Most of these lines run at 9600 baud, or around one hundred fifty words per second. If half the lines are used at any time, I'd have to read well over ten thousand pages every minute. Right. No way could I monitor that kind of traffic on my terminal.

But the high-speed lines come from people at LBL. We'd already traced one suspicious connection to a 1200-baud line. There are fewer of them (we can't afford too many incoming phone lines), and they're slower. Fifty lines at 1200 baud might generate a hundred pages a minute, still far too fast to watch on the screen of my terminal. I might not be able to watch fifty people running at once, but maybe I could print out all their interactive sessions, and read the piles of paper at my leisure. A paper printout would provide hard proof of someone messing around; if we found nothing suspicious, we could drop the whole project.

I'd record everything that happened during each 1200-baud connection. This would be technically challenging—since I didn't know which line the hacker was calling, I'd have to monitor four dozen. More worrisome was the ethical problem of monitoring our communications. Did we have the right to watch the traffic running through our lines?

My sweetheart, Martha, was just finishing law school. Over a deep-dish pizza, we talked about the implications of someone breaking into a computer. I wondered how much trouble I'd be in by listening to incoming traffic.

"Look," she mumbled, burning the roof of her mouth on the vulcanized mozzarella. "You're not the government, so you don't need a search warrant. The worst it would be is invasion of privacy. And people dialing up a computer probably have no right to insist that the system's owner not look over their shoulder. So I don't see why you can't."

So with a clear conscience, I started building a monitoring system. We had fifty 1200-baud lines, and a hacker might be using any of them. I had no equipment designed to record the traffic.

But there's an easy way to record a hacker's activity. Modify the Unix operating system so that whenever a suspicious person logged in, the system records all the keystrokes. This was tempting because I only had to add some lines of code to the Unix daemon software.

The daemons themselves are just programs that copy data from the outside world into the operating system—the eyes and ears of Unix. (The ancient Greek daemons were inferior divinities, midway between gods and men. In that sense, my daemons are midway between the god-like operating system and the world of terminals and disks.)

I could split the daemon's output like a T-joint in a pipe, so the hacker's keystrokes would simultaneously go to both the operating system and a printer. Software solutions are simple and elegant.

"Muck with the daemons at your own risk," Dave Cleveland said. "Just respect their timing needs."

Wayne also warned me, "Look, if you goof up, you'll break the system for sure. It will turn the system into molasses, and there's no way you'll follow everything that happens. Just wait till you see the system console print out 'Panic kernel mode interrupt'—don't come crying on my shoulder!"

Dave chipped in, "Hey, if your hacker has any Unix experience, he's bound to notice a change in the daemons."

That convinced me. A sharp systems person would notice that

we'd changed the operating system. The moment the hacker knew someone was watching him, he'd trash our databases and scram. Our wiretaps had to be completely undetectable, even to an omnipotent super-user. Silent, invisible monitors to trap the hacker's activity.

Maybe just tape recording the telephone lines would work, but tape recorders didn't feel right, too much of a kludge. We'd have to play them back, and couldn't watch the keystrokes until long after a hacker had disconnected. Finally, where would I find fifty tape recorders?

About the only other place to watch our traffic was in between the modems and the computers. The modems converted the tones of a telephone into electronic pulses, palatable to our computers and the daemons in their operating systems. These modem lines appeared as flat, twenty-five conductor wires, snaking underneath the switchyard's false floor. A printer or personal computer could be wired to each of these lines, recording every keystroke that came through.

A kludge? Yes. Workable? Maybe.

All we'd need are fifty teletypes, printers, and portable computers. The first few were easy to get—just ask at the lab's supplies desk. Dave, Wayne, and the rest of the systems group grudgingly lent their portable terminals. By late Friday afternoon, we'd hooked up a dozen monitors down in the switchyard. The other thirty or forty monitors would show up after the laboratory was deserted. I walked from office to office, liberating personal computers from secretaries' desks. There'd be hell to pay on Monday, but it's easier to give an apology than get permission.

Strewn with four dozen obsolete teletypes and portable terminals, the floor looked like a computer engineer's nightmare. I slept in the middle, nursing the printers and computers. Each was grabbing data from a different line, and whenever someone dialed our system, I'd wake up to the chatter of typing. Every half hour, one of the monitors would run out of paper or disk space, so I'd have to roll over and reload.

Saturday morning, Roy Kerth shook me awake. "Well, where's your hacker?"

Still in my sleeping bag, I must have smelled like a goat. I blinked stupidly and mumbled something about looking at the fifty piles of paper.

He snorted, "Well, before you start poking around those printouts, return those printers. You've been running around here like a maniac swiping equipment used by people who are getting work done. You've pissed off a dozen astronomers. Are *you* getting work done? No. Whaddya think this place is, your own personal sandbox?"

Bleary-eyed, I dragged each printer back to its rightful owner. The first forty-nine showed nothing interesting. From the fiftieth trailed eighty feet of printout. During the night, someone had sneaked in through a hole in the operating system.

# 4

FOR THREE HOURS, A HACKER HAD STROLLED THROUGH my system, reading whatever he wished. Unknown to him, my 1200-baud Decwriter had saved his session on eighty feet of single-spaced computer paper. Here was every command he issued, every typing mistake, and every response from the computer.

This printer monitored the line from Tymnet. I didn't realize it, but a few of our 1200-baud lines weren't dial-in modem lines. Rather, they came from Tymnet, a communications company that interconnected computers around the world.

Before divestment, the Bell system monopolized communications. AT&T was the only way to connect New York to Chicago. By using modems, the phone system could handle data, but the noise and expense of the long-distance service made it unsuitable for computers. By the late '70s, a few other companies dipped their toes in the water, offering specialized services like data phones. Tymnet created a network to interconnect computers in major cities.

Tymnet's idea was simple and elegant: create a digital communications backbone, let anyone connect to the backbone by making a local telephone call, then send the data to any computer on the network. Tymnet would compress dozens of users' data into a few packets, and economically send these around the country. The system was immune to noise, and each user could run as fast as he wished. Customers saved money because they could access a distant computer by making a local call.

To satisfy scientists around the country, LBL subscribed to Tymnet. When a researcher in Stonybrook, New York, wanted to connect to our computer, he dialed his local Tymnet number. Once his modem was connected to Tymnet, he just asked for LBL and worked as if he were in Berkeley. Physicists from far away loved the service, and we were delighted to find them spending their research dollars on our computers, rather than their home machines.

Someone was breaking in, using the Tymnet line. Since Tymnet interconnected the whole country, our hacker might be anywhere.

For the moment, though, I was fascinated not by where the hacker came from, but what he had done in three hours. My guess was right: Sventek's account was being used to break into our Unix computer.

Not just break in. This hacker was a super-user.

The hacker had sneaked through a hole in our system to become a super-user—he'd never even logged into the system manager's account. He was like a cuckoo bird.

The cuckoo lays her eggs in other birds' nests. She is a nesting parasite: some other bird will raise her young cuckoos. The survival of cuckoo chicks depends on the ignorance of other species.

Our mysterious visitor laid an egg-program into our computer, letting the system hatch it and feed it privileges.

That morning, the hacker wrote a short program to grab privileges. Normally, Unix won't allow such a program to run, since it never gives privileges beyond what a user is assigned. But run this program from a privileged account, and he'll become privileged. His problem was to masquerade this special program—the cuckoo's egg—so that it would be hatched by the system.

Every five minutes, the Unix system executes its own program named *atrun*. In turn, atrun schedules other jobs and does routine housecleaning tasks. It runs in a privileged mode, with the full power and trust of the operating system behind it. Were a bogus atrun program substituted, it would be executed within five minutes, with full system privileges. For this reason, atrun sits in a protected area of the system, available only to the system manager. Nobody but the system manager has the license to tamper with atrun.

Here was the Cuckoo's nest: for five minutes, he would swap his egg for the system's atrun program.

For this attack, he needed to find a way to move his egg-program into the protected systems nest. The operating system's barriers are built specifically to prevent this. Normal copy programs can't bypass them; you can't issue a command to "copy my program into systems space."

But there was a wildcard that we'd never noticed. Richard Stallman, a free-lance computer programmer, loudly proclaimed that information should be free. His software, which he gives away for free, is brilliantly conceived, elegantly written, and addictive.

Over the past decade Stallman created a powerful editing program called Gnu-Emacs. But Gnu's much more than just a text editor. It's easy to customize to your personal preferences. It's a foundation upon which other programs can be built. It even has its own mail facility built in. Naturally, our physicists demanded Gnu; with an eye to selling more computing cycles, we installed it happily.

Just one problem: there's a bug in that software.

In the way it was installed on our Unix computer, the Gnu-Emacs editor lets you forward a mail file from your own directory to anyone else in an unusual way. It doesn't check to see who's receiving it, or even whether they want the file. It just renames the file and changes its ownership label. You've just transferred ownership of the file from you to me.

No problem to send a file from your area to mine. But you'd better not be able to move a file into the protected systems area: only the system manager is allowed there. Stallman's software had better make sure this can't happen.

Gnu didn't check. It let anyone move a file into protected systems space. The hacker knew this; we didn't.

The hacker used Gnu to swap his special *atrun* file for the system's legitimate version. Five minutes later, the system hatched his egg, and he held the keys to my computer.

He had used this technique to fool the computer into giving him power. He planted his phony program where the system expected to find a valid one. The instant that Unix executed his bogus *atrun* program, he became super-user. The whole operation depended on his being able to move a file anywhere he wished.

Gnu was the hole in our system's security. A subtle bug in an obscure section of some popular software. Installed blindly by our systems programmers, we'd never thought that it might destroy our whole system's security.

Now I understood. Our friend must have entered a guest account, leveraged his privileges using Gnu's hole, and then added a new account to the computer's files.

In front of me, the first few feet of the printout showed the cuckoo preparing the nest, laying the egg, and waiting for it to hatch. The next seventy feet showed the fledgling cuckoo testing its wings.

As super-user, he had the run of our system. First thing he did was erase his tracks: he switched the good copy of *atrun* back where it belonged. Then he listed the electronic mail of all our users, reading news, gossip, and love letters. He learned of the past month's computer changes, grant proposals, and new hires. He searched for changes in the system managers' files, and discovered that I'd just started work. He checked my salary and résumé. More worrisome, he realized that I was a system manager, and my account name.

Why me? What did I do? At any rate, from now on, I'd better use a different name.

Every ten minutes, the hacker issued the command, "who," to list everyone logged onto the computer. Apparently, he worried that someone might see him connected, or might be watching. Later, he searched for any changes in the operating system—had I modified the daemons to record his session, as I'd first planned to do, he would surely have discovered it. I felt like a kid playing hide-and-seek, when the seeker passes within inches of his hiding place.

Within the first hour, he wrote a program to scan everyone's mail messages for any mention of his activity. He searched for the word, "hacker," and "security."

One scientist had started a program that assembled data from an experiment over the weekend. Running under the name "gather," this program innocuously collected information every few minutes and wrote it to a file. The hacker saw this program, spent ten minutes trying to understand what it did, and killed it.

Yow! Here's someone looking over his shoulder every few minutes, checking to see if anyone's around. He kills any jobs that he thinks might monitor him. He opens my mail, checking to see if anyone's written about hackers. Wayne was right: if you stay in the open, he'll know you're watching. From now on, we'd have to be subtle and invisible.

When he wasn't looking back over his shoulder, the hacker was reading files. By studying several scientists' command files and scripts, he discovered pathways into other lab computers. Every night, our computer automatically calls twenty others, to exchange mail and network news. When the hacker read these phone numbers, he learned twenty new targets.

From the mail file of an engineer:

```
Hi, Ed!
I'll be on vacation for the next couple weeks. If you need to get any
of my data, just log into my account on the Vax computer. Account
name is Wilson, password is Maryanne (that's my wife's name). Have
fun!
```

The hacker had fun, even if Ed didn't. He connected through our local area network into that Vax, and had no problem logging into Wilson's account. Wilson wouldn't notice the hacker reading his files, and probably wouldn't care. They contained numerical data, meaningless to anyone but another nuclear physicist.

Our visitor knew about our lab's internal networks. Our dozen big computers were tied to a hundred laboratory computers using ethernets, serial lines, and chewing gum. When physicists wanted to get data from a computer at the cyclotron into our big computer, elegance meant nothing. They'd use any port, any line, any network. Over the years technicians had woven a web of cables around the lab, interconnecting most of the computers with whatever seemed to work. This local area network reached into every office, connecting PC's, Macintoshes, and terminals to our mainframe computers.

Often, these networked computers had been arranged to trust each other. If you're OK on that computer, then you're OK on this one. This saved a bit of time: people wouldn't need to present more than one password when using several computers.

The hacker exploited that trust to enter a half dozen computers. As super-user on our main Unix computer, he disguised himself under someone else's account name. Then he just knocked on the door of another networked machine, and he was admitted without even whispering the password. Our visitor couldn't know what these systems were used for; still, he felt his way around the net, searching for connections into unexplored computers.

By the end of the session, the printer's ribbon had run out of ink. By rubbing a pencil lightly over the paper, I could just make out the impressions left from the printhead: the hacker had copied our password file, then disconnected.

A bass guitar note took my attention from the hacker's trail. The Grateful Dead were playing outdoors at the Berkeley Greek Theater, only a hundred yards downhill from the lab. The police couldn't keep people from sitting in the field overlooking the concert, so I skipped over there, mingling with a thousand others in tie-dyed shirts. Burnt-out panhandlers, left over from the sixties, worked the crowd, begging tickets and selling posters, buttons, and grass. The drum solo in the second set echoed from Strawberry Canyon, adding a weird backbeat appreciated only by us cheapskates in the fields. Life was full: no hacker is worth missing a Dead concert for.

# 5

MONDAY MORNING MARKED MY SECOND WEEK ON THE job. I was an uneasy computer jockey: surrounded by over-worked experts, yet not knowing what tasks I ought to be doing. Something fun would turn up; in the meantime, I might as well finish this hacker project.

Like a freshman in physics lab, I wrote about the weekend's activity in a logbook. Not that I planned to use this logbook: it was a chance to learn a word processor on my Macintosh. The astronomer's rule of thumb: if you don't write it down, it didn't happen.

I passed the results to the gang, hoping nobody would notice that I'd slept overnight in the machine room.

The boss wanted to see me as soon as he arrived.

I suspected he was mad about my grabbing all those terminals. Management might be loose, but computer jocks still weren't supposed to borrow piles of lab equipment without telling anyone.

But Roy didn't even grinch about the terminals. He wanted to know about the hacker.

"When did he show up?"

"Sunday morning at five for three hours."

"Delete any files?"

"Killed one program that he thought was monitoring him."

"Are we in danger?"

"He's super-user. He can wipe out all our files."

"Can we shut him down?"

"Probably. We know the one hole; it's a quick patch."

"Think that'll stop him?"

I could sense where his thoughts were leading. Roy wasn't concerned about slamming the door. He knew we could easily deactivate the stolen Sventek account. And now that we understood it, fixing the Gnu-Emacs hole wasn't difficult: just add a couple lines of code to check the target directory.

Should we close our doors or remain open? Closing up shop was the obvious reaction. We knew how this hacker entered our system and knew how to kick him out.

But what else was wrong? What other gifts had our mysterious visitor left for us? How many other accounts did he access? What other computers did he break into?

There was the worry. The printout showed the hacker to be a competent systems programmer, able to exploit obscure bugs that we'd never seen before. What else had he done?

When you're super-user, you can modify any file in the system. Did the hacker modify a system program to open a backdoor entrance? Had he patched our system to recognize a magic password?

Did he plant a computer virus? On home computers, viruses spread by copying themselves into other pieces of software. When you give an infected piece of software to someone else, the virus copies itself into other software, spreading from disk to disk.

If the virus is benign, it'll be hard to detect and probably won't do much damage. But it's easy to build malicious viruses which duplicate themselves and then erase data files. Just as easy to create a virus that lies dormant for months and then erupts some day in the future.

Viruses are the creatures that haunt programmers' nightmares.

As super-user, the hacker could infect our system in a way that would be almost impossible to eradicate. His virus could copy itself into systems software and hide in obscure areas of the computer. By copying itself from program to program, it would defy our efforts to erase it.

Unlike a home computer, where you can rebuild the operating system from scratch, we had extensively modified our operating system. We couldn't go to a manufacturer and say, "Give us an original copy." Once infected, we could only rebuild our system from backup tapes. If he'd planted a virus six months ago, our tapes would be infected as well.

Maybe he'd planted a logic bomb—a program timed to blow up sometime in the future. Or perhaps this intruder had only rifled our files, killed a couple jobs, and screwed up our accounting. But how could we tell that he hadn't done much worse? For a week, our computer was wide open to this hacker. Could we prove that he hadn't tampered with our databases?

How could we again trust our programs and data?

We couldn't. Trying to shut him out wouldn't work, as he'd only find another way in. We needed to find out what he had done and what he was doing.

Most of all, we needed to know who was at the other end of the line.

"It's gotta be some student on the Berkeley campus," I said to Roy. "They're the Unix wizards, and they think of us as bozos."

"I wouldn't be too sure." Roy leaned back in his chair. "Why would someone from Berkeley come in through Tymnet, when they could more easily have dialed our system over the telephone lines?"

"Maybe Tymnet is just a cover," I said. "A place to hide. If he dialed the lab directly, we'd trace him. But now, we've got to trace both Tymnet and a telephone call."

My hand waving didn't convince the boss. Perhaps from his scientific experience or maybe as a cynical ploy, Roy kept an open mind: it's not a student until he's dragged in. Sure, the weekend's printouts showed a good programmer, but we might be watching any competent computer jockey, anywhere. Tracking the guy meant tracing telephone lines. The price of hard evidence was hard work.

Confronted with traces of a mysterious visitor, Roy only saw footprints. I saw an intruder.

Roy decided not to decide. "Let's close down all network connections for the day. Tomorrow morning, I'll talk to the lab director, and get a sense of what to do." We could delay, but sooner or later we'd have to either start tracing, or lock the guy out.

Did I want to track someone through the city? It would keep me from scientific computing. It had nothing to do with astronomy or physics. And it sounded like cops and robbers—or a game of hide-and-seek.

On the plus side, though, I might learn about phone traces and networks. Best of all was imagining the look on some kid's face when we barged into his dorm room, shouting, "Freeze! Drop that keyboard!"

Tuesday afternoon, Roy called. "The director says, 'This is electronic terrorism. Use all the resources you need to catch the bastard. Take all the time you want. Spend three weeks, if you have to. Nail the bastard.' "

If I wanted to hunt the hacker, management backed me.

# 6

I BIKED HOME, THINKING OF DEVIOUS HACKER-TRAPPING schemes. As I came closer to home, though, my thoughts turned to dinner. So great to have someone to come home to.

Martha Matthews and I had lived together for a few years now, and been friends for almost ten. We'd known each other so well that it was hard to remember a time before I knew her.

Old friends shook their heads. They'd never seen me stay with one woman this long. I'd fall in love, hang around for a couple years, and then we'd grow tired of each other and move on. I was still good friends with several former lovers, but the romance never seemed to last. I'd always been cynical and sarcastic, protecting myself from getting too close to anyone.

But life with Martha felt different. Barrier after barrier came down, slowly, over time. She insisted on talking out our differences, demanded to know the reasons for my moods and tempers, demanded that we think of ways to get along better. It was unbearable sometimes—I hated to talk when I was mad—but it usually seemed to work.

I found myself feeling nesting instincts. The perfect afternoon was to tinker around the house, rewiring a switch, planting some bulbs, or soldering a stained-glass window. We spent many a quiet evening, sewing or reading or playing Scrabble. I began to feel . . .

Married? Who, me? No. Definitely not. Marriage was stultifying, a trap for the conventional. You married someone and they expected you to stay the same forever, never changing, never doing anything new. There'd be fights and you couldn't leave, you'd get tired of the same person every evening, every morning. Limiting, dreary, artificial, and conventional.

Living together was different. We were both free. We freely chose to share each day, and either of us could leave if the relationship was no longer good for us. It was better this way, and Martha seemed content.

Uh, right.

I wondered if she'd remain cheerful if I spent the next few weeks sleeping at work.

Three weeks to catch a hacker. How long should this take? Perhaps a couple days to set up traces, another few days to track him through the networks, and then bust him. Probably we'd need the cooperation of the police, so add a day or two. We could wrap it up in two weeks, then I'd be back to managing a computer, and maybe a bit of astronomy on the side.

We needed to weave a net fine enough to catch the hacker, but coarse enough to let our scientists through. I'd have to detect the hacker as soon as he came on line and call Tymnet's technicians to trace the call.

Detecting the hacker was easy: I'd just camp out in my office alongside two terminals. One terminal for working, another to watch the system. Each time someone logged onto the computer, two beeps would tell me to check out the new user. As soon as a stranger showed up, I'd run down to the switchyard and see what they were doing.

Theoretically foolproof. Impossible in practice. From a thousand users, I knew about twenty. The other 980? Well, I had to check each one. So every two minutes I'd jog down the hall, thinking that I'd caught someone. And since I'd miss the signal if I went home, I ignored Martha and slept under the desk.

The rug smelled like a seat on a crosstown bus and whenever the terminal beeped, I'd sit up and gouge my head on the bottom of a drawer. A couple nights of slicing my forehead convinced me that there had to be an easier way.

If I knew the stolen account names, it would be easy to write a program that watched for the bad guy to show up. No need to check out every person using the computer; just ring a bell when a stolen account was in use. But I also remembered Wayne Graves' warning—stay invisible.

That meant no jobs running on the main computer. But I could watch from another computer. We'd just installed a new Unix computer, our Unix-8 system. Nobody had used it yet, so it might not be secure, but it surely wasn't contaminated. I could connect it to our local area network, secure it against all possible attacks, and let it watch the Unix-4 and Unix-5 computers.

I'd protect my Unix-8 castle with a one-way moat. Information could come into the computer, but nothing could go out. Dave Cleveland, hardly excited about chasing a hacker, smiled slightly and told me how to se Unix-8 to reject all log-in attempts, yet covertly scan the other Unix machines for signs of bad guys.

The program wasn't hard—just a few dozen lines of code to get a status block from each of the local computers. From long tradition, astronomers have programmed in Fortran, so I wasn't surprised when Dave gave me the hairy eyeball for using such an antiquated language. He challenged me to use the C language; in a few minutes he'd reduced it to twenty lines of tightly written code.

We fired up Dave's watchdog program on the Unix-8 computer. From the outside, it looked like just one more laboratory system. Anyone inquiring about its status received an invitation to log in. But you couldn't log on, since that computer rejected everyone except Dave and me. The hacker shouldn't be suspicious, since that computer didn't appear to be hooked up.

From this high ground, a network messenger asked each of the other Unix computers, "Hey, who's logged on?" Each minute, the Unix-8 program analyzed these reports, and searched for Sventek's name. When Sventek showed up, my terminal beeped, and it was forehead-gouging time.

But alarms alone wouldn't catch the hacker. We needed to track him through our system, and back to his lair. And to protect ourselves, we had to know what he was doing.

There was no way to grab fifty printers again to monitor all the traffic through our system, so I had to watch only those lines that he'd be likely to use. Saturday morning, he'd entered through one of our four Tymnet connections, so that seemed like a good place to start.

I couldn't buy, steal, or borrow four printers for a few weeks, so I went out begging. One physics professor gave me a beat-up old Decwriter, delighted that someone would take the ten-year-old heap off his hands. A secretary donated a spare IBM PC in exchange for my teaching her how to use spreadsheet programs. A combination of cookies, coaxing, and conniving led to two more obsolete printers. We were back in business, recording all our Tymnet traffic.

Wednesday afternoon marked a week since we'd first detected the hacker. Berkeley was sunny, though I could barely see the windows from across the maze of cubicles. Dave's watchdog was awake, the printers busy chattering with every keystroke, and I was absentmindedly thinking of infrared emissions from the Pleiades star cluster. Suddenly, the terminal beeped twice: Sventek's account was active. My adrenaline pumped as I ran to the switchyard; the top of the ream of paper showed the hacker had logged in at 2:26 and was still active.

Letter by letter, the printer spat out the hacker's keystrokes.

Logged into the Unix-4 computer as Sventek, he first listed the names of everyone connected. Lucky—there was nobody but the usual gang of physicists and astronomers; my watchdog program was well concealed within the Unix-8 computer. "Looking over your shoulder again," I thought. "Sorry, nobody here but us astrophysicists," I whispered to the terminal.

All the same, he scanned all the processes running. The Unix command *ps* prints the status of other processes. Habitually, I usually typed in *ps -axu,* the last three characters telling mother Unix to tell everyone's status. The intruder, however, entered *ps -eafg*. Strange. I'd never seen anyone use the *g* flag. Not that he discovered much: just a few scientific analysis programs, and a cranky typesetting program—and a network link to the Unix-8 system.

It'd taken him just three minutes to discover the Unix-8 computer, loosely linked to the Unix-4 system. But could he get in? With the Unix *rlogin* command he tried a half-dozen times, knocking on the door of the Unix-8 machine with Sventek's account name and password. No luck. Dave had nailed that door closed.

Apparently satisfied that nobody was watching him, he listed the system password file. There wasn't much for him to see there: all the passwords are encrypted and then stored. An encrypted password looks like gibberish; without solving an extremely difficult cipher, the password file gave the hacker little more than a dream.

He didn't become super-user; rather he checked that the Gnu-Emacs file hadn't been modified. This ended any doubts about whether the same hacker was connected: nobody else would search out the security hole in our system. At 2:37, eleven minutes after he logged in, he abruptly logged off the Unix-4 computer. But not before we'd started the trace.

Tymnet! I'd forgotten to warn their network operations center that they'd have to trace some connections. I hadn't even asked whether they could trace their own network. Now, watching the printer copy every key that the hacker pressed, there were only minutes to get the trace.

Ron Vivier traces Tymnet's network within North America. While I talked to him on the phone, I could hear him punching keys on his terminal. In a staccato voice, he asked for our node's address. At least I'd prepared that much. In a couple minutes, Ron had traced the connection from LBL's Tymnet port into an Oakland Tymnet office, where someone had dialed in from a telephone.

According to Ron, the hacker had called Tymnet's modem in Oakland, just three miles from our lab.

It's easier to call straight into our Berkeley lab than to go through Oakland's Tymnet office. Why call through Tymnet when you can dial directly into our system? Calling direct would eliminate Tymnet's intermediate connections and might be a tad more reliable. But calling via Tymnet added one more layer to trace.

The hacker had called the local Tymnet access number instead of our lab. It was like taking the interstate to drive three blocks. Whoever was at the other end of the line knew how to hide. Ron Vivier gave his condolences—I hadn't wanted just some Tymnet telephone number; I was hunting for a person.

Well, we were on the trail, but there were bends in the road. Somehow, we'd have to trace the phone call, and phone traces meant court orders. Phooey.

When the hacker logged off, I looked up from the printout. Like a firehouse dog, Roy Kerth had picked up the news and made it down to the switchyard. So had Dave and Wayne.

When Ron hung up, I announced, "He's calling Oakland Tymnet. So he must be from around here. If he were in Peoria, he'd save his nickel and call the Peoria Tymnet modem."

"Yeah, you're probably right." Roy didn't look forward to losing a bet.

Dave wasn't thinking about the phone trace. "This *ps -eafg* command bothers me," he said. "I can't say why—it just doesn't taste right. Maybe it's just paranoia, but I'm sure that I've seen that combination before."

"To hell with Unix. Serves us right for running such a dog operating system." Wayne saw a chance to bait Dave. "Hey, that password file isn't much use to him, is it?"

"Only if he owns a supercomputer. You'd need one to unravel the encryption. Unix isn't VMS—it's got the tightest cypher locks around," Dave countered.

Roy had heard it before; he saw himself as above the war of the operating systems. "Looks like *you* need some phone traces, Cliff."

I didn't like his choice of pronoun, but, yes, that was the point. "Any ideas on where to start?"

"Let your fingers do the walking."

# 7

THE MORNING AFTER WE WATCHED THE HACKER BREAK into our computer, the boss met with Aletha Owens, the lab's attorney. Aletha didn't care about computers, but had a wary eye for problems on the horizon. She wasted no time in calling the FBI.

Our local FBI office didn't raise an eyebrow. Fred Wyniken, special agent with the Oakland resident agency, asked incredulously, "You're calling us because you've lost seventy-five cents in computer time?" Aletha tried explaining information security, and the value of our data. Wyniken interrupted and said, "Look, if you can demonstrate a loss of more than a million dollars, or that someone's prying through classified data, then we'll open an investigation. Until then, leave us alone."

Right. Depending on how you looked at it, our data was worth either nothing or zillions of dollars. How much is the structure of an enzyme worth? What's the value of a high-temperature superconductor? The FBI thought in terms of bank embezzlement; we lived in a world of research. Classified data? We weren't a military base or an atomic weapons lab.

Yet we needed the FBI's cooperation. When the hacker next popped his periscope above the water, we'd probably track him to the Tymnet's Oakland telephone access number. From there, I hoped a phone trace would lead to him. But I'd heard that the phone company wouldn't trace a line without a search warrant. And we needed the FBI to get that warrant.

After hitting the FBI's brick wall, Aletha called our local District Attorney. The Oakland DA didn't fool around: "Someone's breaking into your computer? Hell, let's get a warrant and trace them lines." The FBI might not give a damn, but our local prosecutors took us seriously. Still, they would have to convince a judge. Our warrant was at least a week away.

Just after five, Dave stopped by and started talking about the break-in.

"Cliff, the hacker's not from Berkeley."

"How do you know?"

"You saw that guy typing in the *ps -eafg* command, right?"

"Yeah, here's the printout," I replied. "It's just an ordinary Unix command to list all the active processes—'ps' means print status, and the four letters modify the display. In a sense, they're like switches on a stereo—they change the way the command works."

"Cliff, I can tell you're used to Berkeley Unix. Ever since Berkeley Unix was invented, we've mechanically typed 'ps' to see what's happening on the system. But tell me, what do those four letters modify?"

Dave knew my ignorance of obscure Unix commands. I put up the best front I could: "Well, the *e* flag means list both the process name and environment, and the *a* flag lists everyone's process—not just your process. So the hacker wanted to see everything that was running on the system."

"OK, you got half of 'em. So what are the *g* and *f* flags for?"

"I dunno." Dave let me flounder until I admitted ignorance.

"You ask for a *g* listing when you want both interesting and uninteresting processes. All the unimportant jobs, like accounting, will show up. As will any hidden processes."

"And we know he's diddling with the accounting program."

Dave smiled. "So that leaves us with the *f* flag. And it's not in any Berkeley Unix. It's the AT&T Unix way to list each process's files. Berkeley Unix does this automatically, and doesn't need the *f* flag. Our friend doesn't know Berkeley Unix. He's from the school of old-fashioned Unix."

The Unix operating system was invented in the early 1970s at

AT&T's Bell Laboratories in New Jersey. In the late '70s, Unix zealots from Bell Labs visited the Berkeley campus, and a new, richer version of Unix was developed. Along with hot tubs, leftist politics, and the free speech movement, Berkeley is known for its Unix implementation.

A schism developed between advocates of the small, compact AT&T Unix and the more elaborate Berkeley implementation. Despite conferences, standards, and promises, no consensus has appeared, and the world is left with two competing Unix operating systems.

Of course, our lab used Berkeley Unix, as do all right-thinking folks. East Coast people were said to be biased towards AT&T Unix, but then, they hadn't discovered hot tubs either.

From a single letter, Dave ruled out the entire computing population of the West Coast. Conceivably, a Berkeley hacker might use an old-fashioned command, but Dave discounted this. "We're watching someone who's never used Berkeley Unix." He sucked in his breath and whispered, "A heathen."

Wayne didn't give a damn about Unix. As a VMS junkie, Wayne was an infidel. Moreover, he felt the hacker couldn't learn anything from our password file: "Look, there's no way that anyone can decrypt those passwords. About all he's learned is our names. Why bother?"

I'd rolled this around in my mind. Passwords are at the heart of security on a big computer. Home computers don't need passwords: there's only one user. Anyone at the keyboard can access any program. But when there's ten or twenty people using a single system, the computer must be certain that the person behind the terminal isn't an imposter.

Like an electronic signature, passwords verify the authenticity of a transaction. Automatic teller machines, telephone credit cards, electronic funds transfer networks, even some home telephone-answering machines depend on passwords. By filching or forging passwords, a hacker can create counterfeit wealth, steal services, or cover bounced checks. When money was stored in vaults, safecrackers attacked the combination locks. Now that securities are just bits in a computer's memory, thieves go after the passwords.

When your computer has fifty or a hundred users, you might just store each person's password in a file. When the user tries to log on, ask for her password and compare that to what's in your file. In a friendly environment, no problem. But how do you keep someone from sneaking a peek at that password file? Well, protect the password file so that only the system can read it.

Even if you protect the password file, every now and then all the files will be copied onto backup tapes. Even a novice programmer could read those tapes on another computer and list the contents of the password file. File protection alone isn't enough.

In 1975, Bob Morris and Fred Grampp of Bell Laboratories developed a way to protect passwords, even when files weren't secure. They would rely on encryption, rather than file protection. If you chose the password "cradle," the computer doesn't simply store your choice into a file of passwords. Instead, Unix scrambles the letters into an encrypted word, say, "pn6yywersyq." Your encrypted password is stored, not the plain text.

So a Unix password file might look something like this:

```
Aaron:  fnqs24lkcvs
Blacker:  anvpqw0xcsr
Blatz:  pn6yywersyq
Goldman:  mwe785jcy12
Henderson:  rp2d9c149b7
```

Following each account name is the encrypted password. Like Wayne said, stealing the password file just gives you a list of people.

The computer program that encrypts "cradle" into "pn6yywersyq" is built upon a trapdoor algorithm: a process that's easy to do, but difficult to undo. When Sally Blatz logs in, she types in her account name, Blatz, and then her password, cradle. The system encrypts the password into pn6yywersyq, and compares that to the entry in the password file. If the encrypted entries don't match, Sally is booted off the machine. The plain text password itself isn't compared, its encryption is. Password security depends on the trapdoor function.

Trapdoor functions are mathematical ratchets: you can turn them forwards, but not backwards. They quickly translate text into ciphers. To make these locks pickproof, it's got to be impossible to reverse the algorithm.

Our trapdoors were built upon the Data Encryption Standard (DES), created by IBM and the National Security Agency. We'd heard rumors that the electronic spooks of NSA weakened the DES. They hobbled it just enough to be crackable by NSA, but kept it strong enough to resist the efforts of ordinary mortals. The grapevine said that this way NSA could crack the code and read messages, but nobody else could.

The cryptographic DES program within our Unix computer was public. Anyone could study it. NSA had analyzed its strengths and weaknesses, but these reports were secret. Occasionally, we'd heard rumors of someone cracking this cipher, but none of these panned out. Until NSA published its analyses of the DES, we'd have no choice but to trust that our encryption was strong enough.

Wayne and I had watched the hacker break in and steal our password file. The hacker now knew the names of a few hundred scientists. He might as well have asked for our telephone book—at least that included addresses. Unless he owned a Cray supercomputer, he couldn't invert the trapdoor function, and our passwords remained safe.

Wayne was still worried. "Maybe this guy's stumbled on some brilliant way to reverse the trapdoor function. Let's be a tad careful and change our important passwords."

I could hardly object. The system password hadn't been changed for a couple years, and outlasted people who had been hired and fired. I didn't mind changing my password; to make sure, I used a different password on each computer. If the hacker managed to figure out my password from the Unix-4 computer, he'd still have no way to guess it on the others.

Before pedaling home, I again studied the printout of the previous day's session. Buried in the ten pages were clues to the hacker's persona, location, and intentions. But too much conflicted: we traced him through Tymnet into Oakland, California. But Dave didn't believe he was from Berkeley. He copied our password file, yet our encryption made those passwords into gibberish. What was he doing with our encrypted passwords?

In some ways, this was like astronomy. We passively observed a phenomenon, and from a few clues tried to explain the event and find the location of the source. Astronomers are accustomed to quietly gathering data, usually by freezing behind a telescope on a mountaintop. Here the data appeared sporadically, from an unknown source. Instead of thermodynamics and optics, I needed to understand cryptography and operating systems. Somehow, a physical connection existed between our system and a distant terminal. By applying ordinary physics, it must be possible to understand what was happening.

Physics: there was the key. Record your observations. Apply physical principles. Speculate, but only trust proven conclusions. If I were to make any progress, I'd have to treat the task as a freshman physics problem. Time to update my notebook.

# 8

AND JUST IN TIME. WEDNESDAY, SEPTEMBER 10, AT 7:51 A.M., the hacker appeared in our system for six minutes. Long enough to ring the alarm on my terminal, but not enough time to do anything about it. I had stayed at home that night: "Five days at the lab are enough," Martha said.

I wasn't at the lab to watch, but the printer saved three pages of the hacker's trail. He had logged into our Unix-4 computer as Sventek. Well, I understand that—he had Sventek's password, and had entered from Tymnet.

But he didn't hang around my Unix-4 computer. Instead he leapfrogged through it and landed in the Milnet. Now it was no news flash that the Milnet existed—it's a part of the Internet, a computer network that cross-links a hundred other networks. From our Unix computer, we can reach the Internet, and from there, the Milnet.

The Milnet belongs to the Department of Defense.

My hacker connected to Milnet address 26.0.0.113, logged in there as "Hunter," and checked that he had a copy of Gnu-Emacs, then disappeared.

When I biked in around noon, there was no trace to follow upstream. Bu the hacker left an indelible trail downstream. Where was that Milnet address? The Network Information Center decoded it for me: the U.S. Army Depot, in Anniston, Alabama. The home of the Army's Redstone missile complex, two thousand miles away from Berkeley.

In a couple minutes, he'd connected through our lab and into some Army base. The printout left little doubt that this was the hacker. Nobody but the hacker would use Sventek's account. And who else would check for the Gnu-Emacs security hole on some computer in Alabama?

Nobody was around to tell me to ignore it, so I called Anniston information. Sure enough, the Anniston Army Depot had a computer center, and eventually I found Chuck McNatt, the Anniston Unix wizard.

"Hi, Chuck. You don't know me but I think we found someone screwing around with your computer."

"Who are you? How do I know *you're* not trying to break in?"

After a few minutes of disbelief, he asked for my phone number, hung up, and called me back. Here's someone that doesn't trust strangers. Or did he call me back on a secure phone line?

"Bad news," I said. "I think I saw someone breaking into your system."

"Aw, hell—that son of a bitch, Hunter?"

"Yeah. How'd you know?"

"I've seen his ass before."

Chuck McNatt explained through a thick Alabama drawl that the Army's Redstone Missile Arsenal kept track of its supplies on a couple of Unix computers. To get orders processed quickly, they'd hooked up to Chuck's computer at the Anniston Depot. Most of their traffic was news updates—not many people logged in remotely.

One Saturday morning, to escape the August heat, Chuck had gone into work and checked the users on his system. Someone named Hunter was using up an enormous amount of computing time. Surprised to see anyone on a Saturday, Chuck had flashed a message on Hunter's screen, saying, "Hey! Identify yourself!"

The mysterious Hunter typed back, "Who do you think I am?"

Chuck wasn't that gullible. He sent another message, "Identify yourself now or I'll knock you off the system!"

Back came Hunter's reply, "I cannot answer."

"So I bumped him off the machine," Chuck said. "We called the FBI, but they didn't give a damn. So we talked CID into tracing every damn connection coming in on our phone lines."

"What's the CID—Chestnut Inspection Department?"

"Be serious," Chuck said. "The CID's the Army's cops. The criminal investigation division. But they're not doin' much."

"No classified material lost, huh?"

The FBI in Montgomery, Alabama, told Chuck about the same story as Oakland had told me. They'd investigate when a million dollars disappeared. Until then, don't bother 'em. Computer crimes weren't sexy.

"Who'd you find?"

"The weirdest thing," Chuck continued. "I caught Hunter sneaking into my computer two or three more times, but my telephone recorders didn't show a thing."

"Betcha I know why. He's been coming in through your back door. Your Milnet connection. Some hacker's been breaking into our system, and he got into your computer this morning."

Chuck cursed—he'd missed the three-minute connection. He had set traps on all his telephone lines, but hadn't thought to watch his network links.

"We're trying to find out who's hacking our system," I said. "We figure he's a student here in Berkeley, and we're gearing up to track him down. Our first trace points to Oakland or Berkeley."

"Well, I know how you feel. We all suspect it's a student here in Alabama," Chcuk said. "We thought about closing up, but we're out to git him. I'd rather see him behind bars than behind a terminal."

For the first time, I worried for this hacker's welfare. If the Army caught the guy, he'd have a rough time.

"Hey, Chuck, have I got a kicker for you. Betcha this guy's super-user on your system."

"Naw. He might have stolen an account, but no way he'd get to be super-user. We're an Army base, not some goofball college."

I let the swipe at Berkeley pass. "He went looking for your Gnu-Emacs move-mail file."

"Yeah. So what?"

"What do you know about the nesting habits of cuckoos?" I explained the workings of the Gnu-Emacs security hole.

Chuck was taken aback. "You mean we've had this hole since

White Sands sent us this Gnu file?" Chuck whistled. "I wonder how long he's been poking around." He understood the hole and the implications.

The hacker listed files at the Anniston system. Judging from the dates of these files, he'd been in Anniston's computers since early June. For four months, an illegitimate system manager used an Alabama Army computer. Yet he'd been discovered by accident, not through some logic bomb or lost information.

No obvious damage.

Looking closely at the morning's printout, I saw that the hacker had executed the change password command. On the Anniston computer, he had changed Hunter's password to be "Hedges." A clue at last: of zillions of possible passwords, he'd chosen Hedges. Hedges Hunter? Hunter Hedges? A hedge hunter? Time to flip through the H's in the Berkeley telephone book.

Three phone calls to H. Hunter turned up Harold, Heidi, and Hilda Hunter. "Hi, are you interested in a free subscription to *Computer Reviews?*" No dice. None of them said they cared about computers.

What does a physics lab in Berkeley have in common with an Army depot in Anniston, Alabama? You couldn't find more politically opposite locations: a good-old-boy Army base and a radical hippie town. Yet technically, we shared quite a bit. Both our computers ran Unix and connected through the Milnet network.

But wait—Anniston's system ran AT&T Unix, not the Berkeley dialect. If I believed Dave Cleveland, then the hacker was at home on Anniston's system. Might it be a Southern hacker?

# 9

I COULDN'T STAND THE STERILE, FLUORESCENT LIGHTED halls of the lab anymore, so I went outside to look at the panoramic view of the Bay Area below me. The Berkeley campus lay directly beneath my laboratory. Once the home of the free speech movement and antiwar protests, the campus is still known for its wild politics and ethnic diversity. If I were a little closer, I could probably hear the Young Republicans baiting the Socialist Workers, while the Chinese Club looked on in amazement.

Smoky coffeehouses crowded next to the campus, where haggard grad students scribbled their theses, fueled by espresso. At nearby ice cream shops, giggling sorority girls mingled with punks in black leather and spiked hair. Best of all—Berkeley's bookstores.

From the front of the lab, I could look farther south, to the pleasant streets of north Oakland, where we lived. There I shared an old bungalow with an assortment of zany roommates. Across the bay, shrouded in fog, was San Francisco—Oz.

Three years ago, Martha had moved here to study law and I'd tagged along. She'd been worth crossing the country for. She was a damned good hiking partner and caver. I first met her when I fell thirty feet inside a cave; she came to the rescue, rappelling down to where I lay incapacitated by a bad sprain and utter infatuation. My injuries healed, thanks to her chicken soup; my affection for the smart-aleck kid who climbed rocks so fearlessly ripened into love.

Now we lived together. She actually enjoyed studying law. She didn't want to be a lawyer, but a legal philosopher. She was obsessed with aikido, a Japanese martial art, and often came home bruised but grinning. She cooked, gardened, pieced quilts, did carpentry, and made stained-glass windows. For all our zaniness, we wallowed in disgustingly wholesome domestic bliss.

I bicycled home and told Martha about the Alabama break-in, speculating about who might be behind it.

"So there's technocratic vandals," she said. "What else is new?"

"That's news in itself. Technicians now have incredible power to control information and communication," I said.

"So what? Somebody's always had control over information, and others have always tried to steal it. Read Machiavelli. As technology changes, sneakiness finds new expressions."

Martha was still giving me a history lesson when Claudia bustled in, complaining about her fifth graders. Life in Berkeley usually includes a roommate or two. Claudia was ours, and a perfect one at that. She was generous and cheerful, eager to share her life, her music, and her kitchen gadgets with us. She was a professional violinist eking out a living by playing in two symphony orchestras and a chamber music trio, and giving lessons to kids.

Claudia was seldom still or quiet. In her few moments between jobs, she simultaneously cooked meals, talked on the phone, and played with her dog.

At first I listened, but soon her voice became like the background chirp of a parakeet while I worried about how malicious this hacker might be. While I'm at home, how do I know what he's up to?

Claudia knew how to take my mind off the hacker: she brought home a video, *Plan 9 from Outer Space*—aliens in tinfoil flying saucers drag vampires from graves.

Wednesday, September 17, was a drizzly Berkeley day. As the only California couple without a car, Martha and I had to bicycle through the rain. On my way into the lab, I visited the switchyard, to check for any visits by the hacker. Water dripped off my sopping hair onto the printout, smudging the ink on the paper.

Sometime during the night, someone had connected to our computer, and methodically tried to log into the Unix-4 computer. First they tried to log into the Guest account, using the password "Guest." Then they tried the Visitor account, with password "Visitor"; then accounts Root, System, Manager, Service, and Sysop. After a couple of minutes, the attacker left.

Could this be a different hacker? This guy didn't even try valid accounts like Sventek or Stoll. He simply tried obvious account names and simple passwords. I wondered how often such an attack might succeed.

Not often—with six-letter passwords a hacker had a better chance of winning the lottery than randomly guessing a particular password. Since the computer hangs up after a few log-in failures, the attacker would need all night to try even a few hundred possible passwords. No, a hacker couldn't magically enter my system. He'd need to know at least one password.

By 12:29, most of my clothes had dried off, though my sneakers still squished. I was part way into a soggy bagel, and most of the way through an astronomy article about physics of the icy satellites of Jupiter. My terminal beeped. Trouble in the switchyard. A quick (though squeaky) trot down the hallway let me watch the hacker connect into our system as Sventek.

Again the adrenaline rush: I called Tymnet and quickly found Ron Vivier. Ron started the trace, and I huddled over the Decwriter, which now tapped out the hacker's commands.

The hacker wasted no time. He issued commands to show all the active users and any background jobs running. He then fired up Kermit.

Named after the Muppet hero, Kermit is the universal language for connecting computers together. In 1980, Frank da Cruz of Columbia University needed to send data to a number of different computers. Instead of writing five different, incompatible programs, he created a single standard to exchange files between any systems. Kermit's become the Esperanto of computers.

Absentmindedly chewing on a bagel, I watched as the hacker

used Kermit to transfer a short program into our Unix computer. Line by line, faithful Kermit reassembled it, and soon I could read the following program:

```
echo -n "WELCOME TO THE LBL UNIX-4 COMPUTER"
echo -n "PLEASE LOG IN NOW"
echo -n "LOGIN:"
read account_name
echo -n "ENTER YOUR PASSWORD:"
(stty -echo; \
read password; \
stty echo; \
echo" "; \
echo $account_name $password >> /tmp/.pub)
echo "SORRY, TRY AGAIN."
```

Yikes! Now here was a strange program! This program, when installed in our computer, would prompt a user to enter his name and password. An ordinary user who ran this program would see on his screen:

```
WELCOME TO THE LBL UNIX-4 COMPUTER
PLEASE LOGIN NOW
Login:
```

His terminal would then wait until he entered his account name. After he typed his name, the system responds:

```
ENTER YOUR PASSWORD:
```

And he'd naturally type in his password. The program then stashes the unlucky user's name and password into a file, tells the user,

```
SORRY, TRY AGAIN
```

and then disappears.

Thinking they've mistyped their passwords, most people will just try to log in again. By then, their password will already have been stolen.

Four thousand years ago, the city of Troy fell when Greek soldiers snuck in, hidden inside the Trojan horse.

Deliver a gift that looks attractive, yet steals the very key to your security. Sharpened over the millennia, this technique still works against everyone except the truly paranoid.

The hacker's Trojan horse program collected passwords. Our visitor wanted our passwords badly enough to risk getting caught installing a program that was bound to be detected.

Was this program a Trojan horse? Maybe I should call it a mockingbird: a false program that sounded like the real thing. I didn't have time to figure out the difference—within a minute, he was bound to install his program in the systems area, and start it running. What should I do? To disable it would show him that I was watching him. Yet doing nothing would give him a new password every time someone logged in.

But legitimate super-users have power too. Before the hacker could run his program, I changed one line in it, making it look like he'd made a trivial error. Then I diddled a couple system parameters to slow down the system. Slow enough that the hacker would need ten minutes to rebuild his program. Enough time to let us respond to this new attack.

I shouted down the hall for Guru Dave.

"What do you feed a Trojan horse?"

Dave came running. We shifted the computer into high speed, and prepared a fodder of bogus accounts and false passwords.

But our panic wasn't necessary. The hacker rebuilt his Trojan horse, but didn't install it properly. Dave instantly realized that it had been placed in the wrong directory. His Trojan horse would be happy in standard AT&T Unix, but couldn't cavort in the fields of Berkeley Unix.

Dave grinned. "I won't say, 'I told you so,' but we're watching someone who's never been to California. Every Unix jockey on the West Coast would use Berkeley style commands, yet your hacker's still using AT&T Unix."

Dave descended from his tower to explain what he meant. "The spelling of his commands is different from Berkeley Unix. But so is the very feel of the program. Kinda like how you can tell that a writer is British rather than American. Sure, you'll see words like 'colour' and 'defence,' but you can feel the style difference as well."

"So what's the difference?" I asked.

Dave sneered, "The hacker used the command 'read' to get keyboard data. Any civilized programmer would use the 'set' command." For Dave, civilized computers spoke Berkeley Unix. All others were uncouth.

The hacker didn't realize this. Confident that he'd put his Trojan horse in the right pasture, he ran it as a background process, and logged off. Before he disconnected, Ron Vivier had traced the hacker through Tymnet's network, and into an Oakland, California, telephone line. The dust hadn't yet settled on our court order, so we couldn't start the phone trace.

The hacker had left, but his Trojan horse stayed behind, running as a background task. As Dave predicted, it collected no passwords, for it had been installed in a place that wasn't referenced during log-in. Sure enough, twenty minutes later, the hacker reappeared, searched for a collection of passwords, and must have been disappointed to find his program had failed.

"Look, Dave, the poor guy needs your help," I said.

"Right. Should we send him some electronic mail telling him how to write a Trojan horse program that works?" Dave replied.

"He's got the basics right—imitating our log-in sequence, asking for the username and password, then storing the stolen information. All he needs is a few lessons in Berkeley Unix."

Wayne stopped by to watch the hacker flounder. "Aw, what do you expect? There's just too many varieties of Unix. Next time make it easier on those inept hackers, and give them Digital's VMS operating system. It might not be easier to hack, but at least it's standardized. IOTTMCO." Intuitively obvious to the most casual observer.

Wayne had a good point. The hacker's Trojan horse attack had failed because the operating system wasn't exactly what he was accustomed to. If everyone used the same version of the same operating system, a single security hole would let hackers into all the computers. Instead, there's a multitude of operating systems:

Berkeley Unix, AT&T Unix, DEC's VMS, IBM's TSO, VM, DOS, even Macintoshes and Ataris. This variety of software meant that no single attack could succeed against all systems. Just like genetic diversity, which prevents an epidemic from wiping out a whole species at once, diversity in software is a good thing.

Dave and Wayne continued bickering as they left the switchyard. I hung around a few more minutes, reloading paper. At 1:30 P.M., the hacker reappeared; I was still adjusting the printer when he started typing.

This second session was predictable. Our visitor looked at his special file for passwords and found none. He listed his Trojan horse program and tested it a couple times. It didn't work. Apparently, he didn't have a Dave Cleveland for help. Obviously frustrated, he erased the file and logged off in a couple minutes.

But even though he'd been on for only a few minutes, Tymnet managed to trace him, again into Oakland. Ron Vivier, who'd traced Tymnet's connections, apparently welcomed any emergency that might extricate him from a meeting, so he jumped when I called. If we could only get the phone company to continue the trace, we could wrap up everything in a couple days.

Dave felt he could exclude anyone coming from the West Coast. Chuck in Anniston suspected a hacker from Alabama. Tymnet's traces pointed to Oakland.

Me? I didn't know.

# 10

OUR TYMNET TRACES REACHED INTO OAKLAND, AT VARIous times the home of Jack London, Ed Meese, and Gertrude Stein. A twenty-minute bike ride from the Berkeley campus led to the Oakland Paramount Theater, with its sublime art-deco architecture and eye-popping murals. A few blocks away, in the basement of an ugly modern building, Tymnet rents space for fifty dialup modems. Ron Vivier had traced the hacker from our lab into this bank of modems. Now it was my local telephone company's turn.

A two-inch-thick cable runs under Broadway, connecting Tymnet's modems to an unmarked, windowless building. There, Pacific Bell's Franklin office houses an electronic switch to handle ten thousand telephone lines in area code 415 with the prefix 430. Tymnet leases fifty of these lines.

From somewhere, the hacker had dialed 415/430-2900. The path to our mysterious visitor led to Pac Bell's ESS-5 switch.

Across San Francisco Bay, Lee Cheng's office overlooks a grungy alley off Market Street. Lee is Pac Bell's bloodhound; from his office or up on a telephone pole, he traces phone lines.

Lee's degree is in criminology, and his graduate work is in accident reconstruction and causation. But eight years of telephone tracing gives him an engineer's view of the phone company and a cop's view of society. To him, communities are split by area codes, exchanges, and trunk lines, as well as precincts and neighborhoods.

With advance warning, Lee starts a software program in the computer that runs the telephone exchange. At the switching control center, he logs onto the ESS maintenance channel, brings up line-condition-monitoring software, and starts a trap program.

The automatic trap program monitors the status of an individual telephone line. It records the date, time, how many rings before an answer, and where the call came from.

If the call came from a nearby phone—one from the same exchange—then the trace is complete, and Lee's job is easy. More often, the call comes from another exchange, and Lee has to coordinate traces at perhaps five different phone exchanges.

When a technician at an exchange receives a trace call, he drops what he's doing—Lee's traces take precedence over everything except firefighting. He logs into the control computer, commands his computer to display the phone number's status (busy, idle, off-hook), and executes programs to show where the connection came from (routing index, trunk group number, adjacent exchange name).

With luck, the trace might take a few seconds. But a few exchanges, left over from the 1950s, still use mechanical-stepping switches. When you dial through these exchanges, you can hear a soft pulsing in the background, as relays move a lever in tune with your dialing. The old grackles of the telephone system are proud of these antiques, saying, "They're the only switches that'll survive a nuclear attack." But they complicate Lee's job: he's got to find a technician to run from rack to rack tracing these calls.

Local telephones can only be traced while connected. Once you hang up, the connection evaporates and can no longer be traced. So Lee races against time to finish a trace before the connection is lost.

Phone companies view phone traces as a waste of time. Only their most skilled technicians know how to trace a phone connection. Worse, traces are expensive, generate lawsuits, and upset customers.

Lee, of course, sees things otherwise. "Yesterday was a drug bust, today, it's an extortion racket, tomorrow we're tracing a burglary ring. Obscene phone calls around the full moon. Lately, we've been tracing call girls' pocket pagers. Slice of life in the big city." Still, the fear of lawyers keeps him from unofficially helping out.

Our conversation in September 1986 was curt:

"Hey, we need a telephone line traced."

"Got a search warrant?"

"No, do we need one?"

"We won't trace without a warrant."

That was quick. No progress until Aletha Owens got the court order.

After yesterday's attack, we couldn't wait. My searches through the phone book were leading nowhere. A more competent Trojan horse would panic my boss into closing down the investigation. And my three-week allowance was down to ten days.

Sandy Merola was Roy Kerth's sidekick. When Roy's acid tongue got to one of the staff, Sandy applied balm. On a mission to the Berkeley campus, Sandy noticed a set of IBM personal computers in a public section of the library. Like any computer jock would do, he wandered over and tried to use them. Just as he suspected, these computers were programmed to automatically dial Tymnet and log into the Dow Jones Information Service.

Tymnet? Sandy spent a few minutes diddling on the terminal, and discovered that he could find the latest stock quotations and financial rumors from *The Wall Street Journal*. More important, when he signed off the Dow Jones service, the terminal prompted him for, "Tymnet username?" Seemed like nothing to lose by trying, so he entered, "LBL." Sure enough, Sandy connected to my lab's computers.

Maybe these public terminals explained things. Anyone could use them; they dialed the Oakland Tymnet number; and the library was all of a hundred feet away from Cory Hall, where the Berkeley Unix jockeys hang out.

Sandy was a jogger the way some people are Catholics. He trotted up Cardiac Hill and told the police of his discovery. Here was a way to avoid a phone trace—the next time the hacker appeared, we'd just duck over to the library and grab the bastard. We didn't even need a court order.

Sandy returned from the police station, still sweating. He caught me practicing a yo-yo trick.

"Cut the clowning, Cliff. The police are all set to run over to the campus and arrest whoever's using those terminals."

Being more accustomed to parking tickets and medical emergencies, the LBL police don't understand computers and are pretty wary of telephone traces. But they had no problem with busting someone breaking into a computer.

"Hadn't we better make sure that it's the hacker, first?" I had visions of some undercover cops staking out a terminal and dragging a librarian into the paddy wagon for checking the Dow Jones industrials.

"It's easy. Call me the next time the hacker shows up. I'll drive down to the library with the police, and we'll see what's on the screen. If it's data from LBL, then we'll leave it to the police."

"Are they gonna stake out the terminal? You know, like in 'Dragnet'? With one-way mirrors and binoculars?"

"Huh? Be serious, Cliff." Sandy jogged away. I guess scientists are graded in seriousness. It reminded me of when I'd filed a student health report, listing under complaints, "Potato Famine." The doctor called me aside and lectured me, "Son, we take health seriously around here."

We got our chance to test Sandy's theory soon enough. Two days after his failed Trojan horse, the hacker returned at 12:42 P.M. Lunch hour. The perfect time for a Berkeley student to wander over to the library and use their terminals.

At the alarm, I called Sandy. Five minutes later, he appeared with two undercover police agents, wearing suits, ties, and winter coats. Nothing could be more conspicuous on a campus of hippies on a hot summer day. I glimpsed a large revolver under one of the cops' coats. They were serious.

For the next twenty-five minutes, the hacker didn't do much. He became super-user via the Gnu-Emacs hole, listed the day's electronic mail, and scanned through our processes. Ron Vivier skipped lunch to trace the Tymnet connection into Oakland. Any minute, I expected to see the printer suddenly stop, signaling that Sandy and the constabulary had caught their man. But no, the hacker took his time and logged off at 1:20.

Sandy returned a few minutes later.

"No luck, huh?" His face said it all.

"Nobody was at the library's terminals. Nobody even near them. Are you sure the hacker was on?"

"Yeah, here's the printout. And Tymnet traced it into Oakland again."

Sandy was let down. Our shortcut hit a dead end: progress now depended on a telephone trace.

# 11

THAT EVENING, MARTHA WAS SUPPOSED TO BE STUDYING constitutional law, but was actually piecing a calico quilt. I came home discouraged: the library stakeout had seemed so promising.

"Forget the hacker. You're home now."

"But he might be in my system right now." I was obsessing.

"Well, there's nothing you can do about it, then. Here, thread a needle and help with this seam." Martha escaped law school by quilting; surely it would work for me as well. After twenty minutes of silence, while she studied, my sewing started to get crooked.

"When we get the warrant, we'll have to wait until the hacker shows up. For all we know, that'll be at 3 A.M., and nobody will be around."

"I said, forget the hacker. You're home now." She didn't even look up from her book.

Sure enough, the hacker didn't show up the next day. But the search warrant did. It was legal now. Of course, I couldn't be trusted to start anything as important as a phone trace: Roy Kerth was explicit that only he was to talk to the police.

We went through a couple dry runs, making sure we knew who to call and checking that we could unwind our own local network. Then I got bored and went back to writing some software to analyze optical formulas for an astronomer.

In the afternoon, Roy called our systems people and operators together. He lectured us about the need to keep our traces secret—we didn't know where the hacker was coming from, so we mustn't mention our work to anyone outside the lab. I figured that people would talk less if they knew what was going on, so I gave a chalk talk about what we'd seen and where we were heading. Dave Cleveland chipped in about the Gnu-Emacs hole, and Wayne pointed out that we'd better discuss the hacker strictly by voice, since he regularly read our electronic mail. The meeting broke up with Boris and Natasha imitations.

Tuesday, at 12:42 in the afternoon, Sventek's account lit up. Roy called the laboratory police—they wanted to be in charge of the phone traces. By the time Tymnet had unwound their network, Roy was shouting over the phone. I could hear his side of the conversation.

"We need a number traced. We have the search warrant. Now."

Silence for a moment. Then he exploded.

"I don't give a damn about your problems!! Start the trace now!"

More silence.

"If you don't get a trace immediately, you'll hear about it from the lab director." Roy slammed down the receiver.

The boss was furious—his face turned purple. "Damn our police! They've never handled a phone trace, and they don't know who to call at the phone company!" Sheesh. At least his anger was aimed elsewhere.

Perhaps it was for the best. The hacker disconnected within a couple minutes, after just listing the names of the active users. By the time the phone trace was started, there'd be no connection to trace.

While the boss cooled off, I took the printout to study. There wasn't much to summarize in my logbook. The hacker had just logged in, listed the users, then logged off. Didn't even check the mail.

Aah! I saw why he logged off so fast. The system operator was around. The hacker must know the sysop's name. He had raised periscope, seen the enemy, then disappeared. Sure enough, looking back to other printouts, he stayed around only when no operators were around. Paranoid.

I talked with each of our operators, explaining this discovery. From now on, they would run the system covertly, using pseudonyms.

September 16 marked the end of the second week on the trail. I tried working on optics again, but my mind kept drifting to the printouts. Sure enough, just after noon, my terminal beeped: the hacker had returned.

I called Tymnet, and then the boss. This time, we set up a conference call, and I listened to the trace as I watched the hacker walk through our system.

"Hi, Ron, it's Cliff. We need another trace on our Tymnet line, LBL, Tymnet node 128, port 3."

A minute of fumbling on the other end.

"Looks like it's the third modem in our block of 1200-baud lines. That would make it line 2903. That's 415/430-2903."

"Thanks, Ron." The police heard this, and relayed it to Lee Cheng at the phone company.

"That's coming from the Franklin switch. Hold on." I was accustomed to being put on hold by the phone company.

I watched the hacker fire up the Gnu-Emacs move-mail file. He was becoming super-user. He'd be on for at least another ten minutes. Maybe long enough to complete a trace. Come on, Pac Bell!

Three minutes passed by. Lee came back on line.

"The line's active, all right. Connects to a trunk leading into Berkeley. I've got a technician checking that line right now."

Another two minutes pass by. The hacker's super-user now. He goes straight for the system manager's mail files.

"The Berkeley technician shows the line connecting to AT&T long lines. Hold on." But Lee doesn't punch hold, and I listen in on his conversation with the Berkeley office. The guy in Berkeley insists that the line's coming from far away; Lee's telling him to check it again. Meanwhile the hacker is working on our password file. Editing it, I think, but I'm trying to hear what's happening at the phone company.

"It's our trunk group 369, and damn it, that's routed to 5096MCLN." The Berkeley technician was speaking in tongues.

"OK, I guess we'll have to call New Jersey." Lee seemed dismayed. "Cliff, are you still there?"

"Yeah. What's going on?"

"No matter. Is he going to stay on much longer?"

I watched the printout. The hacker left our password file and was cleaning up his temporary files.

"I can't tell. My guess is—oops, he's logged off."

"Disconnected from Tymnet." Ron Vivier had been quiet until now.

"Dropped off the phone line." Lee's trace disappeared.

Our police officer came on line. "Well, gentlemen, what's the story?"

Lee Cheng spoke first. "I think the call's coming from the East Coast. There's a slight chance that it's a local Berkeley call, but . . . no, it's from AT&T." Lee was thinking out loud, like a graduate student at an oral exam. "All our Pacific Bell trunk lines are labeled with three digits; only the long-distance trunks have four-digit identifiers. That line . . . let me look it up."

I heard Lee type into his computer.

Lee came back in a minute. "Hey, Cliff, do you know anyone in Virginia? Maybe Northern Virginia?"

"No. There's no particle accelerators near there. Not even a physics lab. Of course, my sister's there . . ."

"Think your sister's breaking into your computer?"

Yeah, sure. My sister was a tech writer for the goddamn Navy. She even attended night school at the Navy War College.

"If she is," I replied, "I'm the pope of San Francisco."

"Well then, we can't go any further today. Next time, I'll make the trace faster."

It was hard to imagine a faster trace. I'd taken five minutes getting everyone on line. Ron Vivier had spent two minutes tracing the call through Tymnet; it had taken Lee Cheng another seven minutes to snake through several telephone exchanges. In a shade under a quarter hour, we'd traced the hacker through a computer and two networks.

Here was a conundrum. Sandy Merola felt the hacker came from the Berkeley campus. Dave Cleveland was certain he came from anywhere except Berkeley. Chuck McNatt from Anniston suspected someone from Alabama. The Tymnet trace led to Oakland, California. Now Pacific Bell said Virginia. Or was it New Jersey?

With each session my logbook grew. It wasn't enough to just summarize what had happened. I began to annotate each printout and search for correlations between sessions. I wanted to know my visitor: understand his wishes, predict his moves, find his address, and learn his name.

While trying to coordinate the traces, I'd pretty much ignored what the hacker was actually doing. After the tension died down, I hid in the library with the printout from his most recent connection.

Right off, it was obvious that the fifteen minutes which I'd watched were only the coda of the hacker's work. For two hours, he had been connected to our system; I'd only noticed him during the last quarter hour. Damn. If only I'd detected him right away. Two hours would have been enough to complete a trace.

More damning, though, was why I hadn't noticed him. I'd been watching for activity on Sventek's account, but he had used three other accounts before touching Sventek's account.

At 11:09 in the morning, some hacker had logged into an account belonging to a nuclear physicist, Elissa Mark. This account was valid, billed to the nuclear sciences department, though its owner had been on sabbatical at Fermilab for the past year. It took just one phone call to find that Elissa was unaware of anyone using her computer account; she didn't even know if it still existed. Was this the same hacker that I'd been following? Or someone else?

I had no way of knowing in advance that the Mark account had been hacked. But paging through the printout left little doubt.

Whoever was using the Mark account had become super-user by crawling through the Gnu-Emacs hole. As system manager, he searched for accounts that hadn't been used in a long time. He found three: Mark, Goran, and Whitberg. The latter two belonged to physicists long departed from our lab.

He edited the password file and breathed life into the three dead accounts. Since none of these accounts had been deleted, all their files and accounting information remained valid. To steal these accounts, the hacker needed to learn their passwords. But the passwords were protected by encryption: our DES trapdoor functions. No hacker could cut through that armor.

With his purloined super-user powers, the hacker edited the system-wide password file. He didn't try to decrypt Goran's encrypted password; instead, he erased it. Now that the account had no password, the hacker could log in as Goran.

With this he disconnected. What's he up to? He couldn't crack passwords, but as super-user, he didn't have to. He just edited the password file.

He reappeared a minute later as Goran, then chose a new password for this account—Benson. The next time Rodger Goran tried to use our Unix computer, he'd be frustrated to find his old password no longer worked.

Our hacker had stolen another account.

Aah—here's why the hacker stole old accounts. If he stole active accounts, people would complain when their familiar passwords no longer worked. So my adversary stole old accounts that weren't used anymore. Robbing the dead.

Even as super-user, he couldn't undo the DES trapdoor. So he couldn't figure out someone else's password. But he could swipe passwords, with a Trojan horse, or steal a whole account, by changing the password to a new word.

Having stolen the Goran account, he then grabbed the Whitberg account. The hacker now controlled at least four accounts, Sventek, Whitberg, Goran, and Mark, on two of our Unix computers. How many other accounts did he hold? On which other systems?

While running under Whitberg's pseudonym, the hacker tried to connect through our Milnet link into three Air Force systems. After waiting a minute for those distant computers to respond, he gave up, and started listing files belonging to LBL folks. He grew tired of this after reading a few scientific papers, several boring research proposals, and a detailed description of how to measure the nuclear cross section of some beryllium isotope. Yawn. Breaking into computers sure wasn't the key to power, fame, and the wisdom of the ages.

Getting into our two Unix systems hadn't satisfied my voracious foe. He'd tried hurdling the moat around our secured Unix-8 computer, but failed—Dave had sealed off that machine. Frustrated at this, he printed a list of remote computers available from our site.

Nothing secret there, just the names, phone numbers, and electronic addresses for thirty Berkeley computers.

# 12

WITH THE FULL MOON, I EXPECTED MORE HACKING AND planned on sleeping under the desk. The hacker didn't show up that evening, but Martha did. Around seven, she biked up, bringing a thermos of minestrone and some quilting to keep me occupied. There's no shortcut to hand stitching a quilt. Each triangle, square, and parallelogram must be cut to size, ironed, assembled, and sewn to its neighbors. Up close, it's hard to tell the pieces from the scraps. The design becomes visible only after the scraps are discarded, and you stitch the pieces together. Hmmm. A lot like understanding this hacker.

Around 11:30, I gave up my watch. If the hacker wanted to show up at midnight, the printers would catch him anyway.

The next day, the hacker turned up once. I missed him, preferring to share lunch with Martha just off campus. It was worth it: on a street corner, a jazz band played 1930s tunes.

The singer belted out some '30s ditty, "Everybody loves my baby, but my baby loves nobody but me."

"That's absurd," Martha said between tunes. "Logically analyzed, the singer must be his own baby."

"Huh?" It sounded fine to me.

"Look. 'Everybody' includes my baby. Since 'Everybody loves my baby,' then my baby loves herself. Right?"

"Uh, yeah." I tried to follow.

"But then he says, 'My baby loves nobody but me.' So my

baby, who must love herself, cannot love anyone else. Therefore, my baby must be me."

She explained it twice before I understood. The singer had never learned elementary logic. Neither had I.

By the time I returned from lunch, the hacker was long gone, leaving his trail on a paper printout.

For once, he didn't become super-user. Yes, in his paranoid way, he checked for systems people and monitoring processes, but he didn't sneak through the hole in the operating system.

Instead, he went fishing over the Milnet.

A single isolated computer, out of communication with the world, is immune to attack. But a hermit computer has limited value; it can't keep up with what's happening around it. Computers are of the greatest use when they interact with people, mechanisms, and other computers. Networks let people share data, programs, and electronic mail.

What's on a computer network? What do computers have to say to each other? Most personal computers satisfy the needs of their owners, and don't need to talk to other systems. For word processing, accounting spreadsheets, and games, you really don't need any other computers. But hook up a modem to your computer, and your telephone will report the latest from the stock market, news wires, and rumor mills. Connecting to another computer gives you a powerful way to tune in the latest news.

Our networks form neighborhoods, each with a sense of community. The high-energy physics networks transfer lots of data about subatomic particles, research proposals, as well as gossip about who's pushing for a Nobel prize. Unclassified military networks probably pass along orders for shoes, requests for funding, and rumors of who's jockeying for base commander. Somewhere, I'll bet there are classified networks, to exchange secret military orders and top secret gossip like who's sleeping with the base commander.

These electronic communities are bounded by the limits of their communications protocols. Simple networks, like public bulletin boards, use the simplest ways to communicate. Anyone with a personal computer and a telephone can link into them.

Advanced networks require leased telephone lines and dedicated computers, interconnecting hundreds or thousands of computers. These physical differences set boundaries between networks. The networks themselves are linked together by gateway computers, which pass reformatted messages between different networks.

Like Einstein's universe, most networks are finite but unbounded. There's only a certain number of computers attached, yet you never quite reach the edge of the network. There's always another computer down the line. Eventually, you'll make a complete circuit and wind up back where you started. Most networks are so complicated and interwoven that no one knows where all their connections lead, so most people have to explore to find their way around.

Our lab's computers connect to a dozen computer networks. Some of them are local, like the ethernet that ties computers in one building to a lab next door. Other nets reach to an extended community: the Bay Area Research Net links a dozen northern California universities. Finally, the national and international networks let our scientists connect to computers around the world. But the premier network is the Internet.

In the mid 1950s, the Federal government started building the interstate highway system, a twentieth-century marvel of pork-barrel public-works politics. With memories of wartime transportation shortages, military leaders made certain that the interstate system could handle tanks, military convoys, and troop carriers. Today, few think of interstate highways as a military system, though they're just as capable of sending tanks across the country as trucks.

With the same reasoning, the Department of Defense began developing a network to link military computers together. In 1969, the Defense Advanced Research Projects Agency's (DARPA) experiments evolved into the Arpanet and then into the Internet: an electronic highway interconnecting a hundred-thousand computers around the world.

In the world of computing, the Internet is at least as successful as the interstate system. Both have been overwhelmed by their success, and every day carry traffic far beyond what their designers dreamed. Each regularly inspires complaints of traffic jams, inadequate routes, shortsighted planning, and inadequate maintenance. Yet even these complaints reflect the phenomenal popularity of what was an uncertain experiment only a few years ago.

At first, DARPA's network was simply a testbed to prove that computers could be linked together. Since it was seen as an unreliable experiment, universities and laboratories used it, and mainstream military people ignored it. After eight years, only a few hundred computers connected into the Arpanet, but gradually, others were attracted by the network's reliability and simplicity. By 1985 the network directory listed tens of thousands of computers; today, there must be over one hundred thousand. Taking a census of networked computers would be like counting the cities and towns reachable from the interstate system—it's hard to name many places which can't be reached via some convoluted route.

The network's growing pains have been reflected in name changes. The first Arpanet was a backbone connecting random university, military, and defense contractor computers. As military people grew to depend on the network for carrying messages and mail, they decided to split the network into a military portion, the Milnet, and a research section, the Arpanet.

But there's not much difference between the military and academic nets, and gateways let traffic flow between them. Indeed, any Arpanet user can connect to any Milnet computer without so much as an invitation. Together, the Arpanet, Milnet, and a hundred other networks make up the Internet.

There are thousands of university, commercial, and military computers connected through the Internet. Like buildings in a city, each has a unique address; most of these addresses are registered at the Network Information Center (NIC) in Menlo Park, California. Any one computer may have dozens or hundreds of people using it, so individuals as well as computers are registered in the NIC.

The NIC's computers provide a directory: just connect to the NIC and ask for someone, and it'll tell you where they're located. They don't have much luck keeping their database up to date (computer people change jobs often), but the NIC still serves as a good phone directory of computer people.

During my lunch break, the hacker ducked into the NIC. Our printer quietly saved the session as he searched the NIC for the abbreviation, "WSMR":

```
9
LBL> telnet NIC.ARPA The hacker asks for the Network Information Center
Trying . . .
Connected to 10.0.0.51.
Escape character is '^]'.
+ -------------------------DDN Network Information Center---------------------------
|
| For user and host information, type: WHOIS <carriage return>
| For NIC information, type: NIC <carriage return>
|
+------------------------------------------------------------------------------------
@ whois wsmr He searches for WSMR
White Sands Missile Range     WSMR-NET-GW.ARMY.MIL        26.7.0.74
White Sands Missile Range     WSMR-TRAPS.ARMY.MIL         192.35.99.2
White Sands Missile Range     WSMR-AIMS.ARMY.MIL          128.44.8.1
White Sands Missile Range     WSMR-ARMTE-GW.ARMY.MIL      128.44.4.1
White Sands Missile Range     WSMR-NELARMY.MIL            128.44.11.3
```

WSMR? White Sands Missile Range. With two commands and twenty seconds, he found five computers at White Sands.

Astronomers know Sunspot, New Mexico, as one of the finest solar observatories. Clear skies and great telescopes make up for the utter isolation of Sacramento Peak, a few hundred miles south of Albuquerque. The only road to the observatory runs through White Sands, where the Army tests their guided missiles. Once, when I was studying the solar corona, an observing run took me to Sunspot, past the desolation of White Sands. The locked gates and guardhouses discourage onlookers; if the sun doesn't fry you, the electric fences will.

I'd heard rumors that the Army was designing rockets to shoot down satellites. Seemed like an SDI/Star Wars project, but civilian astronomers can only guess. Maybe this hacker knew more about White Sands than I did.

No doubt, though, that the hacker wanted to know more about White Sands. He spent ten minutes trying to log into each of their computers, connecting to them over the Internet.

The printer recorded his steps:

| | |
|---|---|
| LBL> telnet WSMR-NET-GW.ARMY.MIL | Connect to a White Sands |
| Trying . . . | computer |
| Connected to WSMR-NET-GW.ARMY.MIL | |
| | |
| 4.2 BSD UNIX | |
| Welcome to White Sands Missile Range | |
| login: guest | Try the guest account |
| Password: guest | Guesses a password |
| Invalid password, try again | But no luck |
| login: visitor | Try another likely account name |
| Password: visitor | |
| Invalid password, try again | No luck |
| login: root | He tries yet another account |
| Password: root | |
| Invalid password, try again | Still no luck |
| login: system | And a fourth try |
| Password: manager | |
| Invalid password, disconnecting after 4 tries | |

For each computer, he tried to log in as guest, visitor, root, and system. We saw him failing, time after time, as he tried to guess passwords. Perhaps those accounts were valid; the hacker couldn't enter them because he didn't know the right passwords.

I smiled at the printout. No doubt, the hacker wanted to get into White Sands. But they didn't fool around with security. Between their electric fences and passwords, neither tourist nor hacker could enter. Someone at White Sands had locked their doors.

With a snicker, I showed his attempts to the boss, Roy Kerth.

"Well, what do we do about it?" I asked. "Since he didn't get into White Sands, should we tell them?"

"Hell, yes, we'll tell them," Roy responded. "If someone tries to break into my neighbor's house, I'll tell 'em. I'll call the cops, too."

I asked what cops were in charge of the Internet.

"Damned if I know," Roy said. "But here's our policy, from here out: anyone that's attacked, we tell them. I don't care if the hacker didn't get in, you call them on the phone and tell them. Remember, keep this out of electronic mail. And find out who the cops are."

"Yessir."

It took only one phone call to find out that the FBI wasn't policing the Internet. "Look, kid, did you lose more than a half million dollars?"

"Uh, no."

"Any classified information?"

"Uh, no."

"Then go away, kid." Another attempt at rousing the feds had failed.

Maybe the Network Information Center would know who policed their net. I called Menlo Park and eventually found Nancy Fischer. To her, the Internet wasn't just a collection of cables and software. It was a living creature, a brain with neurons extending round the world, into which ten thousand computer users breathed life every hour. Nancy was fatalistic: "It's a miniature of the society around us. Sooner or later, some vandal's going to try to kill it."

It seemed that there were no network police. Since the Milnet—now called the Defense Data Network—isn't allowed to carry classified data, nobody paid much attention to its security.

"You ought to be talking to the Air Force Office of Special Investigations," she said. "They're the narcs of the Air Force. Drug busts and murders. Not exactly white-collar crime, but it can't hurt to talk to them. I'm sorry I can't help you, but it's really not my bailiwick."

Three phone calls later, I'm in a conference call with Special Agent Jim Christy of the AFOSI and Major Steve Rudd of the Defense Communications Agency.

Jim Christy made me nervous—he sounded like a narc. "Let me get this straight. Some hacker broke into your computer, then got into an Army computer in Alabama, and is now going for White Sands Missile Range?"

"Yes, that's about what we've seen." I didn't want to explain the Unix Gnu-Emacs security hole. "Our traces aren't complete yet; he might be from California, Alabama, Virginia, or maybe New Jersey."

"Oh . . . you're not shutting him out so that you can catch the bastard." He was ahead of me.

"And if we close him out, he'll just enter the Internet through some other hole."

Steve Rudd, on the other hand, wanted the hacker nailed. "We can't let this continue. Even without classified information, the Milnet's integrity demands that spies be kept out."

Spies? My ears pricked up.

The narc spoke next. "I don't suppose the FBI has lifted a finger."

I summarized our five calls to the FBI in one word.

Almost apologetically, Jim Christy told me, "The FBI isn't required to investigate every crime. Probably they look at one in five. Computer crimes aren't easy—not like kidnapping or bank robbery, where there's witnesses and obvious losses. Don't blame them for shying away from a tough case with no clear solution."

Steve pressed Jim. "OK, so the FBI won't do anything. How about AFOSI?"

Jim answered slowly, "We're the Air Force computer crime investigators. We usually hear about computer crimes only after a loss. This is the first one that we've come across in progress."

Steve cut in, "Jim, you're a special agent. The only difference between you and an FBI agent is your jurisdiction. Doesn't this fall in your court?"

"It does. It's a strange case that falls in several courts." Over the phone, I could almost hear Jim think. "We're interested, all right. I can't tell if this is a serious problem or a red herring, but it's well worth investigating."

Jim continued, "Look, Cliff. Each agency has thresholds. Our resources are finite so we're forced to choose what we investigate. That's why the FBI asked you about the dollar loss—they're looking to get the most bang for their effort. Now if classified stuff gets stolen, it's a different story. National security doesn't equate to dollars."

Steve interrupted, "But unclassified information can also equate to national security. The problem is convincing law enforcement people."

"So what'll you do?" I asked.

"Right now, there's really not much we can do. If this hacker's using the military networks, though, he's walking on our territory. Keep us informed and we'll sharpen our stingers."

In hopes of encouraging AFOSI, I sent Jim a copy of my logbook, and samples of the hacker's printouts.

After this conversation, Jim Christy explained about the Milnet. What I called the Milnet, Jim knew as the unclassified Defense Data Network, run by the Defense Communications Agency. "The Department of Defense runs the Milnet for all the services—Army, Navy, Air Force, and Marines. That way, each service has equal access to the network, and you'll find computers from every branch on the net."

"So why is Steve Rudd in the Air Force?"

"He's really a purple-suiter—he works for all three branches. Naturally, when he smelled a problem, he called the Air Force investigators."

"And you work full time on computer crime?"

"You betcha. We're watching ten thousand Air Force computers."

"Then why can't you wrap up this case in a snap?"

Jim spoke slowly. "We've got to clearly define our territory. Unless we do, we step on each other's toes. You, Cliff, have no worries that you'll be busted by the OSI—our bailiwick is the Air Force base."

Bailiwicks always belong to someone else.

You know, much as I complained about bailiwicks, I realized that they protected my own rights: our constitution prevents the military from grubbing around civilian affairs. Jim had put this into a new light—sometimes these rights actually do interfere with law enforcement. For the first time, I realized that my civil rights actually limit what police can do.

Whoops. I'd forgotten the boss's instructions to call White Sands. Another few minutes on the phone, and I reached Chris McDonald, a civilian working for the missile range.

I outlined the case—Unix, Tymnet, Oakland, Milnet, Anniston, AFOSI, FBI.

Chris interrupted, "Did you say Anniston?"

"Yes, the hacker was super-user at Anniston Army Depot. It's a little place in Alabama, I think."

"I know Anniston, all right. They're our sister Army base. After we test our missiles, we ship 'em off to Anniston," Chris said. "And their computers come from White Sands as well."

I wondered if this was just coincidence. Perhaps the hacker had read data in the Anniston computers, and realized that the good stuff came from White Sands. Maybe the hacker was sampling every site where the Army stored missiles.

Or maybe the hacker had a list of computers with security holes. "Say, Chris, do you have Gnu-Emacs on your computers?"

Chris didn't know, but he'd ask around. But to exploit that hole, the hacker had to log in first. And the hacker had failed, after trying four times on each of five computers.

White Sands kept their doors locked by forcing everyone on their computers to use long passwords, and to change them every four months. A technician wasn't allowed to choose her own password—the computer assigned unguessable passwords, like "agnitfom" or "nietoayx." Every account had a password, and none could be guessed.

I didn't like the White Sands system. I couldn't remember computer-generated passwords, so I'd write them in my wallet or next to my terminal. Much better to allow people to choose their own passwords. Sure, some people would pick guessable passwords, like their names. But at least they wouldn't complain about having to memorize some nonsense word like "tremvonk," and they wouldn't write them down.

But the hacker got into my system and was rebuffed at White Sands. Maybe random passwords, obnoxious and dissonant, are more secure. I don't know.

I'd followed the boss's orders. The FBI didn't care about us, but the Air Force sleuths were on the case. And I'd notified White Sands that someone was trying to break in. Satisfied, I met

Martha at a vegetarian pizza stand. Over slices of thick-crust spinach and pesto, I described the day's events.

"Vell, Natasha, we have accomplished mission one."

"Vonderful, Boris, vhat a victory. Boris . . . vhat is mission one?"

"We have made rendezvous vith ze secret air force police, Natasha."

"Yes, Boris?"

"Ve have alerted ze missile base to ze counter-counter-intelligence efforts."

"Yes, Boris?"

"And we have ordered ze secret spy pizza."

"But Boris, ven do we catch ze spy?"

"Patience, Natasha. Zat is mission two."

It wasn't until we started walking home that we got to the serious side of our game.

"This thing is getting weirder and weirder," Martha said. "It started out as a hobby, chasing some local prankster, and now you're talking to these military people who wear suits and have no sense of humor. Cliff, they're not your type."

I defended myself stuffily. "This is a harmless and possibly beneficial project to keep them busy. After all, this is what they're supposed to be doing—keeping the bad guys out."

Martha wouldn't let that sit. "Yeah, but what about you, Cliff. What are you doing hanging out with these people? I understand that you have to at least talk to them, but how deeply are you getting involved?"

"Every step makes perfect sense from my point of view," I said. "I'm a system manager trying to protect my computer. If someone hacks into it, I have to chase him. To ignore the bastard will let him wreck other systems. Yes, I'm cooperating with the Air Force police, but that doesn't mean I approve of everything the military stands for."

"Yes, but you have to decide how you want to live your life," Martha said. "Do you want to spend your time being a cop?"

"A cop? No, I'm an astronomer. But here's someone threatening to destroy our work."

"We don't know that," Martha retorted. "Maybe this hacker is closer to us politically than those security people. What if you're chasing someone on your own side? Perhaps he's trying to expose problems of military proliferation. Some sort of electronic civil disobedience."

My own political views hadn't evolved much from the late 1960s . . . a sort of fuzzy, mixed bag of the new-left. I'd never thought much about politics, feeling that I was a harmless non-ideologue, trying to avoid unpleasant political commitments. I resisted radical left-wing dogma, but I sure wasn't a conservative. I had no desire to buddy up with the feds. Yet here I was, walking side by side with the military police.

"About the only way to find out who's at the other end is to trace the wires," I said. "These organizations may not be our favorites, but the particular actions that we're cooperating over aren't bad. It's not like I'm running guns to the Contras."

"Just watch your step."

# 13

MY THREE WEEKS WERE ALMOST UP. IF I DIDN'T CATCH THE hacker within twenty-four hours, the lab would shut down my tracking operation. I camped out in the switchyard, jumping at every connection. "Come into my parlor," said the spider to the fly.

Sure enough, at 2:30 in the afternoon, the printer advanced a page, and the hacker logged in. Although this time he used the stolen account, *Goran,* I didn't doubt that it was the hacker: he immediately checked who was on the computer. Finding no operator present, he searched out the Gnu-Emacs security hole, and started his delicate minuet to become super-user.

I didn't watch. A minute after the hacker connected, I called Ron Vivier at Tymnet and Lee Cheng at the phone company. I took notes as Ron mumbled, "He's coming into your port 14, and entering Tymnet from Oakland. It's our port 322 which is, uh, let me see here." I could hear him tapping his keyboard. "Yeah, it's 2902. 430-2902. That's the number to trace."

Lee Cheng popped on the phone line. "Right. I'm tracing it." More keytaps, this time with a few beeps thrown in. "That line is live, all right. And it's coming from AT&T. AT&T in Virginia. Hold on, I'll call New Jersey."

I listened in as Lee talked with some AT&T guy named Edsel (or was it Ed Sell?) in Whippany, New Jersey. Apparently, all of AT&T's long-distance phone lines are traced through New Jersey.

Without understanding the jargon, I transcribed what I heard. "Routing 5095, no that's 5096MCLN."

Another technician's voice broke in. "I'll call McLean."

The New Jersey technician came back. "Yeah. 5096 terminates in 703 land."

There were suddenly six people on the line. The phone company's conference calls were crisp and loud. The newest member of the conference call was a woman with a slight drawl. "Y'all are trunked into McLean, and it's almost dinnertime here at C and P."

Lee's clipped voice interrupted her. "Emergency trace on routing code 5096MCLN, your termination line 427."

"I copy 5096MCLN line 427. I'm tracing right now."

Silence for a minute, then she came back on line. "Here it comes, boys. Hey, it looks like it's from 415 territory."

"Yeah. Greetings from San Francisco Bay," Lee slid in.

She spoke to no one in particular. "Trunk group 5096MCLN, routing 427 winds up in 448. Our ESS4 at 448. Is it a PBX?" She answered her own question: "No, it's a rotary. Frame twenty-four. I'm almost at the tip ring sleeve. Here we are. Five hundred pair cable, group three number twelve . . . that's ten, uh, ten sixty. You want me to confirm with a short drop-out?"

Lee interpreted her jargon. "She's completed the trace. To make sure that she's traced the right number, she wants to turn off the connection for a second. If she does that, it'll hang up the line. Is that OK?"

The hacker was in the midst of reading some electronic mail. I doubted that he'd miss a few characters. "Sure. Tell her to go ahead, and I'll see what happens here."

Lee talked with her a bit, and announced with certainty, "Stand by." He explained that each telephone line has a set of fuses in the central switching office; they protect the equipment from lightning and idiots that plug their phone lines into power outlets. The central office technician can go to the cable room and pull the line's fuse, forcing it to hang up. It wasn't necessary, but it double checked their tracing efforts.

In a minute, the central office tech came onto the line and said,

"I'm popping the fuse . . . now." Sure enough, the hacker dropped off, right in the middle of a command. They'd traced the right line.

The woman's voice came on. "It's 1060, all right. That's all, boys. I'll shuffle some tissues and ship it on upstairs."

Lee thanked everyone, and I heard the conference call clear. "The trace is complete and the technician's writing it up. As soon as I get the trace data, I'll give it to the police."

I didn't understand. Why didn't he just tell me the owner of the phone?

Lee explained that the telephone company dealt with the police, not with individuals. Moreover, he didn't know where the line had been traced to. The tech that completed the trace would fill out the proper papers (aah! "shuffling tissues") and release them to the authorities.

I protested, "Can't you just short-circuit the bureaucracy and tell me who the hacker is?"

No. First, Lee didn't have the trace information. The technician in Virginia did. Until the Virginia phone company released it, Lee knew as little as I did.

Lee pointed out another problem: my search warrant was only valid in California. A California court couldn't compel the Virginia telephone company to turn over evidence. We'd need either a Virginia or Federal court order.

I protested, "The FBI's turned us down five times already. And the guy's probably not breaking any Virginia law. Look, can't you give me the phone number on the side and just wink?"

Lee didn't know. He'd call Virginia and try to convince them to give us the information, but he didn't hold out much hope. Damn. At the other end of the phone line, someone was breaking into military computers, and we couldn't even get his phone number, ten seconds after the line was traced.

The phone trace was complete, though not quite successful. How do we get a Virginia search warrant? My boss, Roy Kerth, was gone for the next couple weeks, so I called the lab's lawyer directly. To my surprise, Aletha paid serious attention to the problem. She'd rattle the FBI again, and see whether we had a case in Virginia. I warned her that, as a peon, I had no authority to even be talking to her, let alone asking for legal services. She reassured me, "Don't be silly. This is more fun than worrying about patent law."

The laboratory police wanted to know all about the phone trace. I told them to prepare to stake out the entire state of Virginia. Despite my cynicism, they were surprisingly sympathetic to my problem with the Virginia search warrant, and offered to use their old-boy-network to get the information through some informal channel. I doubted it would work, but why not let them try?

# 14

THE PHONE COMPANY MIGHT CONCEAL THE HACKER'S phone number, but my printers showed his every move. While I talked to Tymnet and the telephone techs, the hacker had prowled through my computer. He wasn't satisfied reading the system manager's mail; he also snooped through mail for several nuclear physicists.

After fifteen minutes of reading our mail, he jumped back into Goran's stolen account, using his new password, *Benson*. He started a program that searched our user's files for passwords; while that executed, he called up the Milnet Network Information Center. Again, he knew who he was looking for:

```
LBL>telnet Nic.arpa
Trying . . .
Connected to 10.0.0.51.
+--------------------DDN   Network   Information   Center--------------------|
|For TAC news, type:                        TACNEWS <carriage return>
|For user and host information, type:       WHOIS <carriage return>
|For NIC information, type:                 NIC <carriage return>
+ ----------------------------------------------------------------------------|
SRI-NIC, TOPS-20 Monitor 6.1(7341)-4
@Whois cia
Central Intelligence Agency (CIA)
   Office of Data Processing
   Washington, DC 20505
   These are 4 known members:
```

```
Fischoff, J. (JF27)            FISHOFF@A.ISI.EDU    (703) 351-3305
Gresham, D. L. (DLG33)         GRESHAM@A.ISI.EDU    (703) 351-2957
Manning, Edward J. (EM44)      MANNING@BBN.ARPA     (703) 281-6161
Ziegler, Mary (MZ9)            MARY@NNS.ARPA        (703) 351-8249
```

He had asked for the pathway into the CIA. But instead of their computer, he found four people who worked at the CIA.

Whee! I pictured all these CIA spies playing cloak-and-dagger; meanwhile, someone's pushing on their back door.

So I asked myself, "Should I tell them?"

"No. Why waste my time telling them? Let some spy run around in the CIA's backyard. See if I care. My three weeks of chasing the hacker are up. It's about time to shut our doors and work on real problems of physics and astronomy. He's someone else's problem now."

And yet it didn't feel right. The hacker walked through military computers, yet nobody noticed. The CIA didn't know. The FBI didn't care. Who would pick up where we left off?

I reached for the telephone to call the people listed in the CIA, then put it down. What's a long-haired hippie doing calling some spooks? What would Martha say?

Well, whose side was I on? Not the CIA's, for sure. But then, I wasn't rooting for someone to break in there, either. At least I didn't think so.

Foo. The jerk was trying to slither into someone's computer. Nobody else will warn them, so I'd better. I'm not responsible for the CIA's actions, only my own.

Before I could change my mind again, I called the first CIA guy's phone number. No answer. The second guy was on vacation—his answering machine said so. The third person . . .

A business voice answered, "Extension 6161."

I stammered a bit. "Um, hello, I'm looking for Ed Manning."

"Yes?"

I didn't know where to begin. How do you introduce yourself to a spy? "Uh, you don't know me, but I'm a computer manager, and we've been following a computer hacker."

"Uh-huh."

"Well, he searched for a pathway to try to get into the CIA's computers. Instead, he found your name and phone number. I'm not sure what this means, but someone's looking for you. Or maybe they're just looking for the CIA and stumbled on your name." I'm floundering, scared of the guy I'm talking to.

"Who are you?"

Nervously, I told him, expecting him to send over a gang of hit men in trench coats. I described our laboratory, making sure he understood that the People's Republic of Berkeley didn't have official diplomatic relations with his organization.

"Can I send someone over tomorrow? No, that's Saturday. How about Monday afternoon?"

Uh oh. The hit men were on their way. I tried to backpedal. "This probably isn't serious. The guy didn't find anything except four names. You don't have to worry about him getting into your computer."

Mr. Manning wasn't convinced. "I know why my name's listed. Last year I worked on some computers at the Ballistics Research Lab. But we're professionally interested in this, and we'd appreciate a chance to learn more. Conceivably, this might be a serious problem."

Who was I talking to? Weren't these the people who meddle in Central American politics and smuggle arms to right-wing thugs? Yet the guy I'd just talked to didn't sound like a villain. He seemed like an ordinary person concerned with a problem.

And why not set them on the trail of someone just as meddlesome and destructive as I always thought *they* were? Tracking down a real wrongdoer would give the CIA something harmless, perhaps even beneficial, to do—keep them out of trouble.

It was no use arguing. They needed to know, and I couldn't see a good reason to avoid telling them. And talking to the CIA wouldn't hurt anyone—it wasn't like shipping guns to a military dictator. After all, isn't this what they're legitimately supposed to do: protect us from bad guys? If I don't tell them what's happening, who will?

I couldn't help comparing the CIA's immediate reaction with

the response I got from the FBI. Six calls for help, and a half dozen responses, "Go away, kid."

Well, I agreed to meet with his agents, provided they didn't wear trench coats.

"Now I've put my foot in it," I thought. "Not only am I talking to the CIA, but I'm inviting them up to Berkeley. What'll I tell my radical friends?"

# 15

WINDMILL QUARRY IS JUST ACROSS THE NIAGARA RIVER from Buffalo, New York, where I grew up. It's a ten-mile bicycle ride, across the Peace Bridge to Canada and down a few winding roads to the finest swimming hole around. If you dodge the potholes and speak politely to the U.S. and Canadian customs agents, you'll have no problems.

High school had just let out in June of 1968 when I biked over to Windmill Quarry for a Saturday swim. Two other friends and I wore ourselves out trying to swim to the raft in the middle of the water. Around six, we ran out of steam, hopped on our bikes, and headed back to Buffalo.

Three miles shy of the Peace Bridge, we were pedaling along the stony margins of a country road when a pickup truck crowded us off the roadside. Someone swore at us and tossed a half-empty can of Genesee beer, hitting our lead rider. She wasn't hurt but all three of us were furious.

We were on our bikes. No way to catch up with the SOBs. Even if we could, what would we do? We were three miles inside of Canada, after all. We were powerless, unable to retaliate.

But I'd caught a glimpse of the license plate. From New York State. Oh . . . they're returning to Buffalo, too. Then it hit me.

I stopped at the first phone booth—luckily there was a directory—and called the U.S. customs agents. "There's a green Chevy pickup truck heading for the Peace Bridge," I reported. "I'm not sure, but I think they're carrying some drugs." The agent thanked me, and I hung up.

The three of us biked back at a leisurely pace. We got to the bottom of the bridge, looked over at the side of the road . . . and my heart sang! Sure enough, there was that green pickup, hood up, seat pulled out, and two wheels removed. Customs agents were crawling all over it, searching for drugs.

Aah. The sense of recovered dignity.

Years ago, I hadn't asked that clown to throw a beer can at us. Nor today had I asked this hacker to invade my computer. I didn't want to track him around the networks. I'd rather be doing astronomy.

But now that I'd evolved a strategy, I could only follow the hacker by being sneaky and tenacious. And by informing the few authorities that seemed to care. Like the CIA.

Roy was on vacation, so not only couldn't he tell me to drop the investigation now that my three weeks were up, but he couldn't say anything about the CIA visiting. His stand-in, Dennis Hall, was to greet the spooks.

Dennis is a tranquil, introspective Zen master whose job is to link small computers to Cray supercomputers. He sees networks as channels to slosh computing power from laboratories to desktops. Little computers should talk to people; leave the number crunching to the mainframes. If your desktop workstation's too slow, then move the hard work into a bigger computer.

In a sense, Dennis is the enemy of computer centers. He wants people to use computers without the mumbo jumbo of programming. As long as there are software wizards and gurus, Dennis won't be satisfied with the distribution of computing power.

His is a world of ethernets, optical fibers, and satellite links. Other computer folks measure size in megabytes of memory, and speed in megaflops—millions of floating-point-operations per second. To Dennis, size is measured by counting computers on your network; speed is measured in megabytes per second—how fast the computers talk to each other. The system isn't the computer, it's the network.

Dennis saw the hacker problem in terms of social morality.

"We'll always find a few dodos poking around our data. I'm worried about how hackers spoil the trust that's built our networks. After years of trying to hook together a bunch of computers, a few morons can spoil everything."

I didn't see how trust had anything to do with it. "Networks are little more than cables and wires," I said.

"And an interstate highway is just concrete, asphalt, and bridges?" Dennis replied. "You're seeing the crude physical apparatus—the wires and communications. The real work isn't laying wires, it's agreeing to link isolated communities together. It's figuring out who's going to pay for the maintenance and improvements. It's forging alliances between groups that don't trust each other."

"Like the military and universities, huh?" I said, thinking of the Internet.

"Yes, and more. The agreements are informal and the networks are overloaded," Dennis said. "Our software is fragile as well—if people built houses the way we write programs, the first woodpecker would wipe out civilization."

With the CIA due in ten minutes, Dennis and I talked about what to say. I had no idea what they wanted, other than a listing of last Friday's activity. I could imagine them: some secret agent looking like James Bond, or a hit man specializing in rubouts. Of course there'd be Mr. Big behind them all, pulling the puppet strings. They'd all be in dark glasses and trench coats.

Dennis gave me instructions. "Cliff, tell them what we know, but don't speculate. Confine yourself to facts."

" 'S'all reet. But suppose there's a hit man with 'em, who wants to rub me out because I found that they're spying on the military?"

"Be serious." Everyone told me to be serious. "And for once, be polite. They've got enough problems without a raving Berkeley longhair. And skip the yo-yo tricks."

"Yes, Daddy. I'll be good. I promise."

"Don't worry about them. They're like anyone else around here, except a bit more paranoid."

"And a bit more Republican," I added.

OK, so they didn't wear trench coats. Not even sunglasses.

Instead, boring suits and ties. I should have warned them to dress like the natives: beat-up dungarees and flannel shirts.

Wayne saw the four of them walk up the drive and flashed a message to my terminal: "All hands on deck. Sales reps approach through starboard portal. Charcoal-gray suits. Set warp speed to avoid IBM sales pitch." If only he knew.

The four spooks introduced themselves. One guy in his fifties said he was there as a driver, and didn't give his name—he just sat there quietly the whole time. The second spy, Greg Fennel, I guessed to be a computer jockey, because he seemed uncomfortable in a suit.

The third agent was built like a halfback. Teejay didn't give his last name—or did he conceal his first name? If anyone was the hit man, Teejay was. The fourth guy must be the bigwig: everyone shut up when he talked. Together, they looked more like bureaucrats than spies.

The four of them sat quietly while Dennis gave them an overview of what we'd seen. No questions. I walked to the chalkboard and drew a diagram.

Greg Fennel wouldn't let me get away with just a drawing. "Prove the connection from the phone company to Tymnet."

I described the phone trace and the conference calls to Ron Vivier.

"Since he's not erasing anything, how did you detect him?"

"A hiccup in our accounting system; you see, he imbalanced our accounts when he . . ."

Greg interrupted, "So he's super-user on your Unix system? Bad news, huh?" Greg seemed to be a sharp systems guy. I figured I might as well go into detail.

"It's a bug in the Gnu-Emacs editor. Its mail utility runs with root privilege." Technical questions were easy.

We talked Unix for a bit, and Mr. Big started playing with his pencil. "Can you give us a profile of this guy? How old is he? What's his level of expertise?"

Tougher question. "Well, we've only watched him for three weeks, so it's hard to say. He's accustomed to AT&T Unix, so he's not from around Berkeley. Perhaps he's a high school student.

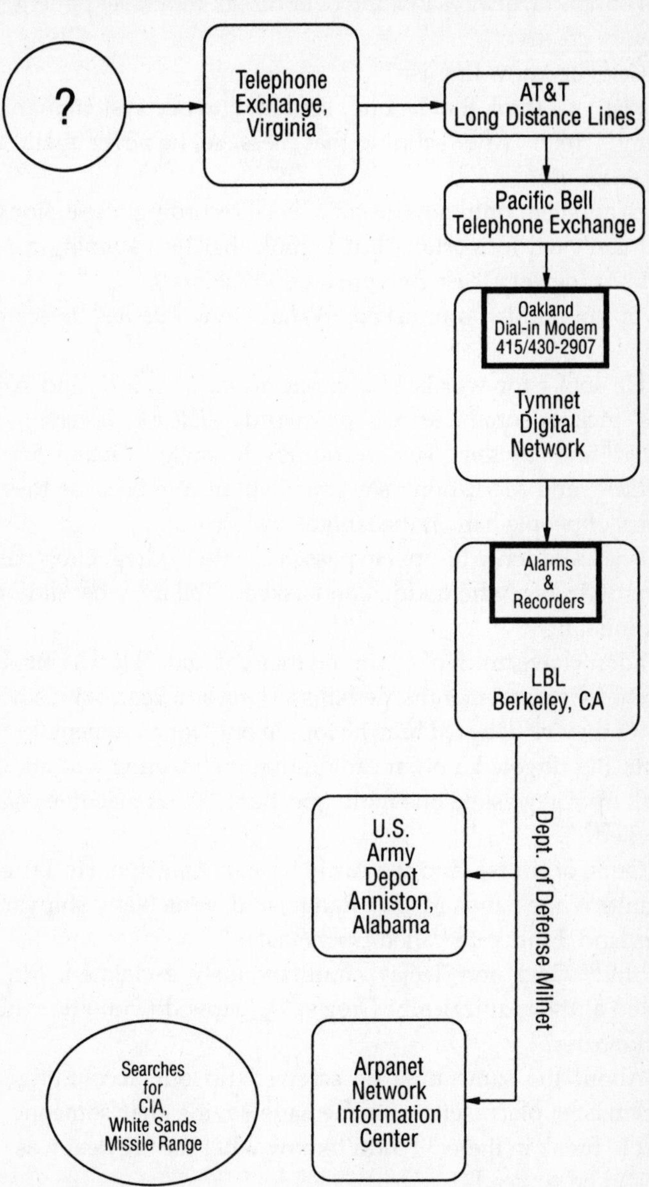
?
Telephone Exchange, Virginia
AT&T Long Distance Lines
Pacific Bell Telephone Exchange
Oakland Dial-in Modem 415/430-2907
Tymnet Digital Network
Alarms & Recorders
LBL Berkeley, CA
Dept. of Defense Milnet
U.S. Army Depot Anniston, Alabama
Arpanet Network Information Center
Searches for CIA, White Sands Missile Range

He's paranoid, always looking over his shoulder, yet patient, and not very creative."

"Does he know English?"

"Well, we think that he once sent mail to our system manager, saying, 'Hello.' After sending that message, he never again used that account."

Teejay, silent until now, asked, "Is he recording his sessions?"

"I can't tell for certain, but I think that he's keeping a notebook. At the very least, he's got a good memory."

Mr. Big nodded and asked, "What keywords has he scanned for?"

"He looks for words like *password, nuclear, SDI,* and *Norad.* He's picked some curious passwords—*lblhack, hedges, jaeger, hunter,* and *benson.* The accounts he stole, *Goran, Sventek, Whitberg,* and *Mark,* don't say much about him because they are names of people here at the laboratory."

Teejay suddenly lit up. He passed a note to Greg. Greg passed it on to Mr. Big, who nodded and asked, "Tell me what did he do at Anniston?"

"I don't have much of a printout there," I said. "He was into their system for several months, perhaps as long as a year. Now, since he knows they've detected him, he logs in only for a moment."

Mr. Big fidgeted a bit, meaning that the meeting was about to break up. Greg asked one more question: "What machines has he attacked?"

"Ours, of course, and the Army base in Anniston. He's tried to get into White Sands Missile Range, and some Navy shipyard in Maryland. I think it's called Dockmaster."

"Shit!" Greg and Teejay simultaneously exclaimed. Mr. Big looked at them quizzically. Greg said, "How do you know he hit Dockmaster?"

"About the same time he screwed up our accounting, this Dockmaster place sent us a message saying that someone had tried to break in there." I didn't know what the big deal was.

"Did he succeed?"

"I don't think so. What is this Dockmaster place, anyway? Aren't they some Navy shipyard?"

They whispered among themselves, and Mr. Big nodded. Greg explained, "Dockmaster isn't a Navy shipyard. It's run by the National Security Agency."

A hacker breaking into NSA? Bizarre. This guy wanted to get into the CIA, the NSA, Army missile bases, and the North American Air Defense headquarters.

I knew a little about the NSA. They're the secret electronics spooks that listen in on foreign radio broadcasts. They launch satellites to listen to Soviet telephone calls. I'd heard (and didn't believe) rumors that they record every overseas phone call and telegram.

Greg explained from his standpoint. "Most of NSA works on collecting and analyzing signals from abroad. One section, however, works on protecting information belonging to the United States."

"Yeah," I said, "like making ciphers that you think the Commies can't break." Dennis shot me a glance and silently mouthed the word "Polite."

"Uh, yeah," Greg said, "that group worries about computer security. They run the Dockmaster computer."

"Sounds like Janus, the two-faced god," I said. "One side tries to crack ciphers of foreign countries; the other side tries to make unbreakable codes. Always pulling in opposite directions."

"Sorta like our own agency." Greg looked around nervously. "We're known for dirty tricks, but we're fundamentally a news organization. Most of our work is just gathering and analyzing information, yet try saying that on campus." Greg rolled his eyes. He'd paid his dues as a college recruiter. Hard to say why, but this spy seemed reasonable. Not arrogant, but sensitive and aware. If we must poke around in dark corners, I'd be more comfortable with him in charge.

"Well then, why can I reach NSA's computers form my unclassified and obviously insecure computer?" If I could reach out and touch NSA, then they could touch me.

"Dockmaster is NSA's only unclassified computer," Greg said. "It belongs to their computer security group, which is actually public."

Mr. Big started talking slowly. "There's not much we can do

about this affair. I think there's no evidence of foreign espionage. Agents on assignment don't send notes to adversaries."

"Well, who should be working on this case?" I asked.

"The FBI. I'm sorry, but this isn't our bailiwick. Our entire involvement has been the exposure of four names—names that are already in the public domain, I might add."

On the way out, I showed our Vax computers to Greg and Teejay. Between rows of disk drives, Greg said, "This is the most serious hacker problem I've heard of. Despite what the boss says, could you keep me informed?"

I decided to trust this guy. "Sure. Want a copy of my logbook?"

"Yes. Send me anything. Even if the agency can't do anything, we need to become aware of this type of threat."

"Why? Do spooks have computers?"

Greg looked at Teejay and laughed. "We've lost count. Our building floats on computers."

"What would the CIA use computers for? Can you overthrow foreign governments with software?" Dennis wasn't around to tell me to be polite.

"Stop thinking that we're arch villains and think of us instead as information gatherers. The information's worthless until it's correlated, analyzed, and summarized. That alone is a lot of word processing."

"Personal computer stuff, I'll bet."

"No, not if you want to do it right. We're trying to avoid the next Pearl Harbor, and that means getting information to the right person fast. Right off, that says networks and computers. To analyze and predict the actions of foreign governments, we use computer-based models. Again, big computers. Nowadays, everything from economic forecasts to image processing requires powerful number crunchers."

I'd never thought of the CIA as needing really major computers. "How do you keep your systems secure?"

"Strict isolation. There's no wires connecting to the outside."

"Can any CIA agent read anyone else's files?"

Greg laughed, but Teejay didn't. "No way. In our world, everyone's compartmentalized. So if one person turns out to be, how should I say, less than trustworthy, the amount of damage is limited."

"Then how do you keep people from reading each other's files?"

"We use trusted operating systems. Computers with thick walls between each individual's data. If you want to read someone else's files, then you've got to get permission. Teejay can tell you some horror stories."

Teejay looked sideways at Greg. Greg said, "Go ahead, Teejay. It's already public."

"Two years ago, one of our contractors built a centralized terminal switchbox," Teejay said. "We needed to interconnect a few thousand terminals to some of our computers."

"Oh, like my lab's switchyard."

"Multiply your switchyard by fifty, and you have some idea."

Teejay continued, "Each employee of this contractor had to pass the same tests as our regular employees—compartmentalized top secret.

"Well, one of our secretaries went on vacation for a month. When she returned and logged onto her computer, she noticed that her account had been accessed a week earlier. You see, every time you sign onto our computers, it shows the date when you last logged on.

"We started sniffing around. The SOB that had connected the terminals wiretapped them from our computer room. He'd capture passwords and text, and then pry into our password disks."

I knew how easy it was to watch the traffic in the LBL switchyard. "Did you bump him off?" I asked, imagining some midnight action with a silenced gun.

Teejay looked at me strangely. "Be serious. Where we come from, it's 'In God we trust, all others we polygraph.' "

Greg finished the story. "We wired him to a lie detector for a week, and the FBI indicted him. It'll be a long time before he sees sunlight."

Walking out of the lab, I asked Teejay, "Looks like the CIA's not going to do much for me, huh?"

"If my superior doesn't think it's serious, there's not much we can do. Ed Manning has the power to make something happen."

"Huh? I thought Ed Manning was a programmer?"

"Hardly. He's director of information technology. When you called him, you hit a central nerve."

A director who knew his way around the networks? Now that's a rare organization. No wonder they flew four people out here. There's a bigger Mr. Big back at the headquarters.

"So when you report that there's nothing shaking here, you'll drop it?"

"Well, there's not much that we can do," Greg said. "It's the FBI's territory."

"Any chance you can rattle their cages and ask them to investigate?"

"I'll try, but don't expect much. The FBI likes to chase bank robbers and kidnappers. Computer crime, well, let's say they've got other worries."

"What I hear you saying is, 'Stop watching and zipper things up.' "

"Not quite. You're watching an extensive attack on our networks. Someone's going after the very heart of our information systems. We've expected minor attacks for several years, but I've never heard of anything this far-reaching. The convoluted connections, the single-minded search for sensitive targets . . . it points to an adversary who's determined to get into our computers. If you close your doors, he'll just find another way in."

"So you're saying, 'Stay open and keep monitoring' even though the FBI ignores us."

Greg looked at Teejay. "I can't buck my management. But you're doing an important piece of, well, research. The FBI will eventually wake up. Until then, keep at it."

I was astonished—these guys saw the severity of the situation but couldn't do anything. Or were they just saying that?

Encouraging words from the CIA.

# 16

IT WOULD HAVE BEEN A FUN SHOW FOR THE SPOOKS IF the hacker appeared while they were visiting. Instead he showed up the next morning at 9:10. Once again we started the traces through Tymnet and the phone company; once again we struck a brick wall somewhere in Virginia. If only our California search warrant were good in Virginia . . .

That day the hacker seemed confident, even arrogant. He performed his usual tricks: checking who's on the system, sneaking through the hole in our operating system, listing electronic mail. In the past he made occasional mistakes as he tried new commands. Today he used no new commands. He was smooth, determined. No mistakes.

As if he were showing off.

He went straight for the Anniston Army Depot and printed out a short file about the combat readiness of Army missiles. He then tried the Army's Ballistic Research Lab's computers in Aberdeen, Maryland. The Milnet took only a second to connect, but BRL's passwords defeated him: he couldn't get through.

He wasted the rest of my morning by raking through my scientists' files, searching for passwords. In a physicist's area, he found one: an old file that described the way to get into a Cray supercomputer at Lawrence Livermore Labs.

To keep people from guessing passwords into their supercomputer, Livermore also used random computer-generated passwords, like *agnitfom* or *ngagk*. Naturally, nobody can remember these passwords. Result? Some people save their passwords in computer files. What good is a combination lock when the combination's scribbled on the wall?

Dave Cleveland, our Unix Guru, watched the hacker. "At least he can't get into the classified computers at Livermore," Dave said.

"Why not?"

"Their classified system is completely off net. It's isolated."

"Then what's the password lead to?"

"Livermore has a few unclassified computers, where they research fusion energy."

"Sounds like bomb making to me," I said. Any kind of fusion seemed like bomb making.

"They're trying to build fusion energy reactors to generate cheap electricity. You know, fusion reactions inside donut-shaped magnetic fields."

"Sure. I played with one when I was a kid."

"I thought so. Since it's not weapons research, that computer's accessible from networks."

"We'd better warn Livermore to disable that account."

"Just wait. You can't reach the Magnetic Fusion Energy computer from here. Your hacker friend's going to wear himself out trying."

"Uh, the ranger's not gonna like this, Yogi . . ."

"Trust me."

The hacker stayed around for a few more minutes, then disconnected. Never even tried to get into Livermore.

"So much for that theory," Dave shrugged.

In hopes that they might be used as evidence, Dave and I signed the printouts. We left the printers in the switchyard and I wandered back to my office. Within an hour my terminal beeped: the hacker was back.

But none of the printers showed him. Checking the Unix systems, I saw him, logged in as Sventek. But he wasn't entering through our Tymnet ports!

Quickly, I scanned the dial-in modems. Two scientists editing programs, a bureaucrat listing boilerplate from a contract, and a student writing a love letter. No obvious hacking.

I ran back to my office and glanced at the Unix computer's status. Sventek, all right. But coming from where?

There: the hacker's port wasn't an ordinary 1200-baud line. That's why he didn't show up in the switchyard. No, he was coming from our local network. Our ethernet. The green cable that interconnected a hundred terminals and workstations around our laboratory.

I ran to Wayne's office. "Look—the hacker's on our local area network."

"Slow down, Cliff. Lemme see." Wayne kept five terminals in his office, each watching a different system. "Yeah, there's Sventek, on the Unix-4 computer. Whatcha wanna do?"

"But he's the hacker. And he's coming from our lab-wide ethernet."

"Big deal. There's a dozen ways to get there." Wayne turned to another terminal. "I'll just switch on my friendly ethernet analyzer, and see who's doing what."

As Wayne typed in the parameters, I thought about the implications of finding the hacker on our local network. Our ethernet was a party line that snaked through every office. That he found a way into the ether was bad news: it meant that the hacker could attack even personal computers attached to the ethernet.

But maybe this would prove to be good news. Perhaps the hacker lived here in Berkeley and worked at our laboratory. If so, we were closing in on him quickly. Wayne would trace the ethernet to within a few feet of the source.

"Here's your connection. He's coming from . . . from the computer that controls the MFE net."

"You mean the hacker is entering our lab through the MFE network?"

"Yeah. He's coming from Lawrence Livermore Laboratory. The Magnetic Fusion Energy Network."

I called down the hallway, "Hey, Dave! Guess who's visiting Livermore?"

Dave ambled over to Wayne's office. "How'd he get there? There's no connection from there into our Unix system."

"I don't know how he got into Livermore, but he's in our ethernet, coming from Livermore."

Dave raised his eyebrows. "I didn't know you could do that. Your hacker found a path to the Unix system that I didn't know about."

Wayne launched into Dave with his usual tirade against Unix. I left the two bosom enemies and called Livermore.

It took three calls to find the system manager of the MFE network. "Hi, you don't know me, but you've got a hacker in your system."

A woman answered, "Huh? Who are you?"

"I work at LBL. Someone's messing around in my computer and he's coming in from the MFE network. It looks like he's logged in from Livermore."

"Oh, hell. I'll scan our users. . . . There's only one job that's connected from Livermore to Berkeley. Account 1674 . . . it belongs to someone named Cromwell."

"That's him," I said. "The hacker found the password a couple hours ago. Got the password from a command file here in Berkeley."

"I'll kill that account. Cromwell can use our system, when he learns to keep his passwords secret." She saw the problem as ignorant users, not unfriendly systems that forced people to use bizarre passwords like *agnitfom.*

"Can you trace the connection?" I wanted Livermore to keep the hacker on line, at least long enough to trace the line.

"No, we're not authorized to make any traces. You'll have to talk to our management first."

"But by the time anyone decides, the hacker will be gone."

"We run a secure installation," she said. "If anyone finds out there's a hacker at Livermore, heads will roll."

"Unless you trace where the hacker's coming from, you'll never know if he's out of your system."

"My job is to run a computer. Not to catch criminals. Leave me out of your wild-goose chase."

She decided to chop off all access and disable the stolen account. The hacker disappeared from Livermore's computer, and from ours.

Maybe it was just as well. Even if she had started a trace, I couldn't monitor what the hacker was doing. I could detect that he was in my computer, all right. But the MFE network connected directly into my computer, without going through the switchyard. My printers wouldn't capture what the hacker typed.

Depressed, I shuffled to lunch. At the LBL cafeteria, Luis Alvarez sat down across from me, Inventor, physicist, and Nobel Laureate, Luie was the twentieth-century Renaissance man. He didn't waste time on bureaucracy; he demanded results.

"How's astronomy?" Even from the stratosphere, Alvarez still found time to talk to pipsqueaks like me. "Still building that telescope?"

"Naw, I'm working at the computer center now. I ought to be writing programs, but I've been spending all my time chasing a hacker."

"Any luck?"

"It's playing hide-and-seek over the wires. First I think he's coming from Berkeley, then Oakland, then Alabama, then Virginia. Lately I've traced him to Livermore."

"Called the FBI?"

"Six times. They've got better things to do. The frustrating part is the complete lack of support." I told him about the morning's activity at Livermore.

"Yes, they've got their jobs to worry about."

"But I'm trying to help them, damn it. They don't care that their neighbor's being burglarized."

"Stop acting like a crusader, Cliff. Why don't you look at this as research. Nobody else is interested—not Livermore, not the FBI. Hell, in a week or two, probably not even our lab's administration."

"They gave me three weeks. It's already up."

"That's what I mean. When you're doing real research, you never know what it'll cost, how much time it'll take, or what you'll find. You just know there's unexplored territory and a chance to discover what's out there."

"That's easy for you to say. But I've got to keep three managers off my back. There are programs to write and systems to manage."

"So what? You're following a fascinating scent. You're an explorer. Think of who might be behind it. Some international spy, perhaps."

"More likely some bored high school kid."

"Well then, forget who's causing the problems," Luie said. "Don't try to be a cop, be a scientist. Research the connections, the techniques, the holes. Apply physical principles. Find new methods to solve problems. Compile statistics, publish your results, and only trust what you can prove. But don't exclude improbable solutions—keep your mind open."

"But what do I do when I hit a brick wall?"

"Like Livermore's system manager?" asked Luie.

"Or the telephone company withholding a phone trace. Or the FBI refusing a court order. Or our laboratory shutting me down in a couple days?"

"Dead ends are illusory. When did you ever let a 'Do Not Enter' sign keep you away from anything? Go around the brick walls. When you can't go around, climb over or dig under. Just don't give up."

"But who's going to pay my salary?"

"Permission, bah. Funding, forget it. Nobody will pay for research; they're only interested in results," Luie said. "Sure, you could write a detailed proposal to chase this hacker. In fifty pages, you'll describe what you knew, what you expected, how much money it would take. Include the names of three qualified referees, cost benefit ratios, and what papers you've written before. Oh, and don't forget the theoretical justification.

"Or you could just chase the bastard. Run faster than him. Faster than the lab's management. Don't wait for someone else, do it yourself. Keep your boss happy, but don't let him tie you down. Don't give them a standing target."

That's why Luie won a Nobel Prize. It wasn't what he did, so much as how he went about it. He was interested in everything. From a few rocks slightly enriched in the element iridium, he'd inferred that meteorites (a source of iridium) must have struck the earth some sixty-five million years ago. Despite skepticism from paleontologists, he recognized those meteors to be the death knell of the dinosaurs.

Luis Alvarez never saw the subatomic fragments that won his Nobel prize. Instead, he photographed their trails inside bubble chambers. He analyzed those trails—from their length, he calculated the particles' lifetimes; from their curvature, their charge and mass.

My research was a far cry from his, but what have I got to lose? Maybe his techniques would work for me. How do you scientifically research a hacker?

At 6:19 that evening, the hacker returned. This time, he came through Tymnet. I didn't bother tracing it—no use rousting everyone from dinner when they wouldn't give me the phone number.

Instead, I sat and watched the hacker deliberately connect to the MX computer, a PDP-10 at the MIT artificial intelligence labs in Cambridge, Massachusetts. He logged in as user Litwin, and spent almost an hour learning how to operate that computer. He seemed quite unaccustomed to the MIT system, and he'd frequently ask for the automated help facility. In an hour, he'd learned little more than how to list files.

Perhaps because artificial intelligence research is so arcane, he didn't find much. Certainly, the antique operating system didn't provide much protection—any user could read anyone else's files. But the hacker didn't realize this. The sheer impossibility of understanding this system protected their information.

I worried about how the hacker might abuse our network connections over the weekend. Rather than camping out in the computer room, I pulled the plugs to all the networks. To cover my tracks, I posted a greeting for every user logging in: "Due to building construction, all networks are down until Monday." It would surely isolate the hacker from the Milnet. By counting complaints, I could take a census of how many people relied on this network.

Quite a few, it turned out. Enough to get me in trouble.

Roy Kerth was first. "Cliff, we're taking a lot of heat for the network being down. A couple dozen people are bitching that they haven't received electronic mail. Can you look into it?"

He must have believed the greeting! "Uh, sure. I'll see if I can get it working right away."

It took five minutes to patch the network through. The boss thought I'd done magic. I kept my mouth shut.

But while the network was down, the hacker had appeared. My only record was a printout from the monitor, but that was enough. He had shown up at 5:15 A.M. and tried to connect into a Milnet site in Omaha, Nebraska. Disappeared two minutes later. From the network directory, I found he tried to get into a defense contractor there, SRI Inc.

I called Ken Crepea of SRI, and he hadn't noticed anyone trying to get in. "But I'll call you back if I see anything strange."

Ken called back two hours later. "Cliff, you won't believe this, but I checked our accounting logs, and someone's broken into my computer."

I believed him. "How do you know?"

"There's weekend connections from several places, on accounts that ought to be dead."

"From where?"

"From Anniston, Alabama, and from Livermore, California. Someone used our old account, *SAC*. It used to be used for the Strategic Air Command, here in Omaha."

"Any idea how it was invaded?"

"Well, it never had much password protection," Ken said. "The password was SAC. Guess we screwed up, huh?"

"What was he up to?"

"My accounting records don't say what he did. I can only tell the times he connected."

He told me the times, and I entered them into my logbook. To protect his system, Ken would change all passwords to all accounts, and make each person show up in person to get a new password.

The hacker was on the Milnet through at least two other computers, Anniston and Livermore. And probably MIT.

MIT. I'd forgotten to warn them. I called Karen Sollins of their computer department and told her about Friday night's intrusion. "Don't worry," she said, "there's not much on that computer, and we're throwing it away in a few weeks."

"That's good to know. Can you tell me who owned the Litwin account?" I wanted to know where the hacker got Litwin's password.

"He's a plasma physicist from the University of Wisconsin," she said. "He uses Livermore's big computers, and ships his results to our system." Doubtless, he left his MIT passwords on the Livermore computer.

This hacker silently followed scientists from one computer to another, picking up the crumbs they left. What he didn't know was that someone was also picking up the crumbs he was leaving.

# 17

THE HACKER KNEW HIS WAY AROUND THE MILNET. NOW I could see the futility of closing him out of our computers. He'd just come in through some other door. Perhaps I could nail my own doors shut, but he'd still climb into other systems.

Nobody detected him. Unmolested, he had sneaked into Livermore, SRI, Anniston, and MIT.

Nobody chased him. The FBI certainly didn't. The CIA and the Air Force Office of Special Investigations couldn't or wouldn't do anything.

Well, almost nobody. I followed him, but I couldn't figure out a way to catch him. The telephone traces wouldn't pan out. And since he used several networks, how was I to know where he came from? Today, he might enter through my lab and break into a computer in Massachusetts, but tomorrow, he might just as well enter the nets in Peoria and break into Podunk. I could monitor him only when he touched my system.

It was time to give up and go back to astronomy and programming, or make my site so inviting that he preferred to use Berkeley as a jumping-off place.

Giving up seemed best. My three weeks had expired, and I heard grumblings about "Cliff's quest for the Holy Grail." So long as it looked like my chase might bear fruit, the lab would tolerate me, but I had to show progress. For the past week, only the hacker had made progress.

"Do research," Luis Alvarez had said. Well, OK, I'd watch this guy and call it science. See what I can learn about networks, computer security, and maybe the hacker himself.

So I reopened our doors and sure enough, the hacker entered and poked around the system. He found one interesting file, describing new techniques to design integrated circuits. I watched as he fired up Kermit, the universal file-transfer program, to ship our file back to his computer.

The Kermit program doesn't just copy a file from one computer to another. It constantly checks to make sure there haven't been any mistakes in transmission. So when the hacker launched our Kermit program, I knew he was starting the same program on his own computer. I didn't know where the hacker was, but he certainly used a computer, not just a simple terminal. This, in turn, meant that the hacker could save all his sessions on a printout or floppy disk. He didn't have to keep notes in longhand.

Kermit copies files from one system to another. The two computers must cooperate—one sends a file, and the other receives it. Kermit runs on both computers: one Kermit does the talking, the other Kermit listens.

To make sure it doesn't make mistakes, the sending Kermit pauses after each line, giving the listener a chance to say, "I got that line OK, go on to the next one." The sending Kermit waits for that OK, and goes on to send the next line. If there's a problem, the sending Kermit tries again, until it hears an OK. Much like a phone conversation where one person says "Uh-huh" every few phrases.

My monitoring post sat between my system's Kermit and the hacker's. Well, not exactly in the middle. My printer recorded their dialogue, but was perched at the Berkeley end of a long connection. I watched the hacker's computer grab our data and respond with acknowledgments.

Suddenly it hit me. It was like sitting next to someone shouting messages across a canyon. The echoes tell you how far the sound traveled. To find the distance to the canyon wall, just multiply the echo delay by half the speed of sound. Simple physics.

Quickly, I called our electronic technicians. Right away, Lloyd

Bellknap knew the way to time the echoes. "You just need an oscilloscope. And maybe a counter." In a minute, he scrounged up an antique oscilloscope from the Middle Ages, built when vacuum tubes were the rage.

But that's all we needed to see these pulses. Watching the trace, we timed the echoes. Three seconds. Three and a half seconds. Three and a quarter seconds.

Three seconds for a round trip? If the signals traveled at the speed of light (not a bad assumption), this meant the hacker was 279,000 miles away.

With appropriate pomp, I announced to Lloyd, "From basic physics, I conclude that the hacker lives on the moon."

Lloyd knew his communications. "I'll give you three reasons why you're wrong."

"OK, I know one of them," I said. "The hacker's signals might be traveling through a satellite link. It takes a quarter second for microwaves to travel from earth to the satellite and back." Communications satellites orbit twenty-three thousand miles over the equator.

"Yeah, that's one reason," Lloyd said. "But you'd need twelve satellite hops to account for that three-second delay. What's the real reason for the delay?"

"Maybe the hacker has a slow computer."

"Not that slow. Though maybe the hacker has programmed his Kermit to respond slowly. That's reason two."

"Aah! I know the third delay. The hacker's using networks that move his data inside of packets. His packets are constantly being rerouted, assembled, and disassembled. Every time they pass through another node, it slows him down."

"Exactly. Unless you can count the number of nodes, you can't tell how far away he is. In other words, 'You lose.' " Lloyd yawned and returned to repairing a terminal.

But there was still a way to find the hacker's distance. After the hacker left, I called a friend in Los Angeles and told him to connect to my computer through AT&T and Tymnet. He started Kermit running, and I timed his echoes. Real short, maybe a tenth of a second.

Another friend, this time in Houston, Texas. His echoes were around 0.15 seconds. Three other people from Baltimore, New York, and Chicago each had echo delays of less than a second.

New York to Berkeley is about two thousand miles. It had a delay of around a second. So a three-second delay means six thousand miles. Give or take a few thousand miles.

Weird. The path to the hacker must be more convoluted than I suspected.

I bounced this new evidence off Dave Cleveland. "Suppose the hacker lives in California, calls the East Coast, then connects to Berkeley. That could explain the long delays."

"The hacker's not from California," my guru replied. "I tell you, he just doesn't know Berkeley Unix."

"Then he's using a very slow computer."

"Not likely, since he's no slouch at Unix."

"He's purposely slowed down his Kermit parameters?"

"Nobody does that—it wastes their time when they transfer files."

I thought about the meaning of this measurement. My friends' samples told me how much delay Tymnet and AT&T introduced. Less than a second. Leaving two seconds of delay unaccounted for.

Maybe my method was wrong. Maybe the hacker used a slow computer. Or maybe he was coming through another network beyond the AT&T phone lines. A network I didn't know about.

Every new piece of data pointed in a different direction. Tymnet had said Oakland. The phone company had said Virginia. His echoes said four thousand miles beyond Virginia.

# 18

BY THE END OF SEPTEMBER, THE HACKER WAS APPEARING every other day. Often, he'd pop up his periscope, look around, and disappear in a few minutes. Not enough time to trace, and hardly worth getting excited about.

I was tense and a little guilty. I often passed up dinner at home to sneak in some extra hacker watching.

The only way I could keep following the hacker was by disguising my efforts as real work. I'd muck around with computer graphics to satisfy the astronomers and physicists, then fool with the network connections to satisfy my own curiosity. Some of our network software actually needed my attention, but usually I was just tinkering to learn how it worked. I called other computer centers ostensibly to clear up network problems. But when I'd talk to them, I'd cautiously bring up the subject of hackers—who else had hacker problems?

Dan Kolkowitz at Stanford University was quite aware of hackers in his computer. He was an hour's drive away from Berkeley, but that was an all-day bicycle ride. So we compared notes on the phone, and wondered if we were watching the same rodent gnawing at our systems.

Since I'd started watching my monitors, I'd seen an occasional interloper trying to get onto my computer. Every few days, someone would dial into the system and try to log on as *system* or *guest.* These inevitably failed, so I didn't bother following them. Dan had it much worse.

"Seems like every kid in Silicon Valley tries to break into Stanford," Dan moaned. "They find out passwords to legitimate student accounts, then waste computing and connect time. An annoyance, but something we'll have to tolerate so long as Stanford's going to run a reasonably open system."

"Have you thought about clamping down?"

"To really tighten up security would make everyone unhappy," Dan said. "People want to share information, so they make most of the files readable to everyone on their computer. They complain if we force them to change their passwords. Yet they demand that their data be private."

People paid more attention to locking their cars than securing their data.

One hacker in particular annoyed Dan. "Bad enough that he found a hole in Stanford's Unix system. But he had the nerve to call me on the phone. He talked for two hours, at the same time pawing through my systems files."

"Did you trace him?"

"I tried. While he was talking on the phone, I called the Stanford police and the phone company. He was on for two hours, and they couldn't trace it."

I thought of Lee Cheng at Pacific Bell. He needed just ten minutes to trace clear across the country. And Tymnet unwound their network in less than a minute.

We compared the two hackers. "My guy's not wrecking anything," I said. "Just scanning files and using my network connections."

"Precisely what I see. I changed my operating system so that I can watch what he's doing."

My monitors were IBM PC's, not modified software, but the principle was the same. "Do you see him stealing password files and system utilities?"

"Yes. He uses the pseudonym of 'Pfloyd' . . . I bet he's a Pink Floyd fan. He's only active late at night."

This was a difference. I often watched my hacker at noon. As I thought about it, Stanford was following different people. If anything, the Berkeley hacker seemed to prefer the name, "Hunter," though I knew him by the several different account names he stole.

Three days later, the headlines of the October 3 *San Francisco Examiner* blared, "Computer Sleuths Hunt A Brilliant Hacker." Reporter John Markoff had sniffed out the Stanford story. On the side, the newspaper mentioned that this hacker had also gotten into the LBL computers. Could this be true?

The story described Dan's snares and his inability to catch Stanford's Pfloyd hacker. But the reporter got the pseudonym wrong—the newspaper reported "a crafty hacker using the name 'Pink Floyd.' "

Cursing whoever leaked the story, I prepared to close things up. Bruce Bauer of our lab's police department called and asked if I'd seen the day's paper.

"Yeah. What a disaster. The hacker won't show up again."

"Don't be so sure," Bruce said. "This may be just the break we're looking for."

"But he'll never show up, now that he knows that we know there's a hacker in our system."

"Maybe. But he'll want to see if you shut him out of the computer. And he's probably confident that if he can outwit the Stanford people, he can sneak past us as well."

"Yes, but we're nowhere near tracing him."

"That's actually what I called about. It'll be a couple weeks before we get the search warrant, but I'd like you to stay open until then."

After he hung up, I wondered about his sudden interest. Could it be the newspaper story? Or had the FBI finally taken an interest?

The next day, doubtless thanks to Bruce Bauer, Roy Kerth told me to keep working on following the hacker, though he pointedly said that my regular duties should take precedence.

That was my problem. Every time the hacker showed up, I'd spend an hour figuring out what he did and how it related to his other sessions. Then a few more hours calling people, spreading the bad news. Then I'd record what happened in my logbook. By the time I'd finished, the day was pretty much wasted. Following our visitor was turning into a full-time job.

In my case, Bruce Bauer's intuition was right. The hacker returned a week after the article appeared. On Sunday, October 12, at 1:41, I was beating my head against some astronomy problem—something about orthogonal polynomials—when my hacker alarm went off.

I ran down the hallway and found him logged into Sventek's old account. For twelve minutes, he used my computer to connect to the Milnet. From there, he went to the Anniston Army base, where he had no trouble logging in as Hunt. He just checked his files and then disconnected.

On Monday, Chuck McNatt from Anniston called.

"I dumped this weekend's accounting logs and found the hacker again."

"Yes, he was on your system for a few minutes. Just long enough to see if anyone was watching." My printouts told the whole story.

"I think I'd better close my doors to him," Chuck said. "There's too much at risk here, and we don't seem to be making headway in tracking him."

"Can't you stay open a bit longer?"

"It's already been a month, and I'm afraid of him erasing my files." Chuck knew the dangers.

"Well, OK. Just be sure that you really eliminate him."

"I know. I'll change all the passwords and check for any holes in the operating system."

Oh well. Others didn't quite have the patience to remain open to this hacker. Or was it foolishness?

Ten days later, the hacker reappeared. I got to the switchyard just as he was trying Anniston.

```
LBL> Telnet ANAD.ARPA
Connecting to 26.1.2.22
Welcome to Anniston Army Depot
login: Hunt
password: jaeger
```

```
Bad login. Try again.
login: Bin
password: jabber
Welcome to Anniston Army Depot.
Tiger Teams Beware!
Watch out for any unknown users
Challenge all strangers using this computer
```

Chuck had disabled the Hunt account, but hadn't changed the password on the system account, *Bin.*

The greeting message warned the hacker that someone had noticed him. He quickly checked his Gnu-Emacs files, and found they had been erased. He looked around the Anniston system and found one file that had been created July 3. A file that gave him super-user privileges. It was hidden in the public directory /usr/lib. An area that anyone could write into. He'd named the file, ".d". The same name he used to hide his files on our LBL system.

But he didn't execute that program. Instead he logged off the Anniston system and disconnected from LBL.

Chuck hadn't noticed this special file. On the phone, he said he'd changed every user's password—all two hundred. But he hadn't changed any of the system passwords like *Bin,* since he assumed he was the only one who knew them. He'd thought that he'd thoroughly eradicated any dangerous files, but he'd missed a few.

That *.d* file at Anniston was a useful benchmark. The hacker had laid this egg on July 3, yet remembered exactly where he'd hidden it three months later.

He didn't guess or hunt around for the *.d* file. No, he went straight for it.

After three months, I can't remember where I stash a file. At least not without a notebook.

This hacker must be keeping track of what he's done.

I glanced at my own logbook. Somewhere, someone was keeping a mirror-image notebook.

A kid on a weekend lark doesn't keep detailed notes. A college joker won't patiently wait three months before checking his prank. No, we were watching a deliberate, methodical attack, from someone who knew exactly what he was doing.

# 19

EVEN THOUGH YOU HAVE TO COAST SLOWLY BY THE guardhouse, you can reach thirty miles an hour by pedaling down the LBL hill. Tuesday evening I was in no hurry, but pedaled anyway: it's a kicker to feel the wind. A mile downhill, then a rendezvous at the Berkeley Bowl.

The old bowling alley was now a huge fruit and vegetable market, the cheapest place for kiwis and guavas. Year 'round, it smelled of mangoes—even in the fish section. Next to a pyramid of watermelons, I saw Martha knocking some pumpkins, hunting for the filling to our Halloween pie.

"Vell, Boris, ze secret microfilm is hidden in ze pumpkin patch." Ever since I met the CIA, I was a spy in Martha's eyes.

We decided on a dozen little pumpkins for a carving party, and one fresh big one for the pie. After stuffing them in our backpacks, we biked home.

Three blocks from the fruit market, at the corner of Fulton and Ward, there's a four-way stop. With a can of spray paint, someone's changed one stop sign to read, "Stop the CIA." Another, "Stop the NSA."

Martha grinned. I felt uneasy, and pretended to adjust my backpack. I didn't need another reminder of Berkeley politics.

At home, she tossed pumpkins to me, and I stashed them in a box. "What you're missing is a flag," she said, throwing the last one low and inside, "some sort of pennant for chasing hackers."

She ducked into a closet. "I had a bit left over from my costume, so I stitched this together." She unrolled a shirt-sized banner, with a snake coiled around a computer. Underneath, it said, "Don't Tread on Me."

In the weeks before Halloween, both of us sewed furiously to make costumes. I'd made a pope's outfit, complete with miter, scepter and chalice. Martha, of course, kept her costume hidden—you can't be too careful when your roommate uses the same sewing machine.

Next day, I hoisted my hacker-hunter flag just above the four monitors that watched the incoming Tymnet lines. I'd bought a cheap Radio Shack telephone dialer, and connected it to an expensive but obsolete logic analyzer. Together, these waited patiently for the hacker to type in his password, and then silently called my telephone.

Naturally, the flag fell down and got caught in the printer, just as the hacker showed up. I quickly unsnarled the shreds of paper and cloth, just in time to see the hacker change his passwords.

The hacker apparently didn't like his old passwords—*hedges, jaeger, hunter and benson.* He replaced them, one by one, with a single new password, *lblhack.*

Well, at least he and I agreed on what he was doing.

He picked the same password for four different accounts. If there were four different people involved, they'd each have a separate account and password. But here in one session, all four accounts were changed.

I had to be following a single person. Someone persistent enough to return over and over to my computer. Patient enough to hide a poisonous file in the Anniston Army base and return to it three months later. And peculiar in aiming at military targets.

He chose his own passwords. "Lblhack" was obvious. I'd searched the Berkeley phone book for Jaegers and Bensons; maybe I ought to try Stanford. I stopped by the library. Maggie Morley, our forty-five-year-old document-meister, plays rough and tumble Scrabble. Posted on her door is a list of all legal three-letter Scrabble words. To get in, you have to ask her one. "Keeps 'em fresh in my mind," she says.

"Bog," I said.

"You may enter."

"I need a Stanford telephone book," I said. "I'm looking for everyone in Silicon Valley named Jaeger or Benson."

Maggie didn't have to search the card catalog. "You need directories for Palo Alto and San Jose. Sorry, but we don't have either. It'll take a week or so to order 'em."

A week wouldn't slow things down, at the rate I was going.

"Jaeger. A word that's been kind to me," Maggie smiled. "Worth sixteen points, but I once won a game with it, when the 'J' landed on a triple-letter score. Turned into seventy-five points."

"Yeah, but I need it because it's the hacker's password. Hey, I didn't know names were legal in Scrabble."

"Jaeger's not a name. Well, maybe it's a name—Ellsworth Jaeger, the famous ornithologist, for instance—but it's a type of bird. Gets its name from the German word meaning hunter."

"Huh? Did you say, 'Hunter'?"

"Yes. Jaegers are hunting birds that badger other birds with full beaks. They harass weaker birds until they drop their prey."

"Hot ziggity! You answered my question. I don't need the phone book."

"Well, what else can I do for you?"

"How about explaining the relationship between the words *hedges, jaeger, hunter and benson?*"

"Well, Jaeger and Hunter is obvious to anyone who knows German. And smokers know Benson and Hedges."

Omigod—my hacker smokes Benson and Hedges. Maggie had won on a triple-word score.

# 20

I WAS ALL SET ON HALLOWEEN MORNING. I'D FINISHED my pope's costume, even the miter. Tonight's party would be a gas: pasta with a dozen lunatics, followed by Martha's fantastic pumpkin pie, and an excursion into San Francisco's Castro district.

But first I had to dodge my bosses at the lab. The physicists were ganging up on the computer center, refusing to pay our salaries. Supporting central computing was expensive. The scientists figured that they could buy their own small machines, and avoid the overhead of paying our programming staff.

Sandy Merola tried to convince them otherwise. "You can hitch a thousand chickens to your plow or one horse. Central computing is expensive because we deliver results, not hardware."

To placate them, Sandy sent me to write a few graphics programs. "You're a scientist. If you can't make 'em happy, at least listen to their problems."

So I spent the morning sitting in the back row of a physics seminar. A professor droned on about the quark function of the proton—something about how each proton has three quarks. I wasn't tired enough to sleep, so I pretended to take notes while thinking about the hacker.

Returning from the seminar, Sandy asked if I'd learned anything.

"Sure." I glanced at my notes. "The distribution function of quarks isn't quantized over the proton. Happy?"

"Be serious, Cliff. What did the physicists say about computing?"

"Not much. They know they need us, but don't want to pay."

"Same as the Air Force," Sandy smiled. "I just got off the phone with one Jim Christy of their Office of Special Investigations."

"Hey, isn't he the narc with the military spooks?"

"Be serious. He's a detective working for the Air Force, please."

"OK, he's an all-American good guy. So what did he say?"

"He says the same thing as our physicists. They can't support us, but they don't want us to go away."

"Did he make any progress with the Virginia phone company?"

"Naw. He called around, and they won't budge without a Virginia search warrant. He checked out the Virginia state law, and the hacker's committing no crime there."

"Breaking into our computer isn't a crime?" I couldn't believe it.

"Breaking into a California computer isn't a crime in Virginia."

"I don't suppose the Air Force can lean on the FBI to get a warrant?"

"Nope. But they want us to keep monitoring, at least until the Air Force decides it's a dead end."

"Did they cough up any dimes?" My time was funded through the grants of astronomers and physicists. They weren't pleased to watch me spend their money chasing some ghost.

"No bucks, nothing but an unofficial request. When I asked for support, Jim gave me the bailiwick story."

Sandy wasn't going to give in. "It's been two months since we started, and nobody's listened to us. Let's stay open for another week, then call it quits."

By five o'clock, I was ready for the Halloween party. On my way out, I checked the floppy disks on the monitors. The printer suddenly started up. There was the hacker. I glanced at the time—17:43:11 PST.

No. Not now. I've got a party to go to. A costume party no less. Can't he choose any other time?

The hacker logged into the old Sventek account, and checked who was on our system. Dave Cleveland was there, running under the alias of Sam Rubarb, but the hacker couldn't know.

He moved over to our accounting files, and collected the past months' files in one place. He scanned that long file, searching for the word "Pink Floyd."

Hmmmm. Interesting. He didn't search for the word "Pfloyd," which was the Stanford hacker's pseudonym. Rather, he searched for the pseudonym that was reported in the newspaper.

My hacker wasn't the same guy as Stanford's. If he were, he wouldn't have to search for "Pink Floyd"—he'd know when he had been active.

In fact, my hacker wasn't even in contact with Stanford's. If the two had met, or even written to each other, my hacker would know to search for "Pfloyd," not "Pink Floyd."

The hacker must have read the news. But it had been almost a month since the article was published. Dave Cleveland must be right: the hacker wasn't from the West Coast.

At 6 P.M., the hacker gave up searching our accounting logs. Instead, he went through our computer onto the Milnet. From there, he went straight for the Anniston army base in Alabama. "Which hole will he sneak into this time?" I wondered.

```
LBL> Telnet Anad.arpa
Welcome to Anniston Computer Center
Login: Hunter
Password: Jaeger
Incorrect login, try again.
Login: Bin
Password: Jabber
Incorrect login, try again.
Login: Bin
Password: Anadhack
Incorrect login, 3 tries and you're out.
```

Chuck McNatt had finally locked him out. By changing all his passwords, Chuck had nailed his door shut. He still might have holes in his system, but this hacker couldn't exploit them.

The hacker didn't give up. He reached over into the building design group.

Some scientists at Lawrence Berkeley Lab worry about how to design energy efficient homes. Most other physicists look down on them—"Yech, applied physics." Protons and quarks are sexy. Saving ten dollars on your monthly heating bill isn't.

The building design group searches for new glasses that let light in, but block the infra-red. They build new insulators to prevent heat leaks through walls. They'd just started analyzing basements and chimneys for thermal efficiency.

The hacker learned this because he dumped all their files. Page after page of thermal emissivity data. Memos about paint absorption in the ultraviolet. And a note saying, "You can move to the Elxsi computer next week."

He didn't need to see that note twice. He interrupted his listing, and commanded my Unix computer to connect him to the Elxsi system.

I'd never heard of this computer. But my computer had. Within ten seconds, he'd made the connection and the Elxsi prompted him for an account name and password. I watched him try to get in:

```
LBL> Telnet Elxsi
Elxsi at LBL
login: root
password: root
incorrect password, try again.
login: guest
password: guest
incorrect password, try again.
login: uucp
password: uucp
WELCOME TO THE ELXSI COMPUTER AT LBL.
```

He got into the UUCP account. No password protection. Wide open.

UUCP is the account for Unix to Unix copying. When one Unix computer wants to copy a file from another, it logs into the UUCP account and gets the file. People should never be able to connect to this special account. The system manager should disable it from human log-ins.

Worse, this Elxsi had its UUCP account set up with system privileges. It took the hacker only a minute to realize that he'd stumbled into a privileged account.

He didn't lose any time. He edited the password file, and added a new account, one with system manager privileges. Named it *Mark.* "Keep it bland," I thought.

But he didn't know much about this computer. He spent an hour dumping its files, and learned about designing energy efficient buildings. Nothing about the computer itself.

So he wrote a program to time the Elxsi computer. A short C program that measured its speed and reported its word length.

He needed three tries to get his program to work, but finally it flew. He found the Elxsi to have thirty-two bit words, and he measured it at about ten million instructions per second.

Eight-bit and sixteen-bit computers are diddlysquat machines; the thirty-two-bit systems are the biggies. Thirty-two bits meant a big machine, ten MIPS meant fast. He'd entered a superminicomputer. One of the fastest in Berkeley. One of the most mismanaged.

As I watched him walk through the Elxsi, I talked to Tymnet. While the hacker tried to understand the new computer, Ron Vivier searched out the needle that pointed where the hacker came from.

"No news. He's coming in from Oakland again." Ron knew that meant a phone trace.

"No use calling the phone company. They'll just tell me to get a Virginia search warrant."

I hung up, disappointed. A long connection like this was perfect for tracing him. I couldn't shut him out of our system when he was into computers I'd never even heard of. When he finally signed off at 7:30, he'd pretty much mapped out our lab's major computers. He might not be able to get into each of them, but he knew where they were.

7:30. Damn, I'd forgotten the party. I ran down to my bike and pedaled home. This hacker wasn't wrecking my computer, he was destroying my life. Being late for a Halloween party—that's a capital crime in Martha's book.

Not only was I late, but I'd shown up without a costume. I slinked guiltily through the kitchen door. What a scene! Princess Diana, tastefully attired in a tailored dress, pillbox hat and white gloves, shuddered as she removed a dripping handful of seeds from a pumpkin. Alice and the Mad Hatter were serving the last of the lasagna. Charlie Chaplin was dipping apples in caramel. In the midst of this swirl of activity stood a small but fierce samurai warrior in full battle gear, shouting orders. "You're late," the samurai scowled. "Where's your costume?"

Buried in the back of the closet, I found my white velvet robe. Worn over Martha's nightgown, with a sheet pinned around my shoulders and a tall, jeweled miter of construction paper and sequins, I suddenly became . . . Pope Cliff the First. I went around blessing the guests. Martha's friend Laurie, who usually wore a crew cut, jeans, and hiking boots, sidled up in a short black cocktail dress and long pearl necklace. "Come on, your holiness, let's go forth and bless the Castro."

We piled into the Mad Hatter's car (Laurie rode her motorcycle) and crossed the bridge to Babylon. Halloween is San Francisco's favorite holiday. Five blocks along Castro Street are cordoned off, and thousands of elaborately costumed revelers jostle up and down, looking at one another and at the drag queens in sequined gowns who lip-sync to Ethel Merman on the fire escapes overlooking the street.

This year's costumes were incredible: a person dressed as a giant bag of groceries, complete with giant paper replicas of vegetables and cans; various creatures from outer space; and several rival samurai, whom Martha fought off with her plastic sword. White-faced draculas mingled with witches, kangaroos, and butterflies. Over near the trolley stop, an assortment of ghouls harmonized with a three-legged pickle.

I offered benedictions left and right—to demons and angels, gorillas and leopards. Medieval knights knelt to me, and nuns (some with mustaches) rushed up to greet me. A trio of sturdy, cheerful fellows in pink tutus and size-thirteen ballet shoes bowed gracefully to receive my blessings.

Despite layoffs at the factories, rent payments due, drugs, and AIDS, somehow San Francisco celebrated life.

Next Monday I showed up late, expecting to find a message from the manager of the Elxsi computer. No such luck. I called around the building design group, and talked with the physicist in charge of the Elxsi computer.

"Noticed anything strange on your Elxsi?"

"No, we've only had it a month. Anything wrong?"

"Who set up your accounts?"

"I did. I just signed on as system manager, then added users."

"Do you run accounting?"

"No. I didn't know you could."

"Someone broke into your computer through the UUCP account. He became system manager and added a new account."

"I'll be damned. What's the UUCP account?"

Here's the problem. This guy's a physicist, bored by computers. He didn't know about managing his machine. Probably didn't care.

This guy wasn't the problem. Elxsi was. They sold their computers with the security features disabled. After you buy their machine, it's up to you to secure it. Just plow through a dozen manuals to find a paragraph saying how to modify the permissions granted to the UUCP account. If you know that account exists.

Right.

The same thing must be happening all over. The hacker didn't succeed through sophistication. Rather he poked at obvious places, trying to enter through unlocked doors. Persistence, not wizardry, let him through.

Well, he wasn't going to get into our Elxsi anymore. Knowing my adversary, I could easily lock him out in a way that would mystify him. I built a trapdoor into our Elxsi: whenever the hacker touched the purloined accounts on that machine, it notified me and pretended to be too busy to accept another user. The Elxsi didn't say, "Go away"; rather, it slowed down to a crawl whenever the hacker showed up. The hacker wouldn't realize that we were on to him, yet the Elxsi was protected against him.

Still, we were treading water. Without search warrants, our phone traces went nowhere. Sure, we read every word he typed into our computer, but how much did we miss? He might be using a dozen other computers to get onto the Milnet.

This much is for sure: I was now dedicated to catching this hacker. The only way to snag this guy was to watch every minute of the day. I had to be ready all the time—noon or midnight.

That was the problem. Sure, I could sleep under my desk and rely on my terminal to wake me up. But at the cost of the domestic tranquility: Martha wasn't pleased at my office campouts.

If only my computer would call me whenever the hacker appeared, then the rest of the time would be my own. Like a doctor on call.

Of course. A pocket pager. I had a bank of personal computers watching for the hacker to appear. I'd just program them to dial my pocket pager. I'd have to rent a pager, but it'd be worth the $20 a month.

It took an evening to write the programs—no big deal. From now on, wherever I went, I'd know within seconds of the hacker's arrival. I'd become an extension of my computer.

It was him against me now. For real.

# 21

LAWRENCE BERKELEY LABS IS FUNDED BY THE DEPARTMENT of Energy, the successor to the Atomic Energy Commission. Perhaps nuclear bombs and atomic power plants are fading into the mists of history, or maybe splitting atoms isn't as sexy as it used to be. For whatever reason, the DOE isn't the same animated team that started atomic energy plants two decades ago. I'd heard rumors that over the years, the organization had silted up like the Mississippi.

The DOE may not be the most nimble of our many Governmental agencies, but they did pay our bills. For over a month, we'd kept silent about our problem, worrying that the hacker might find out we were tracking him. Now that our trace led far from Berkeley, it seemed safe to tell our funding agency about the hacker.

On November 12, I called around the DOE, trying to find out who I should talk to about a computer break-in. It took a half dozen calls to find out that nobody really wanted to listen. Eventually I reached the DOE manager of computer security for unclassified computers.

Rick Carr listened patiently as I told him about the hacker, occasionally interrupting with questions. "Is he still active in your computer?"

"Yes, and we're homing in on him every time he shows up."

He didn't seem especially excited. "Well when you catch him, let us know."

"Want a copy of my logbook?" I asked.

"No. Keep it quiet until you're through."

I explained our need for search warrants and the FBI's lack of interest. "Any chance you might be able to get the FBI to open a case?"

"No, I wish they did, but the FBI doesn't listen to us," Rick said. "I'd like to help, but it's just not my bailiwick."

Bailiwicks again. I mumbled my thanks, and was about to hang up when Rick said, "You might want to call the National Computer Security Center, though."

"Who are they?" Seemed like a group that I should have heard of.

Rick explained, "The NCSC is a sidekick of the National Security Agency. They're supposed to make standards for securing computers." From his emphasis on the word "supposed," it sounded like they weren't.

"Since when does the NSA talk to the public?" I'd always thought that the NSA was the most secret of all government agencies.

"The computer security section of NSA is the only part of NSA that's unclassified," Rick said. "Because of this, they're treated as ugly ducklings within NSA. Nobody from the secret side of the house will talk to them."

"And since they're a part of the NSA, nobody from the public trusts them either." I realized where he was leading.

"Right. They take flak from both sides. But you ought to tell them about your hacker. They're certain to be interested, and they might just rattle the right cages in the bureaucracy."

Next call: the National Computer Security Center. Zeke Hanson was their desk officer. His voice was cheerful and he seemed fascinated by the idea of silently watching a hacker. He wanted all the technical details of our monitors and alarms.

"You're an intercept operator," Zeke informed me.

"What's that?" I'd never heard of it.

He stammered a bit, as if he wanted to unsay his last sentence. I figured out what he meant on my own. NSA must have thousands of people watching teletypes around the world. Intercept operators, huh?

Zeke asked about my computer. I explained, "A couple of Vaxes running Unix. Lots of networks." For the next twenty minutes, I told him about the holes that the hacker exploited—Gnu-Emacs, passwords, Trojan horses. It hit him where he lived.

But when I asked if there was any way that he could finagle a search warrant, he clammed up tight.

"I'll have to talk to my colleagues about this."

Well, what did I expect? Ideally, I'd call an electronic spy on the phone, explain my need for a search warrant, and he'd kick the FBI into acting. Right. How would I react to someone calling my observatory, reporting an invader from some unknown planet?

Still, I might as well explain our problem. "Look, we're about to call it quits. If someone doesn't help out, we're giving up on this monitoring. I've had it with being a volunteer intercept operator."

Not a dent. "Cliff, I'd like to take over, but our charger prevents it. NSA can't engage in domestic monitoring, even if we're asked. That's prison term stuff."

He took this seriously. NCSC or NSA, whichever he worked for, wouldn't monitor my hacker. They'd advise me on how to protect my computers and serve as a liaison to the FBI, but they wouldn't take over my monitoring.

Getting a search warrant? Zeke would look into it, but didn't offer much help. "If you can't interest the FBI, I doubt that they'll listen to us. We're here to make computers more secure, not to catch criminals."

Another bailiwick problem.

I hung up, discouraged. Five minutes later, I walked down the hallway and asked myself what I was doing talking to the NSA.

Maybe Martha was right. She'd said I was on a slippery slope that led into deep water. First you call the FBI, then the CIA, now the NSA.

But it wasn't the spooks that bothered me. It was their inaction. Sure, they all listened to my troubles, but not one would lift a finger.

Frustrating. Every agency seemed to have a good reason to do nothing. Disgusted, I paced the halls.

The hallways at Lawrence Berkeley Labs look like a plumber's nightmare. There's no suspended ceiling tiles to hide the pipes, cables, and ducts. Looking up, I recognized the steam pipes, and the orange ethernet cables. The steam runs at about one hundred pounds per square inch, the ethernet at around ten million bits per second.

My networks were as essential to the lab as steam, water, or electricity.

Did I say, "my networks"? The networks were no more mine than the steam pipes belonged to the plumbers. But someone had to treat them as his own, and fix the leaks.

Something strange was happening to me. In a daze, I sat down on the hallway floor, still staring up at the pipes. For the first time in my life, something important was entirely up to me. My attitude at work had always been like my days as an astronomer—I'd write proposals, observe at the telescope, publish papers, and stand cynically apart from the struggles and triumphs of the world around me. I didn't care if my research led anywhere.

Now, nobody was telling me what to do, yet I had a choice: should I quietly let things drop? Or do I take arms against this sea of troubles?

Staring at the pipes and cables, I realized that I could no longer fool around behind the scenes, an irreverent, zany kid. I was serious. I cared. The network community depended on me, without even knowing it. Was I becoming (oh, no!) responsible?

# 22

THAT EVENING, MARTHA STUDIED CRIMINAL PROCEDURE at Boalt Hall Law Library. I stopped by to deliver some bagels and cream cheese, the high-octane fuel of law students. We necked and pecked among the books, occasionally dodging a zombie cramming for the bar exam. Aah, Boalt library, where the law never sleeps.

In a back room, she showed me the law school's Lexis computer. "Hey, want to play with a fun toy while I study?" she asked.

Without waiting for a reply, she switched on the Lexis terminal. She pointed to the sign giving instructions on how to log into the document search system. She dived back into her books, leaving me with some unknown computer.

The instructions couldn't be plainer. Just press a couple buttons, type the account name, a password, and begin searching judicial records for whatever seems interesting. Next to the instructions were scribbled five account names and passwords, so I picked a pair and logged in. Nobody had thought to protect its passwords. I wondered how many former law students were still freeloading from the library.

So I logged into the law computer and searched on the keywords *telephone trace.* It took a while to understand the legal jargon, but eventually I stumbled on the law regulating telephone traces. It turned out that a search warrant wasn't necessary to trace a phone call made to your own telephone, so long as you wanted the trace made.

This made sense. You shouldn't need a court order to find out who was calling you. Indeed, some telephone companies now sell phones that display the digits of the calling telephone as your phone is ringing.

But if we didn't legally need a search warrant, why were the phone companies so insistent? Monday morning, clutching a xerox of 18 USCA §3121, I called Lee Cheng at the phone company. "Why do you make us get search warrants, when the law doesn't require it?"

"It's partly to protect ourselves from lawsuits and partly to filter out worthless traces," Lee said.

"Well, if the warrant isn't required, why won't the Virginia phone company release the information?"

"I dunno. But they won't. I've spent half an hour talking to them, and they won't budge." If they wouldn't release the number to another phone company, there wasn't much chance they'd tell my lab. Looked like the phone trace was a dead end after all.

Aletha Owens, our lawyer, called. "The FBI won't give us the time of day, let alone a search warrant."

Same story with our lab police. They'd called around and got nowhere. Dead end.

Over lunch at the lab cafeteria, I described the past week's adventures to two astronomer pals, Jerry Nelson and Terry Mast.

"You mean to say that they traced the call and won't tell you the number?" Jerry asked incredulously.

"That's about the size of it. No tickee, no laundry."

Between sandwiches, I showed them my logbook. A couple weeks ago, while the phone technician was tracing the line, I'd copied all her jargon into my logbook. Now, Jerry started interpreting like a palm reader.

"Hey, look, Cliff—the phone technician said 703," Jerry said. "Area code 703 is in Virginia. And C and P . . . I bet that's Chesapeake and Potomac. Yeah. They're the phone company for northern and western Virginia."

Terry Mast is an experimentalist. "You copied those numbers that the phone technician said. Why not call every permutation of those numbers in area code 703, and find out if there's a computer there?"

Jerry Nelson looked at my notes. "Yeah, that oughta work. The technician said 1060 and 427 and 448. Try calling 703/427-1060. Or maybe 448-1060. There's only a few combinations."

It was worth a try. But I'd be slightly more devious.

I called my local telephone business office and said, "I have a couple calls on my bill that I don't remember making. Could you tell me who I dialed?"

The operator was completely cooperative. "Just read me the numbers and I'll check them for you."

I told her six possible numbers, all in area code 703. Ten minutes later, she called back. "I'm very sorry, but five of those numbers are nonexistent or out of service. I don't know how you got billed for them."

Five of the six were bad numbers! One might just do it. I said, "Oh yes, that's all right. Who is the owner of the sixth number?"

"That's Mitre Incorporated, spelled M-I-T-R-E, at 703/448-1060. Would you like me to start a refund for those five other calls?"

"I'm in a hurry right now. I'll take care of it later."

Nervously, I dialed the phone number, ready to hang up when I heard a voice. A computer's modem answered with a high-pitched whistle. Far out!

Mitre. I knew of a defense contractor, Mitre, in Massachusetts. But not in Virginia. I'd seen their ads in electronics magazines—they were always looking for programmers who were U.S. citizens. Digging through the library, I found that, yes, Mitre did have a branch in Virginia. McLean, Virginia.

Strange. Where had I heard of that city? The library's atlas told me.

The CIA's headquarters are in McLean.

# 23

I COULDN'T BELIEVE IT. THE HACKING SEEMED TO BE coming from Mitre in McLean, Virginia—a couple of miles from CIA headquarters. Time to call the boss.

"Hey, Dennis, the calls are coming from Mitre. It's a defense contractor just down the road from CIA headquarters. What do you think Teejay will say to that?"

"How do you know it's Mitre?"

"Well, during the phone trace, I copied down all the numbers and digits that I heard from the technician. I called all combinations of them, and ended up at a computer modem at Mitre."

"So you're not certain." Dennis saw the hole in my argument. "If we spread this around and we're wrong, we'll be in hot water."

"But what are the chances of randomly dialing a telephone and getting a computer to answer?"

"I don't care. Until you find some proof, don't act on it. Don't call Mitre. And don't tell our spooky friends."

Back to square one. I think I know the phone number of the hacker but how to prove it?

Aah! Just wait until the hacker calls back again. Then see if the phone is busy. If it's busy, then likely I've got the right number.

There was another way to get the phone number. Less sophisticated, but more reliable.

Back in graduate school, I'd learned how to survive without

funding, power, or even office space. Grad students are lowest in the academic hierarchy, and so they have to squeeze resources from between the cracks. When you're last on the list for telescope time, you make your observations by hanging around the mountaintop, waiting for a slice of time between other observers. When you need an electronic gizmo in the lab, you borrow it in the evening, use it all night, and return it before anyone notices. I didn't learn much about planetary physics, but weaseling came naturally.

Still, I couldn't finagle a federal search warrant. All I had were the standard tools of astronomers. Exactly enough to get the information I needed.

I dialed Chesapeake and Potomac's business office and asked for the security office. After a few transfers, I recognized the voice of the technician that had traced last week's call.

After a few minutes of casual chat, she mentioned that her eleven-year-old kid was fascinated by astronomy. I saw my opening. "Think he'd like some star charts and posters of the planets?"

"Sure! Especially that ringed thing, you know, Saturn."

One of the few resources that I've plenty of: pictures of planets and galaxies. We talked a bit about her kid, and I returned to the matter on my mind.

"By the way, I think the hacker is coming from Mitre, over in McLean. 448-1060. Does this agree with your trace?"

"I'm not supposed to release this information, but since you already know the number. . . ."

Aah! Grad school comes through.

I rolled a dozen posters into a mailing tube. Today, somewhere in Virginia, a kid's wall sports a collection of planetary and galactic photos.

McLean, Virginia . . . I knew more about Mars than McLean. I called my sister, Jeannie, who lived somewhere near there. At least she had the same area code.

Jeannie had, indeed, heard of Mitre. They weren't just a defense contractor grabbing secret Pentagon contracts. They also had ties to the CIA and the NSA. Among thousands of other projects, Mitre tested computers for security. When someone needed a secure computer, Mitre certified it.

Odd. The hacker came from a company that certifies secure computers. Maybe one of their testers was fooling around on the side? Or did Mitre have some secret contract to explore security on the military networks?

Time to call Mitre. It took five phone calls to pierce their veil of secretaries, but eventually I reached a man named Bill Chandler.

It took fifteen minutes to convince him that there really was a problem. "Simply impossible. We're running a secure shop, and nobody can break in." I described my traces, leaving out the missing search warrants.

"Well, I don't know if someone's hacking from our computers, but if they are, they're sure not coming from the outside."

It took another ten minutes before he'd accept that it was *his* problem. Five more to decide what to do.

I proposed a simple solution. Simple for me, at least. "The next time the hacker's connected to Berkeley, just examine Mitre's telephone line. Find out who's connected to it."

Bill Chandler agreed. He'd round up some technicians and quietly watch Mitre's telephone line, 448-1060. As soon as I'd call him, he'd trace his internal network and find the culprit.

"I doubt we'll find much," he said. "It's impossible to break into our secure site, and all our employees have clearances."

Right. If he wanted to keep his head in the sand, it was all right with me. Maybe one of Mitre's employees was screwing around the military networks, just for kicks. But what if this was an organized effort?

If so, who was behind it? Could some secret agency have hired Mitre? If so, it had to be someone right around the corner. Someone just a couple miles away. Time to call the CIA.

Ten minutes later, I'm on the phone with Teejay. "Uh, I don't know how to ask this, and you probably can't tell me anyway, but what are the chances that our hacker is someone from the CIA?"

Teejay wouldn't consider it. "Absolutely zero. We don't pry into domestic affairs. Period."

"Well, I can't say for certain, but it looks like our phone traces lead to Virginia, and I was just wondering if . . ." I let my voice trail off, hoping Teejay would pick up.

"Where in Virginia?" Teejay asked.

"Northern Virginia. Someplace called McLean."

"Prove it."

"We got a telephone trace, but it hasn't been officially released. We don't have a search warrant, but there's no doubt it's from McLean."

"How do you know?"

"Standard techniques I picked up in graduate school," I said. If I told him how, he wouldn't believe me. Anyway, he'd never reveal his methods to me.

"What else do you know about this McLean connection?"

"A little bit. Know any defense contractors there?" For once I played cat and mouse.

"Cut the crap. Who is it?"

"Mitre."

"Come on. Be serious."

"Would you believe 1820 Dolly Madison Road?"

"Are you trying to tell me that someone from Mitre is hacking into military computers?"

"That's what our phone trace says."

"Well, I'll be damned. . . . No, it's just not possible." Teejay went silent for a second. "Mitre's a secure site. . . . Do you know anything more about this hacker?"

"I know what brand of cigarettes he smokes."

Teejay laughed over the phone. "I guessed that last month."

"Then why didn't you tell me?" Teejay wanted my news, but wasn't forthcoming with his own. "Look, I've got to know one thing. Mitre's a mile from you. They work on classified projects. Are you sure the hacker's not with the CIA?"

Teejay became suddenly bureaucratic. "I can only say that nobody in our agency is authorized to observe domestic activities, with or without a computer." On the side, he added, "Damned if I know who this guy is, but he'd better not be one of us."

"Can you find out?"

"Cliff, this is a domestic problem. I'd love to help, but we can't touch it."

Well, the CIA was interested, but not much help. Time to call the FBI. For the seventh time, the Oakland FBI office didn't raise an eyebrow. The agent there seemed more interested in how I traced the call than in where it led.

Still, there was one more place to call. The Defense Communications Agency. They seemed to be on good terms with the Air Force Office of Special Investigations—maybe they could scare up some official interest.

Despite ten thousand computers on the Milnet, only one person managed security. A month ago, Major Steve Rudd had asked about our problems. He hadn't promised any action, just wanted to hear any news. Maybe the word Mitre would wake him up.

I called him, and mentioned that we'd traced things back to McLean, Virginia. "I hope you're kidding," Steve said.

"No kidding. The hacking's coming from a defense contractor in McLean."

"Who?"

"Can't say till I check with my boss." I wondered if he'd play cat and mouse.

Despite his protests, I stood my ground. Maybe by keeping quiet, I could keep him interested. After a few more minutes on the phone, he gave up, exasperated. "Look, talk to your boss and see if he'll tell us. We might be able to help if we know who to lean on. Unless you tell us, though, we can't do much."

While it was fresh in my mind, I typed the day's events into my logbook. The phone rang, and when I picked it up, a recorded message was playing: "This phone line is not secured. Do not discuss classified information." It repeated a couple times, so I hung up. I didn't know anything classified, and didn't want to.

Three minutes later, the same message came on my phone. By listening carefully, you could hear where the tape was spliced. I was just getting into the rhythm of the mechanical voice when an angry army officer interrupted.

"Hello, is this Doctor Stoll?" People only used titles on me when I was in trouble. "This is Jim Christy of the OSI."

The Air Force narcs were on the phone. The Defense Communications Agency must have rung their bell.

The narc had just one question. "Where did you trace the hacker in Virginia?"

"Uh, I can't tell you. This line isn't secure."

"Be serious."

There wasn't any reason not to tell him. At worst, he'd do nothing. At best, he might armtwist Mitre into cooperating. So I explained the traces to Jim Christy, and he seemed surprised, but satisfied.

"I'll call the Virginia FBI," Jim said. "Maybe we can get some action from our end."

"Then you know something I don't. The Oakland office won't lift a finger unless there's a million dollars involved."

Jim explained that the FBI offices are pretty much autonomous. What excites one agent, another won't consider worthwhile. "It's the luck of the draw. Sometimes you get the elevator . . ."

". . . and sometimes you get the shaft." I wished him luck, asked him to keep me posted, and went back to my logbook. Seemed like the rumors were true. No police agency trusted another. The only way to solve the problem was to tell everyone who might be able to help. Sooner or later, someone might take action.

None of us, at that time, would have guessed anything close to the truth. None of us—not the CIA, not the FBI, not the NSA, and certainly not me—knew where this twisted path would lead.

# 24

THE NEXT MORNING I ARRIVED AT THE LAB TO FIND nothing more than a couple stale phone messages. My boss wanted me to call our funding agency, the Department of Energy—"Give them a heads-up." And Dan Kolkowitz called from Stanford.

"I would have sent you electronic mail," Dan said, "but I'm worried that someone else might read it." We both had learned that hackers scan electronic mail. The simple solution was to use the phone.

In between bites of a cashew-butter sandwich, I told Dan about my traces to Mitre, omitting any mention of the CIA. No need to start rumors about someone in Berkeley cooperating with Big Brother.

Dan took it all in. "Strange. I called you to say that we've just traced our hacker into Virginia. McLean."

My tongue stuck to my mouth—maybe it was cashew-butter—and it took a moment to talk. "But your hacker's not the same guy that I'm following."

"Yeah. Maybe a group of hackers are using the same methods to attack different computers. In any case, I know the name of the hacker that's breaking into Stanford."

"How'd you get that?"

"Simple. We did the same thing as you: printed out everything the hacker typed. Well, one night, the hacker logged into our

Stanford Unix computer and tried to solve his homework. It was a simple calculus problem, solving the area under a curve by counting squares. But the hacker loaded the entire problem into our computer, including his name and his instructor's name."

"Ha! So who is he?"

"I'm not sure. I know his name is Knute Sears. He's in the fourth period math class, taught by a Mr. Maher. But I haven't any idea where he is. I've searched the phone books in Stanford, and I can't find him."

Dan and I both realized that his hacker must be a high school student. Finding the area under a curve is introductory calculus.

"So how do you find a high school student named Sears?" Dan asked. "Ever heard of a directory of all kids in high school?"

"No, but maybe there's a directory of high school math teachers." There's a directory of everyone else, I figured.

We compared our logs, and again decided that we were following two different people. Perhaps Knute Sears did know the hacker that was breaking into my system, but they certainly weren't the same guy.

After I hung up, I hopped on my bike and coasted down to campus. Surely the University library would have a directory of high school teachers. No luck. Finding an individual isn't easy when you know their name but not their city.

As a last straw, I could call my sister, Jeannie, in Virginia. Life was a little zooey for her. What was it like, from my sister's perspective, to be sucked into this ever-widening vortex of computocrud?

All I needed at first was a little telephone work. I'd be most appreciative if she could call around the McLean area high schools to try and locate the mystery math teacher, Mr. Maher. Compared to the FBI's foot-dragging, any help on the East Coast, no matter how minor, would amount to a substantial dragnet. Furthermore, Jeannie had experience with the Department of Defense—well, anyone was more experienced with the military than me. I trusted Jeannie's discretion; even if she did no more than just listen, it would be a service.

I phoned Jeannie at work and launched into the requisite background explanation, but as soon as I dropped the words "hacker" and "Milnet," she said, "Okay, what do you want from me?" It turned out that the Navy research and development center she worked for had warned its support staff about the risks of leaky computers.

Jeannie did attach one thin string to her offer of help. "It would be real sweet if you could get someone to write me a nice, official thank-you note. Say, from the OSI or the FBI, or whoever."

When I next spoke to the OSI, I relayed Jeannie's request. They assured me that this was easy for them. . . . "We're really good at writing notes." (Hardly. Despite abundant promises in the next year, from majors, colonels and generals, my sister was never to receive her official pat on the back. Eventually, we concluded that it's just not possible for someone in one part of the federal bureaucracy to officially thank someone in another.)

At any rate, Jeannie decided to start her investigation during her lunch break. And she called back with something to report within an hour.

"The public high school that's closest to Mitre is McLean High School, so I started there," she said. "I asked to talk to a math teacher named Mr. Maher. They repeated the name, said, 'One moment please,' and connected me to someone. At that point, I hung up."

Could it have been that my sister, in one phone call, had gotten more done than the FBI? Gee, maybe I should impose on her further. "How about dropping by that school and see if you can spot any computers—most schools have 'em. Also, see if you can find Knute Sears in their yearbook. But be careful. The way I've got him scoped, he's extremely skittish. Don't spook the guy."

"Okey doke, I'll take a long lunch tomorrow."

The next day, while I pedaled the verdant hills of Berkeley, my sister circumnavigated the Washington, D.C., beltway, feeling alternately exhilarated and foolish.

It turns out that McLean is the home of loads of elected officials, policymakers, and upper-end military leaders. Jeannie reports that it looks like the "apotheosis of the affluent second-ring suburb," though I'm not sure what that means.

And on that bright Virginia autumn day, its high school seemed a distillation of all the myths surrounding the Great American High School. Classes had just let out. Expensively dressed kids spilled out of the front door. The student parking lot included Mercedes, BMWs, and an occasional Volvo. Jeannie's pride and joy, a beat-up '81 Chevy Citation, shrank to the remote outskirts of the lot in self-conscious mortification.

Jeannie reported that, like her car, she felt discomfort, not to mention an attack of absurdity, snooping around a suburban school.

Now, my sister has better reason than most to hate being in a high school. In her younger and more vulnerable years, she taught eleventh-grade English. Now, teenagers give her the hives, especially teenagers that don't belong to her. Really affluent ones are the worst, she reports.

Under the guise of a concerned parent, Jeannie visited the school office and sat for half an hour, scanning yearbook listings of the swim team, the Latin scholars, the debaters, for just one mention of the apocryphal Knute Sears. No dice.

Having thoroughly exhausted the resource material and convinced that there was no Knute at McLean, she turned her attention to the teachers' mailboxes. Sure enough, one was labeled "Mr. Maher."

Abruptly, a clerk appeared and asked what she wanted to see. With a ditsiness reminiscent of Gracie Allen, my sister burbled, "Gee, I don't know, dear. . . . Well, well, what do you know? Here it is, right in front of my eyes." The clerk smiled patronizingly as Jeannie grabbed a brochure from the nearest pile on the counter—it turned out to explain how to register for night school. Half covering a silly-me smirk with her hand, she waved bye-bye with the other hand and booked out of there.

Her covert operation complete, Jeannie called me that afternoon. Stanford's mythical Knute Sears was to remain a myth. He'd never registered at McLean High School. And their Mr. Maher wasn't a math teacher. He taught history, part time.

Another dead end. Even today, I can't talk to my sister without feeling acute embarrassment for sending her on a wild-goose chase.

I called Dan at Stanford with the bad news. He wasn't surprised. "It'll take a long investigation. We're giving up on the FBI. The Secret Service has a computer crime division that's eager to work on the case."

The Secret Service was helping Stanford? Weren't they the people that caught counterfeiters and protected the president?

"Yes," Dan said, "but they also investigate computer crimes. The Department of the Treasury tries to protect banks from computer fraud, and the Secret Service is a branch of the Treasury Department."

Dan had found a way around a recalcitrant FBI. "They don't know much about computers, but they've got moxie. We'll provide the computer expertise, and they'll get the warrants." Moxie?

It was too late for me, though. Our local FBI still didn't care, but the FBI office in Alexandria, Virginia, had noticed. Someone—Mitre, the Air Force, or the CIA—had leaned on them, and Special Agent Mike Gibbons called.

In a couple minutes, I realized that at last I was speaking to an FBI agent who knew computers. He'd written Unix programs, used modems, and wasn't scared by databases and word processors. His latest hobby was playing Dungeons and Dragons on his Atari computer. J. Edgar Hoover must be rolling in his grave.

Better yet, Mike didn't mind communicating by electronic mail, although since anyone might intercept our traffic we used an encryption scheme to keep our conversations private.

From his voice, I guessed Mike wasn't over thirty, but he knew computer law thoroughly. "There's at least a violation of U.S. Code Section 1030. Probably breaking and entering as well. When we find him, he'll be looking at five years or $50,000." I liked how Mike said "when" rather than "if."

I explained my agreement with Mitre. "When the hacker next shows up in Berkeley, Bill Chandler will trace Mitre's network from the inside. We'll find him then."

Mike wasn't so sure, but at least he didn't object to my plan. The only missing piece was the hacker: he hadn't shown up since Halloween—a two-week hiatus. Each morning, I'd check the recorders. Day and night, I'd wear my beeper, waiting for the hacker to step on our invisible tripwire. But not a peep.

Finally, on November 18, my hacker returned to his Sventek account. He entered at 8:11 in the morning and stayed around for half an hour. Immediately, I called Mitre in McLean. Bill Chandler wasn't in, and a stuffy manager told me that only Bill Chandler was authorized to trace Mitre's internal network. He talked about "strict guidelines" and "certified secure networks." I cut him off. With the hacker live on my system, I didn't need to listen to some big-shot manager. Where were the technicians, the people who actually knew how Mitre's system worked?

Another chance to catch the hacker—foiled.

He showed up again in the afternoon. This time I got through to Bill Chandler, and he ran over to check his outbound modems. Sure enough, someone had dialed out through Mitre's modem, and it looked like a long-distance call. But where was the connection originating?

Bill explained, "Our network within Mitre is complex, and it's not easy to trace. We don't have individual wires connecting one computer to another. Instead, a lot of signals travel on a single wire, and connections have to be traced by decoding the addresses of each packet on our ethernet."

In other words, Mitre couldn't trace the calls.

Damn. Someone was calling out from Mitre, but they couldn't find where the hacker was coming from. We still didn't know if it was a Mitre employee or someone from the outside.

Furious, I looked over the printout from the hacker. Nothing new there. He tried once again to slip into the Army base in Anniston but was turned away. The rest of the time he spent searching my Berkeley computer for words like "nuclear bomb," and "SDI."

Bill promised to get his best technicians on the problem. A few days later, when the hacker showed up, I heard the same story. No doubt that someone was dialing out from Mitre's computer system. But they couldn't trace it. They were baffled. Who was behind it? And where was he hiding?

On Saturday, Martha dragged me on a day's outing to Calistoga, where the geysers and hot springs attract butterflies, geologists, and hedonists. For the latter, there are mud baths, said to be the height of Northern California decadence. For twenty dollars, you can be parboiled in an ooze of volcanic ash, peat, and mineral water.

"It'll take your mind off your work," Martha said. "You've been all twisted up over this hacker—a break will do you good." Mired in an oversized bathtub didn't sound like a recipe for rejuvenation, but I'll try anything once.

Wallowing in this private swamp, my mind drifted off to thoughts of Mitre. My hacker used Mitre's outgoing telephone lines to cross the country. Stanford had traced one hacker to McLean; likely he came through Mitre. Maybe Mitre provided a central point for hackers, a sort of switchboard to place their calls. That would mean the hackers weren't Mitre employees, but were from outside the company.

How could this happen? Mitre would have to make three mistakes. They'd have to create a way for anyone to connect freely to their local network. Then, they'd have to allow a stranger to log onto their computer. Finally, they'd have to provide unaudited outgoing long-distance telephone service.

They'd met the third condition: the modems connected to their internal network could call all over the country. We'd traced our troubles into those very lines.

But how could someone connect into Mitre? Surely they wouldn't allow just anyone to dial into their network. As Bill Chandler had said, they're running a secure shop. Military secrets and stuff like that.

What other ways could you get into Mitre? Over some network, perhaps? Could a hacker get there through Tymnet? If Mitre paid for Tymnet service and didn't protect it with passwords, you could call them from anywhere for free. Once connected, Mitre's internal network might let you turn around and call out. Then you could dial anywhere, with Mitre picking up the tab.

It would be easy to test my hypothesis: I'd become a hacker.

I'd go home and try to use Tymnet to connect to Mitre, trying to break into a place I wasn't supposed to be.

The mud smelled of sulfur and peat moss, and felt like a hot primordial ooze. I enjoyed the mud bath and the sauna that came afterward, but I still couldn't wait to get out of the mud and return home. I had a lead. Or at least a hunch.

# 25

LOGBOOK, SUNDAY, NOVEMBER 23, 1986

10:30 A.M. Oakland Tymnet access number is 415/430-2900. Called from my Macintosh at home. 1200 baud, no parity. Tymnet asked for a username. I entered *MITRE.* Response: *Welcome to Mitre-Bedford.*

10:40 A.M. Mitre has an internal network which gives a menu. Fourteen choices, apparently different computers within Mitre. I try each in succession.

10:52 A.M. One choice, *MWCC,* leads to another menu. That menu has twelve choices. One choice is *DIAL.* I try:

*DIAL 415 486 2984* no effect

*DIAL 1 415 486 2984* no effect

*DIAL 9 1 415 486 2984* Connected into Berkeley computer.

Conclusion: An outsider can connect into Mitre through Tymnet. No password necessary. Once in Mitre, they can dial out, either locally or long distance.

MWCC means "Mitre Washington Computing Center"; Bedford means "Bedford Massachusetts." I'd entered Mitre in Bedford, and popped out five hundred miles away in McLean.

11:03 A.M. Disconnect from Berkeley computer, but remain at Mitre. I request connection into system AEROVAX. It prompts for username. I enter "Guest." It accepts and logs me in, without any password. Explore Aerovax computer.

Aerovax has programs for some sort of airport flight safety.

Program to find allowable landing angles for high-speed and low-speed aircraft approaches. Presumably funded by government contracts.

Aerovax connects to several other computers over Mitre's network. These are password protected. "Guest" is not a valid username on these other Mitre computers. (I'm not sure they're even at Mitre.)

Wait—something's wrong here. The network controlling software doesn't seem normal—its greeting message shows up too quickly, but it completes its connection too slowly. I wonder what's in that program. . . .

Aha! It's been modified. Someone has set a Trojan horse in the Aerovax network software. It copies network passwords into a secret file for later use.

Conclusion: someone's been tampering with Mitre's software, successfully stealing passwords.

11:35 A.M. Disconnect from Mitre and update logbook.

Today, reading my logbook, I remember an hour of poking around Mitre's internal network. At once it felt exciting and forbidden. Any minute, I expected someone to send a message on my computer screen, "We caught you. Come out with your hands up."

No doubt Mitre had left a gaping hole in their system. Anyone could make a local telephone call, tell Tymnet to connect to Mitre, and spend an afternoon fooling around with Mitre's computers. Most of their machines were protected with passwords, but at least one was pretty much wide open.

I remembered Mitre's pious disclaimer, "We're running a secure shop, and nobody can break in." Right.

The "Guest" account on their Aerovax let anyone on. But the Trojan horse was deadly. Someone had tampered with their network program to copy passwords into a special area. Every time a legitimate employee used the Aerovax computer, her password was stolen. This gave the hacker keys to other Mitre computers. Once the hacker penetrated their armor, he could roam anywhere.

How deeply was Mitre's system infested? By listing their

directory, I saw that the Trojan horse was dated June 17. For six months, someone had silently booby-trapped their computers.

I couldn't prove that it was the same hacker that I was dealing with. But this morning's exercises showed that anyone could enter Mitre's system and dial into my Berkeley computers. So the hacker wasn't necessarily at Mitre. He might be anywhere.

In all likelihood, Mitre served as a way station, a stepping stone on the way to breaking into other computers.

The McLean connection became clear. Someone dialed into Mitre, and turned around and dialed out from them. This way, Mitre paid the bills both ways: the incoming Tymnet connection and the outgoing long-distance telephone call. Even nicer, Mitre served as a hiding place, a hole in the wall that couldn't be traced.

Mitre, the high-security defense contractor—I'd been told that you can't get past their lobby without showing picture ID. Their guards wear guns, and their fences are barbed. Yet all it takes is a home computer and a telephone to prowl through their databases.

Monday morning, I called Bill Chandler at Mitre and told him the news. I didn't expect him to believe me, so I wasn't disappointed to hear him insist that his company was "highly secured and sensitive to any security problems."

I'd heard it before. "If you're so concerned about security, why isn't anyone auditing your computers?"

"We do. We keep detailed records of how each computer's used," Bill said. "But that's for accounting, not to detect hackers." I wondered what his people would do about a 75-cent accounting error.

"Ever hear about a system called the Aerovax?"

"Yeah, what about it?"

"Just wondering. Hold any classified data?"

"Not that I know. It's for an airport control system. Why?"

"Oh, just wondering. You ought to check it over, though." I couldn't admit that I'd danced through his system yesterday, discovering the Trojan horse. "Know any way for a hacker to enter your system?"

"It had better be impossible."

"You might check out your public access dial-in ports. While you're at it, try accessing Mitre's computers over Tymnet. Anyone can connect to your system, from anywhere."

This latest news woke him up to some serious problems in his system. Mitre wasn't inept. Just semi-ept.

Bill wasn't sure how to react, but he wouldn't keep his system open any longer. I couldn't blame him. His computers were naked.

Mostly, he wanted me to keep my mouth shut.

I'd shut up, all right, on one condition. For months, Mitre's computers had called around the country, using expensive, AT&T long-distance telephone lines. There must be phone bills for those calls.

In Berkeley, five of us shared a house. We had a monthly dinner party when the phone bill arrived. With poker faces, each of us would deny making *any* of the calls. But somehow, eventually, every call was accounted for, and the bill paid.

If the five of us could haggle through a phone bill, Mitre must be able to as well. I asked Bill Chandler, "Who pays the phone bills for your computer?"

"I'm not sure," he replied. "Probably central accounting. I never see them."

That's how the hacker got away with it for so long. The people paying the phone bills never talked to the managers of the computers. Strange. Or was it typical? The computer's modems run up a long-distance phone bill. The phone company sends the bill to Mitre, and some faceless accountant signs a check. Nobody closes the loop. Nobody asks about the legitimacy of those dozens of calls to Berkeley.

Bill wanted me to be quiet about these problems. Well, yes, but I had a price. "Say, Bill, could you send me copies of your computer's phone bills?"

"What for?"

"It might be fun to see where else this hacker got into."

Two weeks later, a thick envelope arrived, stuffed with long-distance bills from Chesapeake and Potomac.

At home, my housemates and I haggled over a twenty-dollar phone bill. But I'd never seen thousand-dollar bills. Every month, Mitre had paid for hundreds of long-distance calls, all over North America.

But these weren't people reaching out to touch each other. These bills showed Mitre's computer dialing hundreds of other computers. (I proved this to myself by calling a few. Sure enough, in each case, I heard a modem answer with a whistle.)

Now here's some useful information. Mitre might not be interested in analyzing it, but together with my logbook, I might be able to understand how far the hacker had penetrated. I'd just have to somehow separate the hacker's calls from the normal calls.

Plenty of the calls were obvious hacking. On the list were lots of calls to Anniston, Alabama. And there were the calls to Tymnet in Oakland—they'd cost me a galaxy to trace.

But some of the calls on the bills must be legitimate. After all, Mitre's employees must call computers to transfer data or copy the latest software from the West Coast. How could I separate the hacker's calls?

Back home, when our phone bill arrived, Martha cooked up dinner, Claudia did the salad, and I baked cookies.* Afterward, stuffed on chocolate chips, we'd divvy up the phone bill.

Sitting around the dining table, my housemates and I had no problem figuring out who'd made which long-distance calls on our bill. If I had made a call to Buffalo from 9:30 until 9:35 and another to Baltimore from 9:35 to 9:45, then it was likely that I'd made the call to New York from 9:46 to 9:52.

Looking at Mitre's phone bills, I knew that only the hacker would call the Army base in Anniston, Alabama. Pretty likely that a phone call made a minute after calling Anniston belonged

*Two eggs, 1 cup brown sugar, ½ cup regular sugar, 2 sticks softened butter. Fold in 2¼ cups flour, ½ teaspoon salt, 1 teaspoon baking soda, and a couple tablespoons of vanilla. For an extra chocolate jag, toss in 3 tablespoons of cocoa. Oh, don't forget 2 cups of chocolate chips. Bake 'em at 375 degrees for 10 minutes.

to the hacker. Same for a call that ended just before dialing Alabama.

In physics, this is correlation analysis. If you see a solar flare today and tonight there's a bright aurora, chances are that these are correlated. You look at things that occur close together in time, and try to find the probability that they're somehow connected.

Correlation analysis in physics is simply common sense.

Well, here were six months of phone bills. Dates, times, phone numbers, and cities. Probably five thousand in all. Enough that I couldn't analyze it by hand. Perfect for analyzing on a computer—there's plenty of software written to search out correlations. All I had to do was enter them into my Macintosh computer and run a few programs.

Ever type five thousand phone numbers? It's as boring as it sounds. And I had to do it twice, to make sure I didn't make any mistakes. Took me two days.

Two days to enter the data, and an hour to analyze it. I told my program to assume that the hacker made all calls to the Anniston Army base. Find all calls that immediately preceded or trailed those calls. It took a minute, and showed me that the hacker had called Oakland's Tymnet many times. Aah, the program behaved reasonably.

I spent the afternoon tinkering with the program, refining its statistical techniques and watching the effect of different algorithms on the output. It determined the probability that each call was made by the hacker. Cute—just the thing to settle arguments at home.

It wasn't until the evening that I realized what the program was telling me: this hacker hadn't just broken into my computer. He was into more than six, and possibly a dozen.

From Mitre, the hacker had made long-distance connections to Norfolk, Oak Ridge, Omaha, San Diego, Pasadena, Livermore, and Atlanta.

At least as interesting: he had made hundreds of one-minute-long phone calls, all across the country, to Air Force bases, Navy shipyards, aircraft builders, and defense contractors. What can you learn from a one-minute phone call to an Army proving ground?

For six months, this hacker had broken into Air Force bases and computers all across the country. Nobody knew it. He was out there, alone, silent, anonymous, persistent, and apparently successful—but why? What's he after? What's he already learned? And what's he doing with this information?

# 26

MITRE'S PHONE BILLS SHOWED HUNDREDS OF TELEphone calls all around the country, most of them a minute or two long. But no human voice spoke over that line—it was one computer dialing another.

My boss's voice, though, was singularly human. Around the end of November, Roy Kerth stopped in my office, and found me asleep under my desk.

"Whacha been doing for the past month?"

I could hardly say, "Oh, typing in phone bills from some East Coast defense contractor." Reminding him of my chase would jog his memory of a three-week limit. Quickly, I thought of our department's new graphics terminal—a spiffy new toy that displays three-dimensional images of mechanical devices. I'd fiddled with it for an hour, just long enough to learn how difficult it was to use. But it was an excuse to get the boss off my back, and I told him, "Oh, I'm helping some astronomers design their telescope with our new display terminal." This wasn't a total lie, since we'd talked about doing this. For all of five minutes.

My maneuver backfired. Roy smiled slyly and said, "OK. Next week show us some pretty pictures."

By never showing up before noon, I'd managed to avoid half of the department's meetings. If I didn't have something by next week, no doubt my wings would get clipped.

Time to slide the hacker onto the back burner—and just as the trail was heating up.

One week to learn how to program the beast, figure out what the astronomers needed, and get something on the screen. I knew zero about computerized design. And the programming language was from the twenty-first century: it claimed to be "an object-oriented language with graphical inheritance." Whatever that meant.

So I wandered over to the telescope design team, where Jerry Nelson and Terry Mast were arguing over how much their telescope would bend due to gravity. When looking at stars straight overhead, gravity wouldn't bend the telescope tube. But when pointing near the horizon, the tube would bow slightly. Just enough to upset the delicate optical alignment. They wanted to know how much, and could I show the effect on the computer.

This seemed like fun—at least more fun than figuring out what "graphical inheritance" meant. We talked for a while, and Jerry mentioned that Professor Erik Antonsson had written a program to display the telescope on a graphics display terminal. The same type as I was supposed to program.

"You mean that someone has already written the program to solve your problem and display a picture on the screen?" I asked.

"Yes," the astronomer explained. "But it's down at Caltech in Pasadena. Doesn't do us much good four hundred miles away. We need the results now."

I just had to get the Caltech program up to Berkeley and fit it into my Vax computer. No need to even figure out how to program the beast.

I called Professor Antonsson at Caltech. He'd be happy if we used his program, but how would he send it to us? Mail would take a week. Faster to send it electronically. Aah—when you need a program, don't mail a tape. Just ship it over the network. In twenty minutes, the program percolated across the wires, and settled into my computer.

Well, Professor Antonsson had done a super job of programming the problem. By nine that evening, I'd customized his program for my system and the new telescope data.

Amazingly, the damn thing worked, though not quite the first time. By 2 A.M., I got it to draw a multicolored picture of the Keck Telescope, complete with struts, bearings, and mirrors. You could see where the tube bent, where the stresses built up, and which sections needed reinforcing. Technology comes through again.

One evening of real work, and I was off the hook. The hacker was back on the front burner.

But not a peep from him. My alarms were set, the monitors active, but he'd been invisible for two weeks. On my way home, I wondered if he too might have an urgent project that kept him away from my computer. Or had he found a new way to enter the Milnet, completely bypassing my traps?

As usual, I slept late the next morning. (No need to work early when Thanksgiving weekend was coming up.) At 11:30, I pedaled up the hill and ducked into work, ready to show off my zero-work computer display. But once in my office, I went back to wondering why the hacker wasn't showing up. Time to call Mitre, and find out what they'd done.

Bill Chandler's voice crackled through a noisy long-distance connection. Yes, a week ago, he'd disconnected their outgoing modems. The hacker could no longer leapfrog through Mitre's local network.

The gig was up. We didn't know where he came from, and we'd never find out. Since Mitre had corked up their hole, the hacker would have to find another path into my system.

Not likely. If someone had bolted my door shut, I'd be suspicious that they were about to bust me. And I knew this hacker was paranoid. He'd disappear for sure.

So all my traps had been set in vain. The hacker was gone, and I'd never find out who he was. Three months of searching, with only a fuzzy question mark at the end.

Not that I should complain. Without a hacker to occupy my time, there was plenty of worthwhile work waiting. Like designing a telescope. Or managing a computer. And building scientific software. Jeez—I might even do something useful.

But I'd miss the excitement. Running down the hallway and jumping to a printer. Crowding around a computer screen, trying to trace connections through my computer out somewhere across the country.

And I'd miss the satisfaction of building tools with which to follow him. By now, my programs were almost instant. Seconds after the hacker touched my computer, my pocket pager beeped. It didn't just tell me that the hacker was around. I'd programmed my pager to beep in Morse code, telling me the hacker's target computer, his account name (usually Sventek), and which line the hacker had entered from. Backup alarms and monitors made the system fail-safe.

Somewhere out there, a stranger had come close to getting nailed. If only I'd been able to make one more trace.

Just one more trace.

The hacker was gone, but I had a few loose ends. Mitre's long-distance phone bills showed dozens of calls to a number in Norfolk, Virginia. By calling around (standard graduate school technique: keep pestering), I eventually found that the hacker had been dialing the Navy Regional Automated Data Center.

Well, nobody's stopping me, so I called the Navy data center and talked to their system manager, Ray Lynch. Ray seemed to be an outgoing, competent guy who took his job very seriously. He ran an electronic mailbox system—pigeonholes for electronic mail.

Ray reported that back on July 23, from 3:44 until 6:26 P.M., someone had broken into his Vax computer, using the account belonging to the field service engineers. Once inside his system, the hacker had created a new account named Hunter.

There's that name again. Same guy, no doubt.

The episode normally would have escaped Ray's attention. With three hundred Navy officers using his computers, he'd never have noticed someone illegally adding a new account.

But the next day, he received a phone call from Jet Propulsion Laboratory in Pasadena, California; the same people that run interplanetary spacecraft. An alert JPL operator had detected a new system manager at their mail management computer. This new user had entered from the Milnet, coming in from Virginia.

JPL called Ray Lynch, and asked him why his field service

people had been fooling with their computer. Ray didn't wait around to ask questions. He shut down his computer and changed all its passwords. The next day, he reregistered each of his users.

So my hacker had broken into JPL and a Navy computer. Months before I'd detected him in Berkeley, he had been fooling around the Milnet.

These targets were news to me. Were they a clue to where the hacker was? Well, if you live in California, there's no reason to go through Virginia to reach a computer in Pasadena. And why would someone in Virginia go through Mitre to dial another Virginia phone?

Suppose this hacker had used Mitre to dial all his calls, except for local ones. That meant that any state that showed up on Mitre's phone bills was not the hacker's home. Ruled out Virginia, California, Alabama, Texas, Nebraska, and a dozen others. This didn't lead anywhere, and hardly seemed convincing.

I called some of the other places listed on Mitre's phone bills. The hacker had hit a college in Atlanta, Georgia. The system manager there hadn't detected it, but he wasn't likely to, either. "We run a pretty open system. Lots of students know the system password. The whole thing depends on trust."

That was one way to run a computer. Leave all the doors open. Like one of my physics profs: anyone could wander into his office. Didn't do much good, though. He kept his notes in Chinese.

From talking to Ray, I learned one new wrinkle about the hacker. Up until now, I'd watched him exploit Unix systems. But Ray's system was a Vax computer running the VMS operating system. The hacker might not know the Berkeley variant of Unix, but he certainly knew how to break into Vax VMS systems.

Since 1978, Digital Equipment Corporation had been making Vaxes, their first thirty-two-bit computers. They couldn't make them fast enough: by 1985, over fifty thousand had been sold, at $200,000 each. Most of them used the versatile, friendly VMS operating system, although some contrary cusses threw away the VMS system, preferring the power of Unix.

Both Unix and VMS divide up the computer's resources to give a separate area for every user. There's space reserved for the system and common space that can be shared by everyone.

Somehow, when you uncrate the machine and first switch it on, you've got to be able to create places for your users. If the machine comes to you protected with passwords, you won't be able to log on the first time.

Digital Equipment Company answered this problem by packaging every Vax-VMS computer with three accounts, each with its own password. There's the SYSTEM account, with the password "MANAGER." An account named FIELD, password "SERVICE." And an account USER with the password "USER."

The instructions say to start the system running, create new accounts for your users, and then change these passwords. Starting up a computer is a bit tricky and, well, some system managers have never changed these passwords. Despite Digital's best efforts to make the system managers change those passwords, some never do. The result? Today, on some systems, you can still log in as SYSTEM, with the password "MANAGER."

That system account is completely privileged. From it, you can read any file, run any program, and change any data. Seems nutty to leave it unprotected.

The hacker either knew about these backdoor passwords, or else he knew some very subtle bug in the VMS operating system. Either way, there was little doubt that he was skilled in two operating systems: Unix and VMS.

Some high school students are impressive computer jockeys. But it's a rare high school student who's both deeply skilled and versatile—experienced in several computers. That takes time. Years, usually. Yes, most Unix systems folks could exploit the Gnu-Emacs hole, once they realized its weakness. And most VMS system managers knew about the not-so-secret default passwords. But each operating system took a couple years to become proficient in, and the skills weren't very portable.

My hacker had a couple of years of Unix experience, and a couple of years in VMS. Probably had been system manager or administrator along the way.

Not a high school student.

But not an experienced wizard, either. He didn't know Berkeley Unix.

I had been following someone in his twenties who smoked Benson and Hedges cigarettes. And broke into military computers, searching for classified information.

But was I following him anymore? No, not really. He wouldn't show up again.

Teejay called from the CIA. "I'm just checking to hear what's new about our boy."

"No, nothing really. I think I know how old he is, but not a whole lot." I started explaining about the Navy data center and the backdoor passwords, but then the CIA agent interrupted.

"Got printouts of those sessions?"

"Well, no, my direct evidence is Mitre's phone bills. If that's not convincing, there's other pointers. He created an account with the name Hunter. Same as at Anniston."

"Did you write this in your logbook?"

"Sure. I put everything there."

"Could you send me a copy?"

"Well, it's kinda private. . . ." Teejay wouldn't send me copies of *his* reports.

"Come on, be serious. If we're ever going to light a fire under the 'F' entity, I've got to know what's happening."

The "F" entity? I searched my memory. Fourier transform? Fossils? Finger painting?

"What's the 'F' entity?" I asked, somewhat humiliated.

"You know, the entity in Washington," Teejay replied, with a touch of annoyance. "J. Edgar's boys. The Bureau."

Why not just say the FBI?

"Oh, I get it, you want my logbook to convince the 'F' entity to do something." Entity, indeed. Spooktalk.

"Yeah. Just send it to me."

"What's your address?"

"Just mail it to Teejay, Zip Code 20505. It'll reach me."

Now there's status. No last name, no street, no city, no state. I wondered if he ever got junk mail.

With the CIA off my neck, I might as well go back to real work. I played around with Professor Antonsson's graphics program for a while, and found that it was amazingly simple to understand. All this hype about object-oriented programming just meant that you didn't write programs using variables and data structures; instead, you told the computer about things. To describe a robot, you'd detail its feet, legs, joints, torso, and head. No need to talk about X's and Y's. And "graphical inheritance" just meant that when the robot moved its leg, the feet and toes moved automatically. You didn't have to write a separate program to move each object.

Neat. After a day or two of fooling with the Caltech program, its simplicity and elegance came shining through. What seemed a hairy programming challenge turned out to be easy. So I spiffed up the display, adding colors and titles. The boss wanted me to jump through hoops; I'd put up a three-ring circus.

# 27

THANKSGIVING WOULD BE A CORKER. WITH HER BICYCLE and backpack, Martha had hauled home forty pounds of groceries. She made only a few sarcastic comments about roommates who sleep late, and set me to putting stuff away and cleaning the house.

"Put away the veggies, honey," she said. "I'm going to the Safeway." How could there possibly be more food to get? Seeing my amazement, she explained that this was just the fresh stuff, and she still had to get the goose, flour, butter, cream, and eggs. A corker, for sure.

I put the food away and climbed back in bed. I woke up to the smell of biscuits and goose wafting through the house. We expected Martha's grad school friends who couldn't go home (or preferred Martha's cooking to mom's), a couple of law professors, a few hungry warriors from her aikido dojo, and her zany friend Laurie. My conscience finally responded to all Martha's bustling, and I revved up our 250-horsepower Hoover.

As I vacuumed the room, our roommate Claudia returned from a violin rehearsal. "Oh, don't do that," she exclaimed, "that's my job." Imagine—a roommate that enjoyed doing housework. Her only fault was playing late-night Mozart.

Thanksgiving passed by idyllically, with friends wandering in, helping in the kitchen, talking, and lounging around. It was an all-day feed, starting with fresh oysters from the San Francisco wharf, moving on leisurely to Martha's wild mushroom soup, then the goose. Then we lay around like beached whales until we worked up the energy to take a short walk. Over pie and herbal tea, the talk turned to law, and Martha's friend Vicky held forth on environmental regulation while a couple of professors argued over affirmative action.

Finally, too full and contented for intelligent conversation, we lay in front of the fire and roasted chestnuts. Vicky and Claudia played piano duets; Laurie sang a ballad, and I thought about planets and galaxies. Worries about computer networks and spies seemed unreal in this warm world of friends, food, and music. A down-home Thanksgiving in Berkeley.

At the lab, I forgot about the hacker. He'd been gone for almost a month. Why? I didn't know.

The astronomers fiddled with their new graphics display, studying ways to strengthen their telescope. By now, I'd figured out how to animate the display, so they could zoom in on interesting parts, and rotate it on the screen. Object-oriented programming—by accident, I'd learned a new buzzword. The astronomers didn't care, but I had to give a talk to computer folks.

On Wednesday, I was all set to dazzle the other systems folks. I'd memorized all the jargon and set up the display so that it wouldn't foul up at the last minute.

A dozen computer whizzes showed up at three o'clock. The display system worked flawlessly, and the Caltech software loaded without a hitch. Computer people are accustomed to boring talks on databases and structured programming, so this three-dimensional color graphics display amazed them all.

Twenty-five minutes into the show, I was answering a question about the programming language ("It's object oriented, whatever that means . . .") when my pocket pager beeped.

Three beeps. Morse code for the letter S. S for Sventek. The hacker had connected to our system on the Sventek account.

Damn. A month of quiet, and the SOB shows up now.

Well, the show must go on. I couldn't acknowledge that I was still chasing the hacker—my three-week allowance had long ago been used up. But I had to get over to the monitoring post and watch what he was doing.

Of course. I stopped showing pretty pictures and began describing an obscure area of galactic astronomy. It took five minutes, but people began to squirm and yawn. My boss looked at his watch, and ended the meeting. Another application for advanced astronomy.

I dodged the gang in the hallway, and slipped into the switchyard. The hacker wasn't active on any of my monitors.

He'd left his footprints though. The printer showed him here for two minutes. Long enough to check out our system. He checked that the system manager wasn't around, then looked for the Gnu-Emacs hole—it still hadn't been patched. And he listed his four stolen accounts—no change there. Then, poof, gone.

No way to trace him after the fact. But the monitor that caught him was on the Tymnet line. So he was coming in on the same line. Was his path from Mitre to AT&T to Pacific Bell to Tymnet?

Time to call Mitre. Bill Chandler answered. "No, he couldn't have used our modems. They're all turned off."

Really? Easy to check. I called Mitre through Tymnet. I could still reach into Mitre's network, but Bill had indeed shut off his modems. A hacker could fool with his computers, but couldn't get out. My hacker had come from somewhere else.

Should I feel elated or despondent? The varmint was back with super-user privileges. But maybe this time I'd nail the bastard. If he kept returning to his roost, I'd trace him for sure.

I suppressed my vindictive feelings toward my unseen adversary. Research was the answer. The question wasn't, "Who's doing it?" I'd get no satisfaction if a postcard showed up saying, "Joe Blatz is breaking into your computer."

No, the problem was to build the tools to find who was there. What if I traced the whole connection, and it turned out to be a red herring? At least, I'd understand the phenomenon. Not all research yields exactly the results you expect.

My tools were sharp. The alarms triggered as soon as he entered his stolen account names. If they failed, a backup program hidden behind my Unix-8 computer would detect him within a minute. When the hacker touched the tripwire, my beeper told me about it instantly.

The hacker could hide, but he couldn't violate physics. Every connection had to start somewhere. Whenever he showed up, he exposed himself. I just had to be alert.

The fox was back. This hound was ready for the chase.

# 28

AFTER A MONTH'S DISAPPEARANCE, THE HACKER WAS back on my system. Martha wasn't happy about this; she began to see a mechanical rival in my pocket pager. "How long before you're free from that electronic leash?"

Just a couple more weeks. It'll be over by New Year's Day, for sure." Even after three months of chasing, I still thought I was close to the end.

I was sure I'd catch him: since the hacker couldn't hide behind Mitre anymore, the next trace would move us one step closer. He didn't know it, but he was running out of space. In a few more weeks he'd be mine.

Friday, December 5, the hacker showed up again at 1:21 in the afternoon. He raised periscope, looking for our system manager, and then listed our password file.

This was the second time he'd ripped off my password file. What for? There's no key to unlock these encrypted passwords: they're just goulash until they're decrypted. And our encryption software is a one-way trapdoor: its mathematical scrambling is precise, repeatable, and irreversible.

Did he know something that I didn't? Did this hacker have a magic decryption formula? Unlikely. If you turn the crank of a sausage machine backwards, pigs won't come out the other end.

Four months from now, I'd realize what he was doing, but for now, I had my hands full trying to trace him.

Nine minutes after he showed up, he disappeared. Enough time for me to trace the connection to Tymnet. But their network sorcerer, Ron Vivier, was taking a long lunch. So Tymnet couldn't make the trace. Another chance lost.

Ron returned my call an hour later. "It was an office party," he said. "I thought you'd given up on chasing this guy."

I explained the month-long hiatus. "We tracked him into Mitre, and they plugged the hole he was using. Stopped him for a month, but now he's back."

"Why don't you cork up your hole, too?"

"Guess I ought to," I said, "but we've sunk three months into this project. We can't be far from solving it."

Ron had been in the middle of every trace. He'd invested plenty of time, all voluntary. We didn't pay Tymnet to trace hackers.

"Hey, Cliff, how come you never call me at night?" Ron had given me his home number, but I only called him at his office.

"Guess the hacker doesn't show up at night. I wonder why." He started me thinking. My logbook recorded every time the hacker had shown up. On the average, when was he active?

I'd remembered him on at 6 A.M. and at 7 P.M. But never at midnight. Isn't midnight operation the very image of a hacker?

As of December 6, the hacker had connected to us one-hundred-thirty-five times. Enough times for a statistical analysis of his work habits. In a couple of hours, I'd entered all the dates and times into a program. Now just average them.

Well, not exactly a simple average. What's the average of 6 A.M. and 6 P.M.? Is it noon or midnight? But this is bread and butter for statistics folks. Dave Cleveland showed me the right program, and I spent the rest of the day making all sorts of averages.

On the average, the hacker showed up at noon, Pacific time. Because of daylight savings time, I could stretch this to 12:30 or even 1 P.M., but there was no way that he was an evening person. Though sometimes he showed up in the morning, and occasionally at night (I still resented him spoiling Halloween for me!), he generally worked in the early afternoon. On the average, he stayed connected twenty minutes. A lot of two- or three-minute connections, and a few two-hour runs.

So what does this mean? Suppose he lives in California. Then he's hacking during the day. If he's on the East Coast, he's three hours ahead of us, so he works around three or four in the afternoon.

This doesn't make sense. He'd work at night to save on long-distance telephone fees. To avoid network congestion. And to avoid detection. Yet he brazenly breaks in during the day. Why?

Confidence? Perhaps. After he made certain that no system operator was present, he roamed the insides of my computer without hesitation. Arrogance? Possibly. He was shameless in reading others' mail and copying their data. But this hardly could account for his showing up during midday.

Maybe he felt he was less likely to be noticed when dozens of others were using our computer. Although lots of programs ran at night, most of these were batch jobs, submitted during the day and postponed until evening. By midnight, only a couple of night owls were logged in.

Whatever his reason, this peculiar habit made life slightly easier for me. Fewer interruptions when sleeping with Martha. Less need to call the police at night. And a greater chance that I'd be around when he showed up.

As we chopped onions at the kitchen table, I told Martha about my results. "I'm tailing a hacker that avoids the dark."

She wasn't impressed. "This doesn't make sense. If the guy's an amateur, then he'd be breaking in during off-hours."

"So you say he's a professional, keeping regular office hours?" I could picture someone punching a time card in the morning, spending eight hours breaking into computers, then punching out.

"No," Martha said, "even professional burglars keep odd hours. What I want to know is whether his hours change on weekends."

I couldn't answer that one. I'd have to go back to the lab, cull out all the weekend times, and average them separately.

"But suppose the hacker really only shows up around noon," Martha continued. "It might be nighttime where he lives."

When it's noon in California, where is it evening? Even

astronomers get confused by time changes, but I know it gets later as you move east. We're eight hours behind Greenwich, so lunchtime in Berkeley is bedtime in Europe. Is the hacker coming from Europe?

Improbable, but worth thinking about. A month or two ago, I'd measured the distance to the hacker by timing echoes when the hacker ran Kermit. What I found didn't make much sense: the hacker seemed to be around six thousand miles away.

Made sense now. It's five thousand miles to London. Small world.

But how do you get from Europe into our networks? Phoning across the Atlantic would cost a fortune. And why go through Mitre?

I had to keep reminding myself that these were just weak pointers. Nothing conclusive. But it was hard to fall asleep that evening. Tomorrow I'd go up to the lab and reread my logbook with a new hypothesis: the hacker might be coming in from abroad.

# 29

SATURDAY MORNING I WOKE UP NESTLED IN MARTHA'S arms. We fooled around for a while, and I made a batch of my quasi-stellar waffles—the ones that are advertised all over the Andromeda galaxy.

Despite the early hour, I couldn't resist heading over to the lab. I bicycled along side streets, scanning for yard sales. Right along the way, someone was selling their household, well preserved from the 1960s. Rock posters, bell-bottom jeans, even a Nehru jacket. I picked up a Captain Midnight Secret Decoder Ring for two dollars. It still had an endorsement for Ovaltine.

At the lab, I started analyzing the hacker's log-in times, separating out his weekend sessions. It took a while, but I managed to show that on weekdays he showed up from noon to three P.M.; on weekends he'd show up as early as six A.M.

Suppose this sneak lived in Europe. He might break in at any hour on the weekend, but confine himself to evenings during the week. The log-in times agreed with this, but agreement is hardly proof. A dozen other theories could satisfy the data.

I'd ignored one source of information. The Usenet is a nationwide network of thousands of computers, tied together by telephone links. It's a wide-area electronic bulletin board, a sort of networked classified newspaper. Anyone can post notes; every hour, dozens of new messages show up divided into categories like Unix Bugs, Macintosh Programs, and Science Fiction Discussions. There's nobody in charge: any Unix computer can link to Usenet, and post messages to the rest. Anarchy in action.

System managers post a lot of the messages, so you'll find notes like, "We have a Foobar model 37 computer, and we're trying to hook up a Yoyodyne tape to it. Can anyone help?" Often someone will respond, solving the problem in minutes. Other times, it's a lone voice in an electronic wilderness.

I couldn't post a note saying, "Hackers are breaking into my computer. Any idea where they're coming from?" Since most systems folks read these bulletin boards, the hacker would find out right away.

But I could scan for information. I started a text search, hunting for the word, "Hack." Any messages with that keyword would pop out.

Oops. Bad choice of keyword. The word hacker is ambiguous. Computer people use it as a compliment to a creative programmer; the public uses it to describe a skunk that breaks into computers. My search turned up lots of the former usage and not many of the latter.

A few useful notes turned up, though. A guy in Toronto reported that his computer had been attacked by a group from Germany. They called themselves the Chaos Computer Club and seemed to be technocratic vandals. Another note talked about hackers in Finland trying to extort money from a corporation by holding their computers hostage. A third mentioned that a hacker in London ran a credit card scam, where he sold credit card information over the telephone lines.

None of these seemed to describe what my hacker was doing. Nor was it much comfort to realize that others face similar varmints.

I walked out on the roof of the building and looked out over the bay. Below me, Berkeley and Oakland. Across the water, San Francisco and the Golden Gate Bridge. For all I knew, someone within a few blocks was playing an elaborate practical joke on me. I was fiddling with my secret decoder ring when my beeper went off. Three dots. Sventek again, and on my Unix machine.

I ran down the staircase and into the switchyard. The hacker was just logging in. Quickly I called Ron Vivier at Tymnet. No answer. Of course, dummy, it's a Saturday. Another call to his home. A woman answered.

"I need to talk to Ron right away. He's got to make a panic network trace right now." I was out of breath and panting. Five flights of stairs.

She was taken aback. "He's in the yard washing the van. I'll get him." A few centuries later, Ron showed up. There were a couple kids screaming in the background.

"I've got a live one for you," I gasped. "Just trace my port 14."

"Right. It'll take a minute. Good thing I've got two phone lines here." I hadn't realized that he didn't have a whole switchboard at his fingertips. He must be dialing into his computer.

Another couple eons passed, and Ron came back on the line. "Hey Cliff, are you certain that it's the same guy?"

I watched him searching for the word SDI on our computer. "Yes, it's him." I was still wheezing.

"He's coming in from a gateway that I've never heard of. I'm locked onto his network address, so it doesn't matter if he hangs up. But the guy's coming from somewhere strange."

"Where's that?"

"I don't know. It's Tymnet node 3513, which is a strange one. I'll have to look it up in our directory." In the background, Ron's keyboard clicked. "Here it is. That node connects to ITT node DNIC 3106. He's coming from the ITT IRC."

"Huh? What's that mean to me?" His ante was beyond my purse.

"Oh, I'm sorry," Ron said. "I keep thinking that I'm talking to another Tymnet guy. Your hacker is coming from outside the Tymnet system. He's entering Tymnet from a communications line operated by the International Telephone and Telegraph company."

"So what?"

"Tymnet moves data between countries using International Record Carriers, or IRCs. Once, international agreements forced us to use IRCs; now we choose the cheapest carrier around. The IRCs are the go-betweens that link countries together."

"Are you saying that the hacker is coming from abroad?"

"No doubt. ITT takes a Westar downlink. . . ." Ron spoke quickly and used plenty of acronyms.

"Huh? What's that mean?" I interrupted.

"You know," Ron said, "Westar 3." I didn't know, but I was learning by listening.

He continued, "The communications satellite over the Atlantic. It handles ten or twenty thousand phone calls at once."

"So my hacker is coming from Europe?"

"For sure."

"Where?"

"That's the part I don't know, and I probably can't find out. But hold on, and I'll see what's there." More keyboard clicks.

Ron came back to the phone. "Well, ITT identifies the line as DSEA 744031. That's their line number. It can connect to either Spain, France, Germany, or Britain."

"Well, which is it?"

"Sorry, I don't know. You'll have to call ITT. In three days, they'll send us billing information, and then I can find out. Meantime, I can't tell you much more than that."

From twenty-three thousand miles over Brazil, the Westar-3 satellite watches Europe and America at the same time. It relays microwave signals between the continents, each signal in its own channel. ITT, the multinational giant, leases a few thousand of Westar's channels.

Ron went back to washing his car and I crossed the room to the monitoring printer. Twenty minutes had passed, and my hacker hadn't wasted a moment. Everything he typed was saved on my printer and displayed on my computer's screen. If he started to wreck our system, I could pull his plug by just reaching behind the table.

But he wasn't interested in my lab's computer. He first made sure that nobody was watching him by seeing who was logged on, and listing their jobs. Good thing my monitors were concealed.

Then, he went directly to our network links and logged into the Network Information Center. This time, he searched for key-words like CIA, ICBM, ICBMCOM, NORAD, and WSMR. After picking up a few computer names, he methodically tried to log into each of them, using default account names like Guest and Visitor. He didn't get far. Five systems bumped him off with bad passwords.

Like a month ago, when he spent a while trying to get into the Army's White Sands Missile Range. Over and over, he tried to log onto their computers. He had no problem finding the names of people working there—he just scanned the network directory. But he couldn't guess their passwords.

The Milnet connects to thousands of computers. Yet he wanted to get into White Sands. Why bother?

Why's this guy only interested in military stuff? There's a whole world of computers, yet he's targeting Army bases. Something serious is going on—it would be a long time before I found out what.

After half an hour, he gave up on White Sands and tried to get back into our Elxsi computer. On Halloween, he'd sneaked in there and added a new account.

Along with the physicist that managed the Elxsi, I'd planted a trap there. The computer looked like it was still wide open, but when the hacker touched it, it slowed down. The more the hacker tried to use it, the slower it went.

Our electronic tar baby worked like an ace. The hacker tried to log into the Elxsi, and the machine coasted slower and slower. Not quite halting; he could see that he was making progress, but at an appalling rate. Elxsi, Inc. would have been ashamed—theirs is the zippiest of all minicomputers.

Took him ten minutes to throw in the towel. But he came right back to our Unix machines, and right out onto the Milnet. This time, he spent an hour trying to break into forty-two military computers, literally around the world.

With a single command, *telnet,* he'd connect to a military system, and spend one minute trying default account names and passwords. If he couldn't guess his way in with four tries, he'd go on to the next computer.

He knew how to guess. When greeted by the Unix response *login:*, he'd try default accounts like *guest, root, who,* and *visitor.* The Vax-VMS operating system greets you with *Username:*; on those systems he tried the defaults *system, field, service,* and *user.* He'd done this before, and I'm sure that hackers will do it again.

If the Milnet was a roadway, connecting thousands of computers together, then he was a burglar, patiently visiting each house. He'd twist the front doorknob to see if it was unlocked, then walk around and try the back door. Maybe try lifting a window or two.

Most of the time, he found the doors and windows locked. After a minute pushing them, he'd move on to the next place. Nothing sophisticated: he wasn't picking locks or digging under foundations. Just taking advantage of people who left their doors open.

One after another, he tried military computers: Army Ballistics Research Lab; U.S. Naval Academy; Naval Research Lab; Air Force Information Services Group; and places with bizarre acronyms, like WWMCCS and Cincusnaveur. (Cincus? Or was it Circus? I never found out.)

Today wasn't lucky for him. None of his guesses panned out. Forty-two at-bats, forty-two outs.

Clearly, he was going to be on a long time. I reached into my pocket for a Milky Way candy bar—what else, for an astronomer?—and sat back to watch the hacker on my green monitor. I could imagine the far end of that long connection. The hacker sitting behind his monitor, watching the same green characters on his screen. Probably chewing on his own Milky Way bar. Or smoking a Benson and Hedges.

It was Saturday, but I figured I'd try to call the Air Force Office of Special Investigations. They'd told me to call if anything bubbled up, and the cauldron was boiling now. But no answer. Anyway, there wasn't much they could do. I needed to know who was at the other end of ITT's satellite channel.

Only two people knew where I was—Ron Vivier and Martha. Ron was washing his car. So when the phone rang in the switchyard, I answered, "Hello, sweetie!"

Silence, then, "Aah, I've probably got the wrong number. I'm looking for Cliff Stoll." A man's voice with a profound English accent. Had some British spies found me? Or was the hacker in London? What a mindgame.

Turned out to be nothing so subtle. Ron Vivier had called

Tymnet's international department, where their experts in transatlantic communications took over. One of Tymnet's international specialists, Steve White, started tracing.

Steve works in Vienna, Virginia, making certain that Tymnet's customers can communicate worldwide. He grew up in Dorset, England, and first learned to program a computer by mail: he'd write a program at school, send it to a computer center, and receive the printout a week later. Steve claims that this makes you write good programs the first time, since each mistake wastes a week of your time.

Steve had studied zoology at the University of London, and found it just like astronomy: fascinating but impoverishing. So he moved to the states, and began working in his other specialty: digital communications. Steve troubleshoots international communications systems.

There's a dozen ways to tie computers together—telephones, optical fibers, satellite links, and microwave links. At my laboratory, I didn't care how my data moved, so long as a scientist in Podunk could reach my computer in Berkeley. It was Steve's job to make sure that data funnelled in one end of Tymnet reached me at the far end.

Every communications company has someone like Steve White, or at least the successful ones do. To him, the network is a gossamer web of connections: invisible threads that appear and disappear every few seconds. Each of his three thousand nodes have to be able to instantly talk to each other.

You could build a network by stringing a wire to every computer, and then connecting them together in one big switch. With a thousand terminals at our lab, that's exactly how we did things; a zillion wires in the switchyard. Local phone companies still work that way: they route all the neighborhood telephone wires to a single building, where mechanical switches make connections.

With thousands of computers spread around the country, Tymnet couldn't have a central exchange. Mechanical switches were out of the question: too slow and unreliable. Instead, Tymnet creates virtual circuits between computers. Across the country, Tymnet's switching computers, called nodes, communicate with each other over leased cables.

When your computer sends a message to mine, Tymnet treats it like a piece of mail: it squeezes your data into an envelope and sends it to one of Tymnet's nodes. There, Tymnet's computers stamp the envelope with the forwarding address, along with your own calling address. Like a post office running at the speed of light, special software grabs each envelope and tosses it to a node nearer its destination. When the envelope finally reaches my computer, Tymnet removes the address, opens the envelope, and delivers the data.

There's not one giant switch hooking your computer to mine. Instead, each network node knows where to toss every data packet—a central computer tells it the shortest path.* In crossing the country, a dozen Tymnet nodes may forward an envelope.

When your computer's silent, the network sits back and handles other envelopes, but each Tymnet node still remembers where to send your packets. Every node has a thousand pigeonholes, and is constantly sorting envelopes.

There's no wire to trace; rather, there's a thread of addresses between your computer and mine. Ron and Steve, the Tymnet guys, could trace the hacker's connections by untangling this thread. The tail of the thread originated at an ITT earth station. Beyond there, who could tell?

---

*The Internet, too, doesn't have one central switch, but instead has many local switches, all around the country. The lowest-level switches (really, computers) are tied together, forming local networks. These, in turn, are grouped together into regional networks, which connect to national backbones. The Internet, then, connects networks together—like the Arpanet, the Milnet, and its hundred other networks.

While Tymnet (and its many cousins) builds virtual circuits from one point to another, the Internet is hierarchical. An Internet message moves from local roads, to state roads, onto the highways, and then down through state roads to a specific street address.

Envelopes for messages on Tymnet can be simple—once the virtual circuit is established, each node knows where to toss the message. Internet messages, however, have envelopes with complete destination and return addresses, so that each network can figure out how to send it one step closer to the ultimate destination. Those more complex envelopes let Internet packets get through even when the system's congested.

Which is better? Don't ask me.

# 30

SO AFTER MONTHS OF TRACKING, THE HACKER'S COMING from Europe. He was still on my computer, trying to chisel into the Navy Research Labs, when Steve White called.

"Tymnet's connection begins at ITT," Steve said.

"Yes, Ron Vivier already told me that. But he says that it could be from any of four countries."

"Ron can't trace any farther," Steve said, typing on his terminal. "I'll do the trace myself."

"You can trace ITT's lines?"

"Sure. The international record carriers give Tymnet permission to trace their links, in case of problems. I'll just log into ITT's switch and see who's calling." Steve made it sound simple.

I kept watching the hacker on my screen, hoping that he wouldn't hang up while Steve made the trace.

Steve came back on the line. In his modulated, almost theatric British accent, he said, "Your hacker has the calling address DNIC dash 2624 dash 542104214."

I'd grown accustomed to not understanding the jargon, but on principle, I dutifully wrote it down in my logbook. Fortunately, Steve translated for me.

"You see, as far as Tymnet's concerned, the hacker's coming from ITT's satellite. But from inside of ITT's computers, I can see past their satellite link and trace the connection all the way back."

Steve had X-ray vision. Satellites didn't stop him.

"That DNIC number is the data network identifier code. It's just like a telephone number—the area code tells where the call originates."

"So where's the hacker coming from?"

"Germany."

"East or West?"

"West Germany. The German Datex network."

"What's that?" Steve lived in a universe of networks.

"Datex is the German equivalent of Tymnet. It's their national network to connect computers together," Steve explained. "We'll have to call the Bundespost to find out more."

I forgot about the hacker on my computer, and listened to Steve. "You see, the DNIC completely identifies the computer that's making the call. The first four digits tell me that it's from the German Datex network. The Bundespost can look up that number in their catalog, and tell us exactly where it's located."

"Who's the Bundespost?" It sounded vaguely German.

"They're the German national postal service. The government communications monopoly."

"Why's the post office running networks?" I wondered out loud. Here, the post office delivers letters, not data.

"In a lot of countries, the post office owns the phone service. An historical outgrowth of government regulation. Germany's probably the most centralized of all. You can't get a telephone answering machine without government approval."

"So the hacker is coming from a government computer?"

"No, it's a private computer, probably. But the communications link is operated by the Bundespost. And that's our next step. We'll ring up the Bundespost in the morning."

I liked how he said "we" rather than "you."

Steve and I talked for a solid hour. Listening to his descriptions of the network was far more interesting than watching the hacker scan my computer for keywords like SDI. Steve wasn't a technician, but a craftsperson; no, an artist who expressed himself through an invisible tapestry of electronic threads.

To hear Steve speak of it, the network is a living, growing organism. It senses trouble and responds to its environment. To him, the network's elegance lay in its simplicity. "Each node just passes data on to the next.

"Every time your visitor types a key," Steve said, "a character bounces from Datex to ITT to Tymnet and into your system. And between keystrokes, our network wastes no time on him."

With thousands of conversations threaded through his system and millions of bits of data, not one dialogue was lost, and not a byte of data spilled out. The network kept track of the connections, and you couldn't slip through the cracks.

All the same, Steve seemed pessimistic about completing a successful trace. "We know where he connects into the system. But there's a couple possibilities there. The hacker might be at a computer in Germany, simply connected over the German Datex network. If that's the case, then we've got him cold. We know his address, the address points to his computer, and the computer points to him."

"Seems unlikely," I said, thinking of my trace to Mitre.

"It is unlikely. More likely, the hacker is coming into the German Datex network through a dial-in modem."

Just like Tymnet, Datex lets anyone dial into their system, and connect to computers on the network. Perfect for business people and scientists. And hackers.

"The real problem is in German law," Steve said. "I don't think they recognize hacking as a crime."

"You're kidding, of course."

"No," he said, "a lot of countries have outdated laws. In Canada, a hacker that broke into a computer was convicted of stealing electricity, rather than trespassing. He was prosecuted only because the connection had used a microwatt of power from the computer."

"But breaking into a computer is a crime in the USA."

"Yes, but do you think the hacker will be extradited for that?" Steve asked. "Look at the support you got from the FBI. Be serious, Cliff."

Steve's pessimism was contagious. But his trace jagged my spirits: so what if we couldn't nail the hacker—our circle was closing around him.

This hacker, though, knew nothing of our trace. He finally disconnected at 5:22, after two hours of twisting doorknobs and scanning files. My printer captured everything, but the real news was Steve White's work.

Germany. I ran over to the library and dug out an atlas. Germany's nine hours ahead of us. The hacker showed up around noon or 1 P.M.; for him, it's 9 or 10 P.M. He's probably taking advantage of cheap rates.

Poring over the atlas, I remembered Maggie Morley recognizing the hacker's password. "Jaeger—it's a German word meaning hunter." The answer had been right in front of me, but I'd been blind.

This explained the timing of the acknowledgment echoes when the hacker used the Kermit file transfers. I'd measured 6000 miles to the hacker, though I'd never relied much on that figure. I should have. Germany was 5200 miles from Berkeley.

Not just blind. Deaf as well.

I'd been gathering facts. Not interpreting them.

Sitting alone in the library, I was suddenly deeply embarrassed over sending my sister on a wild-goose chase, searching for a high school kid in Virginia; and the Berkeley detectives, running around campus with revolvers.

I'd messed up. For months, I'd scoured North America, searching for the hacker. Dave Cleveland kept telling me, "The hacker's not from the West Coast." No, not by 5200 miles.

Some details were still fuzzy, but I understood how he operated. Somewhere in Europe, the hacker called into the German Datex network. He asked for Tymnet, and the Bundespost made the connection through the international record carrier. Once he reached the States, he connected to my laboratory and hacked his way around the Milnet.

Mitre must have been his stopover point. I could see how he made the connection. He'd entered the German Datex system, asked for Tymnet, and then logged into Mitre. Once there, he could explore their computers at his leisure. When he grew tired of reading the defense contractor's reports, he could dial out from Mitre, connecting anywhere in North America—with Mitre picking up the tab.

But who paid for his transatlantic connections? According to Steve, his sessions cost fifty or one hundred dollars an hour. Walking back to the computer room, I realized that I was following a well-heeled hacker. Or a clever thief.

Now I realized why Mitre paid for a thousand one-minute-long phone calls. The hacker would connect to Mitre, and instruct their system to phone another computer. When it answered, he would try to log in with a default name and password. Usually he failed, and went on to another phone number. He'd been scanning computers, with Mitre picking up the tab.

But he'd left a trail. On Mitre's phone bills.

The path led back to Germany, but it might not end there. Conceivably, someone in Berkeley had called Berlin, connected to the Datex network, connected through Tymnet and came back to Berkeley. Maybe the start of the path was in Mongolia. Or Moscow. I couldn't tell. For the present, my working hypothesis would be Germany.

And he scanned for *military* secrets. Could I be following a spy? A real spy, working for *them*—but who's them? . . . Jeez—I didn't even know who spies work for.

Three months ago, I'd seen some mouse droppings in my accounting files. Quietly, we watched this mouse, seeing him sneak through our computer, and out through a hole and into the military networks and computers.

At last I knew what this rodent was after. And where he was from. I'd been mistaken.

This wasn't a mouse. It was a rat.

# 31

I SPENT SATURDAY EVENING FILLING IN MY LOGBOOK. Now I could tie up loose ends. Anniston's search wouldn't turn up a hacker in Alabama: they were off by five thousand miles. Stanford's hacker was certainly a different guy . . . my hacker would have homework in German, not English. And there wasn't much use in calling around Berkeley, looking for someone named Hedges.

Probably the wrong name. Certainly the wrong continent.

Our stack of printouts was a foot thick. I'd carefully sorted and dated each listing, but I'd never combed through all the listings at one sitting. Most of it was dreary file listings and one-at-a-time guesses at passwords.

Is it easy to break into computers?

Elementary, my dear Watson. Elementary, and tediously dull.

I didn't return home until 2 A.M. Martha waited up, piecing a quilt.

"Out with a hussy?"

"Yeah," I replied. "Spent the day with a mysterious foreigner."

"So the hacker's from Europe after all." She'd guessed what I'd been doing.

"He might live anywhere in the world," I said, "but my bets are on Germany."

I wanted to sleep late Sunday morning, curled up with

Martha. But, dammit, my pager sounded at 10:44, a harsh, insistent squeal followed by a Morse code greeting. The hacker was at it again. In my Unix-5 computer.

I jumped into the dining room and dialed Steve White at his home. While his phone was ringing, I fired up my Macintosh computer. On the fifth ring, Steve answered.

"The hacker is live again, Steve," I told him.

"OK, Cliff. I'll start the trace and call you back."

As soon as I hung up, I reached for my Macintosh. The beast acted like a remote terminal, thanks to a modem and a stellar software program called Red Ryder. Red automagically dialed my lab's computer, logged onto the Vax, and showed me what was up. There was my hacker, traipsing through the Milnet.

Logged on like that, I appeared like an ordinary user, so the hacker could see me if he looked. So I disconnected quickly. Ten seconds was enough to see what my visitor was up to.

Steve called back in a couple minutes. The line didn't come from the ITT international record carrier; today it was from RCA.

"RCA doesn't use the Westar satellite," Steve said. "They talk through the Comsat satellite." Yesterday he used Westar, today Comsat. One elusive hacker—switching communications satellites from day to day.

But I had my facts wrong, and Steve set me straight.

"Your hacker doesn't have any choice in the matter," Steve explained. "To provide redundant service, we use a variety of international routes."

With every call, Tymnet's traffic takes a different route across the Atlantic. As a customer I would never notice, but traffic is spread across four or five satellites and cables.

"Oh, like interstate trucking, before deregulation."

"Don't get me started," Steve said angrily. "You wouldn't believe the international communications laws."

"So where's the hacker coming from today?"

"Germany. Same address. Same place."

There wasn't much more to do. I couldn't monitor the hacker from home, and Steve had finished the trace. I sat shivering next to the Macintosh. Where do I go next?

To the lab. And quick. I scribbled a note for Martha ("The game is afoot"), threw on some jeans, and hopped on my bike.

I wasn't fast enough. The hacker disappeared five minutes before I arrived. I should have stayed in bed.

Well, I paged through Sunday morning's listings—Sunday evening for him—and saw him up to his old tricks. One by one, trying to break into military computers by guessing obvious passwords. Tedious. About as interesting as guessing locker combinations.

Since he'd shown up in the morning, I might as well wait around and see if he'd return. Based on my statistics, he'd be back within an hour or two.

Sure enough, he returned at 1:16 in the afternoon. My pager sounded off, and I ran to the switchyard. There he was, logging into the stolen Sventek account.

As usual, he looked around for others on the computer. Had I been connected from my home, he'd have noticed me. But from my high ground in the switchyard, I was undetectable. He couldn't pierce my electronic veil.

Confident that nobody was watching him, he headed straight out through our Milnet port. With a few commands, he searched the Milnet directory for any locations with the acronym "COC." Huh? I'd never seen such a word. Did he misspell something?

I needn't have wondered. The network information computer cranked for a minute or two, and then returned a half dozen military Command Operations Centers. He kept searching for other keywords: "Cheyenne," "icbm," "combat," "kh11," "Pentagon," and "Colorado."

Sitting there watching him paw through the Milnet directory, I felt like I was watching someone thumbing through the yellow pages. Which numbers would he dial?

All of them. Every keyword brought up a few computer addresses, and after he'd found thirty of them, he closed his connection to the Milnet directory. Then, once again, he methodically tried to break into each of the sites; the Air Force Data Services Center in Arlington, Virginia, the Army Ballistics Research Lab, an Air Force training center in Colorado Springs, the Navy Pacific Monitoring Center in Hawaii, and thirty other places.

But again, he had no luck. By chance, he'd picked places which didn't have obvious passwords. It must have been a frustrating evening for him.

Finally, he tried to break into his old haunt, the Anniston Army Base. Five times. No luck.

So he gave up on the Milnet and returned to messing with my Unix computer. I watched the cuckoo lay its egg: once again, he manipulated the files in my computer to make himself super-user. His same old trick: use the Gnu-Emacs move-mail to substitute his tainted program for the system's atrun file. Five minutes later, shazam! He was system manager.

Now I had to watch him carefully. With his illicit privileges, he could destroy my system, either by accident or on purpose. And it would only take one command, like *rm**—erase all files.

For now, though, he restrained himself. He just printed out phone numbers of different computers, and logged off.

Uh oh. He took a list of telephone numbers that our computer often connects to.

But Mitre had cut off their outbound telephone service. He must have discovered this by now. Yet he still collected phone numbers. So he must have some other way to make phone calls. Mitre wasn't his only stepping stone to the telephone system.

He came back to my system after fifteen minutes. Wherever he'd gone, none of his calls had panned out. Bad passwords, I'll bet.

As soon as he returned, he started Kermit running. He was going to copy a file back to his computer. My password file again? No, he wanted my network software. He tried to export the source code to two programs: *telnet* and *rlogin.*

Whenever one of my scientists connects through the Milnet, they use *telnet* or *rlogin.* Both of them let someone remotely log into a foreign computer. Each of them transfers commands from a user over to a foreign computer. Either is a perfect place to plant a Trojan horse.

By changing a couple lines of code in our *telnet* program, he could make a password grabber. Whenever my scientists connected to a distant system, his insidious program would stash their passwords into a secret file. Oh, they'd log in successfully. But the next time the hacker came into my Berkeley computer, there'd be a list of passwords waiting to be picked up.

Line by line, I watched Kermit shovel the program over to the hacker. No need to time the transfer—I now knew those long delays were caused by satellite and the long hop into Germany.

Watching him, I got annoyed. No, pissed off. He was stealing my software. Sensitive software at that. If he wanted it, he'd have to swipe it from someone else.

But I couldn't just kill Kermit. He'd notice that right away. Now that I was closing in on him, I especially didn't want to tip my hand.

I had to act fast. How do I stop a burglar without letting on that I'm watching?

I found my key chain and reached over to the wires connected to the hacker's line. Jangling the keys across the connector, I shorted out his circuit for an instant. This added just enough noise to confuse the computer, but not enough to kill the connection. To him, it would look like some characters had become garbled. Misspelled words and unintelligible text—the computer equivalent of radio static.

He'd blame it on network interference. He might try again, but eventually, he'd give up. When the connections are lousy, there's no use in talking long distance.

It worked like a charm. I'd jangle my keys, he'd see noise, and his computer would ask for a replay of the last line. I was careful to let a little data get through. But so slowly that the whole file would take all night.

The hacker disconnected and tried again. No way. He couldn't make it through my fog, and he couldn't figure out where the noise was coming from.

He gave up trying to steal our software, and contented himself with just looking around. He found a pathway into Berkeley's Opal computer, but didn't explore it.

Now there's a strange one. The Berkeley Opal computer is the home of some real computer research. You don't have to look far to find some of the finest communications programs, academic software, and games. Apparently this hacker didn't care for the things students might be interested in. But show him something military, and he goes wild.

It was 5:51 in the afternoon when the hacker finally called it quits. I can't say that his every frustration gave me satisfaction. Rather, he responded the way I expected. My work was slowly yielding a solution.

Steve White traced the connections throughout the day. Just as in the morning, they all came from Germany.

"Any chance that it's someone from another European country?" I asked, knowing the answer in advance.

"The hacker could be from anywhere," Steve answered. "My trace only proves a connection from Berkeley into Germany."

"Any idea where in Germany?"

Steve was as curious as I. "There's no way to tell without a directory. Every network has its own way of using the address. The Bundespost will tell us tomorrow."

"So you'll call them in the morning?" I asked, wondering whether he spoke German.

"No, it's easier to send electronic mail," Steve said. "I've already sent a message about yesterday's incident; today's will confirm it, and add a few more details. Don't worry, they'll hop to it."

Steve couldn't hang around this Sunday afternoon—he was cooking a dinner with his lady friend Lynn—which reminded me of Martha. I hadn't called home.

Martha wasn't pleased. She'd left word with Claudia that she'd be out late. Were it not for this hacker, we'd be hiking in the redwoods. Oops.

# 32

LAST NIGHT WAS A TENSE TIME AT HOME. MARTHA didn't talk much. By spending the day watching the hacker, I'd wrecked a fine Sunday afternoon. Progress with the hacker had cost dearly on the home front.

Who should I tell about the latest discovery? My boss, for sure. We'd had a bet on where the hacker came from, and I'd lost. I owed him a box of cookies.

The FBI? Well, they hadn't shown much interest, but this was now out of the league of my local police. Might as well give them another chance to ignore us.

Air Force Office of Special Investigations? They'd asked to be kept aware. With the hacker's attacks on military computers, I ought to tell someone from the defense establishment, no matter how politically awkward I felt.

If it was hard to talk to the military, then calling the CIA was a real hurdle. A month ago, I'd accepted that they needed to know about someone trying to break into their computers. I'd done my duty. Now, should I tell them that it's a foreigner?

But once again, they seemed like the right people to call. I could understand the nodes, and networks, but espionage . . . well, they don't teach you that stuff in grad school.

Surely my friends among Berkeley's flourishing left wing would tell me I'd be co-opted by the State. But I didn't exactly feel like a tool of the ruling class, unless imperialist running-dog puppets breakfasted on stale granola. I argued with myself as I biked through traffic, but my guts told me what to do: the CIA should know, and I ought to tell them.

It had been a constant struggle to get the bureaucracy to move. Maybe I could get someone to notice by waving this flag in front of all the three-letter agencies.

First I'd call the FBI. Their Oakland office hadn't been interested, but maybe I could get a rise out of Mike Gibbons in Alexandria, Virginia. But Mike was on vacation, so I left a message, figuring he'd hear it in a couple of weeks. "Just tell him that Cliff called. And that my friend has a return address in Germany." You can't fit much on a yellow while-you-were-out note.

My second pitch was to the Air Force OSI—the air force narcs. Two people got on the line, a woman's voice and a gravelly man's voice.

The woman, Ann Funk, was a special agent specializing in family crimes. In a serious tone, she explained, "Wife beating, child abuse. The Air Force has the same ugly problems as the rest of the world." Not hi-tech stuff, but even over the phone, her presence inspired respect and sympathy. Now, she worked with the OSI's computer crime group.

A month ago, I'd spoken with Jim Christy. Today, his first question to me was the same as I'd asked Steve: "East or West Germany?"

"West," I answered. "We'll know more in the next couple days."

"Where'd he get into?" Ann asked.

"Nowhere, at least that I saw. Not that he didn't try." I rattled off some of the places he tried to sneak into.

"We'll have to call you back," Jim said. "We have an office in Europe that might be able to work on this."

I'd given the Air Force a heads-up warning. Let's see what they'd do.

Time to call the CIA. Teejay's office answered—he wasn't in. Whew. Off the hook. I felt like a kid who had to give a report to the class, only to find that the teacher was sick.

But having made up my mind to tell the spooks, I called Teejay's fellow spy, Greg Fennel. Greg was in, all right.

"Look, I've got a meeting in three minutes. Keep it short." A busy day at the CIA.

"In short, we traced the hacker to Germany. Goodbye!"

"Huh? Wait! How'd you do it? Are you sure it's the same guy?"

"You've got a meeting now. We can talk tomorrow."

"Forget the meeting. Just tell me what happened. Don't embellish, don't interpret."

Easy to do when you keep a logbook. I read off my weekend's summary. An hour later, Greg was still asking questions, and had forgotten his meeting. It hit him where he lived.

"Fascinating," the spy thought out loud. "Someone in West Germany is breaking into our networks. Or at least they're coming through a West German gateway." He understood that we'd identified one link in the chain. The hacker still could be anywhere.

"Any chance that you'll take action?" I asked.

"That's for someone else to decide. I'll pass it up the chain of command, but I really don't know what will happen."

What did I expect? The CIA couldn't do much to solve the problem—they were information gatherers. I hoped they'd take over the whole mess, but that seemed unlikely. The hacker wasn't in their machines, he was in ours.

Lawrence Berkeley Laboratory was tired of wasting time on the chase. I hid my hacker work, but everyone could see that I wasn't tending to our system. Scientific software slowly decayed while I built programs to analyze what the hacker was doing.

Fearing my vitriolic boss, I polished up on quantum mechanics before talking to Roy Kerth. Maybe if we talked physics for a while, he might overlook my work on the hacker front. After all, he seemed pleased by my graphics software, even though I thought it was comparatively trivial.

But no amount of shop talk could deflect Roy's anger. He was irritated about the time I'd spent tracking this hacker. I wasn't contributing to the department—nothing that he could show off, nothing he could quantify.

At least he didn't shut me down. If anything, he seemed more eager than ever to nail this eggsucker.

I spent a few hours searching bulletin boards on the Usenet network for news about hackers, and found one note from Canada. I called the author on the phone—I didn't trust electronic mail. Bob Orr, a scientist at the University of Toronto, told a sad story.

"We connect to lots of networks, and it's tough to convince funding agencies to pay for it. Some hackers from Germany have invaded our system, changing programs and damaging our operating system."

"How'd they get in?" I asked, already suspecting the answer.

"We collaborate with the Swiss physics lab, CERN. And those vandals have thoroughly walked through their computers. They probably stole passwords to our system, and linked directly to us."

"Did they do any damage?" I asked.

"Damage! Haven't you been listening?" Bob exploded. "Our networks are delicate things—people connect to us in hope of mutual support. When someone breaks into a computer, they destroy that trust. Aside from wasting days of my time, and forcing us to disable our network connections, these hackers undermine the openness that lets us do science together."

"But did they erase your files?" I asked. "Did they change any programs?"

"Well, they modified my system to give them a backdoor password. But if you're looking for headlines like, 'Hacker wipes out entire system,' you won't find them here. These break-ins are far more insidious. They're technically skilled but ethically bankrupt programmers without any respect for others' work—or privacy. They're not destroying one or two programs. They're trying to wreck the cooperation that builds our networks."

Whew! Here was a guy who took his computing seriously. I hadn't learned much about hackers from Germany, but at last I'd spoken to someone who described them with the same expletives that I used. Bob realized that damage wasn't measured in dollars ripped off, but rather in trust lost. He didn't see this as fun and games, but a serious assault on an open society.

Once, I would have argued with Bob, saying that these were only kids fooling around. Once, I might have smiled and respected anyone who could hack around in so many computers. Not anymore.

As an aside, Bob told me the German Chaos Club was attacking the U.S. Fermilab computer as well. I called Fermilab in Illinois and talked with their system manager. "Yes, some German hackers have been giving us headaches. They call themselves the Chaos Computer Club."

"Were they spying?" I asked.

"Be serious. There's no classified work here."

I wondered. Were they vandals or spies? "Can you identify who's breaking in?"

"One guy uses the pseudonym Hagbard. Another, Pengo. I don't know their real names."

"Have you secured your system since you detected them?"

"A little. We're trying to do science, so we don't want to shut our doors to the world. But these vandals are making it tough to run an open computing center. I wish they'd pick on someone else—like the military, for instance. Or NSA."

If only he knew. "I suppose the police haven't been much help?" I asked.

"Not much. They listen, but they're not doing much."

I called Stanford and asked one of their system managers, Dan Kolkowitz, if he'd heard anything from Germany.

"Come to think of it, someone broke in a few months ago. I monitored what he did, and have a listing of him. It looks German."

Dan read the listing over the phone. Some hacker with the nom de guerre of Hagbard was sending a file of passwords to some hackers named Zombie and Pengo.

Hagbard and Pengo again. I wrote them in my logbook.

Still, it seemed like these guys were right. Those hackers were vandals who wanted to create trouble. They attacked universities and scientific institutes—easy pickings. They didn't seem interested in military targets, and didn't seem to know how to navigate the Milnet.

I realized another difference between my hacker and the Chaos Club hoodlums. My hacker seemed at home on Unix; not the Berkeley version, but Unix all the same. The vandals that Bob and Dan described seemed to only attack DEC's VMS operating systems.

From now on, I'd watch for any news about the Chaos Computer Club, but I couldn't assume that all German hackers were in league together.

One good thing was happening. One by one, I was making contact with other people who were losing sleep and slugging down Maalox over the same troubles that obsessed me. It was comforting to learn that I wasn't completely alone.

It was time to take my mind off the hacker and return to astronomy. No such luck—Mike Gibbons of the FBI called.

"I thought you were on vacation," I said.

"I am. At my folks' place, in Denver."

"Then how'd you get my message?" I wondered if the CIA had called.

"Oh, that's easy," Mike said. "We're on two-hour alert. Day or night, the office can reach me. Sometimes makes my marriage uncomfortable."

I understood all too well. My own beeper was an albatross. "Did you hear about the German connection?"

"How about telling me what happened over the weekend." (Just the facts, ma'am.)

Once again, I read from my logbook. I'd reached the part about the DNIC numbers, when Mike interrupted.

"Can you Fed-ex your logbook here?"

"Sure. I'll print out a copy and ship it to you." Easy to do when you keep your notes inside a computer.

"I'll see if we can open a case. No promises, but this looks interesting." By now I'd learned that nobody ever promised to do anything.

I printed out a copy of my logbook and dropped it off at the express office.

When I returned, the phone was ringing. It was Teejay.

"I heard the news," said my CIA contact. "You're sure your friend lives across the puddle?"

"Yes, if you mean the Atlantic." Teejay's shorthand might confuse an eavesdropper, but they threw me for a loop every time. "Almost certainly he's from Germany, and I'd be amazed if he's from the States."

"Do you know his exact location?"

"All I know is the electronic address of a computer. It's a DNIC number, whatever that means."

"Who's going to decode it for you?"

"I expect the Bundespost to tell us who's at the other end. Maybe tomorrow."

"Have you called the, uh, northern entity?"

Northern entity? Who's that? "You mean the 'F' entity?"

"No, the entity in the north. You know, Mr. Meade's place."

Meade. Fort Meade. He must mean the National Security Agency. "No, I called the 'F' entity, though."

"Good. Are they moving or sitting on their butts?"

"I don't know. They might open an investigation, but they wouldn't promise."

"They never do. I'll get in touch with them and see if we can help things along. Meanwhile, why don't you call the northern entity, and see if they'll decode that address."

Of course. NSA must have lists of every telephone number and electronic address in the world. I dialed the National Computer Security Center.

Zeke Hanson answered my call.

"Hey, Zeke, remember that you said that NSA can't help me if the hacker's coming from America?"

"Yeah, so what?"

"Well, he's from Europe."

"You mean that you've been following a foreigner on the Milnet?"

"You heard right."

"Let me call you right back."

By now, I'd gotten used to these call backs. The spooks either have secure telephone lines, or assume that I'm calling from a phone booth.

For the fifth time, I gave a how-I-spent-my-weekend talk. Zeke listened intently, obviously taking notes.

"Think the hacker's on assignment?"

"I can't say. But I suspect he's saving his printouts."

"How about sending me a list of keywords that he's searched for."

"Well, I'd be happy to, but I'm kinda busy today. Mostly, I'm trying to find the electronic address that belongs to that German DNIC number. I'd be glad to swap information."

"You mean you'll send me copies of the traffic in return for looking up that address?"

"Sure. Seems like a fair trade to me." If I simply asked for the address point blank, he'd turn me down.

It didn't work. Zeke stood his ground. "No possible way. I can't even confirm that we have such information."

Stymied. I'd have to decode that address some other way.

Frustrating, too. All day long, secret agencies were asking details from me, but nobody ever told *me* anything.

The day's flurry left me exhausted, but hopeful. This one trace to Germany opened several doors. The spooks could no longer wash this away as a minor domestic disturbance. It still might be minor, but it certainly wasn't domestic.

# 33

I'D KICKED OVER AN ANTHILL. FOR THE NEXT FEW DAYS, I couldn't get away from my phone. The spooks kept calling back, asking for technical details—how do you connect from Europe into military computers? Could I prove that the hacker came from Germany? Where did he pick up passwords? How did he become super-user?

The Air Force OSI, however, worried about how to defend the Milnet. Did the hacker get into this site or that network? What type of computers did he attack? Could we contain him by locking him out of Lawrence Berkeley Labs?

Finally, Steve White called. He'd received a terse message from the manager of the German Datex network:

"The address belongs to a computer in Bremen. We investigate."

Our circle was slowly closing.

I was off to the library again, paging through the atlas. Bremen's a port city in northern Germany, renowned for its medieval paintings and town hall. Momentarily, my thoughts flew across the Atlantic . . . these are places from history books.

On the heels of Steve's call, Mike Muuss of the Ballistic Research Laboratory called. In Aberdeen, Maryland, the Army runs a research and development laboratory; it's one of the last government labs that doesn't farm out its research to private contractors. Mike's their computer honcho.

Mike Muuss—he's famous throughout the Unix community as a pioneer in networking and as a creator of elegant programs to replace awkward ones. As Mike puts it, good programs aren't written or built. They're grown. A six-foot-tall, mustached runner, he's incredibly driven, intense, and obsessed. Mike's paid his dues on ancient versions of Unix, dating back to the '70s. When Mike talks, other wizards listen.

"We detected Joe Sventek probing our system on Sunday," Mike Muuss said. "I thought he was in England."

Do all wizards know each other? Is it telepathy?

"He is," I replied. "You detected a hacker masquerading as Joe."

"Well, keep him off the network. Boot him out."

I'd been through that before. "Closing him from my computer probably won't stop him."

"Oh, he's in a lot of computers, huh?" Mike understood.

We chatted about an hour, and I tried to hide my ignorance. Mike assumed that I knew about the Eniac, the world's first big computer. "Yep, it was right here at Ballistics Research Lab. Back in 1948. Ten years before I was born."

Eniac might have been their first world class computer, but hardly their last. Now, the Army runs a pair of Cray supercomputers—the fastest in the world. Without much modesty, Mike said, "If you want to see the Army in the year 2010, look in my computers today. It's all there."

Exactly what the hacker wanted.

Soon after that call, Chris McDonald of White Sands phoned. He'd also heard someone pounding at his doors and wanted to know what we intended to do about it.

"Nothing," I replied. "Nothing until the bastard's been arrested." A bluff, considering the chances of even discovering where the hacker lived.

The hacker had tried to chisel into eighty computers. Two system managers had detected him.

Suppose you walked along a city street trying to force doors open. How long would it take before someone called the cops? Five houses? Ten?

Well, with the help of the hacker, I knew the answer. On the computer networks, you can bang on forty doors before someone notices. With this kind of guard our computers are sitting ducks. Almost nobody's watching for intruders trying to break in.

My own lab was as blind as anyone else. The hacker had broken in, become system manager, and had full run of my Unix computer before we detected him. Even then, we'd stumbled on him by accident.

It seemed unlikely that computer people could detect hackers in their systems. Well, maybe they could, but nobody was looking. So it was fruitful to keep combing through Mitre's phone bills. The hacker had clearly called TRW, Incorporated in Redondo Beach; he'd spent hours hooked into their computer.

TRW—they're a defense contractor, working for the Air Force and NASA.

When I called Howard Siegal of TRW's signal processing facility, he'd never heard a thing.

"We can't possibly have a hacker here. We're running a secure facility."

By definition, they were secure. I'd heard it before. "Just for my curiosity, could you check your accounting logs for the past couple months?"

He agreed, though I didn't expect to hear back from him. The next morning, though, he called back with bad news.

"You were right," Howard said. "Someone's been in our system, but I can't discuss it. We're closing all access to our computer." He wouldn't describe what evidence had changed his mind, nor would he say if the hacker had become super-user.

I mentioned TRW to my friends at the Keck Observatory. Terry Mast raised his eyebrows: "Hell, they're the defense contractors that built the KH-11."

Wait a second. I'd seen KH-11 before. The hacker scanned for that keyword on Saturday. "Say, Terry, what's the KH-11?"

"It's a spy satellite. A secret spy satellite. KH stands for Key Hole. It's the eleventh in a series. It's obsolete now."

"Replaced by the KH-12, I suppose."

"Yes, in fact. Massive cost overruns, the usual. Both of them are extremely secret projects." Secrecy automatically multiplied the cost of any project.

After a while, Steve White of Tymnet called back. The German Bundespost had determined that the hacker came from the University of Bremen. The address pointed to a Vax computer, not a telephone line, but the University knew nothing of any hacker. Apparently, they doubted that a hacker was on their computer. I wasn't surprised: I'd heard it before. Give 'em a day or two, I thought.

A Vax computer, at a university. A university pointed to a student. I wondered if my gut feeling was wrong: could I just be chasing some poor sophomore prankster?

When talking to the CIA and NSA, I'd been careful to point out that possibility. It was bad enough to waste my time on this quest. I didn't want the spooks to gird up for battle, only to find some kid with a peashooter.

But the spooks asked me speculative questions. Zeke at the NSA: "Can you characterize this person's computer experience?" Well, that's easy. Just list what he's done, and how adept he appears. Then, "How old is he?" and "Is he paid or is this his hobby?" I could only guess at these: the hacker never typed in his age, weight, and occupation.

All my callers wanted to know about the hacker, even if they hadn't the slightest interest in solving the case. My logbook held the information, but was well over fifty pages. To get out from under these phone calls, I wrote a note describing what I knew about him. By bringing together observations about him, perhaps I could paint a profile of this hacker.

Some of their questions I could answer directly: he targeted the military and defense contractors. He guessed and stole passwords. He'd usually work at nights, German time.

Other answers came from indirect observations: he seemed to be in his twenties—his experience in Unix and VMS told me that. Probably out of college—he worked even when school was out. And only a smoker would choose Benson and Hedges as passwords.

I must be watching only one or two people. I inferred this by knowing that he had four purloined accounts on my system, yet he had chosen the same password for all of them. Had there been more than a couple people in on the caper, they would have chosen separate passwords.

In writing this profile, I got an impression of someone methodical and diligent. He'd been active for well over six months—and some of Mitre's records indicated almost a year. He didn't mind spending two hours on Sunday night, slowly trying to guess passwords into military computers. Tedious and tiresome work.

The NSA kept pushing at my conclusions. Zeke asked, "If he's so methodical, how do you know you're not just following some computer program?"

This one threw me for a loop. Zeke had challenged me on a point I hadn't thought of before.

Could I prove that I was following a real person?

I'd once assumed that computer hackers were brilliant geniuses, creatively searching out ways to build new programs. This guy was patient and plodding, repeatedly trying the same tricks. The same sort of behavior you'd expect to find from a computer program.

Suppose someone had programmed a computer to methodically try to log into a hundred other computers. All you'd need would be a home computer with a modem: the programming would be fairly easy. It could guess passwords (like "visitor" and "guest") about as well as a human. And it could run all night long, without anyone nearby.

A momentary panic. Could I prove that I wasn't following such a machine?

Sure. My hacker made mistakes. Occasional typing errors.

I told Zeke, "There's a human behind that keyboard, all right, who's not a perfect typist."

"Can you be sure that the hacker's in the same country as the computer?"

Zeke was on top of this, all right. His questions kept me thinking. I was watching someone, and my guts said he was in Germany. But there's no reason why he couldn't be sitting in Australia, connected into a computer in Germany.

My beeper interrupted my answer. The hacker was back. "Gotta run, Zeke!"

Down the hall again, into the switchyard. There he was, just logging in. I started calling Tymnet, but by the time Steve White answered, the hacker had logged off. Total connect time: thirty seconds.

Damn. All week long, the hacker had been connecting for a minute or two at a time. Every time, he triggered my beeper and siphoned off my adrenaline. But I couldn't trace such short connections. Ten minutes, for sure. Five minutes, maybe. But not one minute.

Fortunately, Steve didn't mind my panic calls, and each time would explain a new wrinkle in Tymnet's switching system. Today, however, Steve mentioned that the Bundespost had talked with the University of Bremen.

After a meticulous search, the systems folks at the University of Bremen had discovered a privileged user: "An expert has created an account for himself and had root privileges. He was last active on December 6, and erased all accounting traces."

Sounded familiar. In fact, the more I read it, the more it said. I could infer that Bremen used Unix, rather than the VMS operating system: on Unix computers, people say "root" access; on VMS, it's "system" privileges. Same concept, different jargon.

Meanwhile, the German Bundespost had determined the account that the hacker used to connect across the Atlantic. They set a trap on that account: the next time someone used that account, they'd trace the call.

The man at the Bundespost thought the account might be stolen. Instead of asking the account owner if he'd authorized the hacker to call America, the Bundespost would quietly watch what was going on.

The Germans weren't sitting around. The University would monitor the suspicious account, and the Bundespost watched the network activity. More and more mouse holes were being watched.

Within an hour, Steve received one more message from Germany: the University of Bremen will be shutting down its computers for the next three weeks. Christmas break.

Maybe this was good news. If the hacker didn't show up during the break, he was likely from Bremen. But if he continued despite the break, he'd have to pick a different route . . . one that might lead directly to him.

The hacker wasn't more than a few minutes from Berkeley. Now, we were only a couple weeks from him.

# 34

DECEMBER WAS TIME TO PRINT GREETING CARDS AND my housemates got together for our annual ink splash. Martha drew the design and Claudia and I cut the silk screens. We figured that we'd avoid offending our zealot friends by keeping the card astronomical: Winter Solstice Greetings!

"We make cards the way you chase hackers," Martha said.

"Huh?"

"Do it yourself," she observed. "Not the way professionals would do it, but satisfying anyway."

I wondered how a real professional would track this hacker. But then, who *were* the professionals? Was anyone dedicated to following people breaking into computers? I hadn't met them. I'd called every agency I could think of, yet nobody had taken over. Nobody had even offered advice.

All the same, the FBI, CIA, OSI, and NSA were fascinated. A foreigner was siphoning data from U.S. databases. The case was documented—not just by my logbook, but also by massive printouts, phone traces, and network addresses. My monitoring station ran full time—the chances for catching the culprit seemed good.

But not a dime of support. My salary was skimmed from astronomy and physics grants, and lab management leaned on me for systems support, not counterespionage. Eight thousand miles away, a hacker was prying around our networks. Three thousand miles east, some secret agents were analyzing my latest reports. But two floors up, my bosses wanted to slam the door.

"Cliff, we've decided to call it quits," Roy Kerth said. "I know you're close to finding the hacker, but we can't afford it anymore."

"How about another two weeks. Until New Year's Day?"

"No. Close things up tomorrow. Revoke everyone's passwords tomorrow afternoon." In other words, slam the door.

Damn. Three, nearly four months' work down the tubes. And just when the trace seemed promising.

Frustrating. The hacker could hide, but he couldn't shake me. My management was the only one who could do that. Just as we were zeroing in on the bastard.

Depressing as well. The hacker wouldn't have any trouble returning to his haunts. He would still roam the networks, breaking in wherever he could. Nobody cared.

I began planning how to pull every user's password. It's easy to do—just rebuild the password file. But how do you tell passwords to twelve hundred scientists? Bring them together in one room? Call everyone on the phone? Mail them notes?

I was still bummed out when Mike Gibbons called from the FBI.

"Just checking to see where the trace has led."

"Into Bremen," I said. "A university there."

"So it's a college student, huh?"

"Not necessarily. But we'll never find out."

"Why not?"

"LBL is closing its doors. Tomorrow."

"You can't do that," the FBI agent said. "We're opening an investigation."

"My boss thinks he can."

"Tell him that we're just making contacts in Europe. Whatever you do, don't stop now."

"You're talking to the wrong guy, Mike."

"OK. What's your boss's phone number?"

I wasn't about to draw fire from Roy Kerth by asking for another extension. If the FBI really wanted us to stay open, let them deal with him.

Anyway, nobody was supporting me. All those fancy three-letter agencies ever said was, "Gimme." Every agency wanted copies of logs and printouts. Every time we completed a trace, four or five people demanded to know where it led.

These were the facts of life in dealing with a bureaucracy: everyone wanted to know what we discovered, but nobody would take responsibility. Nobody volunteered to be the contact point, the center for collecting and distributing information. I'd started out in the center of the study, and it seemed like I'd stay there.

On the other hand, since nobody told me what to do, I could take chances—like remaining open to a hacker who could wipe out my computer in a couple seconds. I could be a one-man band, as in grad school: if it's worth doing, do it for yourself, not to please some funding agency.

If only I could keep Kerth and company off my back.

The FBI did that. Mike Gibbons talked to Roy Kerth. I'm not sure what they said, but half an hour later, Roy told me to remain open for the next few weeks.

"They're finally taking us seriously," Roy said.

"Serious enough to pay our overhead?"

"Are you kidding?"

Rescued from the brink. We'd stay open, though only through the grace of an informal agreement. I had a couple more weeks to catch the hacker.

I might not need much more. Friday, December 19, at 1:38, the hacker showed up again. Stayed around for two hours, fishing on the Milnet.

A pleasant Friday afternoon, trying to guess passwords to the Strategic Air Command, the European Milnet Gateway, the Army's West Point Geography Department, and seventy other assorted military computers.

I got to the monitors within a few seconds, and phoned Steve White at Tymnet. He was getting ready to go home when I called.

"The hacker's on our computer. Tymnet's logical port number 14."

"OK," Steve said. The usual keyboard clatter in the background. Twenty seconds elapsed, and he called out, "Got it!"

Steve had traced a connection from California to Germany in less than a minute.

"How'd you do that?"

Steve laughed. "Now that I know you're looking for traces, I've automated my tracing program. I just have to tell it to fly."

"Where's it point to?"

"You're getting a call from address 2624 DNIC 4511 dash 049136."

"What's that mean?"

"We'll have to ask the Bundespost, but I can tell you a bit about the address. The first digits, 2624, mean Germany."

"We already know that."

"The next four digits, 4511, begin with a 4. That means the hacker's coming through a public dial-in port."

"I don't understand. What's different from the last time you traced the hacker?"

"Last time, we traced him to a computer at the University of Bremen. That time, the digits were 5421. The 5 means that a computer was at the other end."

Oh—the address was coded, like American pay telephones, whose phone numbers always seem to have a fourth digit of 9.

"So the connection isn't coming from the University of Bremen's computer?" I asked.

"That's for certain. But we know more than that. We know that the hacker's coming into a dial-in port. He's connecting from a local telephone."

"Do you know his phone number?"

"No, but the Bundespost can determine what telephone number he called."

Steve's news brought us one step closer. The hacker couldn't hide behind the University of Bremen.

"So when will we find the location of this electronic address?"

"Should be soon. I asked Wolfgang to look it up."

"Who's that?"

"Wolfgang Hoffman. The Datex network manager in Germany."

"You're on the phone with him?"

"Of course not," Steve said. "We're sending electronic mail to each other." I could have guessed.

"And he hasn't decoded today's address, huh?"

"That's right. Until the Bundespost decodes the address, we can't do much . . . hold on, something's showing up . . . it's a message from Germany." Steve apparently had a direct line to Europe, and passed notes between countries the way I might dash off an interoffice memo.

Steve translated the note. "Wolfgang says the hacker came from a dial-in port. He's dialed in over a telephone line."

"We knew that already."

"Yeah, but he's not coming from Bremen. Today, he's dialing from Hannover."

"So where is he? In Bremen or Hannover?"

"Wolfgang doesn't know. For all we know, he could be in Paris, calling long distance."

Another dash to the library. Their atlas showed the city of Hannover, maybe seventy-five miles south of Bremen. Looked like a big city, around half a million people. Jeez—the stuff that travelogues are made from.

Was some student in Bremen dialing Hannover? Not likely. Even with the university closed, he could just call Bremen's Datex port. A Bremen student wouldn't make a long-distance call to Hannover.

Aah, but when the university closed up, students go home.

Was I following some sophomore, home on vacation?

But it didn't feel like a student. College students don't have six-month attention spans. They'd search for games and academic programs, not military keywords. And wouldn't a student leave some kind of signature or joke behind—some way of sticking out his tongue at us?

If this wasn't a student, then why did he come from two places in Germany? Maybe he knew some way to call long distance into Hannover—perhaps from some unprotected computer, or with a stolen credit card. Yesterday it was Bremen. Today Hannover. Where will he hide tomorrow?

The only way to find out was to keep watching. Quietly.

I'd waited four months. I could wait a while longer.

# 35

"YOU NEED A GERMAN SEARCH WARRANT."

Steve White called back from Tymnet. He'd just received electronic mail from Wolfgang Hoffman at the German Bundespost. Wolfgang was hot to pursue the hacker, but needed legal support to trace their lines.

"How do I get a search warrant in Germany?" I asked Steve.

"I don't know, but the Bundespost says they're going to the Hannover courts tomorrow to discuss it."

This was good news. Somewhere in Germany, Wolfgang Hoffman had started wheels turning. With luck, they'd get some court orders, make a couple more traces, and arrest the varmint.

Steve White was less optimistic. "When the hacker shows up, the Germans will have to trace the Datex networks, find the phone number that the hacker is calling, and then trace that telephone line."

"Foo," I said, remembering my traces in Berkeley and Virginia. Unless Wolfgang and his team were patient, competent, and clever, the hacker would evade them.

Too many things could go wrong. The hacker could be from another country. He could be using a phone line from another city, disguised through a wide-area telephone system. The court might not grant the search warrant. Or the hacker might sniff the wind and realize that someone was on his trail.

Wolfgang sent another message: "Until the search warrant appears, we will record the name of the Datex user-identifier."

Steve explained, "Whenever you use Tymnet or Datex, someone pays for the service. When you use the network, you have to type in your account number and password. The Germans are going to find out who's paying for the hacker's connections. When we signal them that the hacker's around, they'll not only trace their Datex network, but also find the account name that's paying for the connection."

I understood. If the hacker had stolen someone else's account number and password, he could be charged with theft, and getting a search warrant would be easy. On the other hand, if he was paying for his own connections, it would be easy to find his name, and a court order wouldn't be necessary. They might not even have to trace his telephone lines.

No doubt, this guy Wolfgang was sharp. He was looking for shortcuts to avoid making telephone traces. At the same time, he was building a case against the hacker.

Saturday, December 20, Steve called me at home. Martha glared at me for letting brunch get cold.

Steve had just received another message from Germany. The Bundespost had contacted the Bremen State Prosecutor, Herr Staatsanwalt Von Vock. ("Now that's a high-class title," I thought.)

The message from Germany read: "The German State Prosecutor needs to contact high-level U.S. criminal justice persons so as to execute proper search warrants. The Bundespost cannot move until officially notified by a high-level U.S. criminal office."

What's a high-level U.S. criminal office? The Mafia? Whatever they meant, I'd better get people moving.

I called my boss, Roy Kerth, who crustily observed that it'd taken the Germans six months to discover this problem. "If they were half competent, the hacker would be behind bars by now."

To catch this snake, we all had to pull in the same direction. My boss's flames didn't promote harmony, so how could they promote international cooperation? Maybe I'd be better off appealing to our legal counsel.

Aletha Owens knew what to do. "I'll call Germany and talk to them directly. They probably need someone in the FBI, but I'll start things moving."

*"Sprechen Sie Deutsch?"*

"Not in twenty years," Aletha said. "But I'll haul out the old Berlitz tapes."

Sunday morning, Aletha called back. "Hey, my German isn't so bad. A few problems with the future tense, but not bad. Not bad."

"Yeah, but what did you learn?"

"Well, I learned all sorts of things about reflexive verbs and . . ."

"What about the hacker?"

"Oh, him. Aah, yes." Aletha adopted a mock academic tone. "The German State Prosecutor is a most kindly gentleman who believes in protecting both liberty and property. So he needs an official request to open an investigation."

"Who's the official?"

"The FBI. We've got to ask the FBI to contact their German counterparts. Or should I say, 'you,' since I'll be gone next week."

It was on my shoulders to get the FBI to call the Germans to open an investigation. Great—another chance for them to say "go away kid." I left a message for Mike Gibbons at the Alexandria, Virginia, FBI office.

Amazingly, Mike called ten minutes later from Colorado.

"Hi, Cliff. This had better be important."

"Sorry to bother you, but the German prosecutor needs to talk to someone in the FBI. We've traced our troubles into Hannover."

"Well, there's nothing I can do tonight," Mike said. "And I don't have any documentation here."

In theory, the FBI's representative in Germany would contact his German counterpart, and things would progress from there. Mike said that this guy, the U.S. Legal Attaché, lived in Bonn and handled communications between the two countries. In a sense, he represents the FBI within Germany.

Over the next few months, I would often hear about the U.S. Legal Attaché. I never learned his name, though plenty of curses were directed his way.

The next day, Mike fished through the crime laws. "It's covered by the computer fraud act. Open and shut case."

"But the guy has never set foot in the States," I observed. "How can you get someone from another country?"

"Well, he probably won't be extradited, if that's what you mean. But we can press charges and get him thrown into a German prison, especially if the German law is similar to ours."

"What's the likelihood that the FBI will drop the whole thing?"

"Not if I can help it," Mike said. "We'll have to work with attorneys at the Justice Department, but I don't see a problem there."

I still didn't believe him. The case was obvious to me, but too complex to describe to a criminal lawyer.

"Is there anything that I can get that will help you?"

"Come to think of it, there is. Could you write up a summary of the hacker? You know, draw up a profile of him and tell us who we're looking for. Things like when he's active, what he's expert in, any idiosyncrasies. Don't speculate, but try to identify our man."

Here was a useful project to keep me from pestering Mike for a few days. I combed through my logbook and drew together a profile of my hacker.

Compiling this profile should have kept me out of trouble for a few days. But trouble came from another front.

Someone at NSA had leaked word of my research to the Department of Energy. In turn, they were pissed that they hadn't heard earlier—and more directly.

Roy Kerth stopped me in the hallway. "DOE is going to reprimand us for not telling them about this incident."

"But we did tell them," I objected. "More than two months ago."

"Prove it."

"Sure. It's in my logbook."

Roy wanted to see it, so we walked over to my Macintosh and brought up the logbook. Sure enough, on November 12th, my logbook said that I'd informed DOE. I'd written a summary of our conversation and even included a phone number. DOE couldn't complain—we could prove that we'd informed them.

Saved by my logbook.

Just like observing at a telescope. If you don't document it, you might as well not have observed it. Sure, you need powerful telescopes and computers. But without a logbook, your observations won't amount to much.

On December 30, my beeper woke me up around 5 A.M. By reflex, I called Steve at his house. He wasn't pleased to hear from me.

"The hacker's on."

"Aaw, I was just in the middle of a dream. Are you sure it's him?" His British accent didn't hide his annoyance.

"I'm not sure, but I'll find out in a minute."

"OK, I'll start a trace." Steve put up with a lot from me.

From home, I dialed my Unix computer. Damn. No hacker. The electricians had tripped my alarm by shutting off a nearby computer.

Sheepishly, I called Steve back.

"Say, Cliff, I can't find anyone connected to your computer." His voice was still sleepy.

"Yeah. It's a false alarm. I'm sorry."

"No problem. Maybe next time, huh?"

Now here's a good guy. If someone I'd never met rousted me out of bed to chase a phantom in a computer . . .

Luckily, only Steve had heard me cry wolf. What would happen to my credibility if I'd passed the word along to Germany or the FBI? From now on, I'd double-check every alarm.

# 36

NEW YEAR'S EVE FOUND US SITTING AROUND THE FIRE with friends, sipping eggnog and listening to the explosions as neighborhood idiots set off cherry bombs in the street.

"Hey," said Martha, "we'd better get moving if we're going to make it to First Night." San Francisco was throwing a city-wide party to welcome in 1987, foster civic pride, and give people an alternative to getting drunk and smashing into each other. There was music, dance, theater, and comedy in a dozen locations across town, with cable-car shuttles between events.

Seven of us piled into a beat-up Volvo and inched into San Francisco, trapped in a raucous traffic jam. Instead of honking, people blew party horns out their car windows. Finally we came to the brightly lit city, ditched the car, and headed for a flamenco concert.

We found our way to the Mission district—the Latin section of town, and discovered a packed Catholic church with an impatient audience. A sheepish face emerged from behind the curtain, explaining, "None of the lights work so we're delaying the performance."

Amid the catcalls and boos, Martha stood up and pushed me forward. I still had my electrician's license, and she'd done tech for many an amateur theatrical. We snuck backstage. The flamenco dancers in their glittering costumes smoked and paced the dark stage like caged tigers, tapping their feet and glancing at us doubtfully. Martha set about untangling the maze of cables strewn in the wings while I located the blown fuse. A quick swap of fuses and, shazam, the stage lights lit.

The dancers stamped and cheered and, as Martha neatly coiled the last cable and adjusted the lighting board, the emcee dragged us on stage to thank us. After we escaped the limelight, we enjoyed the flamenco dancing and *faro* singing; the scowling, nervous creatures we'd seen on the dark stage were transformed into elegant, whirling dancers.

We ducked outside and found a shuttle bus driven by an old lady who could have passed for Tugboat Annie, in appearance and language. She maneuvered the bus gamely through the crowded streets, and we found ourselves at the Women's Building on Eighteenth Street. There the Wallflower Order danced and told stories of feminism and social protest.

One dance was about the Wu-Shu, a legendary Chinese monkey who defeated the greedy warlords and gave land back to the people. Sitting in the balcony, I thought about politically correct monkeys—was I a pawn of the warlords? Or was I really a clever monkey, on the side of the people? I couldn't tell, so I forgot about my hacker and enjoyed the dance.

Finally, we wound up dancing wildly to a rhythm and blues band with lead singer Maxine Howard, a sensational blues singer and the sexiest woman in the history of the world. She was picking people out of the audience to dance with her on the stage, and we soon found ourselves hoisting a protesting Martha onto the platform. Within a few minutes, she and her fellow victims overcame their stage fright and formed themselves into a fairly synchronized chorus line, doing little hand motions like the Supremes. I was never much for dancing, but by two o'clock or so, I found myself jumping and spinning around with Martha, lifting her high in the air . . .

We finally had our fill of high culture and cheap thrills, and went to sleep at a friend's house in the Mission district. What felt like moments after my head touched the pillow (though it was actually nine the next morning), my beeper woke me up.

Huh? The hacker was at work on New Year's Day? Give me a break.

There wasn't much I could do. Hacker or not, I wasn't about to call Steve White on New Year's morning. Anyway, I doubted that the German Bundespost could do much about it on a holiday. Most of all, I was ten miles from my laboratory.

I felt caged in while the hacker had free run. If he wanted to tweak my nose, he'd found the way. Just show up when I couldn't do anything.

Well, I couldn't do much beyond worry, so I tried to sleep. With Martha's arm around me, rest came easily. "C'mon, sweetie," she purred. "Give the hacker a holiday." I sank into the pillows. Hacker or not, we would celebrate the New Year. We slept the rest of the morning. Around noon, we found our way back home. Claudia greeted us with a violin sonata . . . she'd spent New Year's Eve playing at some millionaire's party.

Martha asked about her job. "You should have seen the canapés!" Claudia answered. "We had to sit and stare at them for *hours* before they finally saw us looking pathetic and brought us some. They had a whole smoked salmon and caviar and strawberries dipped in chocolate and—"

Martha cut in, "I meant what music you played."

"Oh, we played that Mozart sonata everyone likes that goes diddle dum diddle da da da. Then they started making requests for really icky things like 'My Wild Irish Rose.' I thought I'd get sick but after all it was $125 for two hours and it was on the way to my mom's so I could drop the dog off there, and do some shopping up at Santa Rosa—"

Martha snuck in a word about brunch. We were all in the kitchen mixing waffle batter and making fruit salad when my beeper sounded.

Damn. The hacker again. Martha cursed, but I hardly heard her: I zipped over to my Macintosh and dialed the lab.

There was the hacker, all right, logged in as Sventek. It looked like he was using the Milnet, but I couldn't be sure until I went to the lab. Meanwhile, I'd better call Steve White at Tymnet.

No time—the hacker disappeared within a minute. He was playing New Year's games.

There wasn't much to do but pick up the pieces. I scarfed

down the waffles and biked over to the lab. There, the hacker's New Year's celebration was saved on my printers. I scribbled notes on the printouts, next to each of his commands.

| | |
|---|---|
| 4.2 BSD UNIX (lbl-ux4) | |
| login: <u>sventek</u> | The hacker logs in as Sventek |
| Password: <u>lblhack</u> | and gives his current password |
| Last login: Mon Dec 29 13:31:43 on ttyi7 | |
| 4.2 BSD UNIX #20: Fri Aug 22 20:08:16 PDT 1986 | |
| z | |
| % <u>telnet</u> | He's going out over the Milnet |
| telnet> <u>open optimis</u> | And into the Optimis Army Database |

******OPTIMIS******

For user assistance, call 695-5772, (AV)225

| | |
|---|---|
| Username: <u>ANONYMOUS</u> | He logs in there as anonymous |
| Password: <u>GUEST</u> | And uses an obvious password |

Welcome to the Army OPTIMIS database
If you use these databases and they achieve a savings in
time spent on a project or money saved to the government or both,
please send a mail message outlining the details to
Maj Gene LeClair, Chief, OPTIMIS

WELCOME TO
OPTIMIS
THE DATA BASE WAS LAST UPDATED
ON 861024 AT 102724
AND CONTAINS 3316 DOCUMENTS

This data base is an extract of AR 25-400-2, Modem Army Record-keeping System (MARKS) to help you identify information for filing.

| | |
|---|---|
| Please enter a word or 'EXIT'. | Looking for SDI dope |
| / <u>sdi</u> | |
| The word "sdi" was not found. | But there's none there. |
| Please enter a word or 'EXIT'. | |

| | |
|---|---|
| / <u>stealth</u> | Any word on the Stealth bomber? |
| The word "stealth" was not found. | No such luck |
| Please enter a word or 'EXIT'. | |
| / <u>sac</u> | Strategic Air Command? |
| The word "sac" was not found. | Nope |

Whee! The hacker had entered an Army database and searched for secret Air Force projects. Even an astronomer would know better. He caught on quickly, though:

```
Please enter a word or 'EXIT'.
/ nuclear
Thank you.
I have found 29 document(s) containing the phrase 'nuclear'.
ITEM #    MARKS #    TITLE
= = =     = = = =    = = = = =
1         20-lf      IG Inspections (Headquarters, Department
                       of the Army)
2         50a        Nuclear, chemical, and biological national
                       security affairs
3         50b        Nuclear, chemical and biological warfare
                       arms controls
4         50d        Nuclear and chemical strategy formulations
5         50e        Nuclear and chemical politico-military affairs
6         50f        Nuclear and chemical requirements
7         50g        Nuclear and chemical capabilities
8         50h        Theater nuclear force structure developments
9         50i        Nuclear and chemical warfare budget
                       formulations
10        50j        Nuclear and chemical progress and statistical
                       reports
11        50k        Army nuclear, chemical, and biological
                       defense program
12        50m        Nuclear and chemical cost analyses
13        50n        Nuclear, chemical warfare, and biological
                       defense scientific and technical information
14        50p        Nuclear command and control
                       communications
15        50q        Chemical and nuclear demilitarizations
16        50r        Chemical and nuclear plans
```

| | | |
|---|---|---|
| 17 | 50-5a | Nuclear accident/incident controls |
| 18 | 50-5b | Nuclear manpower allocations |
| 19 | 50-5c | Nuclear surety files |
| 20 | 50-5d | Nuclear site restorations |
| 21 | 50-5-1a | Nuclear site upgrading files |
| 22 | 50-115a | Nuclear safety files |
| 23 | 55-355FRTd | Domestic shipment controls |
| 24 | 200-1c | Hazardous material management files |
| 25 | 385-11k | Radiation incident cases |
| 26 | 385-11m | Radioactive material licensing |
| 27 | 385-40c | Radiation incident cases |
| 28 | 700-65a | International nuclear logistics files |
| 29 | 1125-2-300a | Plant data |

Well, I'd never come across such things. I'd always thought that a theater was somewhere to watch movies, not a place to develop nuclear forces. This hacker wasn't playing games.

And he wasn't satisfied with the titles to these documents—he dumped all twenty-nine over the line printer. Page after page was filled with army double-talk like:

TITLE: Nuclear, chemical, and biological national security affairs
DESCRIPTION: Documents relating to domestic, foreign, and military police for the
application of atomic energy, utilization of nuclear and chemical weapons, and
biological defense relating to national security and national level crises management. Included are studies, actions, and directives of and related to the
President, National Security Council, Assistant to the President for National Security Affairs, and interdepartmental groups and committees addressing national security affairs regarding nuclear and chemical warfare and
biological
defense.

There, my printer jammed. The old Decwriter had paid its dues for ten years, and now needed an adjustment with a sledge hammer. Damn. Right where the hacker listed the Army's plans for nuclear bombs in the Central European theater, there was only an ink blot.

I didn't know much about movie theaters in Central Europe, so I gave Greg Fennel a call at the CIA. Amazingly, he answered his phone on New Year's Day.

"Hi, Greg—what brings you in on New Year's?"

"You know, the world never sleeps."

"Hey, what do you know about movie houses in Central Europe?" I asked, playing the fool.

"Oh, a bit. What's up?"

"Not much. The hacker just broke into some Army computer at the Pentagon."

"What's that got to do with movies?"

"I dunno," I said, "but he seemed especially interested in nuclear force structure developments in Central European theaters."

"You dunce! That's Army tactical warfare plans. Jeez. How did he get it?"

"His usual techniques. Guessed the password to the Army Optimis database in the Pentagon. It looks like a bibliography of Army documents."

"What else did he get?"

"I can't tell. My printer jammed. But he searched for keywords like 'SDI,' 'Stealth,' and 'SAC.' "

"Comic book stuff." I wasn't sure if Greg was joking or serious. He probably thought the same of me.

Come to think of it, how did the spooks know if I was putting them on? For all they knew, I might be inventing everything. Greg had no reason to trust me—I had no clearance, no badge, not even a trench coat. Unless they were spying behind my back, my credibility remained untested.

I had only one defense against this quicksand of distrust—the facts.

But even if they believed me, they weren't likely to do anything. Greg explained, "We can't just send Teejay overseas and bust down someone's door, you know."

"But can't you, well, sorta snoop around there and find out who's responsible for this?" I imagined spies in trench coats again.

Greg laughed. "That's not how things work. Trust me—we're

working on it. And this latest news will add fuel to the fire." So much for the CIA. I just couldn't tell if they were interested or not.

On January 2, I called the Alexandria FBI office and tried to leave a message for Mike Gibbons. The duty agent who answered the phone said in a dry voice, "Agent Gibbons is no longer working this case. We suggest you contact the Oakland office."

Super. The only FBI agent that knows the difference between a network and a nitwit has been pulled off the case. No explanation given.

And just when we need the FBI. Wolfgang was still waiting for a warrant from the U.S. Legal Attaché in Bonn. A week of waiting, and it still hadn't come through. Time to knock on another door.

No doubt the National Security Agency would want to know about leaks from a Pentagon computer. Zeke Hanson at Fort Meade answered.

"Did the Army information go directly to Europe?" Zeke asked.

"Yeah, though I don't know exactly where," I said. "Looks like Germany."

"Do you know which International Record Carrier they used?"

"Sorry, I don't. But I can fish it out of my records if it's that important." Why would NSA want to know who had carried this traffic?

Of course. NSA is rumored to tape-record every transatlantic telephone conversation. Maybe they'd recorded this session.

But that's impossible. How much information crosses the Atlantic every day? Oh, say there's ten satellites and a half-dozen transatlantic cables. Each handles ten thousand telephone calls. So the NSA would need several hundred thousand tape recorders running full time. And that's just to listen to the phone traffic—there are computer messages and television as well. Why, fishing out my particular session would be nearly impossible, even with supercomputers to help. But there was an easy way to find out. See if NSA could obtain the missing data.

"The New Year's Day sessions were interrupted by a paper jam," I told Zeke, "so I'm missing an hour of the hacker's work. Think you could recover it?"

Zeke was cagey. "What's its importance?"

"Well, I can't quite say, since I haven't seen it. The session started at 8:47 on New Year's Day. Why don't you see if someone in Ft. Meade can find the rest of the traffic from this session?"

"Unlikely at best."

The NSA was always willing to listen but clammed up tight whenever I asked questions. Still, if they were doing their homework, they'd have to call me and see if our results were the same. I waited for someone to ask to see our printout. Nobody did.

Come to think of it, two weeks ago, I'd asked Zeke Hanson at the NSA to find out an electronic address. When I first traced a line into Europe, I passed the address to Zeke. I wondered what he'd done with it.

"Did you ever find out where that DNIC address comes from?" I asked.

"Sorry, Cliff, that information is unavailable." Zeke sounded like one of those Magic-8 balls, the kind that say, "Reply hazy, ask again later."

Fortunately, Tymnet had already figured out the address . . . it only took Steve White a couple hours.

Perhaps NSA has lots of electronics wizards and computer geniuses, listening to the world's communications. I wonder. Here, I'd presented them with two fairly easy problems—find an address and replay some traffic. Maybe they did, but they never told me a whit. I suspect they do nothing, hiding behind a veil of secrecy.

Well, there was one more group to inform. The Air Force OSI. The Air Force narcs couldn't do much about the hacker, but at least they could figure out whose computer was wide open.

Jim Christy's gravelly voice crackled over the phone lines: "So it's the Army Optimis system, huh? I'll make a few calls and bang a few heads." I hoped he was joking.

So 1987 started on a sour note. The hacker still had the free run of our computers. The only competent FBI agent had been pulled from the case. The spooks wouldn't say a thing, and NSA seemed uninspired. If we didn't make some headway soon, I'd give up too.

# 37

AROUND NOON ON SUNDAY, JANUARY 4, MARTHA AND I were stitching a quilt when my beeper sounded. I jumped for the computer, checked that the hacker was around, then called Steve White. Within a minute, he'd started the trace.

I didn't wait while Steve tracked the call. The hacker was on my computer, so I biked up to the lab and watched from there. Another twenty-minute race up the hill, but the hacker took his time: he was still typing when I reached the switchyard.

Underneath the printer, an inch-thick printout had accumulated. The hacker hadn't been lazy today. The top line showed him masquerading behind Sventek's name. After checking that none of our system managers were around, he went back to the Pentagon's Optimis database. Not today: "You are not authorized to log in today," was the Army computer's reply.

Well, hot ziggity! Jim Christy must have bashed the right heads.

Scanning the printout, I could see the hacker going fishing on the Milnet. One by one, he tried fifteen Air Force computers, at places like Eglin, Kirtland, and Bolling Air Force Bases. No luck. He'd connect to each computer, twist the doorknob once or twice, then go on to the next system.

Until he tried the Air Force Systems Command, Space Division.

He first twisted on their doorknob by trying their System account, with the password of "Manager." No luck.

Then Guest, password of "Guest." No effect.

Then Field, password "Service":

```
Username: FIELD
Password: SERVICE

WELCOME TO THE AIR FORCE SYSTEM COMMAND-SPACE DIVISION
VAX/VMS 4.4
IMPORTANT NOTICE
    Computer System problems should be directed to the Information
    Systems Customer Service Section located in building 130, room 2359.
    Phone 643-2177/AV 833-2177.

        Last interactive login on Thursday, 11-DEC-1986 19:11
        Last non-interactive login on Tuesday, 2-DEC-1986 17:30
WARNING - Your password has expired; update immediately with SET
PASSWORD!

$ show process/privilege
4-JAN-1987 13:16:37.56      NTY1:          User: FIELD
Process privileges:
        BYPASS      may bypass all system protections
        CMKRNL      may change mode to kernel
        ACNT        may suppress accounting messages
        WORLD       may affect other processes
        OPER        operator privilege
        VOLPRO      may override volume protection
        GRPPRV      group access via system protection
        READALL     may read anything as the owner
        WRITEALL    may write anything as the owner
        SECURITY    may perform security functions
```

Shazam: the door had swung wide open. He'd logged in as Field Service. Not just an ordinary user. A completely privileged account.

The hacker couldn't believe his luck. After dozens of attempts, he'd made the big time. System operator.

His first command was to show what privileges he'd garnered. The Air Force computer responded automatically: System Privilege, and a slew of other rights, including the ability to read, write, or erase any file on the system.

He was even authorized to run security audits on the Air Force computer.

I could imagine him sitting behind his terminal in Germany, staring in disbelief at the screen. He didn't just have free run of the Space Command's computer; he controlled it.

Somewhere in Southern California, in El Segundo, a big Vax computer was being invaded by a hacker halfway around the world.

His next moves weren't surprising: after showing his privileges, he disabled the auditing for his jobs. This way, he left no footprints behind; at least he thought not. How could he know that I was watching from Berkeley?

Confident that he was undetected, he probed the nearby computers. In a moment, he'd discovered four on the Air Force network, and a pathway to connect to others. From his high ground, none of these were hidden from him; if their passwords weren't guessable, he could steal them by setting up Trojan horses.

This wasn't a little desktop computer he'd broken into. He found thousands of files on the system, and hundreds of users. Hundreds of users? Yep. The hacker listed them all.

But his greediness got in his way. He commanded the Air Force computer to list the names of all its files; it went merrily along typing out names like "Laser-design-plans" and "Shuttle-launch-manifest." But he didn't know how to shut off the spigot. For two hours, it poured a Niagara of information onto his terminal.

Finally, at 2:30, he hung up, figuring that he'd just log back into the Air Force computer. But he couldn't get back on. The Air Force computer informed him:

```
Your password has expired. Please contact the system manager.
```

Looking back over the printout, I realized his goof. The Air Force computer had expired the "field service" password; he'd received a warning when he first broke in. Probably, the system automatically expired passwords after a few months.

To stay on the machine, he should have immediately reset his password. Instead, he ignored the request. Now the system wouldn't let him back.

From thousands of miles away, I could sense his frustration. He desperately wanted to get back into that computer, but he'd been foiled by his own stupid mistake.

He'd stumbled on the keys to a Buick, and locked them in the car.

The hacker's mistake solved one problem: what should I tell the Air Force Space Division? Since it was a Sunday, there was nobody to call today. And because the hacker had locked himself out, he was no longer a danger to the Air Force computer. I'd just report the problem to the Air Force narcs, and let them handle it.

While the hacker stepped through the Air Force computer, Steve White traced Tymnet's lines.

"He's coming through RCA," Steve said. "TAT-6."

"Huh? What's that mean in English?"

"Oh, nothing really. RCA is one of the international record carriers, and today the hacker is coming across the number six transatlantic cable." Steve dealt in worldwide communications like a taxi driver in midtown traffic.

"Why isn't he on a satellite link?"

"Probably because it's a Sunday—the cable channels are less crowded."

"You mean that people prefer cable to satellite links?"

"Sure. Every time you connect through a satellite, there's a quarter-second delay. The undersea cables don't slow down your messages so much."

"Who would care?"

"People on the telephone, mostly," Steve said. "Those delays make for jittery conversations. You know, where each person tries to speak at the same time, then they both back off."

"So if the phone companies try to route over the cables, who wants the satellites?"

"Television networks, mostly. TV signals can't be squeezed into submarine cables, so they grab the satellites. But fiber optics will change everything."

I'd heard of fiber optics. Running communications signals

over strands of glass, instead of copper wires. But who was running fiber-optic cables under the ocean?

"Everyone wants to," Steve explained. "There's a limited number of satellite channels available—you can crowd only so many satellites over Equador. And the satellite channels aren't private—anyone can listen in. Satellites may be fine for television, but cable's the way to go for data."

My conversations with Steve White began with tracing the hacker, but inevitably slipped into other topics. A short talk with Steve usually became a tutorial on communications theory.

Realizing that the hacker was still connected, I asked Steve for the details of the trace.

"Oh yeah. I checked with Wolfgang Hoffman at the Bundespost. Your visitor is coming from Karlsruhe today. The University of Karlsruhe."

"Where's that?"

"I don't know, but I'd guess the Ruhr valley. Isn't that along the Rhine?"

The hacker was still chipping away at the Air Force computer, but after he left, I jogged over to the library. Yes, there's Karlsruhe. Three hundred miles south of Hannover.

Draped across the floor of the Atlantic Ocean, the TAT-6 cable ties together Europe and America. The western end of the connection came through Tymnet, then Lawrence Berkeley Laboratory, across the Milnet, and ended at the Air Force Systems Command Space Division.

Somewhere in Germany, the hacker tickled the eastern end of the connection, unaware that we were zeroing in on him.

Three different places in Germany. My hacker was moving around. Or maybe he was staying in one place, playing a shell game with the telephone system. Perhaps he really was a student, visiting different campuses and showing off to his friends. Was I certain that there was only one hacker—or was I watching several people?

The solution depended on completing a trace. Not just to a country or a city, but all the way to an individual. But how do I get a phone trace from six thousand miles away?

The search warrant! Had the FBI pushed the warrant into Germany? For that matter, had they really opened an investigation? Time to call Mike Gibbons of the FBI.

"I hear you've been pulled off the computer case," I told Mike. "Is there anything I can do?"

"Not to worry," Mike said. "Let me handle it. Just lay low, and we'll make progress."

"Well, is there an open investigation or not?"

"Don't ask me, because I can't say. Just be patient, and we'll work it out."

Mike slipped out of every question. Maybe I could pry some information from him by telling him about the Air Force computer.

"Hey, the hacker broke into an Air Force computer yesterday."

"Where?"

"Oh, somewhere in Southern California." I didn't say that it was at 2400 East El Segundo Boulevard, across from the Los Angeles Airport. He wouldn't tell me what was happening, so I'd play coy with him.

"Who runs it?"

"Someone in the Air Force. Sounds like some Buck Rogers place. I dunno."

"You'd better call the Air Force OSI. They'll know what to do."

"Won't the FBI investigate?"

"I told you. We are investigating. We are making progress. It's just not for your ears to hear." So much for extracting information from the FBI.

The Air Force narcs were a bit more expressive. Jim Christy of the Air Force OSI put it succinctly.

"Systems Command? Son of a bitch."

"Yeah. The guy became system manager there."

"Systems manager at Systems Command. Amusing. Did he get anything classified?"

"Not that I can tell. He really didn't get that much, just the names of a few thousand files."

"Damn. We told them. Twice." I wasn't sure if I should be listening.

"If it makes any difference, he's not going to get back on their system. He's locked himself out." I told him about the password expiration.

"That's fine for the Systems Command," Jim said, "but how many other computers are just as wide open? If the Space Division screws up like that, even after we warn them, then how are we ever going to get the word out?"

"You warned them?"

"Damn straight. We've been telling systems operators for six months to change all their passwords. Don't you think we've been listening to you?"

Smoley hokes! They'd actually heard my message, and were spreading the word. It's the first time that anyone had even hinted that I'd had any effect.

Well, the Air Force OSI in Washington sent the message out to their agent at Vandenberg Air Force Base. He, in turn, was to knock heads at the Space Division. They'd make sure that the hole stayed plugged up.

Two days later, Dave Cleveland and I were sitting in front of his terminal, playing with some broken software. My beeper went off and without saying a word, Dave switched the terminal over to the Unix computer. Sventek was just logging on. We looked at the screen, then nodded to each other. I jogged over to the switchyard to watch the action live.

The hacker didn't bother with my computers, but went straight over the Milnet to the Air Force Space Division. I watched him start to log in there as Field Service, thinking how he would just be booted off again.

But no! He was welcomed back into their system. Someone at the Air Force base had re-enabled the Field Service account with the same old password. The service technician may have noticed that the account had expired, and asked the system manager to reset the password.

Stupid. They'd unlocked the doors and left the keys in the ignition.

The hacker didn't waste a minute. He went straight to the authorization software and added a new account. No, not a new account. He searched for an old, unused account and modified it. Some Air Force officer, Colonel Abrens, had an account, but hadn't been around this computer in a year.

The hacker slightly modified Colonel Abrens' account, giving it system privileges and a new password: AFHACK.

AFHACK—what arrogance. He's thumbing his nose at the United States Air Force.

From now on, he didn't need the Field Service account. Disguised as an officer in the Air Force, he had unlimited access to the Space Division's computer.

Heavy duty. This guy wasn't tinkering around. Air Force OSI had left for the day. What should I do? Leaving the hacker connected would leak sensitive information from the Air Force. But disconnecting him would only cause him to use a different route, bypassing my lab's monitors.

We'd have to chop him off at the Space Command.

But first, I wanted him traced. A call to Steve White started things rolling. Within five minutes, he'd traced the connection to Hannover, and called the Bundespost.

A few minutes of silence. "Cliff, does the connection look like it will be a long one?"

"I can't tell, but I think so."

"OK." Steve was on another telephone; I could only hear an occasional shout.

In a minute, Steve returned to my line. "Wolfgang is tracing the call in Hannover. It's a local call. They're going to try to trace it all the way."

Here's news! A local call in Hannover meant that the hacker's somewhere in Hannover.

Unless there's a computer in Hannover doing his dirty work.

Steve shouted instructions from Wolfgang: "Whatever you do, don't disconnect the hacker. Keep him on the line if you can!"

But he's rifling files at the Air Force base. It was like letting a burglar rob your home while you watched. Should I boot him out or let the trace go ahead? I couldn't decide.

Well, I ought to call some authority. How about Mike Gibbons of the FBI? He's not around.

Hey—the National Computer Security Center might be a good place to call. Zeke Hanson will know what to do.

No luck. Zeke wasn't in and the voice at the far end of the line explained, "I'd like to help you, but we design secure computers. We don't get involved in the operational aspects." I'd heard that before, thank you.

Well, there wasn't anyone else to tell but the Air Force. I hooked into the Milnet Network Information Center and looked up their phone number. Naturally, they'd changed their phone number. They even listed the wrong area code. By the time I reached the right person, the hacker had thoroughly penetrated their computer.

"Hi, I'm looking for the system manager of the Space Command's Vax computer."

"This is Sergeant Thomas. I'm the manager."

"Uh, I don't know how to explain this to you, but there's a hacker in your computer." (Meanwhile, I'm thinking, "He won't believe me and will want to know who I am.")

"Huh? Who are you?" Even over the phone, I could feel him giving me the hairy eyeball.

"I'm an astronomer at Lawrence Berkeley Laboratory." (First mistake, I think, nobody's gonna believe that.)

"How do you know there's a hacker?"

"I'm watching him break into your computer over the Milnet."

"You expect me to believe you?"

"Just look at your system. List out your users."

"OK." I hear typing in the background.

"There's nothing strange here. We've got fifty-seven people logged in, and the system's behaving normally."

"Notice anyone new?" I asked.

"Let's see . . . No, everything's normal." Should I tell him or just beat around the bush?

"Do you know someone named Abrens?"

"Yeah. Colonel Abrens. He's logged in right now. Hey, what are you getting at?"

"Are you sure that Abrens is legit?"

"Hell, yes. He's a colonel. You don't mess with the brass."

I was getting nowhere by asking leading questions. Might as well tell him. "Well, a hacker's stolen Abrens' account. He's logged on right now, and he's dumping your files."

"How do you know?"

"I watched him. I've got a printout," I said. "He came in on the Field Service account, then reset Abrens' password. Right now, he's got system privileges."

"That's impossible. Just yesterday, I reset the password to the Field Service account. It had expired."

"Yes, I know. You set the password to 'service.' The same as it's been for the past year. Hackers know this."

"Well, I'll be damned. Hold on." Over the phone, I hear Sergeant Thomas call someone over. A couple minutes later, he's back on the line.

"What do you want us to do?" he asked. "I can shut off my computer right now."

"No, hold off for a bit," I said. "We're tracing the line right now, and we're closing in on the hacker." This was no fib: Steve White had just relayed Wolfgang Hoffman's request to keep the hacker on the line as long as possible. I didn't want Sergeant Thomas to cut the line before the trace was complete.

"OK, but we'll call our commanding officer. He'll make the final decision." I could hardly blame them. A total stranger calls from Berkeley and tells them that someone's breaking into their system.

Between these phone calls, I watched the printer punch out the hacker's every command. Today, he didn't list the names of every file. Quite the contrary: he listed individual files. He already knew the names of the files he was looking for; he didn't need to scramble around searching for their names.

Aah. This was an important clue. Three days ago, the hacker listed the names of a thousand files. Today, he went straight to those files that interested him. He must have printed out his entire session. Otherwise, he would have forgotten the names of the files.

So the hacker's printing out everything he gets. I already knew that he kept a detailed notebook—otherwise, he'd have forgotten some of the seeds that he'd planted months ago. I remembered my meeting with the CIA: Teejay had wondered if the hacker kept recordings of his sessions. Now I knew.

At the far end of the connection, somewhere in Germany, sat a determined and methodical spy. Every printout that came across my monitor was duplicated in his lair.

Which files did he list? He skipped over all the programs and ignored system management guidelines. Instead, he went for operational plans. Documents describing Air Force payloads for the space shuttle. Test results from satellite detection systems. SDI research proposals. A description of an astronaut-operated camera system.

None of this information had the comment "classified" on it. It wasn't secret, top secret, or even confidential. At least, none of the files carried those labels.

Now, no military computer on the Milnet is allowed to carry classified information. There's another computer network, completely separate, that handles classified data. So in one sense, the Systems Command's Space Division had nothing to lose: its computer is unclassified.

But there's a deeper problem. Individually, public documents don't contain classified information. But once you gather many documents together, they may reveal secrets. An order from an aircraft manufacturer for a load of titanium sure isn't secret. Nor is the fact that they're building a new bomber. But taken together, there's a strong indicator that Boeing's new bomber is made of titanium, and therefore must fly at supersonic speeds (since ordinary aluminum can't resist high temperatures).

In the past, to pull together information from diverse sources you'd spend weeks in a library. Now, with computers and networks, you can match up data sets in minutes—look at how I manipulated Mitre's long-distance phone bills to find where the hacker had visited. By analyzing public data with the help of computers, people can uncover secrets without ever seeing a classified database.

Back in 1985 Vice Admiral John Poindexter worried about just this problem. He tried to create a new classification of information, "Sensitive but unclassified." Such information fit below the usual levels of Top Secret, Secret, and Confidential; but access to it was to be denied to certain foreigners.

Poindexter clumsily tried to apply this to academic research—naturally, the universities refused, and the idea died. Now, standing in front of my monitor, watching the hacker prowl through the Space Command's system, I realized his meaning. Air Force SDI projects might not be top secret, but they sure were sensitive.

What? Me agreeing with Vice Admiral Poindexter? The guy that shipped arms to Iran? How could I have any common ground with Ollie North's boss? Yet dancing across my screen was just what he'd described: sensitive but unclassified data.

Tymnet came back on the line. "I'm sorry, Cliff, but the trace in Germany is stymied."

"Can't they trace the call?" I asked, unsure of who I meant by "they."

"Well, the hacker's line comes from Hannover, all right," Steve replied. "But Hannover's phone lines connect through mechanical switches—noisy, complicated widgets—and these can only be traced by people. You can't trace the call with a computer."

I started to understand. "You mean that someone has to be in the telephone exchange to trace the call?"

"That's it. And since it's after 10 P.M. in Hannover, there's nobody around."

"How long will it take to get someone into the exchange?"

"About three hours."

To trace the line, a Bundespost telephone technician would have to visit the telephone exchange and follow the switches and wires. For all I knew, he might even have to climb telephone poles. Bad news.

Meanwhile, the hacker was slithering through the Air Force computer. Sergeant Thomas was still on hold—he'd probably called all sorts of Air Force brass by now.

I popped my phone to the Air Force line. "Well, we can't trace things any further today."

"Gotcha. We'll cut off the hacker right now."

"Wait for a second," I said. "Don't make it look like you're just booting him off your system. Instead, find a way that he won't suspect that you're on to him."

"Yeah. We figured out a plan," Sergeant Thomas replied. "We'll broadcast an announcement to everyone on the system that our computer's malfunctioning, and will have to be serviced."

Perfect. The hacker will think the system's going down for repairs.

I waited for a minute and in the middle of a page of SDI proposals, this message interrupted the hacker's screen:

```
System going down for maintenance, back up in 2 hours.
```

He saw it right away. The hacker immediately logged off and disappeared into the void.

# 38

HAVING BROKEN INTO ANOTHER MILITARY BASE, THE hacker wasn't about to give up. He returned to our lab, trying over and over to get back into the Air Force Systems Command. But none of his magic charms worked. He couldn't get back into their computers.

They were clever about how they'd locked out the hacker. They didn't just post a notice saying, "Hackers stay out." Instead, they set the hacker's stolen account so that it almost worked. When the hacker logged into his stolen account, Abrens, the Air Force computer appeared to accept it, but then barfed back an error message—as if the hacker had set up his account incorrectly.

I wondered if the hacker realized that he was under my thumb. Every time he succeeded in breaking into a computer, he was detected and booted out.

From his viewpoint, everyone except us detected him. In reality, almost nobody detected him.

Except us.

He couldn't know that he was caged in. My alarms, monitors, and electronic tripwires were invisible to him. Tymnet's traces—through satellites and under the ocean—were totally silent. And the Bundespost was now on his scent.

Wolfgang's latest message said that he was arranging to keep a technician at the Hannover telephone exchange until midnight every night. This was expensive, so he needed to coordinate this with us. More important, the Germans had still not heard from the FBI.

Time to call Mike Gibbons. "The Germans haven't received anything from the FBI," I said. "Any idea why?"

"We're having, er, internal problems here," Mike replied. "You don't want to know."

I did want to know, but there was no use asking. Mike wouldn't say a thing.

"What should I tell the Bundespost?" I asked. "They're getting antsy for some kind of official notification."

"Tell them that the FBI's Legal Attaché in Bonn is handling everything. The paperwork will come along."

"That's what you said two weeks ago."

"And that's what I'm saying now."

Zip. I passed the message back to Steve at Tymnet, who forwarded it to Wolfgang. The bureaucrats might not be able to communicate with each other, but the technicians sure did.

Our complains to the FBI should have been filtered through their office, sent to the American Legal Attaché in Bonn, then passed to the German FBI, the Bundeskriminalamt. The BKA probably inspires the same image of truth and justice in Germany as the FBI does in America.

But someone was plugging up the communications downstream of Mike Gibbons. About all I could do was keep pestering Mike, and stay in close touch with Tymnet and the Bundespost. Sooner or later, the FBI would reach out to the BKA, and the warrants would appear.

Meanwhile, my astronomer buddies needed help. I spent the day trying to understand the optics of the Keck Observatory's telescope. Jerry Nelson needed my programs to predict the telescope's performance; I hadn't made a whit of progress since I'd started chasing the hacker.

The other systems programmers were on my case, too. Crusty Wayne Graves leaned on me to build some disk driver software. ("Screw the hacker. Write some code, already.") And Dave Cleveland gently reminded me he needed to hook up ten new desktop computers to our lab-wide network.

I told each of them that the hacker would be gone "RSN." The ubiquitous statement of software developers everywhere. Real Soon Now.

On my way over to the astronomy group, I ducked into the switchyard for a moment—just long enough to check my monitors. They showed someone working on the Bevatron computer, manipulating the password file.

Bizarre. The Bevatron's one of the lab's particle accelerators, and their programmers all worked at our lab. Only a system manager could manipulate the password file. I stood around, watching. Someone was adding several new accounts.

Well, there's one way to find out if this is legit. Call the Bevatron folks. Chuck McParland answered. "No, I'm the system manager. Ain't nobody else licensed."

"Uh, oh. Then you've got a problem. Someone's playing God on your computer."

Chuck typed a few commands and came back to the phone.

"Son of a bitch."

Chuck's Bevatron particle accelerator used magnets the size of houses to shoot fragments of atoms into thin targets. In the sixties, its ammunition was protons. Now, fed from a second accelerator, it zipped heavy ions up to nearly the speed of light.

After smashing these atomic particles into thin foils, physicists sift through the debris, looking for fragments which may be the fundamental building blocks of the universe. Physicists waited months for time on the beamlines; more important, cancer patients waited as well.

The Bevatron can accelerate helium ions to a fraction of the speed of light, where they'll acquire about 160 million electron volts of energy. At this speed, they travel a few inches and then dump most of their energy.

If you position a cancer tumor at just the right distance beyond this accelerator, most of the particles' energy goes into the tumor. The cancer cells absorb this energy, and the tumor's destroyed without affecting the rest of the person's body. Unlike X rays, which irradiate everything in their path, the Bevatron particles deposit the bulk of their energy at one location. This works especially well on brain tumors, which are often surgically inoperable.

Chuck's Bevatron computers calculate that "right distance." They control the accelerator too, so that the correct energy is used.

Get either of these wrong, and you'll kill the wrong cells.

Every few seconds, a burst of ions spills out of the beamline. By flipping magnets at the right times, Chuck's computers send these to either a physics experiment or a cancer patient. A bug in the program is bad news for both.

The hacker wasn't just poking around a computer. He was playing with someone's brain stem.

Did he know? I doubt it. How could he? To him, the Bevatron's computer was just another plaything—a system to exploit. Its programs aren't labeled, "Danger—medical computer. Do not tamper."

He wasn't innocently looking for information. Having found a way to become system manager, he was fooling with the operating system itself.

Our operating systems are delicate creations. They control how the computer behaves, how their programs will respond. System managers delicately tune their operating systems, trying to squeeze every bit of performance from the computer. Is the program too slow because it's competing with other tasks? Fix it by changing the operating system's scheduler. Or maybe there's not enough room for twelve programs at once. Then alter the way the operating system allocates memory. Screw up, though, and the computer won't work.

This hacker didn't care if he wrecked someone else's operating system. He just wanted to introduce a security hole so that he could reenter whenever he wished. Did he know that he might kill someone?

Chuck nailed his system shut by changing all the passwords. Another door slammed in the hacker's face.

But another worry. I'd been chasing someone around the world, yet I couldn't prevent him from breaking into any computer he wished. My only defense was to watch him and warn people who were attacked.

Sure, I could still boot him out of my computer, and wash my hands of the whole mess. My earlier fears seemed unjustified: I now knew what security holes he exploited, and it didn't look like he'd planted any time bombs or viruses in my computer.

Kicking him off my machine would only black out the window that I used to watch him. He'd continue to attack other computers, using different networks. I didn't have much choice but to let this SOB wander around until I could catch him.

But try explaining that to the FBI. On Thursday, January 8, my local FBI agent Fred Wyniken stopped over.

"I'm here only as a representative of the Alexandria, Virginia, office," Fred said.

"I don't understand," I said. "Why isn't the case being handled from the Oakland office?"

"The FBI's field offices are pretty much independent of one another," Fred replied. "What one office thinks is important, another may well ignore." I could sense in which category he thought my case belonged.

Fred explained that he didn't know the likelihood of prosecution because he wasn't handling the case. "But I'd say it's pretty slim. You can't show any monetary loss. There's no obviously classified data. And your hacker isn't in the States."

"So that's why my local office isn't handling this case?"

"Remember, Cliff, that the FBI only works cases that the Department of Justice will prosecute. Since no classified information's been compromised, there's no reason to commit the resources that it'll take to resolve this."

"But unless you take action, this hacker will keep hammering on our computers until he pretty much owns them."

"Look. Every month we get a half-dozen calls saying, 'Help! Someone's breaking into my computer.' Ninety-five percent of them have no records, no audit trails, and no accounting data."

"Hold on there. I've got records and audit trails. Hell, I've got every keystroke that this bastard's typed."

"I'm getting to that. In a few cases, and yours is one of them, there's good documentation. But that's not enough. The damage must be sufficient to justify our efforts. How much have you lost? Seventy-five cents?"

Here we go again. Yes, our computing costs were small change. But I sensed a larger issue, perhaps one of national importance. My local FBI agent saw only a six-bit accounting error. No wonder I couldn't get any interest—let alone support—from him.

How much longer before someone noticed? Maybe if a classified military computer were hit? Or a high-tech medical experiment damaged? What if a patient in a hospital were injured?

Well, I gave him printouts from the past couple of weeks (after first signing the back of each copy—something to do with "rules of evidence") and a floppy disk with the Mitre telephone logs. He'd send it all to Mike Gibbons at the Alexandria office. Maybe Mike would find them useful in convincing the FBI to talk to the German BKA.

Discouraging. The German telephone technicians still didn't have their warrants, the FBI wasn't responding, and my boss sent me a curt note asking when I'd write some software to link up a new printer.

Martha wasn't happy either. The hacker wasn't just breaking into computers. By way of the beeper, he was invading our home.

"Isn't the FBI or the CIA doing something," she asked, "now that there's foreigners and spies? I mean, aren't they the G-men—Truth, Justice, and the American Way?"

"It's the same old bailiwick problem. The CIA says that the FBI should work it. The FBI doesn't want to touch it."

"Is the Air Force Office of Something or Another doing anything?"

"Same story. The problem starts in Germany, and someone's got to call Germany to solve it. The Air Force Office of Special Investigations can only bang on the FBI's door."

"Then why not punt?" Martha suggested. "Brick up your computer and let the hacker roam around theirs. Nobody appointed you official guardian of America's computers."

"Because I want to know what happened. Who's behind it. What they're searching for. Research." Luis Alvarez's words still rang, months afterward.

"Then think of a way to solve your problem without the FBI. If they won't get the Germans to trace a call, then find some other way."

"How? I can't call the German Bundespost and say, 'Trace this call!' "

"Why not?"

"For one, I wouldn't know who to call. And they wouldn't believe me if I did."

"Then find some other way to home in on the hacker."

"Yeah, right. Just ask him to tell me his address."

"Don't laugh. It might work."

# 39

"THE FBI'S TOSSING IN THE TOWEL."

This was the message Ann Funk of the Air Force Office of Special Investigations left for me. The day before, I'd called her and she said that her group was waiting for the FBI to take action. Now this greeting.

I tried returning Ann's call, but she'd already left Bolling Air Force Base. Not much else to do but call the FBI.

The raspy voice at the Alexandria FBI office didn't want to waste time. "Agent Gibbons is not available right now, but I have a message for you," the guy said officiously. "Your case is closed and you are to shut things off."

"Huh? Who said that?"

"I'm sorry, but that's the whole message. Agent Gibbons will be back next week."

"Did Mike say anything more?" After dozens of conversations, wouldn't he at least tell me in person?

"I told you, that is the entire message."

Great. Pester the FBI for five months. Trace a connection around the world. Prove that the hacker's breaking into military computers. Just when I most needed the FBI's help . . . poof.

Ann Funk called back an hour later. "I just heard that the FBI decided there's insufficient grounds to continue their investigation."

"Do the break-ins at the Air Force Space Command make any difference?" I asked.

"That's the Systems Command, Space Division, Cliff. Get it right, or you'll confuse us." But Space Command sounds neater. Who'd want to command a system?

"OK, but doesn't the FBI care about them?"

Ann sighed. "According to the FBI, there's no evidence of actual espionage."

"Did Mike Gibbons say that?"

"I doubt it," she said. "I got the word from a duty officer who said that Mike's been taken off the case and can't talk about it."

"So who decided?" Mike was the only computer literate FBI agent I'd spoken to.

"Probably some middle management at the FBI," Ann said. "They can catch kidnappers easier than computer hackers."

"So how do you feel?" I asked her. "Should we close up shop or try to catch the bastard?"

"The FBI says to shut down the hacker's access ports."

"That's not what I asked."

". . . and to change all your passwords . . ."

"I know what the FBI says. What does the Air Force say?"

"Uh, I don't know. We'll talk later on and call you back."

"Well, unless someone tells us to continue, we'll close up shop and the hacker can play in your computers all he wants. For five months we've been chasing this spy and not one government agency has contributed a dime." I hung up angrily.

A few minutes later, my local FBI agent called. Fred Wyniken left no doubt about their decision. In an official tone of voice, he informed me that the FBI felt there was no way to extradite this hacker because of unclassified hacking.

"Cliff, if you can show that some classified material has been compromised, or that he's done significant damage to systems, then the FBI will step in. Until that happens, we're not going to move."

"What do you consider damage? If someone rifles my desk drawers and duplicates the plans for a new integrated circuit, is that damage? Who do I turn to?"

Fred wouldn't answer. "If you insist on pursuing this case, the FBI can assist under the domestic police cooperation act. Your lab should contact the Berkeley District Attorney and open an investigation. If your local DA will extradite the hacker, then the FBI will assist in handling the proper paperwork."

"Huh? After five months you're bouncing me back to my local District Attorney?" I couldn't believe what I was hearing.

"If you choose to go in that way, the FBI will serve as a conduit between your local police and the German authorities. The LBL police would be the center of the investigation, and prosecution would be in Berkeley."

"Fred, you can't be saying that. This guy's broken into thirty computers around the country, and you're telling me that it's a local, Berkeley problem?"

"I'm telling you this much," my local G-man continued. "The FBI has decided to drop the case. If you want to continue, you'd better handle it through your local police force."

Not an hour later, Steve White called from Tymnet. He'd just received the following electronic message from the German Bundespost:

"It is most urgent that the U.S. authorities contact the German prosecutor or else the Bundespost will no longer cooperate. We cannot remain hanging, without any official notification. We will not trace phone lines without the proper warrants. You must arrange for the FBI to contact the German BKA immediately."

Oh, hell. Spend months building cooperation between agencies, and the FBI backs out. Just when we need them.

Well, I didn't have much of a choice. We could do what we were told and close up, toss away five months of tracking, or we could stay open and risk censure by the FBI.

Closing down would give the hacker freedom to roam our networks without anyone watching him. Staying open wouldn't lead us to the hacker, since the Bundespost wouldn't trace unless the FBI gave the go-ahead. Either way, the hacker wins.

Time to call on my boss. Roy Kerth believed the news right away. "I never did trust the FBI. We've practically solved the case for them, yet they won't investigate."

"So what do we do?"

"We don't work for the FBI. They can't tell us what to do. We'll stay open until the Department of Energy tells us to shut down."

"Should I call DOE?"

"Leave that to me. We've put in a hell of a lot of work, and they're going to hear about it." Roy mumbled a bit—it didn't sound like praise for the FBI—then stood up and said firmly, "We'll stay open, all right."

But monitoring the hacker in Berkeley wasn't tracing him in Germany. We needed the FBI, even if they didn't need us.

What'll the CIA say?

"Hi, it's Cliff. Our friends at the, uh, 'F' entity have lost interest."

"Who'd ya talk to?" Teejay asked.

"The entity's local representative and an officer from their East Coast office." I was learning spookspeak.

"OK. I'll check into it. Hold still till you hear from me."

Two hours later, Teejay called back. "The word is close up shop. Your contact, Mike, is off the case. His entity is off chasing pickpockets."

"So what do we do?"

"Just sit still," the spook said. "We can't get involved—FCI belongs to Mike's entity. But someone may lean on Mike's entity. Just wait."

FCI? Federal Cat Inspector? Federation of Carnivorous Iguanas? I couldn't figure it out. "Uh, Teejay, what's FCI?"

"Shhh. Don't ask questions. Wheels are turning in places you don't know about."

I called Maggie Morley—our Scrabble whiz and all-knowing librarian. Took her three minutes to find the acronym. "FCI means Foreign Counter-Intelligence," she said. "Met any spies lately?"

So the CIA doesn't handle counterintelligence. The FBI doesn't want to waste time on this one. And the Deutsche Bundespost wants an official notice from the United States. Whee.

One other agency might be able to help. Zeke Hanson at the National Security Agency was sympathetic—he'd watched every step of progress we'd made, and knew how much we needed the FBI's support. Could he help out?

"I'd love to help, Cliff, but we're not able to. The NSA listens rather than talks."

"But isn't this what the National Computer Security Center is for? To solve computer security problems?"

"You know the answer. No and no. We're trying to secure computers, not catch hackers."

"Can't you call the FBI and at least encourage them?"

"I'll spread the word, but don't hold your breath."

At best, NSA's computer security center tried to set standards and encourage computer security. They had no interest in serving as a clearing-house for problems like mine. And they certainly couldn't get a search warrant. NSA had no connections with the FBI.

Teejay called back in a couple of days. "We made a grandstand play," the CIA agent said. "Mike's entity is back on track. Tell me if they give you any more trouble."

"What'd you do?"

"Oh, talked to a couple friends. Nothing much." What kind of friends does this guy have? To turn the FBI around in two days . . . who's he talking to?

It didn't take long before Mike Gibbons of the FBI called. He explained German law to me: hacking into a computer wasn't a big deal there. As long as you didn't destroy the computer, breaking into a system wasn't much worse than double parking.

This didn't make sense to me. If German law was this lenient, why did the Deutsche Bundespost take the case so seriously?

Mike understood my concerns, and at least agreed to keep working on the case. "You should know, though, that last year a German hacker was caught in a Colorado computer, but couldn't be prosecuted."

Would the FBI's Legal Attaché get off his butt?

"I'm working on that," Mike said. "Tell your friends at the Bundespost that they'll hear from us soon."

That evening, we had another chance to catch the guy. While Martha and I waited in line at the grocery store, my beeper chimed in. I dropped my copy of the *National Enquirer* ("Alien Visitors from Mars!") and dashed to the pay phone, dialing Steve White.

"Our friend's on the line," I told him.

"OK. I'll call Germany."

Quick conversation and a quick trace. The hacker was on for only five minutes, yet Steve tracked him into DNIC #2624-4511-049136. A public access dialup line in Hannover, Germany.

Afterwards, Steve White filled me in on the details. Wolfgang Hoffman, awakened at 3 A.M., started tracing that line from Frankfurt. But the telephone engineer assigned to the Hannover exchange had already gone home for the night. Close, but no cigar.

Wolfgang had one question for us. The University of Bremen was willing to cooperate in catching this guy, but who's going to pay? The hacker was wasting the University's money—hundreds of dollars a day. Would we be willing to pay for the hacker?

Impossible. My lab's paper-clip budget was squeezed—no way would they spring for this. I passed the message back that I'd ask around.

Steve pointed out that someone would have to pay, or the Bundespost will just chop the hacker's access. Now that they knew how he's ripping off the Datex network, the Germans wanted to plug the holes.

Yet more news arrived from Germany. A couple of nights ago, the hacker connected into Berkeley for two minutes. Long enough to track him to the University of Bremen. Bremen, in turn, tracked him back to Hannover. It seemed like the hacker wasn't just breaking into our Berkeley laboratory, but snuck into European networks as well.

"Since they had the chance, why didn't the Germans trace him within Hannover?"

Steve explained the problems in Hannover's telephone system. "American telephones are computer controlled, so it's pretty easy to trace them. But they need someone at the exchange to trace the call in Hannover."

"So we can't trace him unless the hacker calls during the day or evening?"

"Worse than that. It'll take an hour or two to make the trace once it's started."

"An hour or two? Are you kidding? Why it takes you ten seconds to trace Tymnet's lines from California across a satellite and into Europe. Why can't they do the same?"

"They would if they could. The hacker's telephone exchange just isn't computerized. So it'll take a while for the technician to trace it."

Lately, the hacker had been showing up for five minutes at a time. Long enough to wake me up, but hardly enough for a two-hour trace. How could I keep him on for a couple of hours?

The Bundespost couldn't keep technicians on call forever. In fact, they could hardly afford to keep them around for more than a few days. We had one week to complete the trace. After next Saturday evening, the telephone technicians would call it quits.

I couldn't make the hacker show up at a convenient time. And I couldn't control how long he hung around. He came and went as he pleased.

# 40

"WAKE UP, YOU SLOTH," SAID MARTHA AT THE OBSCENELY early hour of nine on a Saturday morning. "Today we prepare the ground for our tomato plants."

"It's just January," I protested. "Everything is dormant. Bears are hibernating. I am hibernating." I pulled the covers over my head, only to have them snatched away. "Come on outside," said Martha, taking a viselike grip on my wrist.

At first glance, it seemed that I was right. The garden was dead and brown. "Look," Martha said, kneeling beside a rose bush. She touched the swelling pink buds. She pointed at the plum tree, and looking more closely, I saw a mist of tiny green leaves emerging from the bare branches. Those poor California plants—without a winter to sleep through.

Martha gave me a shovel, and we began the yearly cycle; turning over the soil, adding fertilizer, planting tiny tomato seedlings in their furrows. Every year we carefully planted several varieties that took different amounts of time to ripen, and staggered the planting by several weeks, so we would have a steady supply of tomatoes all summer. And every year, every single tomato ripened on the fifteenth of August.

It was slow, heavy work because the soil was dense with clay and wet from the winter rains. But we finally got the plot spaded, and, dirty and sweaty, stopped to take a shower and have brunch.

In the shower, I felt revived. Martha sudsed my back while I basked in hot water. Maybe the wholesome rustic life wasn't so bad after all.

Martha was in the midst of shampooing my hair when the nasty whine of my beeper, buried in a pile of clothing, destroyed our peace. Martha groaned and started to protest: "Don't you dare. . . ."

Too late. I jumped out of the shower and ran to the living room, switched on my Macintosh, and called the lab computer. Sventek.

A second later, I'm talking to Steve White at his home. "He's here, Steve."

"OK. I'll trace him and call Frankfurt."

A moment later, Steve's back on the line. "He's gone. The hacker was here a moment ago, but he's disconnected already. No use calling Germany now."

Damn. I stood there in utter frustration; stark naked, wet and shivering, standing in a puddle in our dining room, dripping blobs of shampoo onto my computer's keyboard.

Claudia had been practicing Beethoven, but startled by the sight of her roommate charging, naked, into the living room, she'd put down her violin and stared. Then she laughed and played a few bars of a burlesque tune. I tried to respond with a bump and grind, but was too obsessed with the hacker to pull it off.

I wandered sheepishly back into the bathroom. Martha glowered at me, then relented and pulled me into the shower again, under the hot water.

"I'm sorry, sweetheart," I apologized. "It's our only chance to nail him, and he wasn't around long enough to catch."

"Great," Martha said. "Long enough to drag you out of the shower, but not enough time to find out where he is. Maybe he knows you're watching him, and he's purposely trying to frustrate you. Somehow, he telepathically knows when you're in the shower. Or in bed."

"I'm sorry, sweetheart." I was, too.

"Honey, we've got to do something about this. We can't let this guy keep yanking us around. And all those spooks in suits you keep talking to—what have they ever done to help? Nothing. We have to take this into our own hands."

She was right: I'd spent hours on the phone to the FBI, CIA, NSA, OSI, and the DOE. Still others, like the BKA, knew about our problem, yet nobody took the initiative.

"But what can we do without the government's help?" I asked. "We need search warrants and all that. We need official permission to do phone traces."

"Yeah, but we don't need anyone's permission to put stuff in our own computer."

So what?

Under the steaming water, Martha turned to me with a sly look.

"Boris? Darlink, I hev a plan . . ." Martha shaped a goatee and mustache out of soap suds on my face.

"Yes, Natasha?"

"Ees time for ze secret plan 35B."

"Brilliant, Natasha! Zat will vork perfectly! Ah, darlink . . . vhat is secret plan 35B?"

"Ze Operation Showerhead."

"Yes?"

"Vell, you see, zee spy from Hannover seeks ze secret information, yes?" Martha said. "We give him just vhat he vants—secret military spy secrets. Lots of zem. Oodles of secrets."

"Tell me, Natasha dahlink, zees secrets, vhere shall ve get them from? Ve don't know any military secrets."

"Ve make zem up, Boris!"

Yow! Martha had come up with the obvious solution to our problem. Give the guy what he's looking for. Create some files of phony information, laced with bogus secret documents. Leave 'em lying around my computer. The hacker stumbles on them, and then spends a couple hours lapping it up, copying it all.

Elegant.

How much stuff? As I rinsed Martha's hair, I calculated: we want him on for two hours. He's connected over a 1200-baud line, which means he can read about one hundred twenty characters a second. In two hours, he could scan about one hundred fifty thousand words.

"Oh, Natasha, my charming counter-counter-spy, there's just vun problem. Where do ve find five hundred pages of fake secrets?"

"Simple, dollink. Ze secrets, ve invent. Ze regular data, ve use vhat's already lying around."

As the hot water ran out, we clambered out of the shower. Martha grinned as she explained further. "We can't invent that much information overnight. But we can create it as we go along, staying just ahead of him. And we can take ordinary bureaucratic documents, modify them a bit, and give them secret-sounding titles. Real secret documents are probably thick with boring, bureaucratic jargon . . ."

". . . So we'll just take a bunch of those unintelligible Department of Energy directives that are always littering my desk, and change them to look like state secrets."

Martha continued. "We'll have to be careful to keep it bland and bureaucratic. If we head a document with 'CHECK OUT THIS TOP SECRET ULTRA-CLASSIFIED NEAT STUFF,' then the hacker's going to get suspicious. Keep it all low-key. Forbidden enough to keep him interested, but not an obvious trap."

I rolled her ideas around my mind and realized how to implement them. "Sure. We invent this secretary, see, who works for people doing this secret project. And we let the hacker stumble onto her word processing files. Lots of rough drafts, repetitive stuff, and interoffice memos."

Claudia greeted us in the living room, where she had mopped up the pond I'd left behind. She listened to our plan and suggested a new wrinkle: "You know, you could create a form letter in your computer that invites the hacker to write in for more information. If the hacker fell for it, he might include his return address."

"Right," said Martha, "a letter promising more information, of course!"

The three of us sat around the kitchen table with devious grins, eating omelets and elaborating on our plan. Claudia described how the form letter should work: "I think it ought to be like a prize in a crackerjack box. Write to us, and we'll send you, uh . . . a secret decoder ring."

"But come on," I said, "there's no way he'll be stupid enough to send us his address." Seeing that I had thrown cold water on my coconspirators, I added that it was worth a try, but the main thing is to give him something that'll take a couple of hours to chew on.

Then I thought of another problem. "We don't know enough about military stuff to make sensible documents."

"They don't have to make sense," Martha grinned diabolically. "Real military documents don't make sense either. They're full of jargon and double-talk. You know, like 'the procedure for implementing the highly prioritized implementation procedure is hereinafter described in section two, subparagraph three of the procedural implementation plan.' Eh, Boris?"

Well, Martha and I biked up to the laboratory and logged onto the LBL computer. There we shoveled through a mound of real government documents and directives, which were overflowing with far more turgid bureaucratese than we could ever invent, changing them slightly so that they'd look "classified."

Our documents would describe a new Star Wars project. An outsider reading them would believe that Lawrence Berkeley Laboratory had just landed a fat government contract to manage a new computer network. The SDI Network.

This bogus network apparently linked together scores of classified computers and extended to military bases around the world. By reading our files, you'd find lieutenants and colonels, scientists and engineers. Here and there, we dropped hints of meetings and classified reports.

And we invented Barbara Sherwin, the sweet, bumbling secretary trying to figure out her new word processor and to keep track of the endless stream of documents produced by our newly invented "Strategic Defense Initiative Network Office." We named our fictitious secretary after an astronomer, Barbara Schaefer, and used the astronomer's real mailing address. I mentioned to the real Barbara to watch for any strange mail addressed to Barb Sherwin.

Our fake memoranda included budget requests ($50 million for communications costs), purchase orders, and technical descriptions of this network. We cribbed most of them from files lying around the computer, changing the addresses and a few words here and there.

For a mailing list, I grabbed a copy of the lab newsletter's list of names and addresses. I just flipped every "Mr." to "Lieutenant," every "Mrs." to "Captain," every "Dr." to "Colonel," and every "Professor" to "General." The addresses? Just stir in an occasional "Air Force Base" and "Pentagon." In half an hour, my ersatz mailing list looked like a veritable military Who's Who.

Some of the documents, however, we fabricated completely: correspondence between managers and petty bureaucrats. An information packet describing the technical capabilities of this network. And a form letter saying that the recipient could get more information on the SDI Network by writing to the project office.

"Let's label the account, the 'Strategic Information Network Group,' " I said. "It's got a great acronym: STING."

"Naw. He might catch on. Keep it bureaucratic," Martha said. "Use SDINET. It'll catch his eye, all right."

We put all the files under one account, SDINET, and made certain that I was the only one who knew the password. Then I made these files entirely inaccessible to everyone except the owner—me.

Large computers let you make a file world-readable, that is, open to anyone who logs into the system. It's a bit like leaving an office cabinet unlocked—anyone can read the contents when they wish. You might set world-read on a file containing the scores of the office's volleyball tournament.

With a single command, you can make a file readable by only certain people—for example, your co-workers. The latest sales report, or some manufacturing designs, need to be shared among a few people, but you don't want everyone to scan them.

Or a computer file can be entirely private. Nobody but you can read it. Like locking your desk drawer, this keeps everyone out. Well, almost everyone. The system manager can bypass the file protections, and read any file.

By setting our SDI files to be readable only by their owner, I made sure that nobody else would find them. Since I was the owner and the system manager, nobody else could see them.

Except, perhaps, a hacker masquerading as system manager.

For the hacker could still break in and become system manager. It would take him a couple of minutes to hatch his cuckoo's egg, but he'd then be able to read all the files on my system. Including those bogus SDI files.

If he touched those files, I'd know about it. My monitors saved his every move. Just to make certain, though, I attached an alarm to those SDI network files. If anyone looked at them—or just caused the computer to try to look at them—I'd find out about it. Right away.

My snare was baited. If the hacker bit, he'd take two hours to swallow the bait. Long enough for the Germans to track him down.

The next move was the hacker's.

# 41

I'D SCREWED UP AGAIN. OPERATION SHOWERHEAD WAS ready, all right. It might even work. But I'd forgotten an important detail.

I hadn't asked anyone's permission.

Normally, this wouldn't be a problem, since nobody cared what I did anyway. But bicycling up to the lab, I realized that every organization I'd been in contact with would want to know about our phony SDI files. Each place would have a different opinion, of course, but to go ahead without telling anyone would piss them all off.

But what if I asked their permission? I didn't want to think about it. Mostly, I worried about my boss. If Roy stood behind me, then the three-letter agencies couldn't touch me.

On January 7, I went straight to his office. We talked about relativistic electrodynamics for a while—which mostly meant my watching the old professor at the chalkboard. Say what you will about crusty college professors, there's no better way to learn than to listen to someone who's paid his dues.

"Say, boss, I'm trying to get out from under this hacker."

"CIA leaning on you again?"

Roy was joking, I hoped.

"No, but the Germans will only trace the line for one more week. After next weekend, we might as well call it quits."

"Good. It's been too long anyway."

"Well, I was thinking about planting some misleading data in our computer, to use as bait in catching the hacker."

"Sounds good to me. It won't work, of course."

"Why not?"

"Because the hacker's too paranoid. Still, go ahead. It'll be a useful exercise." Hot damn!

My boss's approval insulated me from the rest of the world. Still, I ought to tell the three-letter folks about our plans. I wrote a short proposal, framed as a scientific paper:

Proposal to Determine the Address of the Hacker
Problem:

A persistent hacker has invaded LBL's computers. Because he is coming from Europe, it takes an hour to trace the phone lines. We would like to learn his exact location.

Observations:

1. He is persistent.
2. He confidently works within our computers, unaware that we are watching him.
3. He searches for phrases like "sdi," "stealth," and "nuclear."
4. He is a competent programmer and is experienced at breaking into networks.

Suggested solution:

Provide fictitious information to keep him connected for more than an hour. Complete the phone tracing during this time.

My paper went on and on about History, Methodology, Implementation Details, and had footnotes about the chances of actually catching him. As boring as I could make it.

I sent this paper to the usual list of three-letter agencies: the FBI, CIA, NSA, and DOE. I included a note saying that unless someone objected, we'd carry out this plan next week.

A few days later, I called each agency. Mike Gibbons of the FBI understood what I was getting at, but wouldn't commit his agency one way or another. "What does the CIA have to say about it?"

Teejay at the CIA had also read my proposal, but was equally noncommittal:

"What did the guys at the 'F' entity say?"

"Mike said to call you."

"Well, ain't that dandy. Have you called the northern entity?" Northern entity? What's north of the CIA?

"Uh, Teejay, who's the northern entity?"

"You know, the big Fort M."

Oh—Fort Meade in Maryland. The NSA.

Yes, I had called Fort Meade, and Zeke Hanson at the NSA's National Computer Security Center had read my proposal. He seemed to like it, but he didn't want to have anything to do with it.

"Well, I sure can't tell you to go ahead," Zeke said. "Personally, I'd love to see what happens. But if you get into trouble, we don't have anything to do with it."

"I'm not looking for someone to take responsibility, I'm wondering if it's a bad idea." Sounds strange, but that's just what I was trying to do. Before you start an experiment, get the opinions of people who've been there before.

"Sounds good to me. But you really ought to check with the FBI." That closed the circle—everyone pointed their finger at someone else.

Well, I called the Department of Energy, the Air Force OSI, and a guy at the Defense Intelligence Agency. Nobody would take responsibility, of course, yet nobody blocked the idea. That's all I needed.

By Wednesday, it was too late for anyone to object. I was sold on Martha's idea, and was willing to back it up.

Sure enough, Wednesday afternoon, the hacker showed up. I'd been invited to lunch at the Cafe Pastorale in Berkeley with Dianne Johnson, the field representative of the Department of Energy. Along with Dave Stevens, the computer center's math whiz, we enjoyed some fine fettuccini, while talking about our progress and plans.

At 12:53 PST, in the middle of a cup of cappuccino, my beeper went off. The Morse code said the hacker was into our Unix-4 computer as Sventek. I didn't say a word—just ran to the phone booth and called Steve White at Tymnet ($2.25 in quarters), and he started the trace running. The hacker was on for only three minutes—just long enough to see who was logged onto my computer. I was back at the table before the coffee cooled off.

That spoiled the rest of lunch for me. Why had he stayed around only three minutes? Did he sense a trap? I couldn't tell until I saw the printout up at the lab.

The monitors showed him logging on as Sventek, listing the names of everyone currently logged on, and then disappearing. Damn him. He didn't look around long enough to discover our bogus files.

Oh—maybe our bait was too well hidden. The German phone technician would be around for only a couple more days, so I'd better make it more obvious.

From now on, I'd stay logged on to my computer. I would play sweet Barbara Sherwin, connected to the computer on the SDINET account. The next time the hacker raised his periscope, he'd see SDINET clunking away, trying to edit some file or another. If that didn't catch his attention, then nothing would.

Naturally, he didn't show up the next day, Thursday. We were running out of time. Nothing the next morning. I was about to call it quits, when my beeper sounded at 5:14 P.M., Friday, January 16. There's the hacker.

And I'm here, working in the SDINET account, playing with a word processing program. His first command, "who," listed ten people. I was the seventh on his list:

```
who
Astro
Carter
Fermi
Meyers
Microprobe
Oppy5
Sdinet
Sventek
Turnchek
Tompkins
```

There's the bait. Come on, go for it!

| | |
|---|---|
| **lbl> grep.sdinet/etc/passwd** | He's searching for user "SDINET" in our password file |

**sdinet:sx4sd34x2:user sdinet, files in/u4/sdinet, owner sdi network project**

Ha! He swallowed the hook! He's hunting for information about the user SDINET! I knew what he'd do next—he'd search over in the SDINET directory.

| | |
|---|---|
| **lbl> cd/u4/sdinet** | He's moving over to the SDINET directory |
| **lbl> ls** | and trying to list the file names |
| **file protection violation—you are not the owner.** | But he can't see them! |

Of course he can't read the SDINET data—I've locked everyone out of those files. But he knows how to evade my lock. Just plant a little egg, using the Gnu-Emacs software. Become superuser.

None of my files are hidden from the system manager. And my visitor knows exactly how to grab those privileges. It just takes a few minutes. Would he reach into the monkey bottle?

There he goes. He's checking that the Gnu-Emacs move-mail program hasn't been changed. Now he's creating his own false atrun program. Just like the old days. In a couple more minutes, he'll be system manager.

Only this time, I'm on the phone to Steve White.

"Steve, call Germany. The hacker's on, and it'll be a long session."

"Spot-on, Cliff. Call you back in ten minutes."

Now it's the Germans' turn. Can they pull the plum from the pie? Let's see, it's 5:15 P.M. in Berkeley, so in Germany, it's uh, 2:15 in the morning. Or is it 1:15? Either way, it's sure not ordinary business hours. Sure hope that the Hannover technicians stayed late tonight.

Meanwhile, the hacker's not wasting time. Within five minutes, he'd built a special program to make himself super-user. He twisted the tail of the Gnu-Emacs program, moving his special program into the systems area. Any minute now, Unix will discover that program and . . . yep, there it goes. He's super-user.

The hacker went straight for the forbidden SDINET files. (I'm glued to my monitor, thinking, "Come on, guy, wait till you see what's sitting there for you.") Sure enough, he first lists the file names:

```
lbl> ls
Connections
Form-Letter
Funding
Mailing-Labels
Pentagon-Request
Purchase-Orders
Memo-to-Gordon
Rhodes-Letter
SDI-computers
SDI-networks
SDI-Network-Proposal
User-List
World-Wide-Net
Visitor-information
```

Many of these files aren't just single memos. Some are file directories—whole file cabinets full of other files.

Which one will he look at first? That's easy. All of them.

For the next forty-five minutes, he dumps out file after file, reading all the garbage that Martha and I created. Boring, tedious ore, with an occasional nugget of technical information. For example:

Dear Major Rhodes:

Thank you for your comments concerning access to SDINET. As you know, a Network User Identifier (NUI) is required for access to both the Classified and Unclassified SDINET. Although these NUI's are distributed from different locations, it is important that users who use both sections of the network retain the same NUI.

For this reason, your command center should contact the network controllers directly. At our laboratory in Berkeley, we can easily modify your NUI, but we would prefer that you issue the appropriate request to the network controllers.

Sincerely yours,
Barbara Sherwin

Aah . . . there's a pointer in that letter saying that you can reach the SDINET from Lawrence Berkeley Laboratory. I'll bet that he'll spend an hour or two searching for the portal to reach that mythical SDINET.

Did he believe what I'd fed him? There's an easy way to find out. Just watch what he does—a disbeliever won't go hunting for the Holy Grail.

The files made a believer out of him. He interrupted his listing to search for a connection into our SDI network. On my monitor, I watched him patiently scan all our links to the outside world. Without knowing our system thoroughly, he couldn't search exhaustively, but he spent ten minutes checking the system for any ports labelled "SDI."

Hook, line, and sinker.

He returned to reading our fake SDINET files, and dumped the file named form-letter:

SDI Network Project
Lawrence Berkeley Lab
Mail Stop 50-351
1 Cyclotron Road
Berkeley, CA 94720

name name
address address
city city, state state, zip zip

Dear Sir:
Thank you for your inquiry about SDINET. We are happy to comply with your request for more information about this network. The following documents are available from this office. Please state which documents you wish mailed to you:

#37.6 SDINET Overview Description Document
19 pages, revised Sept, 1985

#41.7 Strategic Defense Initiative and Computer Networks:
Plans and implementations (Conference Notes)
227 pages, revised Sept, 1985
#45.2 Strategic Defense Initiative and Computer Networks:
Plans and implementations (Conference Notes)
300 pages, June, 1986
#47.3 SDINET Connectivity Requirements
65 pages, revised April, 1986
#48.8 How to link into the SDINET
25 pages, July 1986
#49.1 X.25 and X.75 connections to SDINET
(includes Japanese, European, and Hawaii nodes)
8 pages, December, 1986
#55.2 SDINET management plan for 1986 to 1988
47 pages, November 1985
#62.7 Unclassified SDINET membership list
(includes major Milnet connections)
24 pages, November, 1986
#65.3 Classified SDINET membership list
9 pages, November, 1986
#69.1 Developments in SDINET and Sdi Disnet
28 pages, October, 1986
NUI Request Form
This form is available here, but
should be returned to the Network Control Center

Other documents are available as well. If you wish to be added to our mailing list, please request so.
Because of the length of these documents, we must use the postal service.
Please send your request to the above address, attention Mrs. Barbara Sherwin.
The next high level review for SDINET is scheduled for 20 February, 1987. Because of this, all requests for documents must be received by us no later than close of business on 11 February, 1987. Requests received later than this date may be delayed.

Sincerely yours,
Mrs. Barbara Sherwin
Documents Secretary
SDINET Project

I wondered how he'd react to this letter. Would he send us his address?

It didn't make much difference. Steve White called back from Tymnet. "I've traced your connection over to the University of Bremen."

"Same as usual, huh?"

"Yeah. I guess they've reopened for classes," Steve said. "At any rate, the Bundespost has traced the Datex line from Bremen into Hannover."

"OK. Sounds like the hacker's in Hannover."

"That's what the Bundespost says. They've traced the Datex line into a dial-in port located near downtown Hannover."

"Keep going, I follow you."

"Now comes the tough part. Someone has dialed into the Datex system in Hannover. They're coming from Hannover, all right—it's not a long-distance line."

"Does the Bundespost know that phone number?"

"Almost. In the past half hour, the technician traced the line and has narrowed it down to one of fifty telephone numbers."

"Why can't they get the actual number?"

"Wolfgang's unclear about that. It sounds like they've determined the number to be from a group of local phones, but the next time they make a trace, they'll zero in on the actual telephone. From the sound of Wolfgang's message, they're excited about solving this case."

One in fifty, huh? The Bundespost is almost there. Next time, they'll have him.

Friday, January 16, 1987. The cuckoo laid its eggs in the wrong nest.

# 42

THE TRACE ALMOST REACHED THE HACKER. IF HE CAME by once more, we'd have him.

But the deadline was tomorrow night. Saturday, when the German telephone technicians would give up the chase. Would he show up?

"Martha, you don't want to hear this, but I'm sleeping at the lab again. This may be the end of the road, though."

"That's the dozenth time you've said that."

Probably was. The chase had been a constant stream of "I've almost got him" followed by "He's somewhere else." But this time it felt different. The messages from Germany were confident. They were on the right scent.

The hacker hadn't read all our bogus files. In the forty-five minutes that he'd linked into our system, he listed about a third of the data. He knew there was more, so why didn't he stay around and browse?

All the more likely that he'd come back soon. So once again, I crawled under my desk and fell asleep to the sound of a computer disk drive whining in the distance.

I woke up, for once, without a beeper squawking in my ear. Just a peaceful Saturday morning, alone in a sterile office, staring at the bottom of my desk. Oh well, I'd tried. Too bad the hacker didn't show up.

Since nobody else was around, I started to play with an astronomical program, trying to understand how mistakes in mirror-grinding affect images from a telescope. The program was just about working when my beeper called at 8:08 A.M.

A quick jog down the hall, and a glance at the monitor's screen. There's the hacker, just logging into the Unix-5 computer, on one of his old account names, Mark. No time to figure what he's doing here, just spread the word fast. Call Tymnet, and let them call the Bundespost.

"Hi Steve!"

"The hacker's back on, eh?" Steve must have heard it in the tone of my voice.

"Yep. Can you start the trace?"

"Here goes." He was gone for thirty seconds—it couldn't have been a full minute—when he announced, "He's coming from Bremen this time."

"Same as yesterday," I observed.

"I'll tell Wolfgang at the Bundespost." Steve hung up while I watched the hacker on my screen. Every minute the hacker visited, we were that much closer to unmasking him.

Yes, there he was, methodically reading our false data files. With every bureaucratic memo he read, I felt more satisfied, knowing he was being misled in two ways: his information was patently false, and his arrogant strides through our computer were leading him straight into our arms.

At 8:40, he left our computer. Steve White called back within a minute.

"The Germans traced him through the University of Bremen again," he said. "From there, into Hannover."

"Did they make any progress in getting his phone number?"

"Wolfgang says they've got all the digits of his phone number except the last two."

All but the last two digits? That didn't make sense—it meant that they'd traced the call to a group of one hundred phones. "But that's worse than yesterday, when they said they'd isolated him to one of fifty phones."

"All I can tell you is what I hear."

Disturbing, but at least they were tracing the lines.

At 10:17, he came back. By now, Martha had bicycled up to the lab, and the two of us were busy inventing new SDI files to feed him. We both ran to the monitors and watched him, expecting him to discover our latest work.

This time, he wasn't interested in SDI files. Instead, he went out over the Milnet, trying to break into military computers. One by one, trying to guess his way past their password protection.

He concentrated on Air Force and Army computers, occasionally knocking on the Navy's door. Places I'd never heard of, like the Air Force Weapons Lab, Descom Headquarters, Air Force CC OIS, the CCA-amc. Fifty places, without success.

Then he slid across the Milnet into a computer named Buckner. He got right in . . . didn't even need a password on the account named "guest."

Martha and I looked at each other, then at the screen. He'd broken into the Army Communications Center in Building 23, Room 121, of Fort Buckner. That much was obvious: the computer greeted the hacker with its address. But where's Fort Buckner?

About all I could tell was that its calendar was wrong. It said today was Sunday, and I knew it was Saturday. Martha took charge of the monitors, and I ran to the library, returning with their now familiar atlas.

Paging through the back pages, I found Ft. Buckner listed.

"Hey, Martha, you're not going to believe this, but the hacker's broken into a computer in Japan. Here's your Fort Buckner," I said, pointing to an island in the Pacific Ocean. "It's on Okinawa."

What a connection! From Hannover, Germany, the hacker linked to the University of Bremen, across a transatlantic cable into Tymnet, then into my Berkeley computer, and into the Milnet, finally reaching Okinawa. Jeez.

If someone in Okinawa had detected him, they'd have to unravel a truly daunting maze.

Not that this worldwide link satisfied him—he wanted Fort Buckner's database. For half an hour, he probed their system, finding it amazingly barren. A few letters here and there, and a list of about seventy-five users. Fort Buckner must be a very trusting place: nobody set passwords on their accounts.

He didn't find much on that system, outside of some electronic mail messages talking about when supplies would arrive from Hawaii. A collector of military acronyms would love the Fort Buckner computer, but any sane person would be bored.

"If he's so interested in military gobbledegook," Martha asked, "why not enlist?"

Well, this hacker wasn't bored. He listed as many text files as he could, skipping only the programs and Unix utilities. A bit after eleven in the morning, he finally grew tired, and logged off.

While he'd circled the globe with his spiderweb of connections, the German Bundespost had homed in on him.

The phone rang—had to be Steve White.

"Hi, Cliff," Steve said. "The trace is complete."

"The Germans got the guy?"

"They know his phone number."

"Well, who is he?" I asked.

"They can't say right now, but you're supposed to tell the FBI."

"Just tell me this much," I told Steve, "is it a computer or a person?"

"A person with a computer at his home. Or should I say, at his business."

Martha overheard the conversation and was now whistling a tune from *The Wizard of Oz:* "Ding-dong, the witch is dead. . . ."

At last, the trace was over. The police would bust him, he'd be arraigned, we'd press charges, and he'd be pacing a jail cell. So I thought.

But more important, my research was finished. Five months ago, I asked myself, "How come my accounts are imbalanced by 75 cents?" That question had led me across the country, under the ocean, through defense contractors and universities, to Hannover, Germany.

Martha and I biked home, stopping only to pick up a pint of heavy cream. We picked the last of our garden's strawberries and celebrated with homemade milkshakes. No doubt—there's no substitute for mixing 'em yourself. Toss in some ice cream, a couple bananas, a cup of milk, two eggs, a couple spoonfuls of vanilla, and a handful of homegrown strawberries. Thicken it with just enough malt. Now that's a milkshake.

Claudia, Martha, and I danced around the yard for a while—our plans had worked out perfectly.

"In a couple days, the police will bust him, and we'll find out what he was after," I told them. "Now that someone knows who's behind this, it can't be long."

"Yow, you'll get your name in the newspaper," Claudia marveled. "Will you still talk to us?"

"Yeah, I'll even keep washing the dishes."

The rest of the day, Martha and I spent in San Francisco's Golden Gate Park, riding the merry-go-round and roller-skating.

After all these months, the problem was solved. We'd thrown a net around the cuckoo.

# 43

HE STARED BLEAKLY AT THE BROKEN GREASY VENETIAN blinds, a cigarette butt dangling from his clammy lips. The sickly green glow of the screen reflected on his sallow tired features. Silently, deliberately, he invaded the computer.

Six thousand miles away, her longing white arms craved for him. He could feel her hot breath on his cheek, as her delicate fingers curled through his long brown hair. Her negligee parted invitingly, he sensed every curve through the thin silken gauze. She whispered, "Darling, don't leave me. . . ."

Suddenly the night was shattered—that sound again—he froze and stared at the night stand. A red light beckoned across the pitch-black room. His beeper sang its siren song.

Sunday morning, at 6:30, Martha and I were dreaming when the hacker stepped on my electronic tripwire. Damn. Such a great dream, too.

I slid out from under the quilts and called Steve White. He passed the message along to the Bundespost, and five minutes later, the trace was complete. Hannover again. Same guy.

From home, I couldn't observe him—he might notice me watching him. But only yesterday he'd finished reading all our phony SDI files. So why come back now?

It wasn't until I biked into work that I saw the hacker's targets. Milnet again. The printout showed him logging into my Berkeley computer, then reaching out over the Milnet, then trying to log onto a system at the Eglin Air Force Base.

He tried account names like guest, system, manager, and field service . . . all his old tricks. Eglin's computer didn't put up with such nonsense: it kicked him out after his fourth try. So, he went on the European Milnet Control computer, and tried again. Still no luck.

Sixty computers later, he still hadn't gotten into a military computer. But he kept trying.

At 1:39 P.M., he succeeded in logging into the Navy Coastal Systems Center in Panama City, Florida. He got into their system by trying the account "Ingres" with the password "Ingres."

Ingres database software lets you quickly search thousands of accounting records for the one entry you need. You make queries like, "Tell me all the quasars that emit X-rays," or "How many Tomahawk missiles are deployed in the Atlantic fleet?" Database software is powerful stuff, and the Ingres system is among the finest.

But it's sold with a backdoor password. When you install Ingres, it comes with a ready-made account that has an easily guessed password. My hacker knew this. The Navy coastal Systems Center didn't.

Once logged on, he meticulously checked that nobody was watching him. He listed the file structures and searched for links to nearby networks. He then listed the entire encrypted password file.

There he goes again. That's the third or fourth time I'd seen him copy the whole password file into his home machine. Something's strange here—the passwords are protected by encryption, so he can't possibly figure out the original password. Still, why else would he copy the password file?

After an hour inside the navy computer, he grew tired and went back to knocking on doors along the Milnet. That, too, lost its excitement after a while; after fifty or a hundred times, even he tired of seeing the message, "Invalid Login—bad password." So he printed out some SDINET files again, pretty much the same stuff he'd seen in the past couple of days. Around 2:30 in the afternoon he called it quits. He'd spent eight hours hacking on the military networks.

Plenty of time to trace his call. And time enough to learn that the German Bundespost has been in close contact with the Public Prosecutor in Bremen, Germany. They're contacting the authorities in Hannover, and they're also talking to the German BKA. Sounds like someone is about ready to close in on the hacker and make the arrest.

Who should I call about this break-in into the Navy computer?

A week ago, the Air Force OSI warned me not to call the system managers directly. Jim Christy said, "It just runs against military policy."

"I understand," I said. "But is there a clearinghouse to report these problems to?'

"No, not really," Jim explained. "You can tell the National Computer Security Center, but they're pretty much a one-way trap. They listen, all right, but they don't publicize problems. So if it's a military computer, call us," Jim said. "We'll go through channels and get the word to the right folks."

Monday morning brought the hacker again. Time to twist some more doorknobs. One by one, he scanned Milnet computers, ranging from the Rome Air Development Center in New York to someplace called the Naval Electronic Warfare Center. He tried fifteen places before he struck pay dirt—the Ramstein Air Force Base computer. This time, he discovered that the account, "bbncc," wasn't protected. No password needed.

Ramstein's computer seemed to be an electronic mail system for officers. He started listing everyone's mail. Quickly, it opened my eyes—this was stuff that he shouldn't be seeing.

OK, what should I do? I couldn't let him grab this information, yet I didn't want to tip my hand. Disconnecting him won't do much good—he'll just find another pathway. I can't call the place—I've no idea where Ramstein Air Force Base is. I can call Air Force OSI, but I've got to take action now—not in five minutes—before he reads the rest of their data.

I reached for the phone to call Jim Christy of the Air Force OSI. Naturally I can't remember his phone number. There in my pocket is a key chain. Of course, the old key chain trick. Just add some noise to his connection.

I jangled my keys against the connector, shorting out the hacker's communications line. Just enough to appear as noise to the hacker. "Static on the line," he'd think. Every time he asked for electronic mail from Ramstein, I garbled his commands, and Ramstein's computer misunderstood him.

After a few more attempts, he gave up on Ramstein Air Force Base, and went back to scanning the Milnet, trying to get into other places.

I finally reached Jim Christy at Air Force OSI. "The hacker's gotten into someplace called Ramstein Air Force Base. Wherever it is, you'd better tell them to change all their passwords."

"Ramstein's in Germany."

"Huh?" I asked. I'd thought the occupation of Europe had ended in the '50s. "What's the U.S. Air Force doing in Germany?"

"Protecting you. But let's not go into that. I'll warn them right away. Go back to watching the hacker."

I'd missed ten minutes of the hacker. He was trying to break into more military systems, slowly and methodically trying dozens of sites.

The Milnet addresses seemed to be in alphabetical order; right now he was working near the end of the alphabet. Mostly R's and S's. Aha! Yes, that was it. He was working from an alphabetized list. Somehow, he'd obtained the Milnet directory, and was checking off each site after he tried it.

He'd made it halfway through the S's when he tried a computer called Seckenheim. Logged right in as "Guest." No password. This was getting embarrassing.

But though he got into that computer, he didn't stay long. A few minutes to make a couple scans of their system files, then he logged off. I wondered why.

Still, I'd better do something. Time to call the Air Force.

"Hey, the hacker just got into someplace called Seckenheim. It's on the Milnet, so it must be a military computer. But I've never heard of it."

"Snake in the grass," Jim growled.

"Huh?"

"Damn. Seckenheim is the Army Material Command in Europe. Near Heidelberg. Germany again."

"Oops. Sorry about that."

"I'll take care of it." The hacker's success meant problems for the narcs. I wondered how many overseas military bases the United States has. The technology I could handle. It was geography and bureaucracies that tripped me up.

After having cracked three computers today, the hacker was still not satisfied. He continued to bang away on the Milnet, so I kept watch in the switchyard. One by one, I watched as he tried passwords. At 11:37, he got into a Vax computer named Stewart. Logged right in there as "Field," password, "Service." I'd seen it before. Another Vax computer running VMS that hadn't changed their default passwords.

The hacker dived right in. The field service account was privileged, and he wasted no time taking advantage of this. He first disabled accounting, so that he'd leave no tracks behind. Then he went directly to the *authorize* utility—the system software in charge of passwords—and selected one user, Rita, who hadn't used the system for the past few months. He modified Rita's account to give it full system privileges. Then he set a new password. "Ulfmerbold."

Where had I heard that word? Ulfmerbold. It sounded German. Something to figure out later. Meanwhile, I've got to watch my hacker.

Finally, a bit after noon, the hacker left Berkeley. A productive day for him.

The Stewart computer turned out to belong to Fort Stewart, an Army base in Georgia. I called Mike Gibbons of the FBI, and he took care of calling them.

"Mike, have you ever heard of the word 'Ulfmerbold'?"

"Nope. Sounds German, though."

"Just checking. Say, the Germans have completed the trace. The Bundespost now knows who's making the calls."

"Did they tell you?"

"Naw. Nobody ever tells me anything. You know that."

Mike laughed. "That's the way we operate, all right. But I'll get the Legat on the case right away."

"Legat?"

"Oh. Legal Attaché. You know, the guy in Bonn that handles our affairs."

"How soon until they arrest the guy?" I just wanted to know who and why—the last pieces of the puzzle.

"I don't know. But when it happens, I'll tell you. Shouldn't be long now."

By chance, around 3 P.M. Teejay called from the CIA. "What's new?"

"We completed the trace over the weekend."

"Where is he?"

"In Hannover."

"Mmmm. Know the guy's name?"

"No, not yet."

"Does the 'F' entity know?"

"I don't think so. But call them and find out. They never tell me a thing." I doubted that the FBI would tell the CIA, and I didn't want to be squeezed between the two. It was weird enough to talk to either.

"Any clues to his identity?"

"Hard to say. Ever hear of the word Ulfmerbold?"

"Mmmm. What's that from?"

"The hacker chose that as a password when he broke into a computer this morning. At Fort Stewart, Georgia."

"He's not letting the grass grow, huh?" Teejay still tried to sound uninterested, but his voice had a tremor that gave it away.

"Yeah. He got into a couple other places too."

"Where?"

"Oh," I said, "no place special. Just a couple military bases in Germany. And a place called Fort Buckner."

"Son of a bitch."

"You know them?"

"Yeah. I used to work at Fort Buckner. Back in my Army days. Lived on base with my wife." A CIA agent with a wife? I'd never thought of it. Spy novels never mention spouses or kids.

The hacker had chosen a strange password for his use. Ulfmerbold. Nothing in my dictionary. Not in Cassell's German-English dictionary. The trusty atlas showed nothing. Yet I'd heard this word before.

Martha hadn't heard of it. Nor had any of her friends. Not even my sister, the one who'd risked her life prowling around a high school in McLean, Virginia.

It took three days, but my boss, Roy Kerth, figured it out. Ulf Merbold is the West German astronaut who'd made astronomical observations from the space shuttle.

Another clue to Germany, unnecessary, now that the evidence was overwhelming. But why pick an astronaut's name? Hero worship? Or some more sinister motive?

Could this explain why he kept breaking into computers? Could I have been following someone obsessed with the U.S. space program—a guy who dreamed about becoming an astronaut and collected information about the space program?

Nope. This hacker sought out military computers—not NASA systems. He wanted SDI data, not astronomy. You don't search for the space shuttle on Okinawa. You don't find an astronaut's biography by looking up the Army's nuclear warfare plans for Central Europe.

# 44

TUESDAY MORNING GREETED ME WITH A PILE OF MESSAGES from Tymnet. Steve White read some electronic mail from the Deutsche Bundespost. "Since the University of Bremen won't pay for any more international calls, you'll have to carry that cost."

He knew that we couldn't afford it. "Steve, my boss balks at paying my salary, let alone this hacker's connections."

"How much time are you putting in on this chase?"

"Oh, about ten hours a day." I wasn't kidding. Even a five-minute connection by the hacker ballooned into a morning of phone calls. Everyone wanted to hear what had happened. Nobody offered support.

"Well then, I've some good news for you," Steve said. "Wolfgang Hoffman says there's a meeting in Hannover tomorrow. Something about coordinating legal, technical, and law-enforcement activities."

"Why's that good news?"

"Because they expect to make an arrest this weekend."

Finally.

"But there's a couple problems. The Germans haven't heard from the FBI yet. So they're putting things on hold. Wolfgang asks that you pass this message to the FBI."

"Will do."

My next call to the FBI showed the flip side of the coin. Special Agent Mike Gibbons explained the situation.

He'd sent telegrams to Bonn telling the FBI's Legat to contact the German police. At the same time, he shipped by air a folder of information to the Attaché. But somewhere, the messages weren't getting through—Wolfgang still hadn't heard about any warrants from the FBI.

"You see, we can't talk to anyone except through our Legat," Mike said. "Still, I'll rattle the cage again, and see that they're awake in Bonn."

Well, that FBI agent sure wasn't dragging his heels. I never did find out much about the Legal Attaché—do they work for the FBI or the State Department? Is it one part-time person or a whole staff? What do they really do? Who do they talk to in the German government? What do you have to do to wake them up?

The CIA wouldn't leave me alone. Teejay wanted every detail about the past weekend. But the juicy stuff—the guy's name, his motives, and his backers—remained a mystery. All I knew was that he'd been fingered.

"Say, Teejay, if I find out some of this for you, is there any chance you might, uh, trade some gossip?"

"I don't copy," the spook said.

"I mean, suppose you figure out who was behind all this. What'll you tell me about it?" I really wanted to know if he could send some spy over there and find out what this clown was up to.

"Sorry, Cliff. We're listeners, not talkers."

So much for learning anything from the CIA.

Within a day, however, more news came by way of Tymnet. Having traced the hacker's phone number, they compared his name to that on the German Datex accounts.

Hmmm. They're doing their homework!

Seems that the hacker used three different identifiers when he manipulated the Datex network. The first identifier belonged to the hacker. Same name, same address. The second one belonged to another person. And the third . . . well, it belonged to a company. A small company in Hannover that specialized in computers.

Were these identifiers stolen? It's as easy to steal a network user identifier as it is to steal a telephone credit card number—

just watch over someone's shoulder as she makes a call. Perhaps the hacker has ripped off several people's Datex network account numbers. If they worked for big multinational firms, they might never notice.

Or was this guy in collusion with someone else?

I'd pretty much convinced myself that he was acting alone. If a couple people were working together, they'd have to constantly exchange passwords. Moreover, the hacker had a single personality—patient, methodical, an almost mechanical diligence. Someone else wouldn't have quite the same style when prowling around the Milnet.

A few of his targets weren't sleeping. The day after he tried to pry their doors open, two of them called me. Grant Kerr, of the Hill Air Force Base in Utah, phoned. He was annoyed that one of my users, Sventek, had tried to break into his computer over the past weekend. And Chris McDonald of White Sands Missile Range reported the same.

Super! Some of our military bases keep their eyes open. Thirty-nine in forty are asleep. But there are a few system managers who vigilantly analyze their audit trails.

For the next few days, the hacker kept me hopping. He kept scanning my SDINET files, so every few hours, I'd add a couple more. I wanted the files to reflect an active office—a backlog of work and a busy, chatty secretary who didn't quite know how her computer worked. Pretty soon, I was wasting an hour a day generating this flimflam, just feeding the hacker.

Zeke Hanson of the National Computer Security Center helped with these bogus files. I knew nothing about military ranks, so he gave me a few hints.

"The military's just like any other hierarchy. Up at the top, there's the flag officers. Generals. Below them are colonels, except in the Navy, where there's captains. Then there's lieutenant colonels, then majors and captains . . ."

Things are easier in grad school. Just call everyone with a tie "Professor," and anyone with a beard "Dean." When in doubt, just say "Doctor."

Well, every couple days the hacker would log into my system

and read the SDINET files. If he had any doubts about the validity of this information, he never showed it. In fact, he soon began trying to log into military computers using the account SDINET.

Why not? Some of these ersatz files described network links into Milnet computers. I made sure they were crammed with lots of jargon and technobabble.

Still, feeding the hacker bait wasn't leading us to an arrest. Every time he appeared, we traced him all right, but I kept waiting for a phone call saying, "He's at the police station now."

Now that the Germans had a suspect in mind, Mike Gibbons met with the U.S. attorney in Virginia. The FBI's news was mixed: if a German citizen is involved, extradition is unlikely, unless there's underlying espionage.

By the end of the week, the hacker had returned for five more sessions, each an hour or more. He checked into the Navy and Army computers, making sure that they still let him in. I wondered why they hadn't closed their holes yet. Then he played around our laboratory computer, again checking over the SDINET files.

Perhaps he worried that we knew he'd stolen Sventek's account, for he found yet another unused account at our lab, changed its password, and began using it for his hacking.

With all the high-powered computer folks in my department, I worried that one of them would post a notice to an electronic bulletin board, or casually leak the story in a conversation. The hacker still searched our system for words like "security" and "hacker," so he'd stumble onto this news and our bird would fly the coop.

The Germans had promised a bust this weekend. The hacker had what I hoped was his last fling on Thursday, January 22, when he broke into a computer at Bolt, Beranak, and Newman, in Cambridge, Massachusetts. This computer, called the Butterfly-vax, was as unprotected as the rest: you just logged in as "guest," with no password.

I'd heard of BBN—they had built the Milnet. In fact, most of the Milnet would soon be controlled by their Butterfly computers. The hacker had found a particularly sensitive computer—if he planted the right kind of Trojan horse in this computer, he might steal all the passwords that ever crossed the Milnet. For this was where BBN developed their network software.

Stealing passwords at Lawrence Berkeley Labs only gives you access to nearby computers. The place to booby-trap software is where it's distributed. Slip a logic bomb into the development software; it'll be copied along with the valid programs and shipped to the rest of the country. A year later, your treacherous code will infest hundreds of computers.

The hacker understood this, but probably didn't realize that he'd stumbled into such a development system. He searched the system and found one glaring security hole: the root account needed no password. Anyone could log in as system manager without so much as a challenge. Whoa!

Someone was sure to discover such an obvious hole, so he wasted no time in exploiting it. He became system manager and created a new, privileged account. Even if the original flaw was discovered, he'd added a new backdoor into BBN's computer.

He created an account under the name Langman, with a password of "Bbnhack." I understood the password, all right, but why Langman? Could that be his real name? The German Bundespost won't tell me, but maybe the hacker himself did. What's the meaning of the name Langman?

No time to worry about it now. The hacker found a letter on the BBN computer, saying, "Hi, Dick! You can use my account at the University of Rochester. Log in as Thomas, with the password 'trytedj' . . ."

It didn't take him fifteen seconds to reach into the Rochester computer. He then spent an hour reading information about integrated circuit designs. Apparently, a graduate student at Rochester designed sub-micron circuits, using an advanced computer-controlled technique. The hacker started to grab everything, including the programs.

I wouldn't let him: this would be industrial espionage. Every time he started to copy some interesting files, I jingled my keys on the wires. He could look, but he'd better not touch. Finally, at 5:30, he gave up.

Meanwhile, I wondered about the word Langman. Was it someone's name?

Aah—there's a way to find out. Look it up in the phone book. Maggie Morley, our librarian, couldn't find a Hannover telephone directory, so she ordered one. A week later, with suitable aplomb, Maggie delivered the Deutschen Bundespost Telefonbuch, issue number seventeen, covering Ortsnetz and Hannover, with a rubber stamp on the side, "Funk-Taxi, 3811."

My atlas presented a dry, geographic Hannover. And the tourist guides spoke of a historic, scenic city, nestled along the river Leine. But the phone book, well, here's the city: the opticians, the fabric stores, a few dozen autohauses, even a perfumerie. And people . . . I spent an hour just paging through the white pages, imagining a whole different world. There were listings for Lang, Langhardt, Langheim, and Langheinecke, but not one Langman. Bum steer.

Steve White relayed a message from Germany. The Germans had been doing their homework. Apparently, when the hacker called a phone, the German police had printed out that phone number. Eventually, they figured out who was involved, just by piecing together the web of phone calls centered on the hacker.

Were the German authorities planning a simultaneous bust? Tymnet passed along a chilling message: "This is not a benign hacker. It is quite serious. The scope of the investigation is being extended. Thirty people are now working on this case. Instead of simply breaking into the apartments of one or two people, locksmiths are making keys to the houses of the hackers, and the arrests will be made when the hackers cannot destroy the evidence."

# 45

IF YOU PESTER AN ORGANIZATION LONG ENOUGH, eventually they'll hold a meeting. After all my calls to the FBI, NSA, CIA, and DOE, it was the Air Force Office of Special Investigations that gave in first. On February 4, they invited everyone to Bolling Air Force Base, in hopes of resolving the problem.

Suburban Washington's world is measured by position on the beltway. Bolling Air Force Base is somewhere around five o'clock, sort of south by southeast. Even with such explicit directions, I got royally lost: bicycling along Berkeley side streets isn't quite the same as driving a car around a DC highway.

At 11:30, three Department of Energy people met me at a restaurant near the Air Force base. Over some tortellini, we talked about DOE's computer security policies. They worry about atomic bomb secrets. But they're also painfully aware that security gets in the way of operations. High-security computers are difficult to get onto, and unfriendly to use. Open, friendly systems are usually insecure.

Then we went to Bolling. It was the first time I'd ever walked on a military base. The movies are accurate: people salute officers, and some poor guy at the guardhouse spends his day saluting every car that comes through. Nobody saluted me, of course—with long hair, jeans, and a beat-up jacket, a Martian would have been less conspicuous.

About twenty people showed up, from all the three-letter agencies. At last I could hook voices from the telephone to people's faces. Mike Gibbons actually did look like an FBI agent—thirty years old or so, neatly pressed suit, mustache, and probably lifted weights in his spare time. We talked about microcomputers for a while—he knew the Atari operating system inside and out. Jim Christy, the Air Force computer crime investigator, was tall, lanky, and exuded confidence. And there was Teejay, sitting over in the corner of the room, silent as ever.

Barrel-chested and smiling, Zeke Hanson of the NSA greeted me with a slap on the back. He knew his way around both computers and bureaucracies. Occasionally, he whispered interpretations like, "That guy's important to your cause" or "She's just spouting the party line." I felt uncomfortable among all the suits, but with Zeke's encouragement I managed to stand up and talk to the gathering.

I babbled for a while, describing the network connections and weak spots, and then the others discussed national policy on computer security. Seems that there wasn't any.

Through the whole meeting, people kept asking, "Who's in charge?" I looked over at the contingent from the FBI. Mike Gibbons, the agent handling this case, squirmed in his chair. Sitting next to Mike, George Lane of the FBI handled the questions. "Since we can't extradite the guy, the FBI isn't going to devote many resources to this case. We've already done all we can."

The DOE people didn't let this slide. "We've been begging you to call the Germans. They're begging you to contact them. But Bonn still hasn't seen your warrant."

"Uh, we've had a few problems in our Legat office, but that doesn't concern us here," Lane said. "The bottom line is that there's been no damage done by this hacker."

Russ Mundy, a wiry colonel from the Defense Communication Agency, could take it no longer. "No damage! This guy breaks into two dozen military computers and it's no damage? He's stealing computer time and network connections. Not to mention programs, data, and passwords. How long do we have to wait before he gets into something really serious?"

"But no classified data has been compromised," the FBI agent said. "And how much money has been lost—75 cents of computer time in Berkeley?"

I listened as the colonel tried a different approach. "We rely on our networks for communications. Not just military people, but engineers, students, secretaries, hell, even astronomers," he said, gesturing towards me. "This bastard is undermining the trust that holds our community together."

The FBI saw the hacker as a minor annoyance; perhaps just some kid messing around after school. The military people took it as a serious attack on their communications lines.

The Department of Justice backed up the FBI. "Germany won't extradite a German citizen, so why bother? And anyway, the FBI gets a hundred reports like this every year, and we can prosecute only one or two."

He went on to say that we already had enough evidence to convict the hacker: my logbook and printouts would stand up at a trial. And according to U.S. law, we didn't have to catch the hacker *flagrante delicto:* busting in on him while he was connected to a foreign computer. "So you really ought to close up shop. You're not strengthening your case, and we already have enough evidence to bring him to trial."

In the end, the Air Force OSI asked each group for direction. The FBI and Department of Justice wanted us to close up shop and lock the hacker out of our Berkeley computer. Neither Teejay of the CIA nor Zeke of NSA's National Computer Security Center felt there was anything to gain by staying open.

Leon Breault of the Department of Energy stood up. "We've got to support the guys in the trenches and catch this guy. If the FBI won't, then we will," he said, glaring at the Department of Justice attorney.

The people being hit by the hacker wanted to keep the monitoring going. Closing our monitoring station just meant that the hacker would prowl around using a different, unobserved pathway.

But who should we turn to for help? The FBI didn't want to touch the case. The military groups had no authority to issue warrants.

Where was a clearinghouse for reporting problems? This hacker had shown us several novel computer security problems. Who should we report them to?

Why, to the National Computer Security Center, of course. But Zeke told me otherwise: "We set standards for secure computers, and stay away from operational problems. All the same, we're always willing to collect reports from the field."

"Yeah, but will you warn me about others' problems?" I asked. "Will you send me a report describing security holes in my computer? Can you call me on the phone if someone's trying to break into my computer?"

"No, we're an information collection point." Just what I'd expect from an organization run by NSA. The giant vacuum cleaner that sucks in information, yet never says a thing.

Suppose I find a computer security problem, and it's widespread. Perhaps I should keep my mouth shut, and hope that nobody else figures it out. Fat chance.

Or perhaps I should tell the world. Post a notice to lots of electronic bulletin boards saying, "Hey, you can break into any Unix computer by . . ." That would at least wake up the folks who manage the systems. Maybe even prod them into action.

Or should I create a virus, one that takes advantage of this security hole?

If there were a trusted clearinghouse, I could report to them. They, in turn, could figure out a patch for the problem, and see that systems are fixed. The National Computer Security Center seemed like a logical place for this. After all, they specialize in computer security problems.

But they didn't want to touch it. The NCSC was too busy designing secure computers. For the past few years, they'd published an unreadable series of documents describing what they meant by a secure computer. In the end, to prove that a computer was secure, they'd hire a couple programmers to try to break into the system. Not a very reassuring proof of security. How many holes did the programmers miss?

The meeting at Bolling Air Force Base broke up with the FBI and Department of Justice dead set against our continuing to monitor the hacker. The CIA and NSA didn't say much, and the military groups and the Department of Energy wanted us to stay open. Since DOE paid our bills, we'd stay open, so long as an arrest seemed likely.

While I was around Washington, Zeke Hanson invited me to give a talk at the National Computer Security Center. It's just down the road from Fort Meade, NSA's headquarters; even so, I got lost trying to find the place. There, under the exhaust of Baltimore Airport, a guard inspected my backpack for floppy disks, tape recorders, and viewgraphs.

"Hay, what can I steal on a viewgraph?"

The guard scowled. "Them's our orders. Make trouble and you won't pass." He had a pistol on his side. OK.

You enter the meeting room through a door with a combination lock. Twenty people greeted me, leaving one chair empty, up near the front of the room. Ten minutes into my talk, a thin, bearded fellow wandered into the room, sat down in front, and interrupted my description of Tymnet's traces.

"What's the adiabatic lapse rate on Jupiter?"

Huh? I'm talking about transatlantic networks, and this guy asks me about the atmosphere of Jupiter? Well, hot dog—I can handle that.

"Oh about two degrees per kilometer, at least until you reach the two hundred millibar level." By chance, this guy had asked me something straight from my dissertation.

Well, I continued my story, and every ten minutes the bearded guy stood up, left the room, and returned. He'd ask questions about the core of the moon, the cratering history of Mars, and orbital resonances among the moons of Jupiter. Weird. Nobody else seemed to mind, so I dovetailed my talk on the hacker with technical responses to this guy's astronomical interrogation.

About quarter to five, I finished up and was walking out of the room (with a guard standing nearby). The bearded guy pulled me aside and said to the guard, "It's OK, he's with me."

"What are you doing tonight?"

"Oh, going out to dinner with an astronomer friend."

"Cool it. Tell him you'll be a couple hours late."

"Why? Who are you?"

"I'll tell you later. Call your friend now."

So I canceled my Friday evening dinner and was hustled into this guy's dark blue Volvo. What's happening here? I don't even know his name and I'm traveling down the road. Some sort of kidnapping, I guess.

"I'm Bob Morris, the chief scientist at the Computer Security Center," he said once we were on the highway. "We're going to Fort Meade, where you'll meet Harry Daniels. He's the assistant director of NSA. Tell him your story."

"But . . ."

"Just tell him what happened. I called him out of a congressional meeting in Washington to meet you. He's driving up here right now."

"But . . ." This guy wouldn't let me get a word in.

"Look, the atmosphere of Jupiter is fine—though I'd thought all atmospheres were adiabatic so long as they convected—but we've got a serious problem on our hands." Bob chain-smoked and kept the windows rolled up. I gasped for breath. He went on, "We've got to bring it to the attention of people who can do something about it."

"Yesterday's meeting at Bolling was supposed to resolve that."

"Just tell your story."

If security at the Computer Security Center was tough, over at NSA's headquarters—well, it took ten minutes to clear me through. Bob had no problem: "This badge lets me in anywhere, so long as I'm carrying a classified document."

He entered a password and slid the card through the badge reader; meanwhile the guard fumbled with my viewgraphs. By the time we got to the director's office, Harry Daniels had just arrived.

"This had better be important," he said, glaring at Bob. This guy looked impressive—thin and about six-foot-six, he stooped when walking through doors.

"It is. I wouldn't have called you otherwise," Bob said. "Cliff, tell him."

There was no room on his table—it was covered with cryptography equipment—so I spread out a diagram of the hacker's connections on the floor.

Harry Daniels followed the chart meticulously. "Does he use the German Datex-P system to access the international record carriers?"

Holy smoke! How does someone this important know communications networks in such detail? I was impressed. I described the hacker's break-ins, but the two of them wouldn't let me speak two sentences without interrupting with a question.

Bob Morris nodded and said, "Here's your smoking gun, Harry."

The NSA honcho nodded.

The two of them talked for a few minutes, while I played with a World War II Japanese encryption machine. I wished I'd brought my Captain Midnight Secret Decoder Ring to show them.

"Cliff, this is important," Harry Daniels said. "I'm not sure we can help you, but you can sure help us. We've had a real problem convincing various entities that computer security is a problem. We'd like you to talk to the National Telecommunications Security Committee. They make national policy, and we'd like them to know about this."

"Can't you just tell them?"

"We've been telling them for years," Harry Daniels said. "But this is the first documented case."

Bob Morris continued. "Mind you, he said, 'Documented.' The only difference between your case and others is that you've kept a logbook."

"So this has been going on before?"

"I wouldn't have called Harry up from Washington if I didn't think it was serious."

Driving back from Fort Meade, Bob Morris introduced himself. "I've worked on Unix security for the past ten years, up at Bell Labs in New Jersey."

Wait a second. This must be the Morris that invented the Unix password protection scheme. I'd read papers by him about securing computers. Of course—Bob Morris, the violinist. His eccentricity was legendary: I'd heard stories of him eating dessert and lying down so a cat could lick the whipped cream from his beard.

Bob continued. "Next month's meeting will be for policy making. If we're ever going to progress beyond writing standards documents, we've got to demonstrate a danger to these people." At last—someone at NSA who realized that computer security meant more than designing computers. "Any system can be insecure. All you have to do is stupidly manage it."

"Well, yes, that about sums it up," I agreed. "Some of the problems are genuine design flaws—like the Gnu-Emacs security hole—but most of them are from poor administration. The people running our computers don't know how to secure them."

"We've got to turn this around," Bob said. "Secure computers might keep the bad guys out, but if they're so balky that nobody will use 'em, it won't be much progress."

Tightening one computer was like securing an apartment house. But a network of computers, all sharing files and interchanging mail, well, this was like securing a small city. Bob, as chief scientist of the Computer Security Center, directed that effort.

By the time we'd returned, I'd almost grown accustomed to riding in a smoke-filled car. We started to argue about how planetary orbits interact—a subject that I ought to be able to hold my own in. But this guy knew his celestial mechanics. Ouch. I'd been away from astronomy too long if I couldn't bat off his questions.

# 46

IT WAS NEAT TO TALK WITH BOB MORRIS. STILL, I WAS glad to come back home to Martha. I caught the bus home from the airport and jaywalked across College Avenue—striking another blow for anarchy. My roommate, Claudia, was practicing her violin when I walked in the door.

Claudia greeted me with a teasing smile. "Where have you been—running around with loose women, I bet!"

"Nope. Meeting dark, handsome spies with trench coats, in dark alleys."

"Did you bring one home for me?" Claudia was perpetually on the lookout for a good man.

I didn't have time to get out a clever answer, because Martha caught me from behind in a bear hug, and hoisted me into the air. "I missed you," she said, setting me down with a kiss. It's fun, but a little startling, to live with a woman who can beat me in a wrestling match.

I was worried that she'd be mad that I had gone away again, but she shrugged. "You're in time for dinner, so you're fine. Get in the kitchen and help."

Martha was making her famous curry, which started with fresh coconut. I was out on the back porch whacking a coconut with a hammer when I heard Laurie pull up on her motorcycle.

Laurie was Martha's best friend and college roommate. Despite her fierce exterior—crew cut, leather jacket, boots and black muscle shirt—she was a gentle country girl from New Mexico. She and Martha shared a special bond that made me just slightly jealous. But I guess I passed her test, for she treated us both as family.

"Hey, Cliffer," she greeted me, mussing my hair. Looking hungrily at the coconut, she guessed what we were having. She tromped inside, hugged Martha, winked at Claudia, and scooped up the cat.

"Put that lazy thing down and chop some onions." Martha was kitchen despot.

At last, dinner was on the table: a platter of curried rice, and dishes of chopped vegetables, nuts, raisins, fruit, and chutney. If it grows, Martha will curry it.

"Hey, where've you been for the past couple days?" Laurie asked me.

"Oh, I was summoned to Washington—the Reagans, you know, asked me to dinner," I answered. I didn't want to say that I'd just talked to a bunch of spies and spooks. Laurie hated the government, and I didn't want to get her started.

"Oh, do tell what Nancy was wearing," Laurie simpered, taking a third helping of curry. "Hey, what's the latest on that hacker that you were chasing?"

"Oh, we haven't caught him yet. Maybe never will."

"Still think he's a Berkeley student?" I hadn't talked to Laurie about this thing for a couple months.

"Hard to say. For all I know, he's coming from abroad." I was getting nervous, surprised at my own reluctance to tell a close friend what I'd been up to. I wasn't ashamed, exactly, but . . .

"Why are you spending so much time trying to catch some poor computer geek who's just fooling around?"

"Fooling around? He broke into thirty military computers." Whoops. Instantly, I wanted to unsay that.

"So what? That sounds like a good reason not to chase him," Laurie said. "For all you know, he's a pacifist from the German Green party. Maybe he's trying to find out what secret weird things the military is doing, and expose them to public scrutiny."

I'd thought of that months ago and worried about it then. By now I was certain those weren't his motives. I had done the obvious experiment: categorize his interests. Back in January, I'd created a variety of different-flavored baits. Alongside the bogus SDINET files, I'd placed equally counterfeit files about Berkeley's local politics. Other files appeared to be financial statements, payroll accounts, games, and academic computer science topics.

If he were a peace activist, he might look at those political files. A thief, interested in ripping off our lab's payroll, would go for the financial records. And I'd expect a student or computer nerd to reach for the games or academic files. But he wasn't interested in any of these.

Except the SDI files.

This experiment, and a lot of more subtle things about his way of operating, convinced me that he was no idealist. This hacker was a spy.

But I couldn't exactly prove that, and even after I explained my experiment to Laurie, she wasn't convinced.

She still thought of anyone working against the military as one of "us," and in her eyes I was persecuting someone on "our own" side.

How do I explain that, having been mixed up in this thing so long, I had stopped seeing clear political boundaries? All of us had common interests: myself, my lab, the FBI, the CIA, NSA, military groups, and yes, even Laurie. Each of us desired security and privacy.

I tried a different tack. "Look, it's not a question of politics, but simple honesty. This guy violated my privacy and the privacy of all the other users. If someone broke into your house and rifled through your stuff, would you stop to ask if they were a fellow socialist?"

That didn't work either. "A computer system isn't private like a house," Laurie responded. "Lots of people use it for many purposes. Just because this guy doesn't have official permission to use it doesn't necessarily mean he has no legitimate purpose in being there."

"It's damned well exactly like a house. You don't want someone poking around in your diary, and you sure as hell don't want them messing with your data. Breaking into these systems is trespassing without permission. It's wrong no matter what your purpose is. And I have a right to ask these government agencies to help me get rid of this bastard. That's their job!"

My voice had risen, and Martha looked anxiously from my angry face to Laurie's. I realized that I sounded like a shotgun-toting redneck, yelling about law and order. Or worse—was I so blindly patriotic that I thought anyone who had an interest in military secrets was a traitor or a Commie spy?

I felt trapped and confused, and, unfairly, felt it was all Laurie's fault for being so simplistic and self-righteous. She hadn't had to deal with this hacker, and hadn't had to call on the CIA for help, hadn't talked to them and found they were real people. She thought of them as comic-book villains, killing innocent peasants in Central America. And maybe some of them were. But did that make it wrong to work with them at all?

I couldn't talk anymore. I got up, rudely pushing away my half-finished plate of curry. I stomped off to the garage, to sand some bookcases we were making, and sulk in peace.

After an hour or so, it got harder to keep up the sulking. I thought of the fireplace, pie for dessert, and Laurie's great back rubs. But, having grown up in a large, argumentative family, I was a dedicated, world-class sulker. I stayed in the cold garage, sanding furiously.

I suddenly noticed that Laurie was standing quietly by the door. "Cliff," she said softly, "I really didn't mean to give you such a hard time. Martha's crying in the kitchen. Come on, let's go inside."

I thought of how easily I hurt Martha with my temper. I didn't want to spoil the rest of the evening, so I went inside. We hugged, Martha wiped her face, and then served dessert. The rest of the evening, we talked brightly of other things.

But the questions Laurie had stirred up inside me came back to haunt me through the night. I lay awake and wondered where all this was leading me, and what kind of person I was being turned into by this strange chase.

I took flak from all directions, of course. The spooks didn't trust me—I had no security clearance and didn't work for a defense contractor. Nobody had asked me to do this work, and we ran on zero budget. And how do I tell my Berkeley friends that I'd just returned from the CIA?

Since we had neither funding nor authority, the three-letter agencies saw no reason to listen to us. I was little more than an annoyance to them. I felt like a grad student again.

A week after I'd returned, Mike Gibbons called from the FBI. "We're closing our end of the investigation. There's no reason for you to stay open."

"Mike, is that you speaking, or one of your bosses?"

"It's the FBI's official policy," Mike said, obviously annoyed.

"Has the Legal Attaché ever talked to the Germans?"

"Yes, but there's confusion. The German federal police—the BKA—aren't running the phone traces, so not much information filters back to the Legat's office. You might as well close up shop."

"What'll that do for the rest of the sites the hacker decides to hit?"

"Let them worry about it. Most of them won't care anyway."

Mike was right. Some of the places that had been broken into really didn't care if they'd been hit. The Pentagon's Optimis database, for example. Mike had notified them that a foreigner was using their computer. They didn't bat an eyelash. Today, for all I know, anyone can read about the Army's nuclear and biological warfare plans by logging onto their computer as *Anonymous,* with password *Guest.*

But though the FBI wanted us to close up, the Department of Energy still supported us. Halfway between, the CIA and NSA didn't say one way or another.

No support either. For all that we'd told them, the NSA had never coughed up a nickel. And while it might seem fun to rub shoulders with secret agents, it did little for my astronomy, and even less for my reputation.

For several weeks during February, the hacker evaporated. None of my alarms went off, and his accounts remained dormant. Was he on to us? Had someone tipped him off to his impending arrest? Or was he sneaking through other computers?

Whatever the answer, his disappearance relieved some of the pressure to decide. For three weeks, I had nothing to report, so it made no difference if we stayed open. Without a half dozen agencies on my neck, I managed to actually write some software during that time.

Then, routinely scanning my monitor's printouts, I noticed someone using the Lawrence Berkeley Lab's Petvax computer. It looked like they were entering the Petvax from a Caltech computer called Cithex.

I'd been warned about Cithex—Dan Kolkowitz at Stanford had noticed German hackers using that system to break into his computers. So I looked closely at the traffic from our Petvax to the Cithex computer.

Yeah. There it was. Someone had connected into the Caltech machine from the Petvax, and was trying to break into a place called Tinker, in Oklahoma.

Tinker? I looked it up in the Milnet directory. Tinker Air Force Base.

Uh oh. A little bit later, there's a connection into the Optimis database at the Pentagon. Then he tries the Letterman Army Institute. The Comptroller of the Army at Fort Harrison.

Oh hell. If it's not the same hacker, then someone's behaving just like him. That's why the hacker's been quiet for three weeks. He's been using a different set of computers to get onto the Milnet.

Obviously, closing up my laboratory's security holes won't keep him off the networks. This pestilence would have to be eradicated at the source.

The Petvax, of all computers! An outsider would think it's a toy—after all, a pet Vax computer, no?

Hardly. Pet is an acronym for Positron Emission Tomography. It's a medical diagnostic technique to locate where oxygen is consumed in people's brains. By injecting a patient with an activated isotope, LBL's scientists create images of the brain's interior. All you need is a particle accelerator to create radioactive isotopes, a hypersensitive particle detector, and a powerful computer.

That computer is the Petvax. Stored within it are patient

records, analysis programs, medical data, and scans of people's brains.

This hacker was playing games with medical tools. Break this computer, and someone's going to get hurt. A bad diagnosis or a dangerous injection. Or what?

The doctors and patients who used this instrument needed it to work perfectly. This was a sensitive medical device, not a plaything for some cyberpunk. Some poor computer geek, indeed.

Was it the same hacker? Two minutes after he disconnected from the Petvax, he entered my Unix computer, using the name Sventek. Nobody else knew that password.

We locked up the Petvax, changing its passwords and setting alarms on it. But the incident worried me. How many other computers was this hacker slithering through?

On February 27, Tymnet forwarded some electronic mail from Wolfgang Hoffman of the Bundespost. Apparently the German police can only arrest the hackers while they're connected. There's no shortage of evidence to bring them to trial, but without positive identification, the charges won't stick. We had to catch them red-handed.

Meanwhile, one of the LBL computer masters described the whole incident to a programmer at the Lawrence Livermore Lab. He, in turn, sent out electronic mail to several dozen people, saying that he was going to invite me to give a talk on "how we caught the German hackers." Dumb.

Ten minutes after he posted his note, three people called me up, each asking, "I thought you were keeping this hush-hush. Why the sudden publicity?"

Terrific. How do I undo this? If the hacker sees the note, it's all over.

John Erlichman observed that once you squeeze the toothpaste tube, it's tough to get the stuff back in. I called Livermore; it took five minutes to convince them to erase the message from all of their systems. But how do we prevent this kind of leak in the future?

Well, I could start by keeping my officemates better informed. From now on, every week I told them what was happening and why we had to keep quiet. It worked remarkably well . . . tell people the truth, and they'll respect your need for secrecy.

The hacker showed up occasionally during March. Just often enough to upset my life, but not quite enough to let the Germans nail him.

Thursday, March 12, was an overcast Berkeley day. Dry in the morning, so I biked in without a raincoat. At 12:19, the hacker visited his old haunt for a couple minutes. Listed a few of my SDINET files—he found out that Barbara Sherwin had recently bought a car and that SDINET was expanding overseas. He saw the names of thirty new documents, but he didn't read them. Why not?

Steve White had shown up in town, passing through to visit Ron Vivier at Tymnet's office in Silicon Valley. He and Martha and I had a date at a Thai restaurant, so I had to be home by six.

It started to rain about four, and I realized that I would get drenched bicycling home. Not much choice in the matter, so I insanely biked home—the rain turned the bike's brakes into banana peels. My raincoat wouldn't have been much defense against the sheet of water thrown up by an old DeSoto. Traffic splashed me from the side, and my bike's tires got me from below.

By the time I got home, I was sopping wet. Well, I've plenty of dry clothes. But only one pair of shoes. The grungy sneakers I was wearing. And they were soaked. I couldn't dry 'em out in time, so I looked around. There's Claudia's new microwave oven. I wonder . . .

So I popped my sneakers into Claudia's microwave, and pressed a few buttons. The display read "120." I wondered whether that meant 120 seconds, 120 watts, 120 degrees, or 120 light-years. I dunno.

It didn't make any difference. I'd just watch the sneakers through the window and make sure nothing goes wrong. For the first few seconds, no problem. Then the phone rang.

I ran into the front room to answer it. It was Martha.

"I'll be home in half an hour, honey," she said. "Don't forget dinner with Steve White."

"I'm getting ready right now. Uh, Martha, how do I set the microwave oven?"

"You don't need to. We're going out for dinner, remember?"

"Suppose I want to dry out my sneakers," I said. "What should I set on the microwave?"

"Be serious."

"I am being serious. My sneakers are wet."

"Don't you dare put them in the microwave."

"Well, theoretically speaking, how long should I hypothetically set the microwave for?"

"Don't even think about it. I'll come home and show you how to dry them out."

"Well, uh, sweetheart," I tried to interrupt.

"No. Don't touch the microwave," she said. "Just sit tight. Bye for now."

As I hung up the phone, I heard four beeps from the kitchen. Uh oh.

Boiling out of the back of Claudia's new Panasonic microwave oven was an angry cloud of thick, black smoke. The kind you see in newsreels, when the oil refinery blows up. And the stench—it smelled like an old tire burning.

I swung open the microwave, and another cloud of smoke belched out. I reached in and tried pulling out the sneakers—they still looked like sneakers, but had the texture of hot mozzarella cheese. I tossed them and the glass tray out the kitchen window. The tray shattered in the driveway, and the smoldering sneakers lay seething next to the plum tree.

Now I'm in deep yogurt. Martha's due home in half an hour and the kitchen smells like Akron during the tire-burning festival. Time to clean up the mess.

I got out the paper towels and started scrubbing the microwave. Black soot all over. Not the kind of soot that washes away, either. Wiping the glop only spreads the black plague further.

Half an hour. How do you get rid of the delicate fragrance of burning rubber? I swung open the windows and door, letting the wind blow the stench away. It didn't do much for the smell, and now the rain was blowing in the windows.

When you make a mess, cover it up. I remembered a homemakers' column: to mask household aromas, boil a small amount of vanilla on the stove. Well, it can't make things worse. I dump a couple of ounces of vanilla in a pan and crank up the heat.

Sure enough, in a couple minutes, the vanilla works. The kitchen no longer smells like a burning old blackwall tire. No, now it smells like a burning new whitewall tire.

Meanwhile, I'm cleaning the walls and ceiling. But I forgot the vanilla. The vanilla evaporates, the pot burns, and I've now screwed up twice. Three times, if you count the soggy floor.

Fifteen minutes. What to do? Appeasement. I'll bake her some cookies. Reach into the refrigerator for last night's cookie dough, and slap lumps of it onto a cookie pan. Set the oven at 375, just right for chocolate chips.

Well, a third of the cookies slid off the pan and stuck on the bottom of the oven where they turned to cinders.

Martha walks in, takes one sniff, sees the black welt on the ceiling, and says, "You didn't."

"I'm sorry."

"I told you."

"I'm sorry twice."

"But I said . . ."

The doorbell rings. Steve White enters, and with British aplomb says, "I say, old chap. Is there a tire factory nearby?"

# 47

THROUGH MARCH AND EARLY APRIL, THE HACKER LAID low. Occasionally, he'd pop in, just long enough to keep his accounts on the active list. But he seemed uninterested in reaching into other computers, and pretty much ignored my new SDINET files. What was happening to this guy? If he's been arrested, he wouldn't show up here. And if he's busy on other projects, why does he just show up for a minute, then disappear?

On April 14, I was working on the Unix system when I noticed Marv Atchley logged into the system.

Odd. Marv's upstairs, giving a pep talk to some programmers. I wandered over to his cubicle and looked at his terminal. Not even turned on.

Who's using Marv's account? I ran over to the switchyard and saw someone coming in through our Tymnet port. They were connected into the system as Marv Atchley.

I called Tymnet—Steve traced the line quickly. "It's from Hannover, Germany. Are you sure it's not the hacker?"

"Hard to say. I'll call you right back."

I ran up four flights of stairs and peered into the conference room. Yep, there was Marv Atchley, giving an animated talk to twenty-five programmers.

By the time I returned to the switchyard, the pseudo-Marv was gone. But I could see that he'd entered the system without any tricks. Otherwise he would have set off my alarms. Whoever it was must know Marv's password.

When the meeting ended, I showed the printout to Marv.

"Damned if I know who it is. I sure never gave my password to anyone."

"How long since you changed it?"

"Oh, a few weeks ago."

"And what's your password?"

"Messiah. I'll change it right now."

How the hell did this hacker get Marv's password? I would have noticed if he'd set a Trojan horse. Could he have guessed the word "Messiah"?

Uh oh. There's a way he could have.

Our passwords are stored encrypted. You can search the entire computer, and you'll never find the word "Messiah." You will find it encrypted as "p3kqznqiewe." Our password file was filled with such encrypted gibberish. And there's no way to reconstruct the avocado from that guacamole.

But you can guess passwords. Suppose the hacker tried to log in as Marv, then tried the password "Aardvark." My system says, "no good." The hacker, being persistent, then tries again, using the password "Aaron." Again, no luck.

One by one, he tries to log on using passwords that he looks up in a dictionary. Eventually, he tries the password "Messiah." The door opens wide.

Each trial takes a couple seconds. His fingers would wear out before he tried the whole dictionary. Such a brute-force method of guessing passwords will only work on a completely mismanaged computer.

But I saw this hacker copy our password file into his own computer. How could he use a list of our encrypted passwords?

The Unix password scheme uses an encryption program that's public. Anyone can get a copy of it—it's posted to bulletin boards. With a hundred thousand Unix computers in the world, you couldn't keep the program secret.

The Unix encryption program works in one direction only: it will encrypt from English text into gibberish. You can't reverse the process to translate encrypted passwords into English.

But with this encryption program, you can encrypt every word in the dictionary. Make a list of encrypted English words from your dictionary. Then, it's a simple matter to compare what's in my password file to your list of encrypted passwords. This must be how the hacker is cracking passwords.

On his computer in Hannover, he'd run the Unix password encryption program. He'd feed it the whole dictionary, and one by one, his program would encrypt every word in the English language. Something like this:

Aardvark encrypts to "vi4zkcvlsfz." Is that the same as "p3kqznqiewe"? No, so go on to the next word in the dictionary.

Aaron encrypts to "zzolegcklg8." Not the same as "p3kqznqiewe," so go on to the next word in the dictionary.

Eventually, his program would discover that Messiah encrypts to "p3kqznqiewe."

When his program found a match, bingo—it would print it out.

My hacker was cracking passwords using a dictionary. He could find anyone's password, so long as it was an English word.

This was serious stuff. It meant that every time I'd seen him copy a password file, he could now figure out legitimate users' passwords. Bad news. I checked my logbook. He'd copied these files from our Unix computer, the Anniston system, and the Navy Coastal Systems Command. I wondered if he'd be back in those computers.

Hey—I'd proven that he was cracking passwords on his computer. There are around a hundred thousand words in an English dictionary. It had been about three weeks since he copied my password file. If his password cracker worked continually for three weeks, could he have guessed Marv's password?

Well, on an ordinary Vax computer, it takes about a second to encrypt one password. A hundred thousand words, then, would take around a day. On an IBM PC, maybe a month. A Cray supercomputer might take an hour.

But according to Marv, this guy did it in three weeks. So he wasn't using a little home computer. He must be running the password cracker on a Vax or a Sun workstation. I had to be careful about this conclusion, though. He might use a faster algorithm or have waited a few days after cracking Marv's password.

Still, I patted myself on the back. Just by noticing that he'd been cracking passwords, I knew what type of computer he was using. Remote-control detective work.

This explained why he'd always copied our password files to his system. He was cracking our passwords in Germany.

Even one guessed password was dangerous. Now, if I erased Sventek's account, he could sneak in on someone else's account. Good thing that I'd not closed the door on him. What I'd thought to be bulletproof—my passwords—turned out to be riddled with holes.

Password cracking. I'd not come across it before, but I suppose that experts had. Well, what do the experts say about it? I called Bob Morris, the big shot I'd met at NSA. He'd invented the Unix password encryption system.

"I think the hacker's cracking my passwords," I told Bob.

"Eh?" Bob was obviously interested. "Is he using a dictionary or has he actually reversed the data encryption algorithm?"

"A dictionary, I think."

"Big deal. Why, I've got three good password cracking programs. One of them will pre-compute the passwords, so it runs a couple hundred times faster. Want a copy?"

Egads, he was offering me a copy of a password-cracking program! "Uh, no, I don't think so," I said. "If I ever need to decrypt passwords, though, I'll call you. Say, how long have people known about password cracking?"

"This kind of brute force stuff? Oh maybe five or ten years. It's child's play."

Cracking passwords as a game? What kind of a guy is this?

Bob continued. "Guessing won't work when you choose good passwords. Our real concern is with the encryption programs. If someone figures out a way to reverse that software, we're in deep trouble."

I now understood what he meant. The program that translated

"Messiah" into "p3kqznqiewe" is a one-way street. It needs just a second to encrypt your password. But if someone found a way to crank that sausage machine backwards—a way to convert "p3kqznqiewe" into "Messiah"—then they could figure out every password, without guessing.

Well, I'd at least told the NSA. Maybe they'd known these techniques for years, but now they officially knew that someone else was using them. Would they publicize it? Come to think of it, if NSA had known of this for ten years, why hadn't they publicized it already?

Systems designers needed to know about this problem—to build stronger operating systems. Computer managers ought to know, too. And every person who used a password should be warned. It's a simple rule: don't pick passwords that might show up in a dictionary. Why hadn't anyone told me?

The National Computer Security Center didn't seem interested in real-world problems of thousands of Unix computers out in the field. I wanted to know about weaknesses in my Unix system. What problems had been reported? Before, I'd discovered a bug in the Gnu-Emacs editor. A widespread security hole. I'd dutifully reported it to the National Computer Security Center. But they never told anyone about it. Now, I'd discovered that passwords that appeared in dictionaries weren't safe.

How many other security holes were lurking in my system?

The NCSC might know, but they weren't saying.

NSA's motto, "Never Say Anything," seemed to come into play. Yet by keeping silent about these computer security problems, they hurt us all. I could see that the hackers had long ago discovered and exploited these holes. Why wasn't someone telling the good guys?

"It's not our bailiwick," Bob Morris said. "We collect this information so as to better design future computers."

Somewhere, somehow, something was wrong here. The guys in black hats knew the combinations to our vaults. But the white hats were silent.

Well, forget the NSA for now. What more could I do? It was time to prod the other agencies.

By late April the Bundespost still hadn't received the proper papers from the United States. Their traces were based on an official complaint filed by the University of Bremen.

But although the Bundespost had completed several traces, they wouldn't tell me the suspects' names or phone numbers. German law prohibited this. Sounded familiar. Briefly, I wondered if my sister Jeannie would be willing to snoop around Hannover. She'd been the most responsive investigator so far.

I phoned Mike Gibbons. "We're no longer handling this as a criminal case," he said.

"Why give up when the Germans have traced the line and know the suspects' names?"

"I didn't say we were giving up. I just said that the FBI isn't treating this as a criminal case."

What did that mean? As usual, Mike clammed up when I asked questions.

Had the Air Force made much progress? They were quietly getting the word out that reptiles were crawling through the Milnet, trying to break into military computers. One by one, sites were tightening up security.

But the Air Force relied on the FBI to catch the hacker. Ann Funk and Jim Christy wished they could help, but couldn't.

"Tell me anything except, 'It's not my bailiwick,' " I said.

"OK," Ann replied, "it's not within my command."

# 48

I DIDN'T LIKE LEAVING BERKELEY, PARTLY BECAUSE I missed my sweetheart, but also because it left the hacker unwatched.

I was to talk to the NTISSIC, a governmental organization whose acronym has never been decoded. Bob Morris said they set policy for telecommunications and information security, so I could guess some of the letters.

"While you're in the area," Teejay said, "how about stopping by our headquarters in Langley?"

Me? Visit the CIA? I'm in way over my head now. Meeting the spooks on their own ground. I could just imagine it: hundreds of spies in trench coats, skulking around hallways.

Then the NSA invited me to Fort Meade as well. But not quite so informally. Over the phone, Zeke Hanson said, "We'd like you to prepare a talk for the X-1 department. They'll send you questions in advance."

Department X-1 of the National Security Agency? Yow, now this was cloak-and-dagger. As usual, I couldn't get any more information out of them . . . Zeke wouldn't even tell me what X-1 stood for.

Well, I arrived at NSA, and Bob Morris greeted me in his office. The three chalkboards were covered with Russian writing ("They're rhyming riddles," he explained) and a few mathematical equations. Where else but at NSA?

I chalked a short note in Chinese, and Bob hit me with an easy number problem: OTTFFSS. "What's the next letter, Cliff?"

That was an oldie. One. Two. Three. Four. Five. Six. Seven. "The next letter is E for Eight," I announced.

Well, we fooled around with puzzles and palindromes for a while, until he wrote out this series of numbers: 1, 11, 21, 1211, 111221.

"Complete that series, Cliff."

I looked at it for five minutes and gave up. I'm sure it's easy, but to this day, I still haven't solved it.

It was weird. Here I was, hoping to light a fire under NSA's feet. And here was Bob Morris, their top guru, competing with me in number games. Fun, sure. But disquieting.

We drove down to Washington, to the Department of Justice. We talked about computer security, and I pointed out to him that, for all he knew, I could be making up this whole story.

"You don't have a way of checking up on me."

"We don't need to. NSA is a house of mirrors—each section checks on another section."

"You mean you spy on yourself?"

"No, no, no. We constantly check our results. For instance, when we solve a mathematical problem by theoretical means, we check the result on a computer. Then another section might try to solve the same problem with a different technique. It's all a matter of abstraction."

"Think anyone will mind that I don't have a tie?" I'd worn a clean pair of jeans, figuring there might be some important people. But I still didn't own a suit or tie.

"Don't worry," Bob said. "At your level of abstraction, it doesn't make any difference."

The meeting was top secret, so I couldn't listen—someone fetched me when my turn came. In a small room, lit only by the viewgraph machine, there were around thirty people, most of them in uniforms. Generals and admirals, like you see in the movies.

Well, I talked for half an hour, describing how the hacker was breaking into military computers and skipping through our networks. One general in the back kept interrupting with questions. Not easy ones, like "When did you discover this guy?" but toughies, like "How can you prove that electronic mail hasn't been forged?" and "Why hasn't the FBI solved this case?"

Well, the questions didn't let up for another half hour, when they finally let me off the rack. Over cheese sandwiches, Bob Morris explained what had happened.

"I've never seen so many brass in one room before. You know, that one guy who asked the good questions—he's one of the junior people in the room. Just a Major General."

I know as little about the military world as the next person. "I guess I'm impressed, though I'm not sure why," I said.

"You ought to be," Bob said. "These are all flag officers. General John Paul Hyde works at the Joint Chiefs of Staff. And that guy in the front row—he's a big shot from the FBI. It's a good thing he heard you."

I wasn't so sure. I could imagine a honcho in the FBI having a rough time of it: he knows that his agency ought to be doing something, yet something gets corked up. He didn't need flak from some Berkeley longhair; he needed our support and cooperation.

I was suddenly queasy. I pressed the replay button in my mind. Did I screw up? It's a weird feeling of being nervous after you do something. The more I thought about it, the more impressed I was with the military people. They'd zeroed in on the weak points of my talk, and understood both the details and importance of what I'd said.

How far I'd come. A year ago, I would have viewed these officers as war-mongering puppets of the Wall Street capitalists. This, after all, was what I'd learned in college. Now things didn't seem so black and white. They seemed like smart people handling a serious problem.

The next morning I was to speak at NSA's X-1 department. Sure enough, they'd prepared a list of questions, and asked me to concentrate on the following themes:

1. How was the penetrator tracked?
2. What auditing features exist?

3. How to audit someone with system-level privilege?
4. Supply technical details on how to penetrate computers.
5. How were passwords obtained for the Livermore Crays?
6. How were super-user privileges obtained?
7. Did the penetrator guard against detection?

I stared at these questions, and gulped. Oh, I understood what the NSA folks were asking me, but there was something wrong here.

Was it that the answers to these questions could be used to break into systems? No, that wasn't my objection. They covered essentially defensive topics.

Or did I object to NSA's role of gathering information but not sharing it with anyone else? No, not really. I had resigned myself to that.

Reading them a third time, I sensed that they showed an underlying assumption that I found offensive. I scratched my head, wondering what was annoying me.

Finally I realized what galled me about their questions.

It wasn't the content of the questions, it was their intrinsic neutrality. They assumed an impersonal adversary—a sanitized "penetrator." They implied that this was an emotionless, technical problem, to be solved by purely technical means.

So long as you think of someone ripping you off as a "penetrator," you'll never make any progress. As long as they remained impersonal and detached, the NSA people would never realize that this wasn't just a computer being penetrated, but was a community being attacked.

As a scientist, I understood the importance of remaining detached from an experiment. But I'd never solve the problem until I got involved; until I worried about the cancer patients who might be injured by this guy; until I became angry that this hacker was directly threatening all of us.

I rephrased the questions and scribbled a new viewgraph:

1. How does this scoundrel break into computers?
2. Which systems does he slither into?

3. How did this bastard become super-user?
4. How did the louse get passwords to the Livermore Cray?
5. Did the skunk guard against detection?
6. Can you audit a varmint who's system manager?
7. How do you trace an eggsucker back to his roost?

Now *those* questions, I can answer.

These NSA spooks spoke in morally null jargon, while I felt genuine outrage. Outrage that I was wasting my time following a vandal instead of doing astrophysics. Outrage that this spy was grabbing sensitive information with impunity. Outrage that my government didn't give a damn.

So how do you pump up a bunch of technocrats when you're a long-haired astronomer without a tie? Or without any security clearance? (There must be some rule like, "No suit, no shoes, no clearance.") I did my best, but I'm afraid that the NSA people were more interested in the technology than any ethical implications.

Afterwards they showed me a few of their computer systems. It was a bit disconcerting: every room I walked into had a flashing red light on the ceiling. "It warns everyone not to say anything classified while you're here," I was told.

"What's the meaning of section X-1?" I asked my guide.

"Oh, that's boring," she replied. "NSA has twenty-four divisions, each with a letter. X is the secure software group. We test secure computers. X-1 are the mathematical folks who test software theoretically—trying to find holes in its design. X-2 people sit at the computer, trying to break software once it's written."

"So that's why you're interested in computer weaknesses."

"Yeah. One division of NSA may spend three years building a secure computer. X-1 will examine its design and then X-2 will bang on it, searching for holes. If we find any, we'll return it, but we won't tell them where the bug is. We leave it for them to puzzle out."

I wondered if they would have picked up the problem with Gnu-Emacs.

Along the way, I asked several people at NSA if there was any way that they could support our work. Individually, they regretted that our funding came entirely out of physics grants. Collectively, though, they offered no help.

"It would be easier if you were a defense contractor," one spook told me. "NSA shies away from academics. There seems to be a kind of mutual distrust." So far, my total outside support was $85, an honorarium for speaking at the San Francisco Bay Technical Librarians' Association.

The tour of NSA lasted well into lunch, so I left Fort Meade late, and got plenty lost on my way to the CIA in Langley, Virginia. Around 2 P.M., I found the unmarked turnoff and pulled up to the gatehouse, an hour late.

The guard stared at me like I'd recently arrived from Mars. "Who are you here to see?"

"Teejay."

"Your last name?"

"Stoll." The guard looked over her clipboard, handed me a form to fill out, and slipped a blue pass on the rental car's dashboard.

A VIP parking pass from the CIA. That's gotta be worth $5.00 back in The People's Republic of Berkeley. Maybe $10.00.

Me? A VIP? At the CIA? Surreal. I dodged a few joggers and bicycles on my way to the VIP lot. An armed guard assured me that I didn't have to lock the car doors. In the background, the seventeen-year locusts were buzzing and a mallard quacked. What's a flock of ducks doing at the portals of the CIA?

Teejay hadn't said how technical a talk he wanted, so I stuffed my viewgraphs into a grungy envelope. Then, off to the CIA building.

"You're late," Teejay called from across the foyer. What do I tell him? That I always get lost on freeways?

In the middle of the foyer's floor is a five-foot-diameter seal of the CIA, a terrazzo eagle set behind an official seal. I expected everyone to walk around the gray symbol, just as the high school students do in *Rebel Without a Cause.* No such luck. Everyone walks on top of it, showing the poor bird no respect.

On the wall, there's a marble inscription, "The Truth Shall Set You Free." (I wondered why they'd use Caltech's motto—then I noticed the quote came from the Bible.) Four-dozen stars were engraved on the opposite wall—I could only guess about the forty-eight lives they represented.

After a ritualistic search of my belongings, I received a fluorescent red badge with a V. The visitor tag wasn't necessary—I was the only guy around without a tie. Not a trench coat in sight.

The atmosphere was that of a subdued campus, with people strolling the hallway, practicing languages, and arguing around newspapers. Every once in a while, a couple would wander by, arm in arm. This was a long way from Boris and Natasha cartoons.

Well, not exactly like a campus. As Teejay showed me to his first-floor office, I noticed that each door was a different color, but none had cartoons or political posters on them. Some, however, had combination locks, almost like bank vaults. Even the electrical boxes had padlocks.

"Because you're late, we've rescheduled the meeting," Teejay said.

"I've got to select viewgraphs," I said. "How technical a talk should I give?"

Teejay gave me the hairy eyeball and said, "Don't worry about it. You won't need viewgraphs."

I sensed trouble ahead. No escaping this time. While sitting around Teejay's desk, I discovered that he had a fantastic set of rubber stamps. Real "TOP SECRET" stamps, along with things like "CLASSIFIED," "EYES ONLY," "COMPARTMENTALIZED INTELLIGENCE," "SHRED AFTER READING," and "NOFORN." I figured the last one meant "No Fornicating," but Teejay set me straight: "No Foreign Nationals." I stamped each one on a sheet of paper, and stuffed it in my pack of viewgraphs.

Greg Fennel, the other spook who had visited me in Berkeley, stopped by and took me up to the CIA's computer room. More like a stadium. In Berkeley, I was accustomed to a dozen computers in a big room. Here, there were hundreds of mainframe computers packed tightly together in a huge cavern. Greg pointed out that, outside of Fort Meade, it's the world's largest computer installation.

All IBM mainframes.

Now, among Unix aficionados, big IBM systems are throwbacks to the 1960s, when computing centers were the rage. With desktop workstations, networks, and personal computers, Goliath centralized systems seem antiquated.

"Why all this IBM stuff?" I asked Greg. "Those things are dinosaurs." I snidely showed my Unix bias.

"Well, we're changing," Greg answered. "We've got a dedicated artificial intelligence group, active robotics researchers, and our image-processing lab really cooks."

I remembered proudly showing Teejay and Greg through my lab's computing system. Suddenly, I felt incredibly embarrassed—our five Vaxes, scientific workhorses to us, seemed mighty puny next to these.

Yet our purposes were different. The CIA needs a giant database system—they want to organize and associate lots of diverse data. We needed number crunchers: computers that were fast with math. It's always tempting to measure the speed of a computer or the size of its disks, and then conclude that "this one is better."

The question isn't "Which computer is faster," no, not even "Which is better." Instead, ask "Which is more suitable?" or "Which will get your job done?"

After touring the CIA's computing division, Teejay and Greg took me up to the seventh floor. The staircase is labeled with the floor numbers in different languages: I recognized the fifth floor (Chinese) and the sixth floor (Russian).

I was shown to an anteroom with a Persian rug on the floor, Impressionist art on the walls, and a bust of George Washington in the corner. A real mixed bag. I settled down into a sofa with Greg and Teejay. Across from us were two other guys, each with a picture badge. We talked a bit—one of the guys spoke fluent Chinese; the other had been a veterinarian before joining the CIA. I wondered what kind of talk I was expected to give.

The office door swung wide, and a tall, gray-haired man called us in. "Hi, I'm Hank Mahoney. Welcome in."

So this is the meeting. It turns out that the seventh floor is the hide-out for the CIA's high-muckity-mucks. Hank Mahoney's the CIA's deputy director; grinning nearby was Bill Donneley, the assistant director, and a couple others.

"You mean that you've heard about this case?"

"We've been following it daily. Of course, this case alone may not seem like much. But it represents a serious problem for the future. We appreciate your taking the effort to keep us informed." They presented me with a certificate of appreciation—wrapped up like a diploma.

I didn't know what to say, so I stammered out my thanks and looked at Teejay, who was chuckling. Afterward, he said, "We wanted to keep it a surprise."

Surprise? Jeez—I'd expected to walk into a room of programmers and give a shoptalk on network security. I glanced at the certificate. It was signed by William Webster, director of the CIA.

On my way out, sure enough, the guards searched my stack of viewgraphs. Halfway down, there was that page of paper with its telltale stamp, "TOP SECRET." Uh oh.

Red alert—visitor caught leaving CIA with document stamped "TOP SECRET"! Nothing else on the page, of course. Five minutes of explaining and two phone calls later, they let me out. But not without confiscating the rubber stamp sampler. And a lecture on how "we take security seriously around here."

I flew back to Berkeley, sitting next to Greg Fennel, who was flying west for some secret business. Turns out that his background is astronomy—he used to run an observatory. We talked a bit about Space Telescope, the billion-dollar, high-precision instrument that's soon to be launched.

"With a ninety-four-inch telescope in space, we'll be able to see phenomenal detail on planets," I remarked.

"Just think what you could do if you pointed it at the earth," Greg said.

"Why bother? All the interesting things are in the sky. And anyway, the Space Telescope physically can't point to the earth. Its sensors will burn out if you try."

"What if someone made such a telescope and pointed it to the earth. What could you see?"

I fiddled a few numbers in my head. Say, three hundred miles up in orbit, a ninety-four-inch telescope. The wavelength of light is about four hundred nanometers. . . . "Oh, you could easily see detail of a couple feet across. The limit would be around a couple inches. Not quite good enough to recognize a face."

Greg smiled and said nothing. It took a while, but it eventually sunk in: the astronomical Space Telescope wasn't the only big telescope in orbit. Greg was probably talking about some spy satellite. The secret KH-11, most likely.

I returned home, wondering if I should tell Martha what happened. I didn't feel any different— I'd still rather be doing astronomy than chasing some hacker—but I worried that Martha might not approve of who I'd been rubbing shoulders with.

"Have fun?" she asked when I returned.

"Yeah, in a weird way," I answered. "You don't want to know who I met."

"Makes no difference. You've been crunched up in an airplane all day. Let me rub your back."

Home sweet home.

# 49

I STILL SEETHED WITH FRUSTRATION WHEN I THOUGHT of the eight months that we'd been stuck to this tar baby. My boss wouldn't let me forget that I was doing nothing useful.

Then on Wednesday, April 22, Mike Gibbons called to say that FBI Headquarters had decided we should keep monitoring the hacker. It seems the German police wanted to catch this guy; the only way this could happen was if we notified the Germans immediately when our alarms sounded.

Meanwhile, the FBI had put in an official request for cooperation and speedy telephone traces. They were talking to the administrator of justice in Germany, via the U.S. State Department.

Well, yippee. Why this sudden change in policy? Had the NTISSIC committee made a decision? Or was it due to my constant pestering? Or had the Germans finally contacted the FBI?

Although the FBI was only now interested, I'd never disabled my monitoring station. Even when I was away for a couple days, the monitors remained on guard. Last week's printouts showed him on the system from 9:03 to 9:04 A.M. on Saturday, April 19. Later that day, he appeared again for a couple minutes. Quiet for a few days, then he popped up, checked that the SDINET files were still around, and left.

For the past month, I'd been leaving new bait for the hacker. He saw it—at least he glanced at the names of the files—but he didn't read any of it. Was he worried that he was being watched? Did he know?

But if he thought we were watching him, he'd be a fool to show up at all. Maybe he couldn't afford longer connections? No, the Bundespost told us that he was charging these calls to a small company in Hannover.

Throughout the spring, I kept making new bait. To an outsider, the bogus SDINET files were the product of a functioning office. My mythical Barbara Sherwin created memos and letters, requisitions and travel orders. Here and there she sprinkled a few technical articles, explaining how the SDI network interconnected all sorts of classified computers. One or two notes implied that you could use the LBL computers to link into the network.

Every day, I wasted an hour juggling these SDINET files. My hopes were to keep the hacker occupied here, rather than going out into military systems. At the same time, it gave us an opportunity to trace the hacker.

On Monday, April 27, I'd biked in late and began writing a program to let our Unix system talk to Macintosh computers on people's desk tops. If I could connect those together, any of our scientists could use the Macintosh's printer. A fun project.

By 11:30, I'd fouled up two programs—what had worked an hour ago wasn't working now—when Barbara Schaefer called from five floors upstairs.

"Hey, Cliff," the astronomer said, "a letter just arrived for Barbara Sherwin."

"Be serious." For once, it was my turn to say that.

"Really. Come on up and let's open it." I had told Barbara about the dummy SDINET project and mentioned that I was using her mailbox as a mail drop. But I never really expected the hacker to actually send something in the mail.

Good grief! Had this hacker greeted us with a letter?

I ran up the five flights of stairs—the elevator's too slow. Barb and I looked at the letter. Addressed to Mrs. Barbara Sherwin, SDINET project, Mail Stop 50-351, LBL, Berkeley, CA. Postmarked from Pittsburgh, Pennsylvania.

My heart was thumping from the run up the stairs, but I felt the adrenaline rush when I saw that envelope.

We carefully slit the envelope and shook out this letter:

Triam International, Inc.
6512 Ventura Drive
Pittsburgh, PA 15236
April 21, 1987

SDI Network Project
LBL, Mail Stop 50-351
1 Cyclotrov Road
Berkley, California 94720
ATTENTION: Mrs. Barbara Sherwin Document Secretary

SUBJECT: SDI Network Project

Dear Mrs. Sherwin:

I am interested in the following documents. Please send me a price list and an update on the SDI Network Project. Thank you for your cooperation.

Very truly yours,
Laszlo J. Balogh

#37.6 SDI Network Overview Description Document, 19 pages, December 1986

#41.7 SDI Network Functional Requirement Document, 227 pages, Revised September 1985

#45.2 Strategic Defense Initiations and Computer Network Plans and Implementations of Conference Notes, 300 pages, June 1986

#47.3 SDI Network Connectivity Requirements, 65 pages, Revised April 1986

#48.8 How to Link to SDI Network, 25 pages, July 1986

#49.1 X.25 and X.75 Connection to SDI Network (includes Japanese, European, Hawaiian, 8 pages, December 1986)

#55.2 SDI Network Management Plan for 1986 to

1988, 47 pages, November Membership list (includes major connection, 24 pages, November 1986)

#65.3 List, 9 pages, November 1986

Son of a bitch! Someone had swallowed our bait and was asking for more information! I could understand it if the letter came from Hannover. But Pittsburgh? What's happening here?

I asked Barb Schaeffer to tell this to nobody and called Mike Gibbons at the Alexandria FBI office.

"Hey Mike, remember those carrots I left out for bait in January?"

"You mean those SDI files you concocted?"

"Yeah," I said. "Well, my dear, sweet, nonexistent secretary just received a letter."

"Be serious."

"Someone in Pittsburgh wants to learn about SDI."

"And you've got that letter?"

"Right in front of me."

"OK," Mike said. "Listen up carefully. Don't touch that letter. Especially, don't touch around the edges. Go find a glassine envelope. Gently insert the paper in the envelope. Then Fed-ex it to me. Whatever you do, don't handle it. Wear gloves if you must."

"Well, the real Barb Schaeffer's already touched it."

"We may have to fingerprint her, then. Oh, before you put it in the envelope, initial the middle of the back side."

This sounded like Dick Tracy's "Crimestoppers," but I followed orders. I handled it like an astronomical negative—except that I made a photocopy for myself. I suspected that Mike might forget to return the original.

After I'd chased around for an hour (ever hunt for glassine envelopes?) and shipped the letter to the FBI, I dug out my logbook.

The information in that letter showed up in exactly one of my bogus files. That file, named *form-letter,* had been read only once. On Friday, January 16, the hacker had read that file.

I could prove that nobody else had seen it. I'd protected that file, *form-letter,* so nobody could read it except the system manager. Or someone who'd illegitimately become system manager.

Well, maybe someone else had figured out a way to read that file. Nope. Whenever the computer touched that file, for any reason, my alarm sounded and I got a printout. Only one person set off that alarm. The hacker.

I compared Laszlo Balogh's letter from Pittsburgh with my fabricated letter of January 16. He'd pretty much asked for everything that the bait mentioned.

Identical.

Except he'd carefully deleted the word "classified" when asking for document #65.3.

Several errors jumped out: it's Cyclotron, not Cyclotrov. Berkeley, not Berkley. I wondered if the writer's native tongue might not be English—who would say, "Plans and Implementations of Conference Notes"?

Strange. Who's behind this?

Oh—I know what's happening! This hacker lives in Pittsburgh, Pennsylvania. He calls Hannover, connects to the German telephone system, and then invades my computer. What a way to hide!

Naw. That one doesn't hold water. Why wouldn't he call directly—straight from Pittsburgh to Berkeley?

I reread my logbook of January 18. On that day, we'd traced the connection all the way back to the hacker's phone in Hannover. That confirms it. The electronic connection went to someone's home in Hannover, not Pittsburgh.

Information had moved from my computer in Berkeley, across Tymnet, into Hannover, Germany. Three months later, a letter arrives from Pittsburgh.

I scratched my head and looked for a phone number on the letter. None. Maybe Laszlo's listed in the Pittsburgh directory service? Nope. Triam isn't listed either.

That name, though . . . I called my sister Jeannie.

"Hey, sister, what kind of name is Balogh?" Jeannie knows this kind of thing.

"Sounds like Central or Southern Europe. Hungary or Bulgaria. Have a first name?"

"Laszlo."

"Hungary for sure. Why, I had a boyfriend, once, whose father . . ."

"Any chance it's German?" I interrupted.

"Doesn't sound like it to me."

I told her about the letter and the misspellings. "Substituting 'trov' for 'tron' sounds like a Hungarian error," she said. "I'll bet on Hungary."

"Ever hear of the name 'Langman'?"

"No, can't say I have. It means long man in German, if that's any consolation."

"The hacker once created an account for T. G. Langman."

"Sounds like an alias to me," Jeannie said. "And how do you know this Laszlo character is real? Might well be another pseudonym."

Computer hackers hide behind pseudonyms. In the past seven months, I'd come across Pengo, Hagbard, Frimp, Zombie . . . but T. G. Langman and Laszlo Balogh? Maybe.

A hacker in Hannover, Germany, learns a secret from Berkeley, California. Three months later, a Hungarian, living in Pittsburgh, writes us a letter. Fascinating.

Three months, huh? I thought on this for a while. Suppose two friends were communicating with each other. News would take a couple of days to move between them. A week or two, perhaps. But not three months.

So Laszlo in Pittsburgh probably wasn't a close friend of the Hannover hacker.

Now suppose that the information was filtered through some third party. How many people were involved? If two or three people meet, make a decision, and act, it'll only take a week or two. But if five or ten people meet, decide, and act, it'll take a month or two.

Yet I'm pretty sure that only one person is operating the computer. Nobody else would have such a tedious, methodical, and persistent manner. The German Bundespost says they're following at least two guys. What's happening here?

Whatever's going on, I'm in over my head. They don't teach you this kind of stuff in graduate school. Seemed like the CIA's bailiwick. I called Teejay and got two sentences into my description.

"Wait a second. Let me call you back on a different line." A secured phone line.

No doubt, this latest wrinkle hit him where he lived. I had to explain it to him twice—he also wanted an express copy of Laszlo's letter. News travels fast in certain circles: half an hour later, Greg Fennel of the CIA called, asking if Laszlo might have logged into my computer. I explained about my alarms and tripwires. "No, the only guy that's seen that file is a hacker in Hannover."

Greg was quiet on the phone for a second, then said, "A real smoking gun."

That reminded me of the NSA guy's comment. Time to call Bob Morris. I told him about the letter and he seemed mildly interested. "Want me to send you a copy by Federal Express?"

"That won't be necessary. First class is good enough."

He seemed more interested in my techniques of setting alarms than the content of the letter. In a way, that's not surprising—he'd already concluded that something serious was happening.

Air Force OSI sent an investigator over to examine the letter. Their man, Steve Shumaker, had the common sense to show up in dungarees and a T-shirt, so as not to alarm the natives. He asked for a copy of the letter and the printouts from the Air Force System Command Space Division. They were going to do a postmortem analysis of the hacker's break-in.

"I'll give you a copy of the letter—that's no problem," I told Shumaker, "but I can't let you have the original printouts. The FBI's warned me to keep all of this locked up since it might be used as evidence."

"Can you Xerox it?"

Aargh. Xerox five hundred pages of computer printout?

Well, we spent an hour in front of the copier, feeding the damned paper through the machine. I asked the OSI detective what he thought of the letter from Pittsburgh.

"We've been warning everyone that this was bound to happen. Maybe they'll wake up now."

"What have you been doing so far?"

"We visit sites and try to raise their security awareness," he said. "We've formed a team to test their computer security by trying to break into Air Force systems. What we found isn't encouraging."

"You mean you're the only ones who test Air Force computers for security?" I asked. "You must have thousands of computers."

"Well, there's also a group in San Antonio, the Air Force Electronic Security Command, that searches for electronic security breaches," Shumaker said. "They mostly worry about communications security—you know, keeping radio transmissions secret. They're sharpies over there, all right."

Gibbons of the FBI was a sharpie, too. Finally, now that he was actively committed, he wanted to know everything. Every time the hacker appeared, Mike wanted to know about it immediately. Throughout the day, he called repeatedly, asking for my logs and notes, floppy disks and printouts. Descriptions of the monitors. Everything. That's the way to make progress.

I couldn't get this letter out of my mind. I kept searching for some innocent explanation, some way that it might be written off as a fluke.

Finally I gave up and admitted victory. I couldn't explain it any other way: the letter must mean my plan had worked. No, not my plan, it was Claudia's. My sweet, guileless roommate, who didn't know a computer from a toaster, had trapped this cunning hacker!

Cycling home, I swerved suddenly from my usual route, scooted into the Double-Rainbow ice cream store and the video rental place. Then I hurried home, waving a copy of Laszlo's letter. Elated at the news, Martha and Claudia cackled evilly and dropped into Boris and Natasha accents. Zecret plan 35B vas a success!

We crowded into Claudia's room, munched out on popcorn and ice cream, and cheered the monsters in *Godzilla Versus Monster Zero.*

# 50

"DON'T SAY ANYTHING TO ANYONE!"

It was Mike Gibbons on the phone, telling me not to spread the word to the CIA.

"Uh, I'm sorry, Mike, but I've already told this guy Teejay." I wondered if Mike had heard of Teejay.

"I'll take care of it, then. This letter you sent us is intriguing. We ran it through some lab tests."

"What'd you learn?" Mike was being more communicative than usual, so I might as well push my luck.

"Can't tell you, but we're not treating this case lightly. Aspects of it are quite, well, intriguing." That's the second time Mike used that word. Something's up. "Oh, by the way, could you send me a half-dozen sheets of your letterhead?"

The FBI wants my lab's letterhead? Sounds like they're going to reply to Laszlo's letter.

What would "I" tell this guy? How about,

> Dear Mr. Balogh:
>
> You have been selected as a grand prize winner in the SDINET sweepstakes. . . .

The hacker played hide-and-seek for the next few days. He'd show up for three minutes, look at our password file, then log out. My bait grew tastier every day. Yet he wasn't nibbling.

Monday morning, May 18, he came into our system at 6:54 A.M. Awakened by an insistent beep, I reached over and whapped the alarm clock. Wrong noisemaker—the beep continued. Three beeps. S for Sventek. It's the hacker, over on the Unix-4 computer.

Mechanically I ran to my Macintosh, switched it on, and called Steve White at Tymnet.

"Steve, someone's tripped my alarm," I said, still a bit hazy. "I haven't checked it out yet, but could you start the trace?"

"Right-o. It'll be up in ten seconds," he said. "Here it is. Coming through the Westar satellite. Calling address 2624 DNIC 5421-0421. That's Bremen. I'll ring the Bundespost."

I copied down the number; by now my home computer was warmed up. Steve had just completed an international trace in less than a minute. I dialed my lab's system from my pipsqueak home computer and examined the Unix-4 computer. There was Sventek, just leaving.

He'd been on for four minutes. Long enough to detect him and complete a trace. Long enough to ruin my morning. I wouldn't be able to get back to sleep, so I biked up to the lab. Over in the east, the morning star kept me company. Venus.

In four minutes this hacker had pried at a new part of my operating system. He searched for a program called X-preserve on our Unix computer.

Hey—I know what he's doing. He's looking for the X-preserve hole in the VI-editor. Dave Cleveland and I had patched that almost a year ago. But this hacker is only now trying to exploit it.

VI is the Unix screen editor. When Bill Joy wrote it, back in 1980, people thought it was the neatest invention around. It let you watch as you moved words around! If you wanted to remove a word in the middle of a paragraph, you just moved the blinking box to that word, and presto!

VI was predecessor to hundreds of word processing systems. By now, Unix folks see it as a bit stodgy—it hasn't the versatility of Gnu-Emacs, nor the friendliness of more modern editors. Despite that, VI shows up on every Unix system.

What happens if you're writing a long article and the computer hiccups? Say, there's a power blackout or some moron pulls the plug. Used to be that you'd lose everything you had typed in.

The VI editor uses X-preserve to recover what you've done. When the computer returns from the dead, X-preserve will reassemble the pieces of your work. It'll then ask you where to store this knit-together file. Most people will say, "Oh, put it in my home directory."

But X-preserve didn't check where you stashed that file. You could say, "Stick the file in the systems directory," and it would do so.

That's what the hacker tried. He made a file that said, "Grant system privilege to Sventek." He fired up the VI-editor, then tripped up the editor by feeding it an interrupt character. VI, sensing a problem, stored his file in pieces.

The hacker's next step? Tell X-preserve to slip that file into the systems directory. In a couple minutes, Unix would hatch it, and he'd become system manager.

But the cuckoo's egg fell out of this nest. We'd fixed the X-preserve program . . . it now checks who you are and won't let you move a file into the systems area.

Poor guy. He must feel crestfallen. A nifty trick to break into systems, but it just won't work here in Berkeley.

Oh, I'd left our other holes open. He can still use Gnu-Emacs to plant his egg-program in the systems nest. And I've purposely left two other holes in our system waiting around for him to discover. Just to measure his skill. So far, he's batting one for three.

All this took three minutes. He entered his program perfectly—not a single typing error. It's as if he'd done this often. As if he'd practiced breaking into other computers.

How many other system managers hadn't yet patched X-preserve? How many other holes were still waiting to be discovered? Where would I go to warn people about this? How would I tell the people in the white hats, without tipping off the bad guys?

Too late for that. The guys in the black hats already know.

Although this connection lasted only a few minutes in Berkeley, the University of Bremen reported that he was connected for forty-five minutes. In turn, the Bundespost once again traced the entire link back to the same individual in Hannover.

Turned out that the University of Bremen was also printing the hacker's traffic. Two of us were now watching this guy. He could run, but he couldn't hide.

For the past couple months, he'd just nibbled at the SDINET files. He'd seen the names of these files and noticed that every day I added new memos and letters but didn't read them right off. I'd begun having my doubts whether he was still interested in our creative writing.

On Wednesday, May 20, my doubts cleared up. He connected at five in the morning and dumped all the SDINET files. Here was one letter asking the Pentagon for more funding. Another talking about "over-the-horizon radar"—a catch phrase I'd found in an electronics magazine. Yet another note described tests of a new supercomputer, complete with parallel processors. I tried to conceal my utter lack of knowledge of these subjects by filling the letters with jargon.

He swallowed them, all right. One by one. I wanted him to ask for each bogus memo by name rather than saying, "Give me all the files." So I added a few ringers. Files that were far too long to type out. A few short files that were filled with gibberish—computer guacamole. He couldn't print these poisoned files, so he'd have to check each file first. This slowed him down and he stayed on the system longer: more time to trace.

Nine months? We'd been watching this one skunk for the better part of a year. And Mitre's telephone bills said he'd been breaking in for more than a year. What persistence!

I wondered again, what's driving this guy? Sure, I'd get a charge out of fooling around for a night or two. Might even be fun for a couple weeks. But a year? Night after night, patiently twisting doorknobs to computers? Why, you'd have to pay me.

Paid? Was someone paying this hacker?

The next few times he showed up, I hadn't added much more to his SDINET feeding grounds. My puppet secretary, Barbara Sherwin, wrote a word-processed memo asking for a week's vacation. The hacker read this and should have understood why there was so little new information.

Instead of pawing through LBL's files, then, he went out over the Milnet, once again patiently trying to guess passwords. One of my bogus SDINET reports mentioned a special project at White Sands Missile Range; sure enough, he spent fifteen minutes scratching at their door. White Sands' computers recorded a dozen attempts to break in, but none were successful.

Chris McDonald, White Sands' computer security ace, called me within the hour. "Someone's setting off alarms inside my WSMR05 computer."

"I know. It's the same hacker."

"Well, he's trying accounts that don't exist. Names like SDINET. There's no way he'll get in that way," Chris said confidently. "Anyway, that machine needs two passwords, and we changed 'em all last week." White Sands didn't fool around.

He wasted his time trying thirty other computers as well. The Korean Advanced Institute of Science and Technology. The Army Safety Center at Fort Rucker. Strategic Air Command. The Defense Nuclear Agency at Kirtland Air Force Base. Though he still tried account names like "guest" and "system," he used "SDINET" as well. No doubt that he's a believer.

Mostly the hacker's trips through my system were becoming routine. I still ran to the switchyard whenever my beeper called, but I guess I'd become accustomed to having this mouse in a cage.

I'd waited eight months, I could wait some more. Around the second week of June, he stopped into my computer from 3:38 until 4:13 in the afternoon. We traced him completely—Hannover again—and stayed in touch with the FBI throughout.

Immediately after logging onto my Berkeley computer, he jumped onto the Milnet and tried to log onto some computers at the Unisys Corporation, in Paoli, Pennsylvania. Systems named "Omega," "Bigburd," and "Rosencrantz" (I kept waiting to see

Guildenstern, but he never found it). Then he tried the Unisys Burdvax system.

He got in on his first try. Account name Ingres, password, "Ingres." Not bad . . . he remembers the Ingres database. But why did he just try those Unisys computers? What brought them to his attention? Maybe someone told him to look for them.

Maybe Laszlo Balogh in Pittsburgh worked in Paoli. The atlas said otherwise. Paoli's a suburb of Philadelphia, hundreds of miles away from Pittsburgh.

As an Ingres user, the hacker only had limited privileges but he took what he could find. Most useful to him, he found a way to read the Unisys password file. Copied the whole thing to his home computer. Then he listed several files which should never be world-readable: the list of phone numbers that the Unisys computer knew, and Unisys's network address file.

I already knew what he'd do with the Unisys password file. He'd decrypt it by blasting a dictionary at it. Then he'd log into a more privileged account and garner still more power.

Those other files were just as worrisome. They provided the hacker with phone numbers to nearby computers and a map of the Unisys local network. Now he knew how to connect from the Burdvax into other computers . . . he didn't need to explore.

But even as I watched, he disconnected. Was he scared? No, just patient. He was going to check up on other computers. First, the Fort Buckner system in Okinawa. Yes, his password was still good there. Despite our warnings, they hadn't changed a thing.

Next, he tried the Naval Coastal Systems Command in Panama City, Florida. But he couldn't get in on his old Ingres account. They'd changed the password on him.

Didn't faze him for an instant. He turned around and logged in as user "Ovca," password, "Baseball." This worked perfectly.

Aha! More evidence for password cracking. Two months ago, the hacker logged into that naval computer as "Ingres," and copied their encrypted password file. Now, even though they deleted the Ingres account, he can still log in, using some other account. The fools had only changed one password. And their passwords were ordinary English words. Jeez.

While he was at it, he checked into his old haunts. Ramstein Air Force Base. Fort Stewart. University of Rochester. The Pentagon Optimis Data Center. Finally he left the network.

Today he'd broken into a new computer at Unisys. Where had I heard that name? Of course—they're a defense contractor that makes computers for the military. Not just any computers. Unisys builds secure computers, systems that you can't break into.

Right.

Wait a second. What other defense contractors had been hit? I scribbled a list on a pad of paper:

Unisys. Makers of secure computers.
TRW. They make military and space computers.
SRI. They've got military contracts to design computer security systems.
Mitre. They design high-security computers for the military. They're the people that test NSA's secure computers.
BBN. The builders of the Milnet.

What's wrong with this picture? These are the very people that are designing, building, and testing secure systems. Yet hackers traipse freely through their computers.

These companies don't have dinky budgets, either. They charge our government tens of millions of dollars to develop secure software. No doubt about it: the shoemakers' kids are running around barefoot.

I'd seen this guy break into military computers, defense contractors, universities, and laboratories. But no banks. Oh—I know why. Their networks aren't as public as the Arpanet. But if he got on their networks, I'd bet he'd be about as successful.

For it doesn't take brilliance or wizardry to break into computers. Just patience. What this hacker lacked in originality, he made up for in persistence. A few of the holes he exploited were news to me: the Gnu-Emacs problem, for instance. But mostly, he took advantage of administrators' blunders. Leaving accounts protected by obvious passwords. Mailing passwords to each other. Not monitoring audit trails.

Come to think of it, was it foolish to remain open? It had been almost ten months, and he was still free. Despite his breaking into more than thirty computers, despite Laszlo's letter from Pittsburgh, despite all these traces, this hacker was still at large. How much longer would this go on?

# 51

IT WAS JUNE—SUMMER IN PARADISE. I BIKED HOME, enjoying the scene, Berkeley students with Frisbees, sailboards, and an occasional convertible top down in the balmy air. Our garden was full of roses, marigolds, and tomatoes. The strawberries were thriving, promising still more milkshakes.

Inside the house, however, Martha was imprisoned, studying for her bar exam. This last ordeal looked even harder than three years of law school. In summer, when everyone else can go out and play, you're stuck in dreary review classes, cramming your head with legal rules, counting the days until the exam—a three-day ordeal modeled on the Spanish Inquisition.

Martha coped, patiently reading her books, making intricate outlines of each subject with colored pens, meeting with fellow sufferers to quiz each other. She was philosophical about it; she put in exactly ten hours each day, then slammed the books shut. Aikido became her salvation—she took out her frustrations by flipping people over her head.

Martha rarely talked about the lurking horror of the exam itself, but it was always there. Watching her go through this brought back memories of my own grad school days.

In astronomy, you first enjoy three or four years of confusing classes, impossible problem sets, and sneers from the faculty. Having endured that, you're rewarded with an eight-hour written exam, with questions like: "How do you age-date meteorites using the elements Samarium and Neodymium?" If you survive, you win the great honor and pleasure of an oral exam by a panel of learned professors.

I remember it vividly. Across a table, five profs. I'm frightened, trying to look casual as sweat drips down my face. But I'm keeping afloat; I've managed to babble superficially, giving the illusion that I know something. Just a few more questions, I think, and they'll set me free. Then the examiner over at the end of the table—the guy with the twisted little smile—starts sharpening his pencil with a penknife.

"I've got just one question, Cliff," he says, carving his way through the Eberhard-Faber. "Why is the sky blue?"

My mind is absolutely, profoundly blank. I have no idea. I look out the window at the sky with the primitive, uncomprehending wonder of a Neanderthal contemplating fire. I force myself to say something—anything. "Scattered light," I reply. "Uh, yeah, scattered sunlight."

"Could you be more specific?"

Well, words came from somewhere, out of some deep instinct of self-preservation. I babbled about the spectrum of sunlight, the upper atmosphere, and how light interacts with molecules of air.

"Could you be more specific?"

I'm describing how air molecules have dipole moments, the wave-particle duality of light, scribbling equations on the blackboard, and . . .

"Could you be more specific?"

An hour later, I'm sweating hard. His simple question—a five-year-old's question—has drawn together oscillator theory, electricity and magnetism, thermodynamics, even quantum mechanics. Even in my miserable writhing, I admired the guy.

So Sunday morning I'm looking at Martha, calmly working on an outline, the dining table strewn with books. She'll pass, all right, but I also know how scared she is and how an exam can make anyone feel absolutely stupid and helpless. I can't make her ordeal easier, but I can at least make breakfast. I slip quietly into the kitchen and crack a few eggs . . .

At 9:32, the damned hacker steps on my tripwire. The pager

beeps. I call Steve White. He calls Germany. Like the old double play: Tinker to Evers to Chance.

Steve needed a minute to find the hacker coming from address 2624 DNIC 4511 0199-36. Direct from Hannover. (Or as direct as transatlantic satellite connections can be.)

The Bundespost was hot. Took them only a few minutes to confirm that they'd started a trace. Nice. Meanwhile, having started the ball rolling, I pulled on some clothes and biked up to the lab. No time for yard sales this morning.

I arrived with plenty of time to spare. My visitor was still pawing through the bogus SDINET files, carefully copying each one into his own computer. One file described how the Strategic Defense Initiative was to be used in tracking satellites in space. Another file seemed to say that you could connect directly into several Air Force computers from my laboratory.

The hacker wanted to try, but couldn't figure out where we'd installed the network software. So he scoured our entire computer, searching for any program containing the phrase "SDI." He found quite a few, but none seemed to do the job for him.

Then he rifled Dave Cleveland's mail. Dave had prepared for this—he'd written a letter talking about how he'd hidden the SDINET access ports. Dave's letter contained the sentence, "I've concealed the SDI network port, and I doubt that many people will discover it."

That was enough to set the hacker on an hour-long wild-goose chase. He combed through our system, groping for what he knew was a hidden program that would be his northwestern passage to military computers everywhere.

I sat back, smiling at the screen. He'd been suckered in, all right. He still felt challenged to uncover the SDI network connection and truly believed that he could reach those classified computers.

Yet my system looked vanilla. Because it was vanilla. Oh, here and there, I sprinkled hints that other people were using the SDI network. One physicist cooperated and sent a complaint to the system manager, saying that the SDI network wasn't functioning last Tuesday night. Another wrote a mundane program full of subroutines with names like SDI-link and Copy-SDI.

Though it took hours, the hacker eventually discovered these, and must have scratched his head, wondering why others had such an easy time using the network. He tried logging into computers named *Sdi* and *Sdinetwork.* Over and over, he sifted through our system, but to no avail.

Eventually he gave up and let me go home. Martha wasn't pleased, of course. She'd been studying all morning, and she was hungry and grouchy. The two eggs stared at me from the pan, uncooked, just as I'd left them.

So I made a brunch of omelets, hot cocoa, and fruit salad; she dumped her books off the table with a vengeance, and we sat down, enjoying a few moments of peace in the quiet, sunny room. The more strange life gets, the more precious those times are, with food and friends and the Sunday *Times* crossword puzzle.

Monday morning, Teresa Brecken, the Petvax system manager, reported that someone had attacked her computer. He couldn't get into it but had been probing it, searching for weak places. His pounding had set off alarms, and Teresa called me.

He'd come in over her port to the High Energy Physics Network. That didn't mean much—there's a couple thousand other computers on that net. Moreover, the Hepnet ties to SPAN, the Space Physics Applications Network, run by NASA. Altogether there's well over ten thousand computers on those networks.

Had the hacker been laughing at me all the time? While I'd been watching the Tymnet mouse hole, had he been waltzing in through some NASA network?

Teresa's monitors showed the hacker had come from computer 6.133, the National Severe Storms Data Center's computer at NASA's Goddard Spaceflight Center. Not much to do but call them.

I didn't get very far. They were worried about hackers on their computer and had discovered one or two problems, but couldn't go much further. I pestered them, and they finally said that this particular connection had originated at NASA's Marshall Spaceflight Center in Huntsville, Alabama. From there, who knows? Marshall didn't keep records.

Same guy? I doubted it. The NASA computers aren't secret—NASA does civilian space research and has nothing to do with the Strategic Defense Initiative. Still, worth remembering the incident: I wrote it down in my logbook.

I called Mike Gibbons again, wondering how much longer we'd have to wait before the FBI and their German partners began to move.

"Any day now," Mike replied. "The warrants are in order and we're just waiting for the right time."

"Give me a figure, Mike. Do you mean hours, days, weeks, or months?"

"More than days, less than weeks."

I wondered if the FBI was feeding some false information through Laszlo Balogh. "Ever reply to the Pittsburgh letter?" I asked.

"Hey, how about them Yankees winning another game?" As usual, Mike played his cards close to his chest.

Almost every day now, the hacker logged in for a few minutes. Sometimes he'd grab any new files from the SDINET account. Other days he'd try to break into military computers. Once he spent half an hour trying to guess the password for our Elxsi computer—I'd dropped a hint that our Elxsi was a central SDINET controller.

I could embroider fake military documents as fast as he could read them. Knowing that he was passing my handiwork to some agent in Pittsburgh, I added just a dash of verifiable information: the Pentagon was scheduling a secret satellite to be launched on the *Atlantis* space shuttle. This was common knowledge to anyone reading the newspapers. But I imagined that in his quest for secret information, he'd feel that these nuggets of truth confirmed that he'd struck the mother lode.

Sunday, June 21, 1987, at 12:37 P.M., he logged into our Unix computer as Sventek. For five minutes he checked the system status and listed a few mail files. This intrusion seemed just like his others.

But this session was different in one important way.

It was his last.

# 52

"HI, CLIFF, IT'S STEVE." I PUT DOWN MY CHOCOLATE CHIP cookie.

"I just got a message from Wolfgang Hoffman at the German Bundespost. He says that there'll be a full-time policeman outside the hacker's apartment on Monday through Wednesday of next week. They'll keep watch continually, and they'll rush in to make an arrest as soon as he connects to Berkeley."

"How will the cop know when to bust in?"

"You'll give the signal, Cliff."

The next time the hacker touched my system, I would call the FBI and Tymnet. They'd make the trace, tell the German BKA, and the cops would bust into his apartment.

Finally, after ten months.

Will he show up? And what if he doesn't? Will they bust him anyway or give up on the whole thing? With my luck, they'll drop the whole thing.

I spent the weekend at home with Martha, arriving at the lab late Sunday evening. With the best of luck, the hacker would show up on Sventek's account, I'd call the FBI, and while he was dumping a file of my concocted SDI baloney, he'd be busted. I could imagine him frantically trying to conceal his computer as police break down his apartment's door.

With dreams like those, I nestled under my desk, wrapped in the quilt that Martha and I had made last winter. In case my beeper failed, two personal computers stood watch, each wired to a bell. After ten months, I wasn't going to miss my big chance.

Monday afternoon, June 22, Wolfgang Hoffman cabled this message: "Arrests expected shortly. Notify us immediately if hacker shows up."

OK, I'm waiting. Every few minutes, I walk over to the switchyard and everything's quiet. Oh yeah, a couple physicists are using Tymnet to analyze some high-temperature superconductors. But there's no other traffic. My alarms and tripwires are in place, but not a peep.

Another night under the desk.

Tuesday morning, June 23, Mike Gibbons called from the FBI.

"You can close up shop, Cliff."

"What's happened?"

"Arrest warrants were issued this morning at 10 A.M."

"But I didn't see anyone on my system then."

"Makes no difference."

"Anyone arrested?"

"I can't say."

"Where are you, Mike?"

"In Pittsburgh."

Something was happening. But Mike wouldn't say what. I'd wait for a while before closing my doors to this hacker.

A few hour later, Wolfgang Hoffman sent a message: "An apartment and a company were searched, and nobody was home at the time. Printouts, disks, and tapes were seized and will be analyzed in the next few days. Expect no further break-ins."

What does this mean? I guess the police busted his apartment. Why didn't they wait for our signal? Should I celebrate?

Whatever happened, at last we could seal our doors. I changed our Tymnet passwords and patched the hole in the Gnu-Emacs editor. What should we do about everyone's passwords?

The only way to guarantee a clean system would be to change every single password overnight. Then certify each user, one by one, the next morning. Easy if there's only a few people on your system. Impossible for our twelve hundred scientists.

Yet if we didn't change every password, we couldn't be sure

that some other hacker might not have purloined an account. All it takes is one stolen account. In the end we expired everyone's passwords and asked everyone to pick a new one. One that's not in the dictionary.

I set traps on all the hacker's stolen accounts. If anyone tries to log in as Sventek, the system will reject the try—but it'll capture all the information on where the call originates. Just let him try.

Martha and I couldn't celebrate in a big way—her bar-exam cram course was a ball and chain—but we played hooky for a day and escaped to the North Coast. We wandered on the high cliffs covered with wildflowers and watched the waves crash over the rocks a hundred feet below us. We climbed down to an isolated little cove—our own private beach—and for a few hours all my worries were far away, unreal.

Within the next few days, word filtered back from Germany. Apparently the Hannover police had simultaneously searched an office at a small computer company in Hannover, and the apartment of one of their employees. They seized eighty disks at the computer firm, and twice that at the apartment. The evidence? Shipped to somewhere called Wiesbaden for "analysis by experts." Hell, I could analyze it easily enough myself. Just search for the word "SDINET." As the inventor of that word, I could tell instantly whether their printouts were the real McCoy.

What's the hacker's name? What was he up to? What's the connection with Pittsburgh? What's happened to him? Time to ask Mike of the FBI.

"Now that it's all over, can you tell me the guy's name?" I asked.

"It's not all over, and no, I can't tell you his name," Mike replied, showing more than his usual annoyance at my questions.

"Well, can I find out more about this guy from the Germans?" I knew the prosecutor's name, even if I didn't know the hacker's.

"Don't contact the Germans. This is sensitive, and you'll bollix things up."

"Can't you even tell me if the hacker's in jail? Or is he wandering the streets of Hannover?"

"It's not for me to say."

"Then when will I find out what happened?"

"I'll tell you at the right time. Meanwhile, keep all your printouts locked up."

Lock up the printouts? I looked across my office. Sandwiched between bookshelves of computer manuals and astronomy books were three boxes of the hacker's printouts. My office door doesn't have a lock, and the building is open twenty-four hours a day. Oh—the janitor's closet can be locked. I could stash the boxes up over the sink, on the shelf next to the ceiling.

While he was still on the phone, I asked Mike when I could expect to hear back on this case.

"Oh, in a few weeks. The hacker will be indicted and brought to trial," Mike said. "Meanwhile, keep silent about this. Don't publicize it and stay away from reporters."

"Why not?"

"Any publicity may let him off. The case is tough enough without being tried in the newspapers."

"But surely this is an open-and-shut case," I protested. "The U.S. Attorney said that we had more than enough evidence to convict the guy."

"Look, you don't know everything that's going on," Mike said. "Take my word for it: don't talk about it."

The FBI was happy with their work, as well they should be. Despite several false starts, Mike had stuck with the investigation. The FBI wouldn't let him tell me anything; there wasn't much I could do about that. But he couldn't stop me from checking on my own.

Ten months ago, Luis Alvarez and Jerry Nelson had told me to treat the hacker as a research problem. Well, at last the investigation was complete. Oh, there were a few details to figure out, but the real work was over. Yet the FBI wouldn't let me publish what I'd learned.

When you run an experiment, you take notes, think for a while, then publish your results. If you don't publish, nobody will learn from your experience. The whole idea is to save others from repeating what you've done.

It was time for a change anyway. I spent the rest of the summer making weird computer pictures of telescopes and teaching a few classes at the computer center. The pursuit of the German had taught me about how to connect computers together.

Sooner or later, the FBI would let me publish. And when it did, I'd be ready. Around the beginning of September, I started writing a dry, scientific paper about the hacker. I just distilled my lab notebook—all 125 pages of it—into a boring article and got it ready for some obscure computer journal.

Still, letting go of the hacker project wasn't entirely easy. For a year, the chase had consumed my life. In the course of my quest, I'd written dozens of programs, forsaken the company of my sweetheart, mingled with the FBI, NSA, OSI, and CIA, nuked my sneakers, pilfered printers, and made several coast-to-coast flights. I pondered how I would now spend my time, now that my life wasn't scheduled around the whims of some faceless foe from overseas.

Meanwhile, six thousand miles away, someone was wishing that he'd never heard of Berkeley.

# 53

A MONTH BEFORE THE HANNOVER HACKER WAS CAUGHT, Darren Griffith had joined our group, having moved up from Southern California. Darren liked punk music, Unix networks, laser typography, and friends with spiked haircuts—in that order. Besides the coffeehouses and concerts, Berkeley attracted him because of its hundreds of Unix computers tied together with an ethernet, making an intricate maze for Darren to explore.

At work, our boss set him loose to work in his own rhythm and at whatever projects interested him. After five, when the normal folks left, he cranked up the stereo in his cubicle, and wrote programs to the sound of U2. "The louder the music, the better the code."

I filled him in on the past year's hack and figured that he'd be delighted with the hole in Gnu-Emacs, but he just shrugged. "Eeh, anyone could see how to exploit that. Anyway, it's only on a few hundred systems. Now if you want a tasty security hole, check out VMS. They've got a hole you could drive a truck through."

"Huh?"

"Yeah. It's in every Vax computer from Digital Equipment Corporation that runs the VMS operating system Version 4.5."

"What's the problem?"

Darren explained. "Anyone that logs into the system can become system manager by running a short program. You can't stop 'em."

I hadn't heard of this problem. "Isn't DEC doing something about it? After all, they sell those systems."

"Oh, sure, they're sending out patches. But they're real quiet about it. They don't want their customers to panic."

"Sounds reasonable."

"Sure, but nobody's installing those patches. What would you do—some tape shows up in the mail saying, 'Please install this program or your system may develop problems' . . . you'll ignore it, because you've got better things to do."

"So all these systems are open to attack?"

"You got it."

"Wait a second. That operating system was certified by NSA. They tested it and certified it secure."

"Sure they spent a year testing it. And a month after they verified the system, DEC modified it slightly. Just a little change in the password program." The National Computer Security Center's verification program had a hole in it as well.

"And now fifty thousand computers are insecure." I couldn't believe it. If my hacker knew, he'd have a field day. Good thing we'd nailed him.

This problem seemed important, so I called Bob Morris at the National Computer Security Center. He'd not heard of it before, but he promised to check into it. Well, I'd done my job and warned the authorities.

Around the end of July, Darren picked up a message from the network. Roy Omond, a system manager in Heidelberg, Germany, had detected a group called Chaos Computer Club breaking into his Vax computer. They'd used the hole that Darren had described. Omond's message described how these vandals had broken in, set up Trojan horses to capture passwords, then erased their trails behind them.

The Chaos Computer Club, huh? I'd heard rumors that back in 1985, a few German hackers banded together to "explore" computer networks. To them the government monopoly only made trouble—they called it the "Bundespest."* They soon developed

---

*In truth, German telephone rates are exorbitant compared to those in North America.

into a gang that systematically attacked computers in Germany, Switzerland, France, and eventually the United States. Those pseudonyms I'd heard of before—Pengo, Zombie, Frimp—were all members . . . self-styled cyberpunks who prided themselves on how many computers they could break into.

Sounded familiar.

By the end of the summer, the problem had spread. The Chaos gang broke into a hundred computers around the world, using the NASA SPAN network. Wait a second. The Petvax computer! Those alarms in June—I'd traced them back to the NASA network. I'll bet that the connection wended its way all the way back to Germany. Uh oh.

Pretty soon, I realized what was happening. The Chaos Computer Club had broken into computers at the CERN physics laboratory in Switzerland, and caused endless headaches there—they were said to have stolen passwords, destroyed software, and crashed experimental systems.

All for the fun of it.

From the Swiss laboratory, Chaos members had stolen passwords to reach into computers at American physics labs—Fermilab in Illinois, Caltech, and Stanford. From there, it was a short hop to the NASA network and into NASA's computers.

Every time they entered a computer, they used the bug to become system manager. Then they modified the operating system to let them in with a special password—one known only to them. Now, whenever a Chaos Club member used the magic password on an injured Vax computer, they'd get in . . . even if the original hole was fixed!

Whoa! Serious stuff here. Hundreds of computers were at risk. They could easily wreck the software on each system. But what to do? NASA's not responsible for each computer connected to its network. Half of them are at universities, running scientific experiments. NASA probably doesn't even have a list of all the computers attached to its network.

The NASA network, like the Milnet, is a roadway connecting computers around the country. A burglar will naturally use that road, but that's hardly the fault of the road's builder. NASA's only responsible for keeping the road intact. The security of each computer rests in the hands of the people running it.

The Chaos Computer Club created headaches for network folks—they were thumbing their noses at hundreds of system managers and thousands of scientists. If you owned a Vax computer, you had to rebuild the system software from scratch. That's an afternoon's work. Multiply that by a thousand sites. Or was it fifty thousand?

At last the Chaos Club triumphantly announced their break-ins to the press, painting themselves as brilliant programmers. I searched for any mention of my laboratory, of Milnet, or of Hannover. Nothing. It was as if they'd never heard of my hacker. Yet what a coincidence: a couple months after I nail a German hacker breaking into computer networks, a German club goes public, saying that they've prowled through NASA's networks.

Could this be who had broken into my computer? I thought for a while. The Chaos gang seemed to work with the VMS operating system and knew little about Unix. My hacker certainly knew VMS, but he seemed more at home on Unix. And he had no hesitation to exploit any bug in the computer. Hannover is close to Hamburg, the home of Chaos. Less than a hundred miles.

But my hacker was arrested on June 29. The Chaos Club was breaking into systems during August.

Hmmm. If the LBL hacker from Hannover was in contact with the Chaos Club, his arrest would send shock waves through the entire club. They'd evaporate as soon as they heard that one of their members had been arrested.

Another wrinkle . . . NASA doesn't have secrets. Oh, perhaps the military shuttle payloads are classified. But almost everything else about NASA is public. Right down to the design of their rockets. Hell, you can buy the space shuttle's blueprints. Not the place for a spy.

No, my hacker wasn't in Chaos. Probably he was loosely tied into their club . . . perhaps he checked into their electronic bulletin board. But they didn't know about him.

Chaos Club members justify their actions with a peculiar set of ethics. They claim that it's perfectly all right for them to roam through others' databases, so long as they don't destroy any information. In other words, they believe their technicians' curiosity should take precedence over my personal privacy. They claim the right to peruse any computer they can break into.

Information in databases? They've no qualms, if they can figure out how to get it. Suppose it's a list of AIDS patients? Or your last year's income tax return? Or my credit history?

Darren had been great to talk to about all of this, with his knowledge of networks and sharp eye for holes. But whenever we talked, he seemed amused and distant, looking at the hacker problem purely as an intellectual game. I felt that he looked down at me for getting caught up in it, being out to get the hacker.

Finally one afternoon after Darren had patiently listened to my whining about the hacker and my gloomy predictions of future trouble, he fixed me with a stare.

"Cliff," he said, "you're an old fart. Why do you care so much that someone's frolicking in your system. That could have been you, in your distant youth. Where's your appreciation of creative anarchy?"

I tried to defend myself—as I'd tried with Laurie, months ago. I hadn't set out to be a network cop. I'd started with a simple puzzle: why did my accounting show a 75-cent error? One thing led to another, and I ended up on the trail of our friend.

And I didn't just blunder around in a blind rage, trying to nab the guy just because he was there. I learned what our networks are. I had thought of them as a complicated technical device, a tangle of wires and circuits. But they're much more than that—a fragile community of people, bonded together by trust and cooperation. If that trust is broken, the community will vanish forever.

Darren and other programmers sometimes expressed respect for hackers because they test the soundness of systems, reveal holes and weaknesses. I could respect this view—it take a rigorous, honest mind to feel gratitude to someone who exposes our mistakes—but I could no longer agree with it. I saw the hacker not as a chess master, teaching us all valuable lessons by exploiting the weak points in our defenses, but as a vandal, sowing distrust and paranoia.

In a small town, where people never locked their doors, would we praise the first burglar for showing the townspeople how foolish it was to leave their houses open? After it happened, the town couldn't ever go back to open doors.

Hacking may mean that computer networks will have to have elaborate locks and checkpoints. Legitimate users will find it harder to communicate freely, sharing less information with each other. To use the network, we all might have to identify ourselves and state our purpose—no more logging on casually just to gossip, doodle around, see who else is on the net.

There's plenty of room for truly "creative anarchy" on the networks as they are—nobody is in charge of them, nobody makes the rules—they exist purely out of cooperative effort and they evolve freely at the whim of their users. A hacker's abuse of this openness might mean the end of the casual, communal way the networks are run.

I could finally answer Darren. All my buddying up with spooks in suits and playing computer cop *came from* my appreciation for creative anarchy. To have the networks as our playground, we have to preserve our sense of trust; to do that, we have to take it seriously when people break that trust.

But though I finally felt like I knew why I'd done it, I still didn't know what I had done. What was the guy's name in Hannover? Who was behind the whole thing? Nobody would tell me.

As the summer stretched on, the case showed every indication of dying out. Mike Gibbons didn't call and seldom returned my calls. It was as if nothing had happened.

I understood the technical aspects of the case—the computer's holes and the hacker's location. Wasn't that all I'd wanted? But something was wrong. This wasn't satisfying.

I knew the whats and the hows. I wanted to know the whos and whys.

# 54

WHO'S BEHIND IT? ONLY ONE WAY TO FIND OUT. DO research.

The FBI wouldn't tell me anything except, "Be quiet and don't ask questions." Not helpful.

Maybe my poking around would upset some trial that was going on. But if there was a trial, surely they'd need my cooperation. After all, I had the crucial evidence: a couple thousand pages of printouts, all neatly folded into boxes and locked up in a janitor's closet.

Well, even if I couldn't ask questions, I could still do science. Publishing your results is as much a part of research as investigating a weirdness. In my case probably more important. As rumors of this hacker spread, military people began to call, asking for more information. What should I tell them?

The end of August marked a year after we'd first detected this hacker in our computers, and two months after we finally nailed him in Hannover. The FBI still told me to keep quiet.

Of course, the FBI couldn't legally prevent me from publishing, or even poking around. Martha was adamant: "You're free to write what you wish. That's what the First Amendment's all about."

She should know. She was in the midst of studying constitutional law for her bar exam. Just three more weeks, and it'd be all over. To take her mind off the exam, we began sewing a quilt. Just a few minutes here and there, but the design grew and grew, and though I didn't realize it, something wonderful was growing with it.

We split up the work of making the quilt the way we always had. She'd do the piecing, I'd sew the squares, and we'd both share the quilting. We'd just started cutting the pieces when Laurie stopped by for brunch.

Martha showed her the design and explained that the quilt would be called "Garden Star." The central blazing star would be bright yellow and orange, like the peonies in our garden. Surrounding it would be a ring of tulips, and then a border called "snowball," like the snowball bushes we had, the first plants to bloom in spring. Laurie suggested another border, called "flying geese," to represent the birds in the garden.

Listening to Laurie and Martha talk about quilting patterns, each one with its ancient, romantic name, I felt a deep warmth. Here was my home, my love. The quilt we were making now would last our whole lives; in fact, it would outlive us and still be there to comfort our grandchildren . . .

Whoa. I was getting carried away. After all, Martha and I weren't married or anything, just living together, just sharing our lives while it was good for both of us, free to move on if things weren't working out. Yeah. It was better that way, more open and enlightened. None of this old-fashioned "till death do us part" stuff.

Yeah, sure.

Laurie startled me, her words somehow picking up on my private thoughts. "This should be your wedding quilt." Martha and I both stared at her.

"Really. You two are already married—anyone can see it. You've been best friends and lovers for almost eight years. So why don't you make it official and celebrate?"

I was completely at a loss. What Laurie had said was so true and obvious that I'd been blind not to see it. I had been stuck thinking that we should just go on, one day at a time, being together "for now," while things were good. But really, would I leave Martha if we were going through hard times? Would I leave her if someone else attracted me more? Was that the kind of person I wanted to be, and the way I wanted to live the rest of my life?

At that moment I realized what to do, and how I wanted to live. I looked at Martha, her face calm and still, bent over the bright pieces of calico. There were tears in my eyes, and I couldn't speak. I looked at Laurie for help, but the moment she saw my face, she vanished into the kitchen to make tea, leaving Martha and me alone together.

"Sweetheart?"

She raised her head and looked at me steadily.

"When do you want to get married?"

"What about next spring, after the rainy season, when there are roses?"

So it was done. No looking back, no regrets, no glancing around to see if someone better would come along. Martha and me, for the rest of our lives. Laurie poured out the tea, and we all sat together, not saying much, but so happy.

By October I started thinking about the hacker again. Darren and I argued about whether to publish a paper. "If you don't say something," Darren argued, "some other hacker will wreck someone else's computer."

"But if I do publish, it'll teach a dozen hackers how."

That's the problem with talking about security problems. If you describe how to make a pipe bomb, the next kid that finds some charcoal and saltpeter will become a terrorist. Yet if you suppress the information, people won't know the danger.

January marked six months since the hacker had been busted, a year and a half since we'd first detected him. Yet I still didn't know his name. It was about time to publish my results.

So I sent the paper to *Communications of the Association of Computer Machinery.* Though you won't find it on newsstands, *Communications* reaches most computer professionals, and it's a real scientific journal: every article is refereed. Which meant that three other computer scientists checked over my article and made anonymous comments on whether it should be published.

The paper was to come out in the May issue. Together, the

Association for Computer Machinery and Lawrence Berkeley Labs scheduled a joint announcement for May first.

May would be a goofy month. Martha and I planned on getting married at the end of the month. We'd reserved the Berkeley Rose Garden, sewn our wedding clothes, and invited our friends and relatives. Even without the publicity of the hacker, this month wouldn't be calm.

Well, we were pretty much all set when the German magazine *Quick* got there first. On April 14, they printed a story about how a German hacker had broken into three dozen military computers. Although their reporter had managed to meet the hacker, most of their story came from my logbook.

My logbook! How did *Quick* magazine, a cross between *Life* and the *National Enquirer,* manage to get ahold of my laboratory logbook? I'd kept my logbook on my computer—it lived on disks, not on paper. Did someone break into my computer and read my logbook?

Impossible. My logbook was on my Macintosh: I never connected to any network, and I hid the disk in my desk every night.

I reread the translation of the article, and realized that someone had leaked a copy of my logbook from a year ago, January. Before I'd set up the phony SDINET sting. Had I given a copy of that logbook to anyone?

Yes, I had. On January 10, I'd sent the logbook to Mike Gibbons at the FBI. He must have forwarded it to the Legal Attaché in Bonn. Who knew where it landed next?

Someone had leaked it to *Quick* magazine. And they published the story two weeks before I was going to. Damn.

One year of silence. A year of covert cooperation with the authorities. Betrayed to a cheap tabloid in Germany. How ignominious.

Even with a copy of my notebook, *Quick* was anything but accurate. Not much to do but get the facts out ourselves. Damn.

Whatever we did, we'd be late. John Markoff—now at the New York *Times*—had heard about the story and was asking questions. Damn. Only one thing to do: my lab announced a press conference. With me at center stage. Damn.

That evening, at 11 P.M., I was nervous and worried sick. Me? At a press conference? A phone call from the NSA didn't help, either.

Sally Knox, an administrator with NSA's computer security center, was in town. She'd heard about tomorrow's press conference. "Don't you dare mention our name," she barked into my ear. "We get enough bad press as it is."

I look at Martha. She hears this woman's voice from the phone and rolls her eyes. I try to soothe the spook's worries.

"Look, Sally, NSA hasn't done anything wrong. I'm not about to say that your funding ought to be cut."

"It doesn't matter. As soon as the media hears our name, there'll be trouble. They distort everything about us. They'll never publish a fair story."

I look at Martha. She's motioning me to hang up.

"OK, Sally," I said. "I'll make sure that I don't even mention your agency. If anyone asks, I'll just say, 'No comment.' "

"No, don't do that. Then those pigs will sniff around and pick up more. Tell them that we had nothing to do with it."

"Look, I'm not gonna lie, Sally. And anyway, isn't the National Computer Security Center a public, unclassified agency?"

"Yes, it is. But that's no reason to let the press prowl around."

"Then why don't you send one of your people to my press conference?"

"None of our employees are authorized to talk to the media."

With this attitude, it's no wonder her agency gets such bad press.

Martha wrote me a note: "Ask her if she's ever heard of the First Amendment," but I couldn't get a word in edgewise. Sally went on about how the Congress was out to get them, the press was out to get them, and I was out to get them.

She ranted for twenty-five minutes, trying to convince me not to mention NSA or the National Computer Security Center.

It's 11:30 at night, I'm exhausted, and I can't take any more. I'll do anything to get off the phone.

"Listen, Sally," I say, "where do you get off, telling me what I can't say?"

"I'm not telling you what to say. I'm telling you not to mention the Computer Security Center."

I hang up.

Martha rolls over in bed and looks at me. "Are they all like that?"

The next morning's press conference was a zoo. I'm accustomed to scientific meetings and technical seminars. You always hear about press conferences, but I'd never actually seen one. Now I'm the target of one.

It was nuts. Along with my boss, Roy Kerth, I spouted for half an hour, answering questions from reporters. The television reporters asked easy ones ("How do you feel now that it's over?"), while the newspaper people asked jagged, tough questions—"What should be the national policy on computer security?" Or "Was Admiral Poindexter justified in clamping down on sensitive but unclassified material?"

Nobody asked about the NSA. Not a mention of the National Computer Security Center. Sally had blathered for half an hour in vain.

Beforehand, I'd been pretty jaded on the press. Figured that they'd distort whatever happened. Now here was a technical story, spanning two continents and a year's work. How would the American media report it?

Amazingly accurately. My technical article had more details—the Gnu-Emacs hole, how the hacker cracked passwords—but I was astounded by how well newspapers conveyed the story. The important stuff was there—the military computers, the sting, even Operation Showerhead.

And these reporters did their homework. They called Germany and somehow dug up what I had never found: the hacker's name. They phoned the hacker.

# 55

"HELLO, IS THIS MARKUS HESS IN HANNOVER?"

"Yes."

"This is Richard Covey. I'm a reporter here in California. May I talk with you?"

"I cannot talk."

"About this hacker case—could you tell me if you worked alone or with someone else?"

"I cannot answer that. The case is still running in the German courts."

"What were your intentions?"

"It was strictly a hobby."

"Are you a student?"

"Uh, yes. I cannot speak on the phone because I do not trust the lines. They may be tapped."

"Do you have a lawyer?"

"Yes."

"What is his name?"

No answer.

"Do you know Laszlo Balogh in Pittsburgh?"

"No. Never heard of him, except for the newspaper stories."

"Can you speculate on how Balogh got the false data?"

"I cannot answer that question."

"Did you work with anyone?"

"I cannot say. I am not comfortable talking. I am not sure that the lines are clean."

"Were you a spy?"

"Ha. Anyone who believes that is ridiculous. I was just curious."

"Can you guess how the data got to Pittsburgh?"

"No, I cannot guess. I did not show it to anyone. It is dangerous for me to say anything more because I do not know if the telephone lines are clean."

"Were you paid for your work?"

"I must go now. I cannot talk." Click.

Markus Hess. After all this time, my cuckoo's name is Markus Hess.

Well, he speaks English, although without contractions. And he's as paranoid on the telephone as he is on the computer—always looking over his shoulder. German newspapers report that Hess is five foot ten inches, twenty-five years old, broad-shouldered, and known to his friends as a solid but not brilliant Unix programmer. And he chain-smokes Benson and Hedges.

Once again, I page through the Hannover telephone directory. There's his name, all right, but who is he? What's this guy up to? I'll never find out from Berkeley.

Maybe I should call someone in Germany? Who do I know there? A couple students at the Max Planck Institute. Some astronomers in Darmstadt. And a college buddy in Hamburg.

Around the end of the summer, a friend of a friend sent a letter to me: "I need a place to stay while visiting San Francisco. Mind if I sleep on your floor?" Seemed it was a high school student visiting from abroad.

Martha, Claudia, and I don't exactly run a youth hostel, but our door's always open for visitors. Michael Sperber stayed for a couple nights and kept us amused with tales of touring the States. Just as interesting to me: his dad, Jochen Sperber, is a reporter in Northern Germany and could make contact with hackers around Hannover.

I struck paydirt. By chance, I'd found someone who was curious, persistent, and able to dig up the facts in Germany. Over the next five months, Jochen Sperber found enough information to piece together what happened at the other end of the trail.

What really happened? Here's my estimate, based on interviews, police reports, newspaper accounts, and messages from German computer programmers.

I'd been chasing a shadow. Now I could sketch a portrait.

In the early '80s, the Bundespost expanded the German telephone service to include data networking. Their Datex service got off to a slow start, but by 1985 businesses and universities began subscribing. It was a convenient, if not cheap, way to interconnect computers spread across Germany.

As everywhere, students started to exploit this service. First, discovering flaws in the system's protections; later, finding ways to connect abroad through the network. The Bundespost had its hands full in starting up Datex, and pretty much ignored these hackers.

A dozen hackers started the Chaos Computer Club, whose members specialize in creating viruses, breaking into computers, and serving as a computer counterculture. Some are cyberpunks; a few are extremely proficient in computing, others little more than novices. Through electronic bulletin boards and telephone links, they anonymously exchanged phone numbers of hacked computers, as well as stolen passwords and credit cards.

Markus Hess knew of the Chaos Club, although he was never a central figure there. Rather, he kept his distance as a free-lance hacker. During the day, he worked at a small software firm in downtown Hannover.

Over a crackling phone connection, Jochen Sperber said, "You see, Hess knew Hagbard, who kept in touch with other hackers in Germany, like Pengo and Bresinsky. Hagbard is a pseudonym, of course. His real name is . . ."

Hagbard. I'd heard that name before. After I hung up the phone, I searched my logbook for Hagbard. There he was—he'd broken into Fermilab and Stanford. Yet I'd seen it elsewhere. I searched databases at school and asked friends. Not a peep. For the next three days, I asked every person I met, in hopes that it might ring a bell with someone.

At last, at a Berkeley bookstore, the woman behind the counter said, "Why sure. Hagbard is the hero of the Illuminati books." It's a series of science fiction novels, about an international conspiracy that controls the world. The Illuminati run—and ruin—everything. Against this age-old secret cult, Hagbard leads a small band of anarchists.

So Hess's compatriot runs under the alias of Hagbard. He must really believe that there's a conspiracy out there. And he probably feels that I'm one of the secret Illuminati—out to suppress the good guys!

Maybe he's right. A couple of my radical friends would agree with him. But I sure don't know any secrets.

Well, Hagbard worked closely with Markus Hess. The two drank beers together at Hannover bars, and spent evenings behind Hess's computer.

Who's Hagbard? According to the German magazine *Der Spiegel,* Hagbard—Karl Koch—was a twenty-three-year-old programmer who needed money to support a stiff cocaine habit, not to mention monthly telephone bills for overseas hacking adventures.

During 1986, some hackers from Berlin and Hannover discussed (over alcohol and drugs) how to raise some money.

Pengo—real name Hans Huebner—was an accomplished eighteen-year-old programmer who claimed to be in it for the pure technical challenge. He was bored with those computers that he had legal access to, so he started breaking into systems via the international networks. In a message posted to a bulletin board, Pengo said that he was involved with "a circle of persons who tried to make deals with an eastern secret service."

Why? Since the software on the systems that he had legal access to "didn't turn me on anymore, I enjoyed the lax security of the systems I had access to by using [international] networks." Computing had become an addiction for Pengo.

But why sell the information to the Soviet bloc agents? According to *Der Spiegel,* he needed money to invest in his computing company. So Pengo got together with a couple others in West Berlin. One of them, Dirk Brezinski, is a programmer and troubleshooter for the German computer firm Siemens. Another, Peter Carl, also in Berlin, is a former croupier who "always had enough cocaine."

These five worked together to discover new ways to break into computers, exploring military networks and sharpening their skills at cracking operating systems. Pengo specialized in Digital's Vax VMS operating system and frequently talked with Hagbard.

Pengo had no scruples about selling information to Soviet bloc agents. He saw himself as ethically neutral—he didn't want to give the Russians any advantage; he just wanted to have fun on the networks.

And pick up some cash along the way.

Hess, too, just played around the networks, searching for ways to connect around the world. He'd dropped out of the University of Hagen, where he didn't quite finish a degree in mathematics and physics. (Physics? If only he'd known!)

At first, Hess apparently just played around the networks, searching for ways to connect around the world. Like a ham radio operator, he started out a hobbyist, trying to reach as far away as possible. At first, he managed to connect to Karlsruhe; later he reached Bremen over the Datex network.

Soon, he discovered that many system managers hadn't locked their back doors. Usually these were university computers, but Markus Hess began to wonder: how many other systems were wide open? What other ways could you sneak into computers?

In early 1986, Hagbard and Pengo were routinely breaking into computers in North America: mostly high-energy physics labs, but a few NASA sites as well. Hagbard described his exploits to Hess.

The challenge was there. Hess began to explore outside of Germany. But he no longer cared about universities and physics labs—he wanted real excitement. Hess and Hagbard would target the military.

The leaders of the Chaos Computer Club had issued a warning to their members: "Never penetrate a military computer. The security people on the other side will be playing a game with you—almost like chess. Remember that they've practiced this game for centuries." Markus Hess wasn't listening.

Hess found his way into an unprotected computer belonging to a German subsidiary of the U.S. defense contractor, Mitre. Once inside that system, he could have discovered detailed instructions to link into Mitre's computers in Bedford, Massachusetts, and McLean, Virginia.

Why not? The system was wide open, and let him call anywhere in America.

By summer 1986, Hess and Hagbard were operating separately, but frequently comparing notes. They collaborated in methodically twisting all doorknobs as they walked down the streets of the military networks.

Hess soon expanded his beachhead at Mitre. He explored their system internally, then sent out tentacles into other American computers. He collected telephone numbers and network addresses, and methodically attacked these systems. On August 20, he struck Lawrence Berkeley Lab.

Even then, Hess was only fooling around. He'd realized that he was privy to secrets, both industrial and national, but kept his mouth shut. Then, around the end of September, in a smoky Hannover beer garden, he described his latest exploit to Hagbard.

You can't make money by breaking into universities and colleges. Who's interested in data from physics labs, other than a few grad students?

But military bases and defense contractors? Hagbard smelled money.

And Hagbard sensed who to contact: Pengo, in West Berlin.

Pengo, with his contacts to hackers across Germany, knew how to use Hess's information. Carrying Hess's printouts, one of the Berlin hackers crossed into East Berlin and met with agents from the Soviet KGB.

The deal was made: around 30,000 Deutschmarks—$18,000—for printouts and passwords.

The KGB wasn't just paying for printouts, though. Hess and company apparently sold their techniques as well: how to break into Vax computers; which networks to use when crossing the Atlantic; details on how the Milnet operates.

Even more important to the KGB was obtaining research data about Western technology, including integrated circuit design, computer-aided manufacturing, and, especially, operating system software that was under U.S. export control. They offered 250,000 Deutschmarks for copies of Digital Equipment's VMS operating system.

Peter Carl and Dirk Brezinski apparently met with the KGB a dozen times, filling many of their requests: source code to the Unix operating system, designs for high-speed gallium-arsenide integrated circuits, and computer programs used to engineer computer memory chips.

Alone, the source code to Unix isn't worth $130,000. Chip designs? Perhaps. But a sophisticated computer design program . . . well, maybe the KGB did get its money's worth.

Hagbard wanted more than Deutschmarks. He demanded cocaine. The KGB was a willing supplier.

Hagbard passed some of the money (but none of the cocaine) to Hess, in return for printouts, passwords, and network information. Hagbard's cut went to pay his telephone bill, sometimes running over a thousand dollars a month, as he called computers around the world.

Hess saved everything. He kept a detailed notebook and saved every session on a floppy disk. This way, after he disconnected from a military computer, he could print out the interesting parts, and pass these along to Hagbard and on to the KGB.

Also the KGB's wish list was SDI data. As Hess searched for it, I naturally detected SDI showing up in his requests. And Martha's Operation Showerhead fed Hess plenty of SDI fodder.

But could the KGB trust these printouts? How could they be certain that Hagbard wasn't inventing all of this to feed his own coke habit?

The KGB decided to verify the German hacker ring. The mythical Barbara Sherwin served as a perfect way to test the validity of this new form of espionage. She had, after all, invited people to write to her for more information.

But secret services don't handle things directly. They use intermediaries. The KGB contacted another agency—either the Hungarian or Bulgarian intelligence service. They, in turn, apparently had a professional relationship with a contact in Pittsburgh: Laszlo Balogh.

The Bulgarian embassy in America probably has a standing agreement with Laszlo along the lines of "We'll pay you $100 for mailing the following letter . . ."

Laszlo Balogh didn't care one way or another. According to Roger Stuart of the *Pittsburgh Press,* Laszlo billed himself as a Hungarian refugee; a draftsman; a credit corporation employee; a trucking company owner; a diamond dealer; a world traveler; a bodyguard for Kuwaiti princesses; a CIA hit man; and an FBI informant.

The reporter wrote: "Although he has claimed extensive foreign government contacts and driven expensive foreign cars, he once testified that he had difficulty recording an undercover conversation for the FBI because the recorder kept slipping beneath his sweat suit."

Apparently Balogh ran a now-defunct company when a forged check drawn on a nonexistent bank was used to obtain a garbage hauling contract. Other times he was involved in schemes to steal $38,000 in diamonds, and to sell computer equipment to the Soviets. Indeed, he once claimed to have been held captive at the Soviet embassy.

As long as the money was green, Laszlo didn't care where it came from. He knew nothing about SDINET, knew nobody in Hannover, and said he didn't even own a computer.

Hmmm. I looked over Laszlo's letter. It had been word-processed—not a typewriter, but a word processor. If Laszlo Balogh doesn't own a computer, then who'd created this letter? The Bulgarian embassy perhaps?

Does the FBI have enough evidence to indict Laszlo Balogh? They won't tell me. But the way I see it, Laszlo's in deep yogurt: the FBI is watching him, and whoever's pulling his puppet strings isn't pleased.

The West German police, though, have plenty of evidence against Markus Hess. Printouts, phone traces, and my logbook.

When they broke into his apartment on June 29, 1987, they seized a hundred floppy disks, a computer, and documentation describing the U.S. Milnet. Not much doubt there.

But when the police raided Hess's apartment, nobody was home. Though I was waiting patiently for him to appear on my computer, the German police entered his place when he wasn't connected.

At his first trial, Hess got off on appeal. His lawyer argued that since Hess wasn't connected at the moment his apartment was raided, he might not have done the hacking. This, along with a problem in the search warrants, was enough to overturn the case against Hess on computer theft. But the German federal police continued to investigate.

On March 2, 1989, German authorities charged five people with espionage: Pengo, Hagbard, Peter Carl, Dirk Bresinsky, and Markus Hess.

Peter Carl met regularly with KGB agents in East Berlin, selling any data the others could find. When the German BKA caught up with him, he was about to run off to Spain. He's now in jail, awaiting trial, along with Dirk Bresinsky, who was jailed for desertion from the German Army.

Pengo is having second thoughts about his years working for the KGB. He says that he hopes he "did the right thing by giving the German police detailed information about my involvement." But as long as there's an active criminal case, he'll say no more.

All the same, the publicity hasn't helped Pengo's professional life. His business partners have shied away from backing him, and several of his computing projects have been canceled. Outside of his business losses, I'm not sure he feels there's anything wrong in what he did.

Today, Markus Hess is walking the streets of Hannover, free on bail while awaiting a trial for espionage. Smoking Benson and Hedges cigarettes. And looking over his shoulder.

Hagbard, who hacked with Hess for a year, tried to kick his cocaine habit in late 1988. But not before spending his profits from the KGB: he was deep in debt and without a job. In spring 1989 he found a job at the office of a political party in Hannover.

By cooperating with the police, he and Pengo avoided prosecution for espionage.

Hagbard was last seen alive on May 23, 1989. In an isolated forest outside of Hannover, police found his charred bones next to a melted can of gasoline. A borrowed car was parked nearby, keys still in the ignition.

No suicide note was found.

# 56

WHEN I BEGAN THIS HUNT, I SAW MYSELF AS SOMEONE engaged in mundane tasks. I did what I was assigned to do, avoided authority, and kept myself peripheral to important issues. I was apathetic and outside the political sphere. Yeah, I vaguely identified myself with the old '60s left movement. But I never thought much about how my work interacted with society . . . maybe I picked astronomy because it has so little to do with earthly problems.

Now, after sliding down this Alice-in-Wonderland hole, I find the political left and right reconciled in their mutual dependency on computers. The right sees computer security as necessary to protect national secrets; my leftie friends worry about an invasion of their privacy when prowlers pilfer data banks. Political centrists realize that insecure computers cost money when their data is exploited by outsiders.

The computer has become a common denominator that knows no intellectual, political, or bureaucratic bounds; the Sherwin Williams of necessity that covers the world, spanning all points of view.

Realizing this, I've become pro-active—almost rabid—about computer security. I worry about protecting our vulnerable data banks. I wonder what happens on financial networks, where millions of dollars slosh around every minute. I'm ticked that the Feds don't seem to be minding the mint. And I'm upset that looters have proliferated.

It took a lot of crap to make me give a damn. I wish that we lived in a golden age, where ethical behavior was assumed; where technically competent programmers respected the privacy of others; where we didn't need locks on our computers.

I'm saddened to find talented programmers devoting their time to breaking into computers. Instead of developing new ways to help each other, vandals make viruses and logic bombs. The result? People blame every software quirk on viruses, public-domain software lies underused, and our networks become sources of paranoia.

Fears for security really do louse up the free flow of information. Science and social progress only take place in the open. The paranoia that hackers leave in their wake only stifles our work . . . forcing administrators to disconnect our links to networked communities.

Yes, you can make secure computers and networks. Systems that outsiders can't easily break into. But they're usually difficult to use and unfriendly. And slow. And expensive. Computer communications already costs too much—adding cryptographic encoding and elaborate authentication schemes will only make it worse.

On the other hand, our networks seem to have become the targets of (and channels for) international espionage. Come to think of it, what would I do if I were an intelligence agent? To collect secret information, I might train an agent to speak a foreign language, fly her to a distant country, supply her with bribe money, and worry that she might be caught or fed duplicitous information.

Or I could hire a dishonest computer programmer. Such a spy need never leave his home country. Not much risk of an internationally embarrassing incident. It's cheap, too—a few small computers and some network connections. And the information returned is fresh—straight from the target's word processing system.

Today there's only one country that's not reachable from your telephone: Albania. What does this mean for the future of espionage?

Yow! What am I thinking about? I'm not a spy—I'm just an astronomer who's been away from science for too long.

As I turned off my monitors and wound up the cables, I realized that for a year, I'd been caught in a maze. I'd thought I'd been setting traps; actually, I'd been trapped the whole while. While the hacker was searching military computers, I was exploring different communities—on the networks and in the government. His journey took him into thirty or forty computers; mine reached into a dozen organizations.

My own quest had changed. I thought I was hunting for a hacker. I'd imagined that my work had nothing to do with my home or country . . . after all, I was just doing my job.

Now, with my computers serviced and holes patched, I biked home, picked a few strawberries, and mixed some milkshakes for Martha and Claudia.

Cuckoos will lay their eggs in other nests. I'm returning to astronomy.

# Epilogue

WHILE I WAS DESPERATELY TRYING TO WRAP UP THE hacker chase, we also had a wedding to plan. It was a hectic time, and I cursed my work (and Hess) for distracting me from my home life. We were going to be married at the end of May, so the April revelations were particularly awkward, Martha ending up with more than her share of the preparations.

She was coping, however, firmly resolved to make the wedding true to who we were. We silk-screened our own invitations, saying that the two of us, along with our families, were doing the inviting. Naturally, the ink on the silk-screen leaked through, and half the invitations had our fingerprints, but that's a part of the home brew.

Martha decked out in a white dress and veil, and me in a tux? Absurd. And Laurie in a bridesmaid's outfit? Nobody ever made Laurie wear a dress for any reason. Somehow we managed. Laurie wore white linen pants and a tailored jacket, Martha made a simple pale yellow dress, and I sewed my own cotton shirt. (Try sewing your own shirt sometime. You'll learn a new respect for shirtmakers, especially after you sew the cuffs on backward.)

So it rained on our wedding and there wasn't a place to hide in the rose garden. Claudia's string quartet unraveled a tarp, protecting their violins from the downpour. My sister Jeannie showed up, straight from her last class at Navy War College—and straight into a political argument with Laurie. Of course, after the ceremony, we got lost driving to a remote inn by the ocean.

It was wonderful, all the same. Say what you will about marriage, this was the happiest day of my life.

Sure, I could have just stayed living with Martha, never quite committing myself beyond next month's rent. I'd lived with several other people in this casual way, saying we were in love, but always ready to split if things got tough. We dressed it up with talk about openness and freedom from oppressive conventions, but for me it was just an excuse. The truth was, I had never dared to give myself fully to anyone, committing myself to make it work no matter what. But now I'd found someone I loved and trusted enough to gather my courage and stand by, not just for now but forever.

But domestic happiness doesn't solve everything—I still had to figure out what to do next. With Hess unmasked, I could return to astronomy, or at least, computing. Not quite tracking an international spy ring, but then, there's research to do everywhere. The best part is not knowing where your science will lead you.

It wasn't the same. The computer people felt I'd wasted the past couple years rubbing shoulders with spies. The spies didn't have much use for me—who needs an astronomer? And the astronomers knew I'd been away from the field for two years. Where do I go from here?

Martha had passed her bar exam and was clerking for a judge across the bay, in San Francisco. She loved it—taking notes on trials, researching case law, helping to write decisions. A sort of grad school for law.

She found another clerkship in Boston, starting in August '88. Over a strawberry milkshake, she described her possibilities:

"I'd clerk for the circuit court in Boston. It'll be more academic there—no trials, just appeals. Might be fun."

"And the alternatives?"

"Well, I'm thinking about returning to school, to finish my degree in jurisprudence. That'll take a few more years." Always the academic.

Would I leave Berkeley to follow her to Massachusetts?

Simple decision: I'd follow her anywhere. If she's going to Boston, I'd dredge up a job there. Fortunately, the Harvard Smithsonian Center for Astrophysics was looking for a half-breed astronomer–computer jockey, someone to play with their X-ray astronomy database.

I can mess up a database as well as the next person, and they didn't mind my hiatus from astronomy. And, being astronomers, they were already accustomed to people showing up late and sleeping under desks.

It wasn't easy to leave Berkeley—the strawberries, the street vendors, the sunshine—but we signed a nonaggression pact with our roommates: we could visit anytime and wouldn't have to wash the dishes. In return, they could stay at our place in Massachusetts, so long as they brought some California kiwi fruit.

The hardest part was leaving our roommate Claudia. I'd grown accustomed to her late-night Mozart practicing (a long way from the Berkeley Grateful Dead concerts!). She hadn't quite settled down with a mate, although several promising musicians were courting her just as we left. The latest gossip? Oh, there's this handsome orchestra conductor that's simply lusting after her . . .

So, in August 1988, we packed a couple suitcases for a year in Massachusetts.

Being uprooted and towed to the East Coast had a few advantages. My computer network address changed . . . a good thing, since several hackers had tried to break into it after I published my article. One or two had threatened me in various ways—better not to give 'em a standing target. And various three-letter agencies stopped calling me, asking for advice, opinions, and rumors. Now, in Cambridge, I could concentrate on astronomy, and forget about computer security and hackers.

Over the past two years, I'd become an expert on computer security, but hadn't learned a thing about astronomy. Worse, the physics of X-ray astronomy was totally foreign to me: I'm accustomed to planetary science, and planets don't give off X-rays.

So what do X-ray astronomers look at? The sun. Stars and quasars. And exploding galaxies.

"Exploding galaxies?" I asked Steve Murray, my new boss at the Center for Astrophysics. "Galaxies don't explode. They just sit there in spirals."

"Bah. You learned your astronomy in the '70s," Steve replied. "Why, we're looking at stars exploding into supernovas, bursts of X-rays from neutron stars, even stuff falling into black holes. Hang around here for a while and we'll teach you some real astronomy."

They didn't fool around. Within a week, I was settled behind a computer, building databases of X-ray observations. Classical computing, but there's good physics in there. Yow! There really are black holes in the middle of galaxies. I've seen the data.

The Smithsonian Astrophysical Laboratory shares buildings with Harvard Observatory. Naturally, everyone's heard of Harvard Observatory. But the Smithsonian? That's in Washington, isn't it? Only after I moved to Cambridge did I realize that the Smithsonian had a hot-damn astronomy section, the Center for Astrophysics. Makes no difference to me, so long as they're doing good astronomy.

Cambridge, Massachusetts, might be across the country, but culturally, it's just around the corner from Berkeley. Lots of '60s hippies, left-wing politics, bookstores, and coffeehouses. There's street musicians most every night, and you're serenaded at the downtown subway stations by guitars and mandolins. And the neighborhoods—some of these houses are a hundred years old. Bicycling in Cambridge is sheer excitement—the drivers aim right at you. History, weird people, good astronomy, cheap pizza . . . all the ingredients for a good place to live.

Marriage? Except that Martha keeps me away from microwave ovens, it's been a kicker.

Wednesday, November 2, 1988, Martha and I stayed up late, reading a novel out loud. Around midnight we pulled up the quilt and fell asleep.

I was dreaming about floating through the air on an oak leaf when the phone rang. Damn. The glow-in-the-dark clock said 2:25 A.M.

"Hi, Cliff. It's Gene. Gene Miya at NASA Ames Laboratory. No apologies for waking you up. Our computers are under attack." The excitement in his voice woke me up.

"Wake up and check your system," Gene said. "Better yet, stay asleep and check it. But call me back if you see anything strange."

I'd hung up the phone for ten seconds when it rang again. This time, the line just beeped. A Morse code beep.

My computer was calling. It wanted my attention.

Oh hell. Can't hide. I stumbled over to the trusty old Macintosh, dialed into Harvard Observatory's computer, and typed in my account name, Cliff. Then my non-dictionary password, "Robotcat."

Slow logging in. After five minutes, I gave up. My computer just wasn't responding. Something was wrong.

Well, as long as I was awake, I might as well see what's on the West Coast. Maybe there's some electronic mail waiting for me. I connected over Tymnet into Lawrence Berkeley Labs—no long-distance phone calls for me.

The Unix system at Berkeley was slow, too. Frustratingly slow. But only one other guy was using it. Darren Griffiths.

Over the screen, we exchanged a couple notes:

```
Hi Darren—It's Cliff. How's things :-)
Cliff, call me on the phone right away. We're under attack.
OK O-O
```

O-O means Over and Out. And the :-) is a crude smiley face. You look at it sideways, and it smiles at you.

2:15 A.M. in Massachusetts isn't yet midnight in Berkeley. Darren was nowhere near asleep.

"Hi, Darren. What's this attack?"

"Something's eating our system, starting a lot of processes running. Slowing the system down."

"A hacker?"

"No. I'd guess a virus, but I can't tell right now." Darren spoke slowly as he typed. "I've been working on it for ten minutes, so I'm not sure."

Then I remembered Gene Miya's call. "NASA Ames Labs says the same thing."

"Yeah. I bet we're under attack from the Arpanet," Darren said. "Yeah, look at all these network connections!"

I couldn't see any—as long as I talked on the phone, my computer was disconnected and I was blind. With a single phone line, either I could speak on the phone, or my Macintosh could talk to another computer, but not both. I hung up and dialed into my Harvard computer, a desktop computer made by Sun. Slow. Something was chewing on it.

I looked at the processes running (with a *ps* command, like the hacker had taught me). There was the virus. But not just running one or two jobs. Hundreds of connections to other computers.

Each process was trying to talk to some other computer. The connections came from all over: nearby systems at Harvard, distant computers from the Arpanet.

As fast as I'd kill one program, another would take its place. I stomped them all out at once; not a minute later, one reappeared. Within three minutes, there were a dozen. Holy smoke!

What's crawling around my computer?

A biological virus is a molecule which sneaks into a cell and convinces the cell to copy the virus molecule, instead of the cell's DNA molecules. Once duplicated, the virus then breaks out of the cell to infect other cells.

Similarly, a computer virus is a program that replicates itself. Like its biological namesake, it enters a system, duplicates itself, and sends copies of itself to other systems.

To the host computer, a virus looks like a series of commands which appear perfectly legitimate, yet have dire consequences. Often these commands are buried within ordinary programs, hibernating until the program is executed. When the infected program is run, all seems fine until the virus is executed. Then the computer is tricked into copying the virus instructions elsewhere.

Where? Probably the virus will copy itself into another program on the same computer, making it tough to eradicate. Or maybe onto another disk, so that someone will transport it to another computer.

Perhaps the virus will do nothing more than duplicate itself into other programs. A malicious virus maker, however, might throw in a side effect: "Copy yourself four times, then erase all the word processing files."

Computer viruses spread most easily on personal computers: these machines have no protections built into their operating systems. At a PC, you can run any program you wish and change any part of memory. On small computers, it's hard to tell if a program has been changed on a disk.

Bigger computers, like Unix systems, are more resistant: their operating systems isolate one user from another, and set limits on how much you can modify. In addition, you can't change system programs without permission—the operating system's walls seal you out of those sensitive areas.

The virus writer must carefully tailor the program to a target computer. A program that runs on your IBM PC won't work on my Macintosh, or my lab's Unix system. Then too, the virus program can't occupy much space, or it'll easily be discovered and removed.

A virus is a good place to hide time bombs. It's easy to design a virus whose instructions work like this:

"Copy me into four other programs."

"Wait until February 13."

"Erase all the files on the system."

The virus must find a way to propagate. Simply infecting programs on one computer will only hurt one person. The creator of a malicious virus wants the virus to infect hundreds of systems. How do you pass a program to hundreds of others?

People exchange software on disks. Infect one program on a disk, and it'll infect every system that runs that program. As the disk is passed from office to office, dozens of computers can be infected and possibly wiped out.

Public bulletin boards also exchange software. These dial-in computers are run by hobbyists, schools, and a few companies. You dial their number and copy programs from the bulletin board into your home computer. You can just as easily copy a program from your home system into the bulletin board. There it'll wait until someone requests it. And if your program has a virus buried inside, well, you won't discover it until it's too late.

So computer viruses spread by interchanging programs. Someone brings an infected program—a fun game—into work and runs it on her office machine. The virus copies itself into her word processing program. Later she gives her word processing disk to a friend. Her friend's system gets infected. Oh, each program appears to work properly. But when February 13 rolls around . . .

The obvious way to prevent viruses is to avoid exchanging programs. Don't take candy from strangers—don't accept untrusted programs. By keeping your computer isolated from others, no virus program can infect it.

This canonical wisdom overlooks our daily needs. Unless we exchange programs and data, our computers won't be much use to us. There's a wealth of public-domain software—much of it ideal for solving our problems.

Viruses and logic bombs poison this communal well. People stop trusting public software, and eventually the sources of public software dry up.

But there's another way for a virus to propagate: directly over a network.

Our Arpanet interconnects eighty thousand computers across the country. You can send mail to anyone on these computers, send or receive files over the Arpanet, or (as Markus Hess showed) interactively log into computers connected to the Arpanet.

Could a virus propagate over the Arpanet? A program that copies itself from one computer, out over the network, into another . . .

I'd thought of this before, but had always dismissed the possibility. Arpanet computers have defenses against viruses: you need passwords to log into them. Hess got around this by guessing passwords. Could a virus guess passwords?

At 3:30 in the morning, shivering behind my Macintosh at

home, I dialed into my observatory's computer. It's a Sun workstation, running the popular Berkeley flavor of Unix. All those hundreds of jobs were still running . . . my system was grossly overloaded. No hacker was logged in. Just me.

Same symptom at Lawrence Berkeley Labs. And NASA Ames. Smells like a virus.

I called Darren Griffiths at LBL. "It's a virus," he affirmed. "I can watch it replicate. Try killing the jobs. They'll come right back."

"From where?"

"I'm getting connections from five places. Stanford, University of Rochester, Aerospace Company, the Berkeley campus, and somewhere called BRL."

"That's the Army's Ballistics Research Lab," I said, remembering a conversation with BRL's Mike Muuss. "How's the virus getting into your system?"

"I can't tell, Cliff. The connections are all from the Arpanet, but it's not the usual way of logging into the system. Looks like the virus is breaking in through a hole in the mail system."

Someone's built a virus that exploits a security hole in Unix systems. The hole is in the mail system, and the virus spreads over the network. What's the virus doing? Just copying itself, or does it have a time bomb built in?

It's 4 A.M. What to do? I'd better call the Arpanet controllers and warn them. There's a twenty-four-hour duty officer at the Network Operations Center that watches over the network. This morning, they've heard nothing of this virus. "Better call around, because it'll be all over the place by nine this morning."

The Networks Operations Center hasn't heard. The virus is only a few hours old. I'm seeing viruses coming from a dozen other sites. Virulent. By morning it will have spread to scores or even hundreds of systems. We've got a problem. A major problem.

An epidemic.

We've got to understand this virus and spread the word. For the next thirty-six hours I knocked myself out, trying to understand and defeat this thing. I knew I wasn't alone. At the same time, groups at Berkeley, MIT, and Purdue University were already hot on the trail.

Here I'm only describing what I saw, but my struggle was minor compared to the work of Unix wizards across the country. One by one, programmers reacted—gurus like Keith Bostic, Peter Yee, Gene Spafford, Jon Rochlis, Mark Eichin, Donn Seeley, Ed Wang, and Mike Muuss. I was but a small part of an unorganized but dedicated response to this disaster.

I dig into the code in my system in Cambridge. Right off I can see two versions of the virus. One's customized for Vax computers running Unix. The other's for Sun workstations. Each file is forty-five thousand bytes long. If it were English, it would fit in about thirty pages. But it's not text—I dump the file and it looks like gibberish. It doesn't even look like machine code.

Now this doesn't make sense: computer programs *look* like machine code. This one doesn't. There's no header block information and only a few commands that I recognize. The rest is guacamole.

Patiently I try to understand what those few commands do. Suppose I were a Sun workstation, and someone fed those commands to me. How would I respond? With a pad of paper, hand calculator, and a booklet of machine instructions, I start unwinding the virus's code.

The first few commands just strip off some encryption from the rest of the virus. That's why the virus looks strange. The actual commands have been purposely obscured.

Aha! The virus writer has hidden his virus: he's tried to prevent other programmers from understanding his code. Throwing nails on the road to slow down his pursuers.

Diabolical.

Time to call Darren again. It's 5 A.M. and we're comparing notes—he's discovered the same thing and more: "I've unmasked part of the virus, and I can see it's breaking in through the mail system. Then, it uses *finger* and *telnet* to spread itself to other computers. It's decrypting passwords by brute force guessing."

Together, over the phone, we pry apart the program. Its whole purpose seems to be to copy itself into other computers. It searches for network connections—nearby computers, distant systems, anything that it can reach.

Whenever the virus program discovers a computer on the network, it tries to break into it, using several obscure holes in the Unix operating system.

Holes in Unix? Sure.

When you send mail from one Unix computer to another, the Unix *Sendmail* program handles the transfer. A mail message arrives from the network and *Sendmail* forwards it to the addressee. It's an electronic post office that pigeonholes mail.

*Sendmail* has a hole. Normally, a foreign computer sends messages into this program and everyone's happy. But if there's a problem, you can ask the program to enter debug mode—the program's back door.

When you're in debug, *Sendmail* lets you issue ordinary Unix commands from a foreign computer. Commands like "Execute the following program."

So that's how this virus spawned copies. It mailed copies of itself to other computers and commanded them to execute the virus program.

After the virus program started, it searched for other computers to infect and sent mail messages to them.

On some systems *Sendmail* had been fixed. If so, the virus tried yet another hole: the finger daemon.

To see if I've been using a Unix system, you can issue the command, *finger cliff.* If I've been logged in, Unix will respond with my name, phone number, and what I'm up to. It works well over the network; often I'll just finger someone before calling their telephone.

The virus invaded through the program that handled finger requests. The finger daemon has room for 512 characters of data; the virus sent 536 characters. What happened to the extra 24 characters? They got executed as commands to Unix.

By overflowing the finger daemon, the virus found a second way to execute the command "Execute the following program" on someone else's computer.

If that wasn't enough, the virus had a password guesser built in. It tried to log into nearby, trusted computers, using a few hundred common passwords. If it guessed a valid password, it copied itself into the computer and started all over.

Whew! Any one of these ways would impregnate a lot of computers. Taken together, they formed a fiendishly effective virus.

Like a sorcerer's apprentice, the program kept copying itself from one computer to another. Erase one copy, and a new one would spring into its place. Plug up one hole, and the virus would try a different hole.

Did I say virus?

"You know, Cliff, a virus modifies other programs when it runs. This thing doesn't change other programs; it just copies itself," Darren explained. "It's really not a virus, it's a network worm."

A virus copies itself into other programs, changing the program itself. A worm copies itself from one computer to another. Both are contagious; either can spread havoc.

Viruses usually infect personal computers, spreading through floppy disks and copied programs. Worms strike over networks, spreading through the very connections used for electronic mail and communications.

But at 5 A.M., all I knew was that my computers were bogged down and it's the fault of this self-replicating program. It's a cuckoo, laying eggs in other birds' nests.

Worm or virus, whoever built it has deliberately thrown up roadblocks to prevent anyone from understanding it. The code's encrypted, and it hides its internal tables. It erases any evidence of its parent worm. It feints by appearing to send a message to a Berkeley computer, while actually sending nothing at all—an attempt to draw attention away from the real source of the program.

By 6 A.M., Thursday morning, I'm thinking about the effects of this worm: a disaster's brewing, and someone needs to be notified. Who?

I've called the Arpanet Network Operations Center. They can't do much—even if they turn off the whole network, the worm will still breed, moving around local networks. Better call the National Computer Security Center. Who do I know there? Bob Morris, their chief scientist.

* * *

I knew Bob Morris was on his computer at 6:30 A.M. Thursday morning. I could see him logged into NSA's Dockmaster computer. After posting a message to that machine, I called him on the phone.

"Hi, Bob. We've got troubles. A virus is spreading over the Arpanet, and it's infesting Unix computers."

"When did it start?"

"Around midnight, I'd guess. Maybe earlier—I just don't know. I've been up all night trying to understand it."

"How's it spread?"

"Through a hole in the Unix mail program."

"You must mean *Sendmail.* Hell, I've known about that for years." Bob Morris might have known, but he had never told me.

"Whoever wrote the virus must be laughing, but it's going to mean a rough day for everyone."

"Any ideas who started it?"

"Nope."

"Don't worry about it. I'll look into it and see what I can do."

We chatted awhile, then I hung up. Well, I've warned the authorities. As chief scientist of the National Computer Security Center, Bob had a few hours to rouse his troops and begin figuring out what this virus was all about. I stared at my computer screen for a while, then, clad in a bathrobe, fell sleep on the keyboard.

Two hours later the phone rang. It's Don Alvarez from MIT on the line.

"Hey, Cliff," he says, "something weird is going on. There's a hundred jobs running on our computer. Smells like a virus."

"You've got it too, huh?" We compared notes and quickly realized that Unix systems across the country must be infected. There's not much to do but patch the bugs in the systems.

"There are only two ways to understand this virus," Don said. "The obvious way is to disassemble it. Follow the computer code, step by step, and figure out what it does."

"OK," I said, "I've tried that, and it's not easy. What's the other way?"

"Treat it as a black box. Watch it send signals to other computers, and estimate what's inside of it."

"There's a third way, Don."

"What's that?"

"Find out who wrote it."

I scanned the computer network news: Peter Yee and Keith Bostic of the University of California at Berkeley were unraveling the virus; they described the Unix holes and even published a way to patch the software. Well done!

Within the day, Jon Rochlis, Stan Zanarotti, Ted Ts'o, and Mark Eichin of MIT were dissecting the program, translating the bits and bytes into ideas. By Thursday evening—less than twenty-four hours after the virus was released—the MIT and Berkeley groups had disassembled the code and were well along to understanding it.

Mike Muuss of the Ballistics Research Lab was making progress, too. Within a few hours, he built a test chamber for the virus and used his software tools to prod it. From his experiments, he understood how it spread, and which holes it used to infest other computers.

But who wrote it?

Around eleven in the morning, someone from NSA's National Computer Security Center called me.

"Cliff, we've just held a meeting about the virus," the voice said. "I've got just one question for you: did you write the virus?"

I was stunned. Me? Write this virus?

"No, damn it, I didn't write it. I've spent the past night trying to extinguish it."

"A couple people at the meeting suggested that you were the most likely creator. I'm just checking."

You've got to be joking. Me? What could make them think that I had written it? Then I realized: I'd posted a message to their computer. I was the first to call them. What paranoia!

Their call set me to thinking. Who had written the virus? Why? You don't accidentally write a virus. This one had taken weeks to build.

Late Thursday afternoon, I called Bob Morris back. "Any news?" I asked him.

"For once, I'll tell you the truth," Bob said. "I know who wrote the virus."

"Are you going to tell me?"

"No."

Now that's efficient. Ten hours after I call them, the National Computer Security Center has found the culprit.

But I hadn't. He's still a mystery to me, so it's back to snooping around the networks. If I could only find the computer that had been first infected. No, that won't work. There's thousands out there.

John Markoff, a reporter from the New York *Times,* called. "I heard a rumor that the person who wrote the virus has the initials RTM. Is that any help?"

"Not much, but I'll check it out."

How do you find someone from his initials? Of course . . . you look him up in the network directory.

I log into the Network Information Center and search for anyone with the initials RTM. One guy pops up: Robert T. Morris. Address: Harvard University, Aiken Laboratory.

Aiken. I've heard of that. It's three blocks from my house. I think I'll stroll by.

I pull on a coat and walk along Kirkland Street, then over to Oxford Street, where the sidewalks are brick. Across the street from Harvard's Cyclotron Laboratory, there's a lunch truck selling Middle Eastern food. A hundred feet away, Aiken Computer Lab—an ugly modern concrete building surrounded by old Victorian masterpieces.

I walk up to a secretary. "Hi. I'm looking for Robert Morris."

"Never heard of him," she says. "But I'll check my machine." She types into her terminal:

```
Finger Morris
```

Her computer responds:

```
Login name: rtm            In real life: Robert T. Morris
Phone: 617/498-2247
Last login Thu Nov 3 00:25 on ttyp2 from 128.84.254.126
```

Well—the last time that Robert Morris used the Harvard computer was twenty-five minutes after midnight, on the morning that the virus struck. But he's not here in Massachusetts. That address, 128.84.254.126, is at Cornell University. He entered the Harvard system from a computer at Cornell University. Curious.

The secretary sees the message, looks up, and says, "Oh, he must have once been a student here. That phone number is in room 111."

I wander over to room 111 and knock on the door. A student in a T-shirt peers out. "Ever hear of Robert Morris?" I ask.

His face blanches. "Yeah. He's not here anymore." And he slams the door in my face.

I walk away, think for a moment, then return. "Have you heard about the virus?" I ask the guy at the door.

"Oh, RTM wouldn't have done that. I'm sure."

Wait a second. I hadn't even asked if Morris had written the virus and this guy's denying it. There's an easy way to test this guy's veracity. "When's the last time that Morris has used Harvard's computers?"

"Last year, when he was a student. He's at Cornell now, and he doesn't log into our computer anymore."

This guy's story doesn't jibe with the accounting records of his computer. One of 'em's telling the truth. I'll bank on the computer.

We talked for five minutes, and this guy tells me how he's a good friend of Morris, how they were officemates together, and how RTM would never write a computer virus.

"Yeah, right," I'm thinking.

I leave, thinking that Morris's old officemate is covering for him. Morris must be talking to this guy, and they're both frightened. I'd be scared, too, in that squeeze. Half the country's looking for the creator of this virus.

Where did the virus start from? I checked other computers in Cambridge, searching for connections to Cornell. One machine, over at MIT's Artificial Intelligence Lab, showed late-night connections from Robert Morris's computer at Cornell.

Now things made sense. The virus was designed and built at Cornell. Then the creator used the Arpanet to connect to MIT and release the virus there. A while later he panics when he realizes that his creature is out of control. So he logs into the Harvard computer, either to check on the virus's progress, or to ask his friends for help.

The joke was on me, though. It didn't occur to me that Robert T. Morris, Jr., was the son of Bob . . . er, Robert Morris, Sr. Yeah, son of Bob Morris, who only yesterday told me he'd known of the *Sendmail* hole for years. Bob Morris, the head honcho who'd grilled me on astrophysics, then nearly asphyxiated me with cigarette smoke.

So Bob Morris's son froze two thousand computers. Why? To impress his dad? As a Halloween prank? To show off to a couple thousand computer programmers?

Whatever his purposes were, I don't believe he was in cahoots with his father. Rumors have it that he worked with a friend or two at Harvard's computing department (Harvard student Paul Graham sent him mail asking for "Any news on the brilliant project"), but I doubt his father would encourage anyone to create a virus. As Bob Morris, Sr., said, "This isn't exactly a good mark for a career at NSA."

After dissecting the code, MIT's John Rochlis characterized the virus as "not very well written." It was unique in that it attacked computers through four pathways: bugs in the Unix *Sendmail* and Finger programs, guessing passwords, and by exploiting paths of trust between computers. In addition, Morris camouflaged the program in several ways, so as to avoid detection. But he made several programming mistakes—like setting the wrong replication rate—and the worm probably could have been written by many students or programmers.

All it takes is knowledge of Unix flaws and no sense of responsibility.

Once you understand how this particular worm-virus infests computers, the cure becomes evident: repair *Sendmail* and the finger daemon, change the passwords, and erase all the copies of the system's virus. Evident, yes. Easy, no.

Spreading the word isn't easy when everyone's chopping off their electronic mail system. After all, that's how this worm propagates its children. Slowly, using alternate networks and telephone calls, the word went out. Within a couple days, Morris's worm was pretty much squashed.

But how do I protect against other viruses? Things aren't so hopeful. Since viruses masquerade as sections of legitimate programs, they're tough to detect. Worse, once your system is infected, these are difficult beasts to understand. A programmer has to decompile the code: a time-consuming, boring job.

Fortunately, computer viruses are rare. Although it's become fashionable to blame system problems on viruses, they mostly hit people who exchange software and use computer bulletin boards. Fortunately, these are usually knowledgeable people who make backup copies of their disks.

A computer virus is specialized: a virus that works on an IBM PC cannot do anything to a Macintosh or a Unix computer. Similarly, the Arpanet virus could only strike at systems running Berkeley Unix. Computers running other operating systems—like AT&T Unix, VMS, or DOS—were totally immune.

Diversity, then, works against viruses. If all the systems on the Arpanet ran Berkeley Unix, the virus would have disabled all fifty thousand of them. Instead, it infected only a couple thousand. Biological viruses are just as specialized: we can't catch the flu from dogs.

Bureaucrats and managers will forever urge us to standardize on a single type of system: "Let's only use Sun workstations" or "Only buy IBM systems." Yet somehow our communities of computers are a diverse population—with Data General machines sitting next to Digital Vaxes; IBMs connected to Sonys. Like our neighborhoods, electronic communities thrive through diversity.

Meanwhile, how much astronomy was I doing?

None. For thirty-six hours, I worked on disinfecting our computers. Then came meetings and then papers to write. And a couple copycat virus makers—fortunately, none as clever as the original.

The last I heard, Robert T. Morris was lying low, avoiding interviews and wondering about the chances of an indictment. His father's still at NSA, still the chief scientist at their computer security center.

How much damage was done? I surveyed the network, and found that two thousand computers were infected within fifteen hours. These machines were dead in the water—useless until disinfected. And removing the virus often took two days.

Suppose someone disabled two thousand automobiles, say, by letting the air out of their tires. How would you measure the damage? By one measure, there's been no damage at all: the cars are intact, and all you need to do is pump some air.

Or you can measure damage by the loss of the cars. Let's see: how much do you lose if your car is disabled for a day? The cost of sending a tow truck out? Or the price of a rental car? Or the amount of work that you've lost? Hard to say.

Perhaps you'd thank the person who let the air out of your tires—award him a medal for raising your consciousness about automotive security.

Here, someone crippled some two thousand computers for two days. What was lost? Programmers, secretaries, and managers couldn't work. Data wasn't collected. Projects were delayed.

The virus writer caused that much damage at least. Deeper damage, too. A while after the virus hit, some astronomers and programmers took a poll. Some of the computer people felt the virus was a harmless prank—one of the finest jokes ever.

The astronomers had a different opinion: for two days, they couldn't work. Their secretaries and grad students weren't working. Proposals and papers weren't being written. We pay for their network connections out of our pockets—and this caper made it even more difficult to expand their astronomy networks.

Some programmers see this virus as a useful exercise in raising consciousness about computer security. The virus writer should be thanked. Yeah, sure. Like going into a small town and breaking into people's homes, so as to impress upon the townsfolk the need to buy strong locks.

Once, I too would have seen no mischief in this virus. But over the past two years, my interest changed from a micro-problem (a 75-cent discrepancy) to macro-issues: the welfare of our networks, a sense of common fair play, legal implications of hacking, the security of defense contractors, commonweal ethics in computing . . .

Omigod! Listening to myself talk like this, I realize that I've become a grown-up (sob!)—a person who *really has a stake.* My graduate student mentality of earlier days let me think of the world as just a research project: to be studied, data extracted, patterns noted. Suddenly there are conclusions to be drawn; conclusions that carry moral weight.

I guess I've come of age.

The greatest B-movie of all time, *The Blob,* finishes off with the malignant monster being towed off to Antarctica: it's harmless when frozen. Then, the words "The End" flash across the screen, but at the last minute, a blob-shaped question mark appears. The monster isn't dead, only sleeping.

That is how I felt when I finally dismantled my monitors, made the last entry in my logbook, and said good-bye to midnight chases after Markus Hess.

The monster is still out there, ready to come alive again. Whenever someone, tempted by money, power, or simple curiosity, steals a password and prowls the networks. Whenever someone forgets that the networks she loves to play on are fragile, and can only exist when people trust each other. Whenever a fun-loving student breaks into systems as a game (as I might once have done), and forgets that he's invading people's privacy, endangering data that others have sweated over, sowing distrust and paranoia.

Networks aren't made of printed circuits, but of people. Right now, as I type, through my keyboard I can touch countless others: friends, strangers, enemies. I can talk to a physicist in Japan, an astronomer in England, a spy in Washington. I might gossip with a buddy in Silicon Valley or some professor at Berkeley.

My terminal is a door to countless, intricate pathways, leading to untold numbers of neighbors. Thousands of people trust each other enough to tie their systems together. Hundreds of thousands of people use those systems, never realizing the delicate networks that link their separate worlds.

Like the innocent small town invaded in a monster movie, all those people work and play, unaware of how fragile and vulnerable their community is. It could be destroyed outright by a virus, or, worse, it could consume itself with mutual suspicion, tangle itself up in locks, security checkpoints, and surveillance; wither away by becoming so inaccessible and bureaucratic that nobody would want it anymore.

But maybe, if Hess was an exception, if enough of us work together to keep the networks safe and free, this will all be over. I can finally get back to astronomy and have time to spend with my long-suffering bride. I don't want to be a computer cop. I don't want our networks to need cops.

The phone's ringing. It's Lawrence Livermore Laboratory—a place I've stayed away from because they design nuclear bombs. A hacker's breaking into their computer. They want my help. They think I'm a wizard.

**THE END**
**?**

# After the Question Mark

"I couldn't get back to astronomy that easily. A year after moving to Cambridge, my boss still noticed that I was spending time on computer security. "And not enough on astronomy . . ." he added.

Seems that hackers were hunting for me. Anonymous phone calls, threatening letters, nasty electronic mail. People from various three-letter agencies still call. Meanwhile, several individuals wound up in court.

The past year's been hard. Martha has a clerkship at the Supreme Court in Washington: Zooks! But our jobs seem to pull in different directions, so we've been living apart. Her days are spent in lawbooks, mine behind a keyboard in Cambridge.

Plenty to do at the Harvard-Smithsonian Astrophysical Observatory. Bread and butter astronomy: making databases from the high energy astrophysics satellites and connecting a Sun workstation to an X-ray telescope.

Yes, looking at the sky through a telescope is a real charge, but the challenge is to analyze what's there. Suppose you compare the X-ray sky with observations taken through radio telescopes. Plenty of stars give off radio waves. But those objects that show up in both wavelengths might be colliding galaxies.

To search for these, we needed to compare a half-dozen databases. For me, that means programming a Unix computer. Once again, I'm half astronomer, half programmer.

December 1989 letter from the German Oberlandesgericht Court in Celle: "You are respectfully requested to appear at the trial of M. Hess, D. Brysinski, and P. Carl."

Charge: espionage.

Celle is an old town half an hour outside of Hannover . . . Houses from 1550, cobblestone streets, a 200-year-old castle, and the Federal district courthouse.

The trial wasn't like the old Perry Mason shows. There were three days of testimony, all double-translated. A panel of five judges asked questions. The defense attorneys asked questions. The defendants asked questions. The prosecutor remained silent.

How did I feel? Nervous, yet confident in my research. My logbook made all the difference. It was like presenting some observations to a room of astronomers. They may disagree with the interpretation, but they can't argue with what you saw. Still, this wasn't science. I looked across the room and saw three worried guys trying desperately to stay out of prison. In the hallway I heard Peter Carl, the former croupier, telling how good he felt helping the KGB because someone's got to even things out with the CIA. He explained that he carried a gun that he "found in the street."

There was Markus Hess: round faced, slightly overweight, and balding. Chain-smoking Benson and Hedges in the hallway, he admitted that he'd broken into our computers. Some military systems, too. And, yes, he'd sold certain software to the KGB.

As last, here was my adversary, yet I didn't know what to say. Before meeting him, I'd watched him for a year. I already knew him and had classified him as a reptile.

But my opinions softened a bit face-to-face. Up close, well, here was a guy that knew that he'd screwed up and was squirming to escape. Throughout the trial, Hess knew what was incriminating, and tried to chip away at my testimony: Why were some sessions missing from my printouts? Could I prove that nobody else had seen those bogus SDINET files? Might other hackers have been responsible for the theft of this data?

Those missing sessions were from paper jams and disk overflows. Yes, I could tell the difference between the hacker using the

Hunter/Jaeger/Sventek accounts and others just playing around. And my alarms alerted me every time anyone touched those sensitive files.

The trial was tough, but afterward I met some computer programmers and not-quite-hackers from Hannover. They showed me Hess's old apartment on Glockenstrasse, across the street from a community theater. Two years earlier, they'd held regular hacker meetings to compare notes, exchange passwords, and plan future attacks. Now, though, they were staying clear of others' systems: Hagbard's death and Hess's arrest had made an impact.

On February 15, 1990, Hess, Brysinski, and Carl were found guilty of espionage and received one- to two-year sentences. Released on probation, they are now free in Germany. Markus Hess now writes networking software for a company in Hannover.

Back on this side of the ocean, Robert T. Morris went on trial in January 1990 for writing the infamous Internet worm that froze thousands of computers. The federal prosecutor pointed out that Morris had written his program specifically to break into computers. Was there a programming error? Well, yes—his worm wasn't supposed to infect thousands of computers overnight. Rather, it was supposed to happen over a period of weeks, months, and even years. If his code had worked properly, the Morris virus would still be infesting computers today.

The jury in Syracuse found Morris guilty of a felony—the first conviction for writing a computer virus. On May 4, the judge sentenced him to three years of probation, 400 hours of community service, and a $10,000 fine.

A fair sentence? I'd say so. A prison term wouldn't do much except satisfy a desire for revenge. Community service is certainly appropriate, considering that his worm program was an attack on a most delicate community.

Special Agent Mike Gibbons is now at FBI headquarters in Washington. Yow—maybe the system works: A competent FBI special agent is setting policy.

Martha? Working at the Supreme Court and practicing aikido daily . . . got her black belt a few months ago. Sure do miss her.

Without Martha, chocolate chip cookies weren't much fun to make. Instead of gardening, I'd spend Sunday afternoons at work. So at 1:30, March 11, I biked over to the Smithsonian Observatory, looked at my Sun workstation, and noticed something weird. My electronic mail files had been read at 12:57. But I'd been asleep then. Someone had been messing with my files. Reading my network mail. Changing passwords.

Someone's broken in and become super-user. Left a message for me too: "Now the cuckoo has egg on his face." Out to prove he's the fastest gunslinger in the west.

Please, not again.

But sure enough, my lab director ordered our system isolated from the network. For the next two weeks, we scoured our systems software, finding Trojan horses and backdoor passwords that this hacker had left behind. Whee!

He got in through an unprotected astronomy computer run by a couple of infrared astronomers. They didn't care about security . . . they just needed to connect to the network. Because I exchange programs with them, we'd set up our systems to work as one—you didn't need a password to move from their computer to mine.

This hacker guessed a password for their Unix system. From there, he became super-user by planting an egg in the systems area, then sliding into my computer.

A couple days later the SOB called me. Said his name was Dave. From Australia. "I broke in to show you that your security isn't very good."

"But I don't want to secure my computer," I replied. "I trust other astronomers."

Dave had other reasons for breaking in, too. "You think that hackers are bad. This proves otherwise."

"Huh? You break into my computer to show that hackers are good?"

"Yeah," Dave replied. "We're helping you out by finding your security faults."

If you tell some kids that they're behaving like children, they'll get even with you by acting like children.

Last I heard, the Secret Service, FBI, and the Australian police had tracked down three Australian hackers. Charged with theft of telephone service and breaking into computers, they are out on bail. One of them is named Dave.

Hey—the Hubble Space Telescope is in orbit. And the Keck Observatory in Hawaii is nearly finished . . . another nifty telescope that I'd like to write software for. I could have been helping out except that I've been chasing—and being chased by—hackers. I wonder if there's room there for an astronomer who's occasionally mistaken for a computer wizard?

# Bibliography

If you'd like technical details behind this book, read my article, "Stalking the Wily Hacker," in the May 1988 issue of the *Communications of the ACM.* It's an academic paper which highlights the techniques that the hacker used to break into computers.

In addition, I described how to track hackers in "What Do You Feed a Trojan Horse?"—found in the *Proceedings of the 10th National Computer Security Conference* (September 1987). Because I wrote that paper while the hacker was still actively breaking into computers, it's about how to trace networks and doesn't mention our problems.

For more details about the NSA and a bit about their computer security problems, read *The Puzzle Palace* by James Bamford. Bamford describes the tug of war between the code makers and code breakers—he must have had fun prying those details out of the super-secret agency. David Kahn's book, *The Codebreakers,* is a fascinating description and history of ciphers, which suggests how computers use cryptography to protect their data. In *Deep Black* William E. Burrows writes mostly about secret observations from spy satellites, but also hints at the use of computers in espionage.

For more mundane, yet valuable descriptions of the problems and techniques of computer security, read *Defending Secrets, Sharing Data,* available from the U.S. Congress, Office of Technology

Assessment, OTA-CIT-310. For a still more technical discussion, try *Cryptography and Data Security* by Dorothy Denning. The hacker probably wouldn't have broken into our system had we read (and applied) *Unix System Security* by Wood and Kochan. There's a superb report by David Curry: "Improving the Security of Your Unix System." The name says it all—ask for report ITSTD-721-FR-90-21 from SRI International, 333 Ravenswood Avenue, Menlo Park, CA 94025.

Computer security problems are usually heard first on Internet and Usenet network conferences. These are worldwide electronic bulletin boards—this is often where first rumors of trouble show up. To hear about the latest computer security problems, watch the *Unix-wizards, Info-vax, Security, TCP-IP,* and *Virus-L* conferences. There's a lively, moderated discussion on the *Risks-forum* conference, where participants discuss social issues relating to computers. There are a few private security conferences as well; their "invitation only" membership is indicative of the paranoia surrounding the field. There are also anonymous and pirate bulletin boards; these seldom have much useful information—but they do tell you what one segment of the population is thinking.